STOCK INDEX FUTURES

STOCK INDEX FUTURES

A Guide for Traders,
Investors, and Analysts

NEIL S. WEINER

JOHN WILEY & SONS
New York • Chichester • Brisbane • Toronto • Singapore

This publication is designed to provide accurate and
authoritative information in regard to the subject
matter covered. It is sold with the understanding that
the publisher is not engaged in rendering legal, accounting,
or other professional service. If legal advice or other
expert assistance is required, the services of a competent
professional person should be sought. *From a Declaration
of Principles jointly adopted by a Committee of the
American Bar Association and a Committee of Publishers.*

Library of Congress Cataloging in Publication Data:
Weiner, Neil S.
  Stock index futures.

  Includes index.
  1. Stock index futures—Handbooks, manuals, etc.
I. Title.

HG6043.W44   1983   332.63'222   83-17040
ISBN   0-471-89382-X

Printed in the United States of America

10   9   8   7   6   5   4   3   2   1

To my own special futures,

HEATHER L. and GARRETT R.

Preface

Stock index futures contracts started out on the proverbial "dead run." Trading in them began in February 1982 at the Kansas City Board of Trade, and throughout the rest of the year, they grew at a faster rate than any other new futures contract on record. Stock index futures set new trading record volumes on the Chicago Mercantile and New York Futures exchanges. These new futures provide risk management potential to help make the U.S. capital markets more responsive to investors' risk preferences, a need previously left unfilled.

The uproar about stock index futures had started long before the successful inception of trading, during the three to four year approval drama that unfolded at the Commodity Futures Trading Commission. Objections to the innovative proposal arose from all quarters: Capitol Hill, from a variety of other U.S. Governmental regulatory agencies, from within the securities industry, and from some parts of the futures industry as well.

Parts of the controversies and misconceptions were understandable. Putting aside the threats to vested interests, the economic and operational justifications for the proposed new futures contracts constitute a combination of the principles and mechanics of futures trading and the more esoteric developments in quantitative capital market theory. Many in the investment community were just becoming comfortable with such concepts as "systematic risk" and "beta coefficients," and then a bunch of new wrinkles from futures trading were thrown in: hedging, the basis risk, and "spreading."

For those in the futures industry, the concept of "diversifiable risk" might already have had some intuitive appeal, but such concepts as the "market factor" and the use of a stock market index as the "commodity" underlying a futures contract left many shaking their heads. Added to those complexities was yet another "outlandish" feature of no physical, but "cash" delivery. What a mess!

To top it all off, the crucial element for stock index futures, systematic or market risk, wasn't observable—even afterward. Thousands of pages in academic journals had been devoted to "proving" or "disproving" a myriad of related but inconclusive hypotheses. The "market factor" and systematic risk are what we'd have to call "statistical realities": they're there but we can't observe them directly. In the words of "Lord, Mr. Ford," Jerry Reed's song of a few years ago,

> The average American father and mother
> Own one whole car and half another,
> And I'll bet that half-a-car's a trick to drive, don't you?*

Nonetheless, the evidence is irrefutable: over the long haul all stock prices tend to move up and down together. But the extent to which a given stock's price movements are caused by the market influence, as opposed to its own underlying characteristics, cannot be definitively measured. The process of dichotomization can be approximated with a whole host of statistical tools and techniques. But statistics deal with probabilities and not certainties. The "bottom line," unfortunately, is that there is no "quick-and-dirty" way to explain the justification of stock index futures to the average investor in two or three minutes.

To really penetrate the "mystery" of stock index futures, all that is required is a little patience and concentration. It is a building process, but none of the component blocks are too heavy to lift or put in place. This book, for example, literally starts from "square one." As a point of reference, if you know what a simple average is, then you are already part of the way through Chapter 2. It's that simple.

Some recent developments related to stock index futures do not appear in this book. In particular, options on the stock index contracts ("commodity options"), and options on new ("homemade") stock market indexes are beyond the scope of consideration here. Both instruments appeared in early 1983, and therefore market data about them are sparse. Further, the inclusion of these new instruments would only complicate,

---

*Words and music by Dick Feller © 1973 Vector Music Corp. Used by permission. International copyright secured. All rights reserved.

if not confuse, the exposition about the main topic: stock index futures themselves.

Finally, almost every book of this type starts with a disclaimer that it will not make you rich overnight. Sorry, but the same holds true here as well. This is not a tome with which mystics and soothsayers can predict future(s) prices. The purpose here is less ambitious, but in the long run more substantive. This presentation develops the rationale and economic justification for stock index futures from a historical, evolutionary perspective. It proceeds from some familiar aspects of the stock market and portfolio theory, through the mechanics and principles of futures trading, to the actual risk management uses of these financial instruments. Along the way there are accounts of colorful disputes, some ending in litigation, as well as illuminating historical insights. For the more inquisitive, the technical side trips have been relegated to the appendices. At the end, all of the confusion about stock index futures contracts is penetrated and put in perspective. Others may persist in raising "phony" issues about them, but the reader here will know better.

NEIL S. WEINER

Encino, California
October 1983

Acknowledgments

This book is an outgrowth of the various economic justification documents, journal articles, and trading booklets written when I was the consulting economist to the Kansas City Board of Trade (KCBT). The KCBT has been most generous in granting permission for the use of numerous quotations throughout this book. In particular, I am indebted to Walter N. Vernon III, chief executive officer of the exchange, and to J. Frank Baumgartner, past president of the KCBT and chairman of the stock index contract committee.

I must also thank Roy Brady of Arnold Bernhard & Co. for statistical data processing and Perry J. Kaufman for supportive guidance and helpful suggestions.

Finally, the crew behind the scenes rarely receive recognition. My thanks go to those at Wiley who worked diligently to improve the manuscript, especially my editor, Stephen A. Kippur, without whose goading, cajoling, encouragement, and benevolent patience this book would probably still be incomplete. Others at Wiley who deserve special thanks are Carole Schwager, Linda Grady-Troia, and Usha Prakash.

As is customary, I retain sole claim on any errors or omissions.

N.S.W.

Contents

1 Introduction

The pundits of the financial pages have had a real field day. The introduction of trading in stock index futures contracts evidently signaled many to dust off their saltiest lines and sharpen their most sarcastic rapiers. On the editorial page of *The Wall Street Journal,* for example, Richard L. Hudson exhorted: "Drop those dice, tear up those football-betting cards. A new gambling game is coming: the stock-index future" (Hudson, 1982).

One month earlier, even the venerable *New York Times* had contributed to the same level of misconception. An article by William M. Reddig was headlined "How to Bet on a Stock Index: The latest wrinkle on the old commodity contract is scheduled to appear in February. Beware the odds" (Reddig, 1981).

Not to be outdone, the *Los Angeles Times* resorted to somewhat more classical humor:

"If you bet on a horse," a sports columnist once remarked, "that's gambling. If you bet you can make three spades, that's entertainment. If you bet cotton will go up three points, that's business. See the difference?" (Baron, 1982).

When there is access to the printed word, the old adage about a little knowledge being a dangerous thing somehow never seemed truer. Or as a former colleague once remarked about his expertise in a particular area, he felt he knew just enough to hurt himself, but not enough to help.

Why all the hoopla? Why should a new futures contract attract such biting attention? One reason is probably a reflection of the jurisdictional confusion that persisted for over two years in Washington, D.C. Many regulators and legislators felt that the Commodity Futures Trading Com-

1

mission (CFTC) was somehow invading the stock market turf of the Securities and Exchange Commission. Another reason relates to the potential hedging and trading activity of stock index futures: 30 million stock owners, and over $1.5 trillion in common stocks held by individuals and institutions. Less antagonistic commentators have recognized the potential quantum leap in participation for the most successful futures contract yet to be conceived.

GAMBLING REVISITED

On the other hand, perhaps we should not be too critical of the misconceptions. After all, the distinction between "investing" and "gambling" is very often a fairly subtle one, and from the standpoint of the individual, the two different acts may be indistinguishable. One can bet on a horse, and either win or lose. One can also buy 100 shares of IBM, and "win" (if the price increases) or "lose" (if the price goes down). What's the difference anyway?

For the moment, "gambling" can be differentiated from other forms of risk bearing as a situation where the risk is *created* or *contrived* for the sole purpose of someone taking it. Eight individuals sit down to play poker. (In Las Vegas, the situation is frequently seven "shills" and one "pigeon.") The stakes, together with the probabilities of various hands, will determine the risks and rewards (payoffs, or size or pots) of playing. The risk bearing in a poker game is contrived in the sense that it is self-imposed by electing to play; the game may also provide entertainment and satisfaction for the "gambling instinct." Another example is that thoroughbred horse racing could exist without pari-mutuel betting, just as humans compete in track meets without a betting system.

As mentioned, at the level of the individual, the distinctions are often fuzzy and frequently misleading. Using the logic of the opening citations, the act of insuring one's house against fire is "betting" that the house will burn down—a "wager" that most would hope to lose. For a clearer understanding, one must resort to an aggregate, or economy-wide, perspective.

UBIQUITY OF RISK

Risks pervade our economic system. These risks, as opposed to *contrived* ones, exist with or are attendant to the provision of other economic activities. In this regard, Arrow observed:

> Although our economics textbooks have remarkably little to say about the matter, nothing is more obvious than the universality of risks in the economic system. Machines break down from time to time; the coordination of complex production processes can never be perfect; despite the decreasing importance of agriculture, the uncertainties of the elements still play an important role; the search for mineral deposits is notoriously chancy; the demand for a product may change unpredictably in relatively short time spans, due to changing tastes or the development of substitutes; in a capitalist society, the success of new businesses and the *movements of the stock market* cannot be foreseen; and above all, technological progress and the development of new knowledge are by their very nature leaps into the unknown." (Arrow, 1971, p. 135, emphasis added).

In Arrow's view, the shifting of risks, the very essence of insurance, occurs in many different forms in the economic system, but typically with some limits. He sees these limitations as hobbling the system. "It is desirable to extend the scope of risk-shifting, and indeed from time to time new economic institutions arise with precisely this aim in view" (Arrow, 1971, p. 134). Cases in point are the recent evolution of futures contracts on a wide range of debt instruments. Stock index futures—the subject of this book—represent yet another extension of specialized risk shifting.

WHY SHIFT RISK?

What is the social usefulness of reallocating risk? For one thing, "A man's capacity for running a business well need not be accompanied by a desire or ability for bearing the accompanying risks" (Arrow, 1971, p. 135). It is axiomatic in the literature about futures markets that the price risks of inventory ownership inevitably arise in the normal course of commerce. The ever-changing conditions of supply and demand "Are by far the most hazardous of all trade risks, and commodity handlers are anxious to minimize or avoid them entirely whenever possible." The typical merchants are depicted as preferring to forego the "possibility of making a speculative profit in favor of earning an expected normal merchandising or service charge through the efficient operation of their respective businesses" (Horn, 1969, p. 69).

Risk transference in the form of futures markets, hedging operations for price protection, can thus be viewed as a means for the commodity storers, processors, or exporters to be able to concentrate on the efficiency of their particular specializations or functions. Having "insured" against possibly disastrous inventory price fluctuations, they need not be distracted from the fields of their true comparative advantages.

The possibility of shifting risks allows individuals to engage in activities they would not otherwise undertake. On the other hand, if risks are *not* shiftable, many worthwhile projects might not be undertaken. To the extent that risks can be transferred, then each individual investor (risk-bearer), "by diversification, can be fairly sure of a positive outcome, and society will be better off by the increased production" (Arrow, 1971, p. 138).

COMMON STOCKS AND DIVERSIFICATION

The most widespread mechanisms for shifting risks are the various forms of insurance and the futures markets. Arrow pointed out that *common stocks* themselves are yet another device for shifting risk. However, the use of common stocks allows the entrepreneur to disperse risk,

> but only in an undiscriminating way. Suppose he is quite certain about the production costs of a new product but uncertain about the market. He would like insurance only about sales, but the issuance of common shares means that he has to share the fruits of his special knowledge of production methods, about which he is not uncertain, in order to be protected against selling risks. He may therefore be motivated not to enter into production at all.
>
> Another example of the inadequacy of the stock market can be given. Suppose that all firms tend to be profitable or unprofitable together, due, for example to shifts in foreign demand. The investors would like to find

insurance against a generally unfavorable development, but they cannot find it by *any amount of diversification*. There may indeed be individuals or organizations who would be willing at a price to pay compensation for the occurrence of the unfavorable event, but the stock market does not provide any opportunity for a mutually advantageous insurance transaction to occur." (Arrow, 1971, p. 139, emphasis added)

It is this type of portfolio risk that *cannot be diversified away* that is called *systematic risk*. It is the *raison d'être* for stock index futures contracts.

SYSTEMATIC VERSUS UNSYSTEMATIC RISK

Roughly speaking, *systematic risk* is the degree of correspondence of a security's price movements with the general stock market. The statistical evidence is overwhelming to the effect that security prices tend to move up and down together. Therefore, "It might reasonably be thought that they are affected by a common market factor" (Aber, 1973, p. 11).

The type of portfolio risk that can be diversified away is called *unsystematic risk*. Diversification is protection against a decline that has an impact on a particular industry or firm, but it is not protection against a general market decline, as illustrated above by Arrow's foreign demand example. Regardless of portfolio policy or stock selection criteria, the best-reasoned equities position—no matter how well diversified—is not safe from the hazards or risks of a general market downturn. Thus with adequate and proper diversification, the *sole* source of uncertainty about the rate of return of an efficient portfolio is its degree of systematic, or market, risk.

Stock index futures contracts began trading in the United States during the spring of 1982. The purpose of these new futures instruments is to furnish investors a flexible means for safeguarding portfolio values from fluctuations in the general stock market. The data from statistical studies indicate that on the average the systematic market risk accounts for about 30–35 percent of the price variability of common stocks. However, for a large number of individual issues, the market risk can account for as much as 50 percent or more of the variability. And as mentioned above, systematic risk accounts for nearly all of the uncertainty for well diversified portfolios.

ORGANIZATION AND SCOPE OF THIS BOOK

Like Caesar's Gaul, this book is divided into three parts. The first part (Chapters 2–5) acquaints the reader with some indispensable building blocks for understanding stock index futures contracts. Chapter 2 may seem like a detour at the beginning of our journey, a quick review of some basic statistical tools, but without them the reader would not fully enjoy the trip. However, all that is required for Chapter 2 is a working knowledge of English and a little arithmetic. In Chapter 3 the various stock market averages and indicators that are the "underlying commodities" for stock index futures contracts are explained, explored, defined, and distinguished. Chapter 4 summarizes the main diabolical machinations economists and statisticians have contrived in the last twenty years—"capital market theory"—and identifies the sources of controversy. It is very colorful. Really. Chapter 5 is somewhat more standard: a description of the mechanics and principles of futures trading; in particular, the parallels and differences from trading stocks are highlighted.

The second part of this book builds on the first. And at last stock index futures contracts are fully addressed and explained. In Chapter 6 there is a description of the very lively history and litigation surrounding the development of these contracts, and the specifications and differences among the actively traded contracts. Chapters 7 and 8 explain how stock index futures contracts are used to reduce risk for stocks, portfolios, and individual stock options. Chapter 9 is about the money, especially about how futures market performance guarantees, called "margins," resemble and differ from their counterparts in the stock market. In Chapter 10 the 1982 statistical record for stock index contracts is summarized and analyzed: prices, correlations, and various other intrigues of futures trading. The year 1982 was a real zinger for the inception of trading: a fairly humdrum bear market until mid-August, and then a record-setting "bull run" throughout the remainder of the year—perfect laboratory conditions to find out how stock index futures behave. In Chapter 11 we draw together many of the important aspects of stock index trading and confront some of the criticisms.

The third part of the book is for the very curious, or very studious. Appendix A presents more on stock indexes, Appendix B more on the capital asset pricing model (CAPM). Various studies on stock ownership and other technical matters are explored in Appendix C. Appendix D contains more on hedging, especially the "portfolio" approach that has been developed in the last few years. However, the earlier, conventional approach is classic, and is also recounted in Appendix D. Finally, Appendix E contains various systematic risk statistics for 1440 individual stocks. In terms of the concepts developed in this book, it is natural for curious investors to wonder how their portfolios look in the new light.

2 Vital Statistics

Everyone knows that there's no such thing as a "free lunch." Economists usually point out that there is always a cost involved, even if it's only listening to a sales pitch about some privileged investment opportunity. Time very often is a scarce resource, and one may not choose to pay this frequently hidden cost.

Authors of finance texts are equally fond of telling us that there is no such thing as a truly "riskless" asset. For example, all securities and other forms of holding wealth (including cash) are subject to at least one of the following types of risk:

1 Business risk (i.e., a decline in earning power), which reduces a company's ability to pay interest or dividends, or even survive as a commercial enterprise.
2 Market risk (i.e., a change in "market psychology"), which causes a security's price to decline regardless of any truly fundamental change in earning power.
3 Purchasing power risk (i.e., a rise in prices), which reduces the buying power, or *real* value, of income and principal.
4 Interest rate risk (i.e., a rise in market rates), which depresses the prices of fixed-income type securities.
5 Political risk (e.g., wage-price controls, tax increases, changes in tariff and subsidy policies, etc.).

Common stocks are most vulnerable to (1), (2), and (5), although the latter could be interpreted as mainly affecting (1), "unsystematic risk";

(2) is of course "systematic risk." Less widely recognized is that stocks are also exposed to (3).

Bonds are most vulnerable to (1), (3), (4), and (5). As mentioned, no securities are immune to all risks. Even U.S. government bonds are subject to (3) and (4), and cash is subject to (3) (cf. Cohen and Zinbarg, 1967, pp. 119–120).

THE RISKS OF STOCK OWNERSHIP

Common stocks are considered rather "risky" assets because the combined influences of (1) and (2) result in a *price variability* that is usually higher than that of most other financial assets. (Including, by the way, futures prices!) The risk aspect is present because one may have to sell a stock for less than the purchase price, and thereby suffer a loss. On the other hand, if the stock's price always rose, and there were no downside risk in nominal money terms, the holder would still be subject to the purchasing power risk (3), if consumer prices rose at a faster rate.

In general, the riskiness of a stock is framed in terms of how "volatile" its price is, that is, how much does the price vary? Although there are a number of ways to measure a stock's price volatility, the most commonly used measure is its *variance,* or correspondingly, the square root of the variance: the *standard deviation.* The latter are statistical measures used to indicate dispersion.

KEY STATISTICS: CONCEPT AND COMPUTATION

With a minor apology to the reader, at this point it is necessary to define and illustrate a few statistical tools. Without an understanding of these concepts and measures, the rationale for much of what follows about stock index futures would be rather barren. A solid grasp of these statistical concepts adds flesh and substance to the skeleton of the discussion. Instead of whisking along through this pungent forest of empirical flora, the reader is able to stop, as it were, and smell the roses. As promised, the explanations are as simple and brief as possible.

Average

The arithmetic mean, commonly called the "average," of a series or sample is familiar ground from which to start. Unless designated otherwise, it is generally understood that an "average" is an equally weighted statistic. That is, all components or observations used to calculate the arithmetic mean have equal influence. (Otherwise, some weighting scheme is employed to give more weight or importance to some components than to others to compute the average. In Chapter 3 we have occasion to consider, for example, "capitalization-weighted" averages and indexes— measures that, by definition, are not equally weighted.)

Let's start with stocks A, B, and C.

As everyone already knows, for the six periods shown in Table 2.1, the average, or arithmetic mean, prices for the three stocks are calculated by summing the six prices and dividing by the number of periods, or observations:

$$\text{average price of A} = \frac{11 + 9 + 10 + 10 + 11 + 9}{6} = \frac{60}{6} = \$10$$

For ease of reference, let's designate the average price of stock A as $\overline{P}_a$. Similarly, for stock B, the mean price is

$$\overline{P}_b = \frac{6 + 8 + 12 + 14 + 15 + 5}{6} = \frac{60}{6} = \$10$$

and

$$\overline{P}_c = \frac{24 + 22 + 18 + 16 + 15 + 25}{6} = \frac{120}{6} = \$20$$

In each calculation the sum of the observations was divided by 6, giving each component a "weight" of $\frac{1}{6}$ in determining the average, or arithmetic mean, price for stocks A, B, and C.

Variance and Standard Deviation

Now we are ready to consider measuring the volatility of our stocks. An intuitive explanation of variance and standard deviation can be seen in terms of how far, and how often, the price of the stock varied from its *average* price. Both A and B have average prices of $10, but notice that

Table 2.1 Prices for Stocks A, B, and C

Period	Price of A	Price of B	Price of C
1	$11	$ 6	$24
2	$ 9	$ 8	$22
3	$10	$12	$18
4	$10	$14	$16
5	$11	$15	$15
6	$ 9	$ 5	$25
Average price	$10	$10	$20

stock A's price was always within $1 of the average. Stock B, on the other hand (by now you know that this phrase is also a favorite of economists), while having the same arithmetic mean price of $10, never actually traded at that price, but jumped all around $10. We would expect B to have a variance different from, and higher than, stock A. More particularly, we can think of the "average deviation" of a stock's price from its average price. Calculation of the statistical measures of variation follows from that notion.

For example, for stock A in period 1, the deviation of its price from its *mean* price, $\overline{P}_a$, equals $11 - $10 = $1 = $(P_{a1} - \overline{P}_a)$, where P_{a1} is the price of stock A in period 1. For period 2, the deviation of stock A from its average price equals $(P_{a2} - \overline{P}_a) = $9 - $10 = -$1$. For period 3, it's $(P_{a3} - \overline{P}_a) = $10 - $10 = 0. The basic notation is simply $(P_t - \overline{P})$, where t is the particular period under consideration. In this example, t refers to periods 1, 2, . . . , 6.

Notice also that it is important to retain the algebraic sign or direction (i.e., positive or negative) of the deviation. For stock A, both P_{a1} and P_{a2} differ from the average price $\overline{P}_a$ by $1: P_{a1} is $1 over the mean $\overline{P}_a$ at $11, and P_{a2} is $1 under $\overline{P}_a$ at $9 = -$1$. All of the deviations for stocks A, B, and C are shown in Table 2.2 in terms of our basic deviation formula (price of the stock in period t minus the average price of the stock).

Now to compute the "average deviation" for each stock. Our natural impulse might be to add up the deviations and divide by the number of observations, in this case six. Sounds reasonable, but wait a minute. The sum of the deviations for stock A equals zero! A zero value for the variance would mean that the price of the stock never varied from its mean, here $10, and while the price of stock A did not vary far, it did vary from the

Table 2.2   Deviations for Stocks A, B, and C

Period	$P_{at} - \overline{P}_a$	$P_{bt} - \overline{P}_b$	$P_{ct} - \overline{P}_c$
1	$(11 - 10) = 1$	$(6 - 10) = -4$	$(24 - 20) = 4$
2	$(9 - 10) = -1$	$(8 - 10) = -2$	$(22 - 20) = 2$
3	$(10 - 10) = 0$	$(12 - 10) = 2$	$(18 - 20) = -2$
4	$(10 - 10) = 0$	$(14 - 10) = 4$	$(16 - 20) = -4$
5	$(11 - 10) = 1$	$(15 - 10) = 5$	$(15 - 20) = -5$
6	$(9 - 10) = -1$	$(5 - 10) = -5$	$(25 - 20) = 5$

mean. In fact, look at the sum of the deviations for B and C, too. They also equal zero. Actually, that is not really a surprise: it is a mathematical property of the arithmetic mean. The sum of the deviations about the mean always equals zero. No matter how dispersed the values are, or how close to the mean, the sum of the deviations equals zero. That property is consistent with the "central tendency" characteristic of an average.

The way around this problem is to deal with the *squares* of the deviations, and the sum of those squares. That way the negative deviations will be converted to positive values; and the larger the deviation is, the larger will be the squared value of it, for both positive and negative deviations. We could have considered all deviations from the mean as positive, but we'll need to retain the identity of the negative deviations for yet another calculation, to be discussed below. The squared deviations and their sums are shown in Table 2.3.

Table 2.3   Squared Deviations, and Their Sums, for Stocks A, B, and C

	Stock A		Stock B		Stock C	
Period	Deviation	(Deviation)^2	Deviation	(Deviation)^2	Deviation	(Deviation)^2
1	1	1	-4	16	4	16
2	-1	1	-2	4	2	4
3	0	0	2	4	-2	4
4	0	0	4	16	-4	16
5	1	1	5	25	-5	25
6	-1	1	-5	25	5	25
Sum		4		90		90

Table 2.4 Mean Prices, Variances, and Standard Deviations for Stocks A, B, and C

	Stock A	Stock B	Stock C
Mean price	$10	$10	$20
var(P)	.667	15.0	15.0
SD(P)	.816	3.873	3.873

We are now ready to compute the variances of the prices of our stocks A, B, and C.* For this illustration, the variance of each stock's price is simply the sum of the squared deviations divided by N, the number of observations. Therefore, the variance of P_a, denoted as

$$\mathrm{var}(P_a) = \frac{4}{6} = 0.667$$

$$\mathrm{var}(P_b) = \frac{90}{6} = 15.0$$

and

$$\mathrm{var}(P_c) = \frac{90}{6} = 15.0$$

The standard deviations (SD's) follow directly from the calculated variances: they are simply the (positive) square roots. Thus

$$\mathrm{SD}(P_a) = \sqrt{1.667} = .817$$

$$\mathrm{SD}(P_b) = \sqrt{15.0} = 3.873$$

and

$$\mathrm{SD}(P_c) = \sqrt{15.0} = 3.873$$

All of our calculated measures are recapped in Table 2.4.

The variance and standard deviation statistically measure *dispersion* around the arithmetic mean. In terms of stock prices, for the moment,

---

* For purposes of exposition, the variance and standard deviation calculations are presumed to be for entire population parameters. Sampling adjustments to obtain "unbiased" estimators are omitted for simplicity.

let us loosely equate higher volatility, as measured by the standard deviation, with higher "risk." In Table 2.4, stocks A and B have the same average prices but different standard deviations. Stocks B and C, meanwhile, exhibit different average prices but have the *same* standard deviations. The variance (standard deviation) measure of stock price dispersion is thus not necessarily related to the arithmetic mean, or average, price of the stock. Strictly speaking, the standard deviation measures how many points away from the mean price the stock has traded, on the "average," during the period of observation—without regard to what that mean price has been. The average is used in computing the variance, but B and C might be regarded as equally risky stocks since they exhibit the same variances.

As a practical matter, on the other hand, casual observation suggests that higher price stocks tend to have wider, or larger, trading ranges than lower price stocks, at least as measured in nominal (i.e., standard deviation) dollar terms. One way around this problem, for comparative purposes, is to "normalize" for different levels of stock prices by converting to a "percentage variation" approximation. This procedure is accomplished simply by dividing the standard deviation by the average price. The resulting measure is called the *coefficient of variation* (CV). The coefficient of variation is a heuristic statistic, but frequently it is useful for gaining a relative perspective. For Stock A, the coefficient of variation

$$CV(P_a) = \frac{SD(P_a)}{\overline{P}_a} = \frac{.816}{10} = .0816$$

Similarly,

$$CV(P_b) = \frac{SD(P_b)}{\overline{P}_b} = \frac{3.873}{10} = .3873$$

and

$$CV(P_c) = \frac{SD(P_c)}{\overline{P}_c} = \frac{3.873}{20} = .1937$$

Another way to deal with the variability of stock prices in comparative terms is to transform the observations into *logarithmic* form. Unfortunately, there is no readily intuitive way to explain logarithms for the nonmathematical reader. Most texts define the logarithmic function in terms of other mathematical functions. Suffice it for the moment to portray logarithms as dealing with *exponents* (e.g., the "2" of X^2, or the "3" of X^3) and exponential relationships. For our purposes, a logarithmic transformation allows us to immediately treat our data in *percentage* terms. For example, the standard deviation of the logarithms of the six prices of stock A = .0748; this value is fairly close to the $CV(P_a)$ = .0816 shown above. Similarly, $SD(\log P_b)$ = .3837, as contrasted to $CV(P_b)$ = .3873, and $SD(\log P_c)$ = .1801, vis-à-vis the $CV(P_c)$ = .1937.

While the "coefficient of variation" is easier to explain, the logarithmic standard deviation concept has more mathematical validity. We have occasion to utilize both forms throughout this book. For the moment just consider the logarithmic form as a computational transformation or procedure that facilitates the interpretation of data in percentage terms. That's about as painlessly as it can be presented.

As an extreme illustration of the risk reduction aspects of diversification, consider a portfolio consisting of one share of stock B and one share of stock C. Go back and look at Table 2.1, or at the deviations shown in Tables 2.2 and 2.3. The fictitious data show that whenever the price of B varied, the price of C changed in the opposite direction and by the same amount! Although each individually might be considered a somewhat "risky" stock, together stocks B and C form a "riskless" portfolio, at least in nominal dollar terms. The total value of the portfolio remained at $30 throughout the periods of observation. [Such a portfolio would still be subject to the purchasing power risk (3), however.]

In the real world, there are no B and C combinations possible. The prices shown in the example were contrived to illustrate the principle of risk reduction, but it is purposely extreme. As we see later on, the evidence is irrefutable that all stocks are influenced to some degree by the movements of the market as a whole. That is, every stock has some element of systematic risk in its price variability. For two stocks to behave as B and C, always varying inversely, it would be necessary for one of the stocks to *always* move contrary to the market, or for both stocks to be entirely independent of systematic influences. In reality, there are no such stocks.

"Return" Form

Most of the empirical analyses of stock prices in recent years have utilized another form of standardization. Since stocks exhibit prices and volatilities of considerable differences, the concept of "holding period returns" reduces some of the dimensions of comparison. Basically, the "return" format is simply an expression of a stock's percentage change during the holding period. The return variable, Y_t, is defined as the ratio of P_t, the price of the stock at the end of the period, divided by P_{t-1}, its price at the end of the preceding period. That is,

$$Y_t = \frac{P_t}{P_{t-1}}$$

and this is a gross percentage change measure; if P_t increases from P_{t-1}, Y_t takes on values greater than 1.0. Similarly, if P_t results from a price decline, Y_t is less than 1.0, and no change in the stock's price implies that $P_t = P_{t-1}$, and $Y_t = 1.0$. Back to stocks A, B, and C, the return variable is defined only for periods 2, 3, . . . , 6, since P_1 is the first observation. For stock A, $Y_2 = P_2/P_1 = 9/11 = .818$; $Y_3 = P_3/P_2 = 10/9 = 1.111$. The holding period return forms for stocks A, B, and C appear in Table 2.5. The average holding period returns, $\overline{Y}_j$, where j = stocks A, B, and C, are simply the sums of the individual Y_{jt}'s, divided by N—here equal to 5, instead of 6, since one observation is lost due to the percentage change nature of the calculation: P_{j1} is included $Y_{j2} = P_{j2}/P_{j1}$. The "return form" averages for stocks A, B, and C are

$$\overline{Y}_a = .969; \qquad \overline{Y}_b = 1.081; \qquad \text{and} \qquad \overline{Y}_c = 1.046$$

Similarly, the variance and standard deviations are also calculated as before. The respective period deviations are as shown in Table 2.6. Since the "return form" transforms the price changes into percentage change form, the coefficients of variation and standard deviations do not differ very much, since both represent relative variation measures.

Table 2.5   Holding Period Return Forms for Stocks A, B, and C

Period	Stock A	Stock B	Stock C
1	—	—	—
2	.818	1.333	.917
3	1.111	1.500	.818
4	1.000	1.167	.889
5	1.100	1.071	.938
6	818	.333	1.667

Table 2.6 Variances, Standard Deviations and CV's for Stocks A, B, and C

Period	Stock A		Stock B		Stock C	
	deviation	(deviation)^2	deviation	(deviation)^2	deviation	(deviation)^2
1	—	—	—	—	—	—
2	−.161	.023	.252	.064	−.129	.017
3	.142	.020	.419	.176	−.228	.052
4	.031	.001	.086	.007	−.157	.025
5	.131	.017	−.010	.000^a	−.108	.012
6	−.151	.023	−.748	.560	.621	.386
Sum	.002^a	.084	.001^a	.807	.001^a	.492
Variance:	.084/5 = .017		.807/5 = .161		.492/5 = .098	
Standard deviation:		.130		.401		.313
Coefficient of variation ($s/\overline{Y}$):		.135		.371		.299

^{a}Due to rounding.

VOLATILITY OF ACTUAL STOCKS

In order to provide some perspective on the standard deviation measure of stock return variability, Table 2.7 displays the decile range end-values for nearly 1700 stocks. These are the stocks covered in the Value Line Investment Survey and comprise the Value Line Composite Index (VLIC). The ranges of "monthly average" standard deviations are shown for two 5 year periods: July 1977 through June 1982 and July 1972 through June 1977. As indicated, the standard deviations have been calculated in logarithmic return form and therefore can be roughly interpreted as percent-per-month variation.

Each decile interval includes 10 percent of the stocks, ordered from highest volatility to lowest. That is, the stocks with the greatest variation (Decile I) exhibited standard deviation measures ranging from 26.472 to 13.957 in the July 1977–June 1982 period, and from 36.411 to 15.896 in the July 1972–June 1977 period. Decile II is the 10 percent group of stocks with the next highest volatilities, as measured by the logarithmic standard deviation. The ordering continues in terms of decreasing standard deviations, so that Decile X includes the stocks with the lowest variability. As

Table 2.7   Stock Price Standard Deviations, in Logarithmic Return Form, Stocks Comprising the VLIC, Ranked by Deciles from Highest Standard Deviations to Lowest, Monthly Observations

	July 1977–June 1982		July 1972–June 1977	
Decile	Number of Stocks	Standard Deviations	Number of Stocks	Standard Deviations
I	166	26.472 – 13.957	144	36.411 – 15.896
II	167	13.929 – 12.235	144	15.820 – 13.799
III	167	12.225 – 11.055	144	13.701 – 12.210
IV	167	11.044 – 10.034	144	12.207 – 11.103
V	167	10.032 – 9.173	144	11.101 – 10.145
VI	167	9.172 – 8.278	144	10.139 – 9.407
VII	167	8.274 – 7.652	144	9.406 – 8.473
VIII	167	7.644 – 6.874	144	8.465 – 7.708
IX	167	6.872 – 5.834	144	7.705 – 6.716
X	167	5.825 – 3.463	144	6.706 – 4.063
	1669		1440	
Median Standard Deviations:		9.17		10.14
Standard Deviations of VLIC:		5.25		6.46
NYSE:		4.57		4.84

Table 2.7 indicates, the volatilities were greater throughout the decile ranges in the earlier period. That does not mean, of course, that *every* stock was more variable in the earlier period. But on the average, stock prices were more volatile from July 1972–June 1977 than they were from July 1977–June 1982. That is also reflected by the standard deviations shown for the VLIC, as well as for the New York Stock Exchange Composite Index (NYSE). Again, the median standard deviations shown for the entire group of stocks indicate higher overall stock price (return) volatility for 1972–1977 (10.14) than for 1977–1982 (9.17).

A couple of qualifying comments seem in order about Table 2.7. First, not all of the stocks currently covered by the Value Line survey are included. The main reason is that recent additions to the VLIC result in a paucity of observations; for example, as few as three data points. Second, the Decile I category for 1977–1982 excludes the stock with the highest standard deviation of all: Pengo Industries. Its value for 26 months was 45.904, almost double the next highest value of 26.472, for Triton Group. Pengo, however, did exhibit some dramatic price volatility: in

1981, the stock traded in a range from 33⅞ to 15⅞; during 1982, the trading range was 17⅝ to 2¾. Pengo was not included to avoid distorting the practical range continuity of the Decile I standard deviations.

Probably a more familiar point of reference is the volatility of the 30 stocks that make up the Dow Jones Industrial Average (DJIA). The standard deviations are shown in Table 2.8 for two 5 year periods, January 1978–December 1982 and January 1973–December 1977. The 1982 data now include the record-setting bull market move that began in August of that year. However, that modification substitutes only six monthly observations (July–December 1982) for July–December 1977. The standard deviations shown in Table 2.8 still reflect higher variability in the earlier 1973–1977 period. The averages shown at the bottom of the table also indicate lower volatility in the 1978–1982 time frame. Further, on a stock by stock basis, only seven of the Dow Jones Industrials exhibit increased standard deviations: American Brands, American Can, Inco Ltd., International Harvester, Standard Oil of California, United Technologies, and U.S. Steel. The other 23 decreased in measured volatility. While 1982 included a robust bull market, the earlier 5 year period included a 2 year bear market in 1973–1974, during which the Dow Industrials declined by more than 40 percent.

There is one additional point to be made about the standard deviations of the Dow Jones Industrial stocks. If we compare Tables 2.8 and 2.7, it is readily apparent that the large, heavily capitalized Dow Industrials exhibit standard deviations that generally correspond to the lower deciles in Table 2.7. For the 30 DJIA stocks, 5 fall within the range of Decile X, 9 in Decile IX, 6 in Decile VIII, 6 in Decile VII, 2 in Decile VI, 1 in Decile V (Inco Ltd.), and 1 in Decile III (International Harvester). Generally, the larger, more seasoned corporations, and especially the utility stocks, exhibit relatively low price variability. Appendix E shows the 5 year standard deviations for each period (1973–1977 and 1978–1982) for most of the stocks included in the VLIC.

COVARIANCE AND CORRELATION

Now to return to our statistics refresher. For our purposes the important statistical measures relate to the degree of interdependence, or association, between two variables. The concepts and calculations follow quite naturally from our previous examples and statistical computations.

Table 2.8 Stock Price Standard Deviations, in Logarithmic Return Form, for the 30 Stocks of the DJIA, Monthly Observations

Stock	January 1978–December 1982	January 1973–December 77	Stock	January 1978–December 1982	January 1973–December 1977
Allied Corp.	7.995	9.201	IBM	5.522	7.549
Alcoa	7.718	9.296	International Harvester	11.605	8.648
American Brands	6.448	5.010	International Paper	7.622	9.107
American Can	7.554	5.741	Merck	6.119	8.205
American Express	8.176	11.459	MMM	6.290	7.875
American T & T	3.621	4.557	Owens-Ill.	6.825	7.723
Bethelehem Steel	8.247	8.642	Procter & Gamble	4.990	7.094
duPont	7.392	8.156	Sears	6.720	7.428
Eastman Kodak	6.890	8.031	Standard Oil (CA)	8.694	7.160
Exxon	5.588	6.749	Texaco	6.072	6.949
General Electric	5.278	7.608	Union Carbide	6.227	8.483
General Foods	5.961	8.231	United Technologies	8.131	7.827
General Motors	6.415	7.470	U.S. Steel	8.395	7.915
Goodyear	6.294	8.249	Westinghouse	7.599	11.026
Inco Ltd.	9.751	8.028	Woolworth	7.940	10.113

Average of the Standard Deviations of the Dow Jones Industrials Component stocks, 5 year period ending:

December 1982 = 7.069
December 1977 = 7.984

First, let's consider *covariance* (cov). This statistic is the central or core element in determining correlation. The calculation of the covariance of two variables, X and Y, denoted as $cov(X,Y)$, is just the sum of the *paired* (cross) products of the deviations from the mean, divided by the number of observations. Continuing with our previous data about stocks A, B, and C, to obtain the $cov(P_a, P_b)$ we would multiply the deviations of P_a from its mean, $\overline{P}_a$, times the deviations of P_b from its mean, $\overline{P}_b$, period by period. Then we simply add up these cross products and divide by N (here equal to 6), and we've got it: covariance.

To illustrate, for P_a and P_b in period 1, the deviations from the means are 1 and -4, respectively. Thus $(P_{a1} - \overline{P}_a)(P_{b1} - \overline{P}_b) = (1)(-4) = -4$; for period 2, $(P_{a2} - \overline{P}_a)(P_{b2} - \overline{P}_b) = (-1)(-2) = 2$. Table 2.9 develops the covariance calculations for all three stocks' prices; that is, $cov(P_a, P_b)$, $cov(P_b, P_c)$, and $cov(P_a, P_c)$. The deviations used are the same as those that appear in Table 2.2 as well as Table 2.3.

Notice that the $cov(X,Y) = cov(Y,X)$, since the order of the pairwise multiplication of the deviations does not affect the resulting values. Again, it is important to recognize that the covariance statistic is a pairwise concept limited to just two variables at a time. Further, the numerical value of a covariance does not have much significance in and of itself or

Table 2.9   Covariance Calculation

Period	dev(P_a)	dev(P_b)	dev(P_c)	(D_a)(D_b)	(D_a)(D_c)	(D_b)(D_c)
1	1	-4	4	-4	4	-16
2	-1	-2	2	2	-2	-4
3	0	2	-2	0	0	-4
4	0	4	-4	0	0	-16
5	1	5	-5	5	-5	-25
6	-1	-5	5	5	-5	-25
Sum of Deviation Products				8	-8	-90

Since $N = 6$, then $cov(P_a, P_b) = \dfrac{8}{6} = 1.333$

$$cov(P_a, P_c) = \dfrac{-8}{6} = -1.333$$

$$cov(P_b, P_c) = \dfrac{-90}{6} = -15.000$$

much intuitive appeal. Unless normalized in some way (e.g., by expressing the variables in percentage change terms, à la the "return" form), the value of a covariance can be arbitrarily influenced by changing the unit of measurement, for example, measuring in inches rather than feet.

An important standardization or normalization procedure is to divide the covariance value by the product of the standard deviations of the two variables in question. This procedure results in the *correlation coefficient*—a measure that permits ready comparison among different pairwise combinations of variables. The correlation coefficient, conventionally denoted by R, allows us to compare not only cov(X, Y) with the cov(X, Z), but completely different combinations, for example, cov(A, B) with cov(C, D). The formula for R is

$$R(X, Y) = \frac{\text{cov}(X, Y)}{(\text{SD}_x)(\text{SD}_y)}$$

where the cov(X, Y) is calculated as illustrated above, and the standard deviations, SD_x and SD_y, are calculated as demonstrated previously, namely, as the square roots of var(X) and var(Y).

To continue with our data on stocks A, B, and C, the correlation coefficient of the prices of A and B would be computed as follows:

$$R(P_a, P_b) = \frac{\text{cov}(P_a, P_b)}{(\text{SD}_a)(\text{SD}_b)}$$

From Table 2.9, the cov(P_a, P_b) = 1.333, and from Table 2.4 SD_a = .816 and SD_b = 3.873, so

$$R(P_a, P_b) = \frac{1.333}{(.816)(3.873)} = \frac{1.333}{3.160} = .422$$

Similarly,

$$R(P_a, P_c) = \frac{\text{cov}(P_a, P_c)}{(\text{SD}_a)(\text{SD}_c)}$$

$$= \frac{-1.333}{(.816)(3.873)} \text{ from Tables 2.9 and 2.4}$$

$$= \frac{-1.333}{3.160}$$

$$= -.422$$

The correlation coefficient (R) measures the degree of association between two variables. There is a probability distribution that can be used to test hypotheses about the statistical significance of correlation between variables, but that is beyond the scope of our discussion here. It is important to keep in mind that high degrees of correlation do not imply *causation*.

The covariance numerator, as we have seen, can take on negative, as well as positive, values; that is why we retained the algebraic sign of the deviations from the mean. And since the denominator, the product of the standard deviations, must be a positive number, R can take on values ranging from -1 to $+1$. Correlation coefficient values near $+1$ (e.g., .957) suggest strong positive association, while those near -1 (e.g., $-.944$) connote strong negative correlation.

Values at the extrema imply "perfect positive" correlation when $R = +1.0$ and "perfect negative" correlation when $R = -1.0$. For $R(X, Y) = +1.0$, when X deviates above its mean, $\overline{X}$, Y must also deviate above its mean in exactly the same degree, relative to the standard deviations of X and Y in the denominator. Similarly, when X deviates below its mean, the corresponding Y value must deviate below its mean, in the same relative degree.

For perfect negative correlation, i.e., $R(X, Y) = -1$, when X deviates above its mean, the corresponding movement of Y must be below its mean in the same relative degree. Since the cov(X, Y) in the numerator must be negative, it must also equal the product of $(SD_x)(SD_y)$ in order to obtain a perfect negative correlation of -1. Just such an example is provided by our, admittedly artificial, variables: the stock prices of B and C. Let's check to see if the correlation coefficient is -1.

$$R(P_b, P_c) = \frac{\text{cov}(P_b, P_c)}{(SD_b)(SD_c)} \text{ from Tables 2.9 and 2.4}$$

$$= \frac{-15.0}{(3.873)(3.873)} = \frac{-15.0}{15.0} = -1.0$$

Go back and look at Table 2.2. When the price of stock B deviated -4 in period 1, stock C deviated $+4$; in period 2, when B deviated -2, stock C deviated $+2$, and so on, for all six periods, As mentioned earlier, two such stocks as B and C do not really exist. The illustration does demonstrate "perfect negative" correlation, though.

Finally, values of R near zero, that is, .098 or $-.146$, suggest no strong association between the two variables. A firm understanding of this statistic is of great value when we assess the relationships between key variables that underlie and relate to stock index futures.

REGRESSION ANALYSIS

There remains one additional weapon we must add to our statistical arsenal before beginning the frontal assault on stock index futures and related market indicators: regression analysis. One definition of regression is the process of reasoning backward; that is an apt description in this context. Anyway, regression analysis is the birthplace of "beta," a term and concept that has infiltrated empirical research on stock prices and portfolios for over a decade. With a little more apology to the reader, we'd better find out what it is all about.

So far we have considered the variation of individual stock prices and the degree of covariability between any pair of them, that is, correlation. Regression analysis in its simplest form hypothesizes that not only is there a relationship between two variables, but the relationship takes on a particular form: principally, a *linear* one. The assumption is that simultaneous or paired values of X and Y, for example (X_i, Y_i) or (P_{a1}, P_{b1}), . . . , (P_{a6}, P_{b6}), trace out a line, or nearly so. Years of statistical research in economics (a field called econometrics) have resulted in the generalization that almost all important economic relationships are linear in nature or, alternatively, that a linear approximation is adequate for most purposes. The capital asset pricing model, as it applies to stock prices and portfolio risk, is a case in point.

The equation of a line is of the form $Y = A + BX$. In more concrete terms, an example is $Y = 10 + 4X$. That is, $A = 10$ and $B = 4$. So if we plug in any admissible value of X, out comes the corresponding value of Y. If, for example,

$$X = 3, \quad \text{then } Y = 10 + 4(3) = 22$$

and if

$$X = 4, \quad \text{then } Y = 10 + 4(4) = 26$$

and if

$$X = 5, \quad \text{then } Y = 10 + 4(5) = 30$$

A graph of this linear equation is shown in Figure 2.1. What is the value, in Figure 2.1, of Y when $X = 0$? Also, from the equation, if $X = 0$, then $Y = 10 + 4(0) = 10$. That is just the value of A, a coefficient that is called the "intercept" term of the equation, the point where the line intersects the Y axis (i.e., when $X = 0$). But now what is B, the coefficient of X?

Look back at the calculated values of Y, above, when X was set equal to 3, 4, and 5. Every time we changed the value of X by 1, the value of Y changed by 4. The coefficient B is the *slope* of the line, denoting the change in Y for a given change in X.

The linear equation model is easy when we know what the values are for A and B; if we pick an X, we can solve for Y. Conversely, if we want to know what X value corresponds to a particular value of Y, elementary algebra yields the answer. For example, if $Y = 50$, what must the value of X be in our equation $Y = 10 + 4X$? That is, $50 = 10 + 4X$, or $40 = 4X$, and $X = 10$. Notice in Figure 2.2 that A can be negative (e.g., $Y^* = -5 + 2X$), B can be negative (e.g., $Y' = 30 - 3X$), or both A and B can be negative, as in $Y'' = -7 - X$.

Now for regression analysis. Often, if not quite always, we don't know what the values of A and B are. Frequently we have observations on X and Y, that is, in joint form (X_i, Y_i) as we did for the stock prices (P_{at}, P_{bt}). Given a set of such joint (X_i, Y_i) observations (data), how can we determine the values of A and B? We are willing to assume X and Y are linearly related. (This is where the "reasoning backward" comes in.) Also, it is rare that the (X_i, Y_i) will fit exactly on a given line (see Figure 2.3), so we must provide for values that lie off the line. This is accomplished by adding an "error" or disturbance term to our hypothesized relationship; thus the equation becomes

$$Y_i = A + BX_i + u_i \qquad (2.1)$$

Where the u_i's are assumed to satisfy certain conditions, and where i simply refers to each observation, $i = 1, 2, \ldots, N$ when we have N data points, (X_i, Y_i). Moreover, we probably are never going to know the

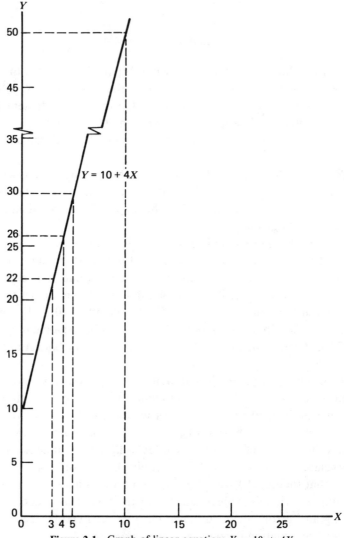

Figure 2.1 Graph of linear equation: $Y = 10 + 4X$.

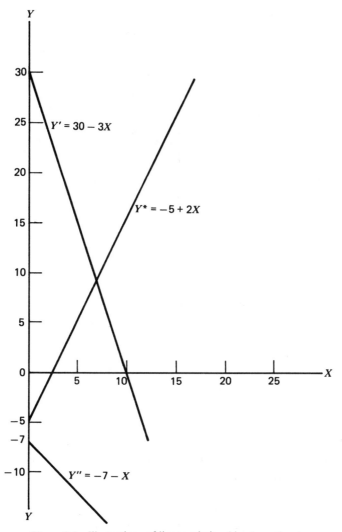

Figure 2.2 Illustrations of linear relationships (equations), when the values of *A* or *B* are negative.

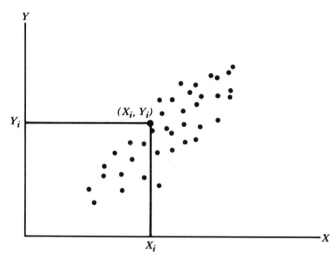

Figure 2.3 Plot of (X_i, Y_i) data points.

"true" values of A and B; we can only estimate them from the available data. In this structure Y is called the "dependent" variable, and X is the "explanatory" variable. More complicated regression procedures (multiple regression) permit us to use more than only one X to "explain" the variations in Y. Here we'll just stick to one X.

Therefore, we rewrite Eq. 2.1 in the form

$$Y_i = \hat{A} + \hat{B}X_i + e_i \tag{2.2}$$

where the carets indicate estimates of the unknown parameters—$\hat{A}$ is an estimate of A, $\hat{B}$ is an estimate of B—and the e_i's that we calculate from the regression procedure are assumed to satisfy the conditions imposed on the original u_i's in Eq. 2.1.

How do we obtain estimates of A and B? We can select values arbitrarily, or perhaps draw a line through the data points and then try to measure geometrically what $\hat{A}$ and $\hat{B}$ might be. Is there a better way? Without subjecting the reader to unnecessary mathematical mumbo jumbo, let us just state that the conventional methodology for estimating A and B is called *least squares regression* or, alternatively, "ordinary least squares." Squares of what? The e_i's that are hypothesized to correspond to the original u_i's. [The e_i's are the deviations of the actual (observed) Y_i's from the estimated regression line Y's, that is, the $\hat{Y}$'s.] Recall that in calculating the variance about the mean, we squared the deviations. Using a similar methodology, the "best" estimators of unknown A and B are obtained by finding $\hat{A}$ and $\hat{B}$ that *minimize* the sum of $(e_i)^2$, hence the description as "least squares." By rearranging Eq. 2.2 we obtain

$$e_i = Y_i - \hat{A} - \hat{B}X_i \quad \text{for } i = 1, 2, \ldots, N \tag{2.3}$$

So given values for $\hat{A}$ and $\hat{B}$, we can obtain an estimated value for Y, denoted $\hat{Y}$. For example, suppose our estimated equation of the line, $\hat{Y} = \hat{A} + \hat{B}X$, is $\hat{Y} = 3 + 2X$; that is, $\hat{A} = 3$ and $\hat{B} = 2$. Suppose further that one of our (X_i, Y_i) data points is $(X = 3, Y = 10)$; from our estimated equation above, if $X = 3$ then $\hat{Y} = 3 + 2(3) = 9$ (see Figure 2.4). But $Y_i = 10$, not 9! That's where e_i comes in: $Y_i - \hat{Y}_i = e_i$, from Eq. 2.3. We only need to write it a little differently:

$$e_i = Y_i - (\hat{A} + \hat{B}X_i) \tag{2.4}$$

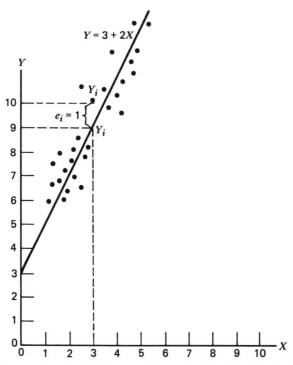

Figure 2.4 Graph of estimated regression line: $Y = 3 + 2X$.

where $\hat{A} + \hat{B}X_i = \hat{Y}_i$ from above; then $e_i = Y_i - \hat{Y}_i$ for every (X_i, Y_i) observation. We can make any one of the e_i's larger or smaller by changing $\hat{A}$ and $\hat{B}$. But when we make one e_i smaller we might make other e_i's larger; what we want are those values of $\hat{A}$ and $\hat{B}$ which make the sum of all the $(e_i)^2$ as small as possible. None of the actual Y_i's may be on the line, but it is the best "average" line, given all of the observations. The actual formulas for $\hat{A}$ and $\hat{B}$ are readily available in most statistics texts and are embedded in the statistical routines of many hand-size calculators. The derivation involves calculus, and we need not pursue the matter further.

THE COEFFICIENT OF DETERMINATION, R^2

One other important statistical tool derives from all this. Recall that R, the correlation coefficient, measures the degree of association between two variables. In the context of regression analysis, it can be shown that the sum of the squared residuals (the e_i^2's) around the "fitted" regression line, $\hat{Y} = \hat{A} + \hat{B}X$, relates to the square of R (i.e., R^2) in such a way that R^2 represents the proportion of the variation of Y "explained" by the particular X used in the regression. The sum of the e_i^2's relates to the unexplained proportion. The derivation is beyond the scope of this discussion, but the result remains an important one: R^2 in a regression analysis is a measure of the proportion, or percent, of Y's variation "attributable" to the variation in X, the independent, or "explanatory" variable. Again, high R^2 values do not necessarily imply causation: in some cases X could be used as the dependent variable Y, and R^2 would remain unchanged.

BETA

In the equations above, we have used A and B to represent the coefficients, the true values and the estimated values. In other presentations of regression analysis, B is usually denoted by the Greek letter β and estimates of it as $\hat{\beta}$. It is the same parameter, the slope of the line. The financial statistical literature seems to have adopted, or more accurately *kidnapped*, "beta" as its own particular parameter, relating the responsiveness of a stock to variations in the "market." We follow that convention also, in order to relate the work of others. But it is fully recognized that beta had a home before the zealots of the capital asset pricing model (CAPM) usurped it.

So much for the methodology. Let's explore an example from the "real world" to demonstrate how regression analysis actually works. Suppose we are interested in the relationship between the price movements of NCR Corp. and the "market" during the fourth quarter of 1982. If we let the weekly closing prices of NCR be the Y's and the corresponding weekly closing values of the DJIA be the X's, then our hypothesized linear relationship is expressed below as

$$\text{NCR}_t = A + B\,(\text{DJIA})_t + u_t \tag{2.5}$$

where NCR_t is the price of NCR at the close of week t, DJIA_t is the week's closing value of the DJIA, and the disturbance term, u_t, is assumed to satisfy the usual spherical conditions. The respective values for NCR and DJIA are shown in Table 2.10; $t = 1, 2, \ldots, 14$, the number of weekly observations from October 1–December 31, 1982. The estimated values for Eq. 2.5 are

$$\text{NCR}_t = -116.607 + .195(\text{DJIA})_t, \qquad R^2 = .7154 \tag{2.6}$$

Interpretation of $\hat{A}$ is somewhat meaningless, since it implies that if $\text{DJIA} = 0$, then the price of NCR would be -116.607. For many forms of this sort of estimation, the constant term is frequently disregarded. More important is the estimate of $\hat{B} = .195$. That estimate is interpreted to mean that for a 1.00 change in the DJIA, the price of NCR changed in the same direction (i.e., positive sign) by about 19.5 cents, *during* the period of observation (October 1–December 31, 1982). Finally, the R^2 statistic suggests that variations of the DJIA "explained" nearly 72 percent of the variation in the price of NCR. The other statistics that we have explored in this chapter are shown in the lower portion of Table 2.10; namely, the respective means, variances, standard deviations, and coefficients of variation and correlation, R.

The form of Eq. 2.5 does not tell us much about the relative responsiveness of NCR's price. A second specification would be in "return" form, shown on the right side of Table 2.10. The equation to be estimated would be

$$\frac{\text{NCR}_t}{\text{NCR}_{t-1}} = \hat{A} + \hat{B}\left(\frac{\text{DJIA}_t}{\text{DJIA}_{t-1}}\right) + e_t \tag{2.7}$$

where t now equals 2, 3, . . . , 14, since the data period now covers
October 8–December 31, 1982. The resulting estimated regression coefficients are

$$\frac{\text{NCR}_t}{\text{NCR}_{t-1}} = -.324 + 1.335 \left(\frac{\text{DJIA}_t}{\text{DJIA}_{t-1}} \right), \qquad R^2 = .5067 \qquad (2.8)$$

In this form, we are dealing with period by period percentage changes;
the interpretation of $\hat{B}$ is that NCR increased 13.35 percent when the DJIA
changed by 10 percent, for the estimation period. Notice that this regression explained less variation, only about 50 percent, than the form in Eq.
2.6. Again, the other statistics are shown in the lower portion of Table

Table 2.10   Example Regression Data: NCR and DJIA—Weekly Observations, October 1–December 31, 1982

			Return Form	
Date	$Y = $ NCR Price	$X = $ DJIA	$Y = \dfrac{\text{NCR}_t}{\text{NCR}_{t-1}}$	$X = \dfrac{\text{DJIA}_t}{\text{DJIA}_{t-1}}$
10/1	62⅝	907.74	—	—
10/8	68¾	986.85	1.0978	1.0872
10/15	68½	993.10	.9964	1.0063
10/22	79¾	1031.46	1.1642	1.0386
10/29	82	991.72	1.0282	.9615
11/5	88	1051.78	1.0732	1.0606
11/12	85	1039.92	.9659	.9887
11/19	85	1021.25	1.0000	.9820
11/26	84⅜	1007.36	.9926	.9864
12/3	91	1031.36	1.0785	1.0238
12/10	86	1018.76	.9451	.9878
12/17	82¼	1011.50	.9564	.9928
12/23	88¾	1045.07	1.0790	1.0332
12/31	86	1046.54	.9690	1.0014
Means:	81.286	1013.172	1.0266	1.0116
Standard deviations:	8.546	37.011	.0664	.0354
Coefficients of variation:	.105	.037	.0647	.0350

	$\hat{A} = -116.607$	$\hat{B} = 0.195$	$\hat{A} = -0.3240$	$\hat{B} = 1.335$
	$R = .8458$	$R^2 = .7154$	$R = .7118$	$R^2 = .5067$

2.10; notice that the coefficients of variation for DJIA did not change very much, but that NCR's did from Eq. (2.6). In addition, both Eq. 2.6 and 2.7 were estimated in logarithms; the statistics are shown below for both log transformations:

$$\log(\text{NCR}_t) = \log \hat{A} + \hat{B} \log (\text{DJIA}_t) + e_t \qquad (2.9)$$

$$= -13.264 + 2.546 \log (\text{DJIA}_t), \qquad R^2 = .7302$$

$$\overline{Y} = 4.3924, \qquad \overline{X} = 6.9202, \qquad SD_y = .1123,$$

$$SD_x = .0377, \qquad R = .8545$$

$$\log \left(\frac{\text{NCR}_t}{\text{NCR}_{t-1}} \right) = \log \hat{A} + \hat{B} \log \left(\frac{\text{DJIA}_t}{\text{DJIA}_{t-1}} \right) + e_t \qquad (2.10)$$

$$= .0101 + 1.311 \log \left(\frac{\text{DJIA}_t}{\text{DJIA}_{t-1}} \right), \qquad R^2 = .5069$$

$$\overline{Y} = .0244, \qquad \overline{X} = .0109, \qquad SD_y = .0638,$$

$$SD_x = .0346, \qquad R = .7120$$

The coefficients of variation are not shown for Eq. 2.9 and 2.10, since the log standard deviations reflect relative variance of the respective variables. Compare the coefficients of variation Eq. 2.6 with the standard deviations of Eq. 2.9, the logarithmic transformation of Eq. 2.6: in the former $CV(X) = .037$ and in the latter, $SD_x = .0377$; similarly, $CV(Y) = .105$ from Eq. 2.6, while $SD_y = .1123$ in Eq. 2.9. In the return form equations, Eq. 2.8 and 2.10, the coefficients of variation and the standard deviations are all very close in value, about .035 for X and .064 for Y.

Given these four different forms of estimating the same relationship, which is the one to use? The straight linear specifications (Eq. 2.6 and 2.9) "explain" about 20 percent more of the variation in NCR than do the return (Eq. 2.8) or log return (Eq. 2.10); however, the beta coefficient estimated in the latter forms is easier to interpret, and does not differ in estimated value by very much, that is, $\hat{B} = 1.3+$. If we look at the estimated β values for NCR (monthly data, 5 year period) in Appendix E, with NYSE as the explanatory variable, the value is 1.37 for 1978–1982, and with VLIC, for the same 5 year period, the estimated beta is 1.24. It should be emphasized that these estimates pertain to *past* behavior, and may not apply in the future; but for the moment we can consider the "return" form (Eq. 2.8) or its log transformation (Eq. 2.10) as probably the superior specifications.

SUMMARY

Variation has been called the heart of statistics. It is also at the heart of financial asset risk. The most prevalent form is variation in the prices of the assets held—exposing the investor to possible losses in monetary value, as well as possible gains. Sometimes the "variation" occurs in a more subtle form: changes in consumer or producer prices which affect the "real value" of assets held, even though their nominal dollar values remain fixed, for example, savings accounts and cash.

In this chapter we have explored more observable variation: the volatility of stock prices. In that context, we have reviewed some valuable statistical tools with which to confront a world of constantly fluctuating economic asset values. Starting with the familiar arithmetic mean, or "average," the discussion developed the statistical concepts and measures of dispersion: the variance and its square root form, the standard deviation. These same measures applied to stock price variability, for many purposes, define "risk." The connection to stock index futures may seem remote at this point, but mitigating the systematic risk, or market-related variation in the prices of stocks, is a key focal point for these financial instruments.

Along the way, standard deviations of actual stocks were examined: with respect to the entire ranges of stock price variability during the last decade, and for somewhat more familiar reference, the individual standard deviation measures for the stocks comprising the DJIA. Generally, the variability of these latter prominent issues ranks in the less volatile strata (deciles).

More of the statistical bridgework built upon relative measures of stock price variability, or those "normalized" in percentage terms. Among these were the heuristic "coefficient of variation" (CV) statistic, the logarithmic transformation of stock prices, and the percentage change "return form" (P_t/P_{t-1}). The latter is the archway leading from the theoretical evolution of portfolio theory, as we see in Chapter 4, to the concept of *systematic risk*.

Finally, statistical measures of association and correspondence, that is, covariance and correlation, emerged as the core elements of *regression analysis*. This latter methodology has been the proverbial workhouse for testing various propositions of capital market theory and for isolating empirically the different types of influences on stock price variation. Regression analysis is the underpinning for bringing stock index futures into the appropriate focus.

3 Stock Market Indicators

Common stocks are traded in a number of different locations. The largest and best known is the New York Stock Exchange. In addition, stocks are bought and sold on the American Stock Exchange, the National Association of Securities Dealers' over-the-counter system (NASDAQ), and on various other regional exchanges. The stocks of the dominant U.S. corporations are traded on the New York Stock Exchange, about 1500–1600 issues. In the aggregate, there are over 5000 issues traded publicly. In commodity market parlance, these are the "cash" or "spot" market assets.

Since the evidence is overwhelming that stock prices tend to move up and down together, a convenient way to summarize general market movements is to use stock price averages or indexes. These market indicators provide a summary of the direction and extent of "average" changes of stock prices. However, the covariability of stock prices should be kept in perspective; on any given day, there are always some issues that move contrary to the general trend (e.g., the advance-decline ratio), even when a market move is an extreme one. But over reasonable time intervals, all stocks—even the so-called contra-cyclicals, have a positive correlation with general market movements.

Stock market indicators come in a variety of forms; the differences among them in terms of issues included or method of calculation result in slight or purposeful divergence of short term movements. For example, some indexes include only stocks from a particular industrial sector (e.g., utilities), and some indicators relate to stocks on one exchange only (e.g., the American Exchange Market Value Index). Although there are a fairly wide variety of indicators, we consider here only those that are relevant to stock index futures contracts.

THE DOW JONES INDUSTRIAL AVERAGE

Even though there is not (at this writing) a futures contract based on it, the Dow Jones Industrial Average (DJIA) has played a central role in the development and regulatory approval process (see Chapter 6) for those stock index contracts that are in existence. Another reason for including the DJIA is that it is probably the most widely followed and recognized stock market indicator. When an investor asks a stockbroker "How is the market doing?" the response is almost always in terms of the DJIA. In addition to the 30 industrials, there are also the Dow Jones Transportation Average (20 stocks), the Dow Utilities Average (15 stocks), and the Dow Jones 65 stock Composite Average. But it is the change in the Dow Jones Industrial Average that is routinely reported daily on both national and local newscasts.

In the simplest terms, the DJIA is just an "average" price of its component stocks. This can be easily illustrated. Suppose there were only 3 stocks in the DJIA, instead of the actual 30, with the price of stock A being $20, that of stock B, $10, and that of stock C, $30. The value of the "average" would be $(20 + 10 + 30)/3 = 60/3 = 20$. Instead of a value of 20 (dollars) for the average, we are familiar with values ranging from 500, in 1956, to over 1000, but the principle is the same. If there had never been any stock splits, or stock dividends, or changes in the components of the DJIA, the "average" would simply be the sum of the 30 stock prices divided by 30.

The splits and changes are the source of the DJIA "divisor syndrome." To illustrate, suppose that stock C above splits 2 for 1, so that its postsplit price is $15 instead of $30. If the divisor were left at 3, for the moment, the "average" would suddenly be changed to $(20 + 10 + 15)/3 = 45/3 = 15$ instead of its previous value of 20. However, the decline in stock C's price is due not to a change in the market's valuation of the company but to the company issuing an additional one share for every one previously outstanding. Twice the number of shares times half the price leaves the aggregate market value of stock C unchanged! Should the Dow average show a decrease because of that? Obviously not. The intent of the average is to depict what is transpiring in the market. Therefore some adjustment is in order.

The "adjustment" is arrived at in the following way. If the average was 20 before the split, by what do we have to divide 45 (the sum of stocks A, B, and C's current prices) to get back to 20? The answer is $45/D^* = 20$, and $D^* = 45/20 = 2.25$. So instead of dividing the sum of the prices by 3, we divide by an adjusted divisor (D^*) to allow the average to be unaffected by the split. The divisor for the DJIA is adjusted regularly to accommodate stock splits, and not distort the average. Instead of a divisor of 30, by August 1965, for example, the original divisor of 16.67 had been reduced through stock splits and substitutions (changes in the 30 companies, like the recent addition of American Express in place of Johns Manville) to 2.278 (cf. Eiteman et al., 1966, p. 177) and by the end of 1975, the divisor was 1.6 (Fosback, 1976, p. 284). The current value of the divisor (June, 1983) is 1.248.

In actuality, the divisor for the DJIA has never been 30! Before publication of the *Wall Street Journal* began on July 8, 1889, the Dow Jones averages were published in a business and finance daily letter, and consisted of eleven stocks, nine of which were railroads. In order to recognize that the industrial structure had changed, by the growth of the various "trusts" (tobacco, whisky, sugar, oil, and steel), two averages appeared in the June 1896 *Wall Street Journal:* one for 20 railroad stocks, and another for 12 "active, representative industrial stocks." By 1916, the industrials had been expanded to 20 stocks; and until October 13, 1915, the industrial averages had been computed on a percentage basis. On that date, however, the Exchange ruled that all stock transactions be put in terms of dollars per share.

The present computation method of divisor adjustment for the DJIA began on September 10, 1928. Prior to that date, stock splits were adjusted in the *numerator,* a procedure that rendered the average susceptible to distortions. However, confining the adjustments to the denominator has not eliminated the distortions, either. The change on September 10, 1928 resulted in an adjusted divisor of 12.7 for the 20 industrials. When the DJIA increased to 30 stocks on October 1 1928, the divisor changed from 12.7 to 16.67 (Eiteman et al., 1966, p. 177). As indicated, stock splits and substitutions of particular stocks in and out of the DJIA have resulted in continual decreases in the divisor, to its current value, which is less than 2.0. It never equalled 30.

The divisor adjustment method used for the DJIA is not without some impact, especially in terms of an implicit "weighting" of the average. For example, in our illustration, before stock C split at a price of 30, it had a "weight" in the average of .5 (i.e., 30/sum of prices, 60); at the postsplit price of 15, stock C's weight declined to $\frac{1}{3} = \frac{15}{45}$. This is the so-called splitting bias, which results from the divisor adjustment procedure: implicitly more weight shifts to the stocks that remain unsplit.

Other criticisms have been leveled at the DJIA. Among them are its "anti-growth bias" (which assumes that growth stocks split more than nongrowth stocks); a "blue chip bias" (due to the sample used), and its "arithmetic mean bias" (which gives equal weight to equal absolute rather than percentage changes in stock prices) (cf. Latane et al., 1971, pp. 75–76). In addition, the small sample bias has provoked observations that the DJIA may not be truly "representative of the market." An interesting example of this aspect was pointed out by Norman Fosback: "If IBM had not been pulled from the Dow Jones Industrial Average in 1939 in favor of American Tel. & Tel, the DJIA today [ca. 1976] would be more than twice its current level [i.e., around 1500–1600 at that time]" (Fosback, 1976, p. 282).

CAPITALIZATION-WEIGHTED INDEXES

Two of the existing stock index futures contracts are based on indexes of stock prices which are structured to reflect relative weights based on each company's capitalization. The relative weights are determined by the price of the stock multiplied by the number of shares outstanding. That is a company's "market value" and, relative to the total of all companies' market values in the index, is its relative weight in the index.

A simplified example can be extended from our micro Dow Jones illustration. Capitalization values for each stock are obtained by multiplying each stock's price by the number of shares outstanding:

Stock	Price	Number of Shares	Capitalization Value
A	$20	2 million	$ 40 million
B	$10	10 million	$100 million
C	$30	2 million	$ 60 million
Total capitalization value			$200 million

Each stock's relative weight in the capitalization-weighted index is simply its proportion of the total index's capitalization value. The relative weights for this illustration are shown below:

Stock	Proportion of Total	Weight	"Dow" Average Weights
A	40/200	.20	20/60 = .33
B	100/200	.50	10/60 = .17
C	60/200	.30	30/60 = .50
Total		1.00	1.00

The prices shown above correspond to the "presplit" prices of the preceding illustration. Notice how the relative weights differ; stock C, for example, carried a weight of .50 in the "micro Dow" example, but in the capitalization-weighted index, stock C has a relative weight of .30.

Now let's again consider the two-for-one split for stock C; the capitalization data would be the following, postsplit:

Stock	Price	Number of Shares	Capitalization Value
A	$20	2 million	$ 40 million
B	$10	10 million	$100 million
C	$15	4 million	$ 60 million
Total capitalization value			$200 million

Stock C's relative weight in the index is *not changed;* the total capitalization is still $200 million, and stock C's weight is still 60/200 = .30 as before. Recall that in our "mini Dow" example, the postsplit weight declined from .5 to .333; here it remains unaffected by the split.

INDEX FORM

A convention common to almost all market indicators (except the Dow Averages and the Wilshire 5000) is that they are typically expressed in *index number* form. All that means is that some previous period's value is selected as the "base" (I_0) and set equal to some arbitrary value (e.g., 10, 50, 100). Any period's total capitalization, for example, can be converted to index number form, simply by dividing through by the base period value (I_0).

This index number conversion can be shown in terms of our capitalization-weighted illustration. Suppose we choose the $200 million total as the base for an index, $I_0 = $200 million, and express our index numbers so that $I_0 = 100.00$. Let's consider two subsequent time periods, time 1 and time 2, and the respective prices of stocks A, B, and C. The number of shares outstanding for the stocks are assumed to remain unchanged.

			Time 1		Time 2
Stock	Number of Shares	Price	Capitalization Value	Price	Capitalization Value
A	2 million	$22	$ 44 million	$24	48 million
B	10 million	$13	$130 million	$13	$130 million
C	4 million	$14	$ 56 million	$ 8	$ 32 million
Total captalization value			$230 million		$210 million

The index values for time 1 and time 2 can readily be calculated by dividing through by the index base value ($200 million) and then multiplying by the base number selected for the index, in this case 100.00. Thus the index values for time 1 and time 2 are computed below:

$$\text{time 1} = \frac{230}{200} = 1.15 \, (\times \, 100.00) = 115.00$$

$$\text{time 2} = \frac{210}{200} = 1.05 \, (\times \, 100.00) = 105.00$$

Alternatively, if we had selected $I_0 = 50$ as the base value, then the corresponding index values for time 1 = 1.15 ($\times$ 50) = 57.50, and for time 2 = 1.05 ($\times$ 50) = 52.5. In passing, it is useful to note that the choice of base period is completely arbitrary, as is the "scale" value of the index (i.e., 10, 50, 100). Also, any period can serve as the base period, since all other "raw" values are divided by a constant, the base period capitalization value. The consequent index series values retain relative proportions, independent of the base period and scale value chosen.

THE STANDARD & POOR'S 500 STOCK INDEX

The "underlying commodity" for the Chicago Mercantile Exchange's stock index futures contract is the S&P 500. The S&P 500 Index is computed just like the capitalization example shown above. As its name suggests, the S&P index consists of 500 stocks, with the price of each "weighted" by its capitalization, or "market value." For example, in S&P's publication "Stocks in the Standard & Poor's 500," September 29, 1978, General Motors had a market value of $18,030.14 million and represented a weight of 2.75 percent of the total market value of the S&P 500 of $655,789.0 million. A stock's weight in the index changes as its capitalization value changes, relative to the index base.

The base value for the S&P 500 is the average market value of those 500 stocks during the period 1941–1943, and that value was set (scaled) equal to 10. Others have observed that $10 closely approximated the average price of a share of stock on the New York Stock Exchange during that period. During 1982, values for the S&P 500 Index ranged from about 103.00 to slightly over 143.00.

Like the Dow Jones averages, there are sectoral subindexes maintained by Standard & Poor's: 400 industrials, 40 utilities, 20 transportation companies, and 40 financials. Also like the current DJIA 30 stocks, the S&P index has not always had 500 component stocks. Before 1957, there were 90 stocks in the S&P index: 50 industrials, 20 rails, and 20 utilities (Eitemen et al., 1966, p. 184). Prior to the middle of 1976, all issues in the S&P 500 were listed on the NYSE. At that time, however, the index was altered to include some financial stocks and insurance companies that were traded in the over-the-counter market. When issues are added and deleted from the index, adjustments are made in the index base to retain consistency.

As stated by Standard & Poor's, the selection of issues for the S&P 500 index is "with the aim of achieving a distribution by broad industry groupings that approximates the distribution of these groupings in the New York Stock Exchange common stock population" (Standard & Poor's Corp., p. 1). Further, each stock included in the index is intended to be a viable representative within its industry group, without regard to its investment appeal. And while the S&P 500 are not the 500 largest companies, the total market value of the index is approximately 80 percent of the capitalization value of all stocks listed on the New York Stock Exchange (cf. Chicago Mercantile Exchange, 1981a, p. 5).

THE NEW YORK STOCK EXCHANGE COMPOSITE INDEX (NYSE)

The New York Stock Exchange Index is very similar to the S&P 500. Like the S&P 500, the NYSE index is capitalization-weighted, but instead of a selected sample of 500 issues, the NYSE index includes *all* of the common stocks traded on the "Big Board." As of April 30, 1982, the NYSE index covered 1520 issues, over three times the number included in the S&P 500 (New York Futures Exchange, 1982a, p. 3). The NYSE also contains subindexes: financials, transportation, utility, and industrials. In late 1982, the New York Futures Exchange (NYFE) began trading a futures contract based on the financials subindex.

The base for the NYSE index is the total market value of all common stocks listed on the New York Stock Exchange on December 31, 1965. Scaled to a base of 50, this index value was about the average price of a NYSE common share on that date. The method of calculation is completely analogous to the capitalization-weighted illustrations shown above, as is the method for the S&P 500. During 1982, the NYSE index ranged from around 58.00 to slightly over 82.00.

Both the NYSE index and the S&P 500 have been extrapolated backward, to cover periods when the indexes did not actually exist. The S&P 500 was extended back to 1871 on a monthly basis by the Cowles Commission (Eiteman et al., 1966, p. 184), and the NYSE index was computed on a weekly close basis, back to 1939.

Since the NYSE index and the S&P 500 are both capitalization-weighted, and since both contain the heaviest capitalized companies, it is not surprising to find that the two indexes move in close concert. (The statistics about their correlation appear in this chapter.) The 30 stocks that comprise the DJIA account for about 26–27 percent of the total market value of the S&P 500. In the NYSE, those same 30 issues account for roughly 21–22 percent. Since the capitalization-weighted structure is the same for the S&P 500 and NYSE index, the only difference between them is that the NYSE contains about 1000 more stocks. However, since the S&P 500's total market value is about 80 percent of all the issues listed on the New York Stock Exchange, those 1000 stocks account for only about 20 percent of the NYSE total capitalization. In effect, the NYSE and S&P 500 are virtually the same index.

THE VALUE LINE COMPOSITE INDEX

The remaining stock market indicator that serves as the basis for a stock index contract is the Value Line Average, also referred to as the Value Line Composite Index (VLIC). As in the cases of the other indexes discussed so far, there are subindexes for the Value Line also: industrials, rails, and utilities. The VLIC consists of those issues covered in the Value Line Investment Survey, about 1700 stocks. These VLIC components account for about 96 percent of the dollar trading volume in U.S. equity markets. A previous estimate (1979) indicated that about 88.4 percent of the stocks in the VLIC traded on the New York Stock Exchange, 1.3 percent on the American Stock Exchange, about 9.5 percent traded in the over-the-counter market, and the remaining .8 percent traded on the regional exchanges. In terms of issues covered, then, the VLIC differs somewhat from the NYSE, but all of the S&P 500 stocks are included in the Value Line. The more important differences between the VLIC and the S&P 500 and NYSE indexes relate to their mathematical construction.

First, the VLIC is an equally weighted index, in terms of each stock's percentage change. Even though the 30 Dow Jones Industrials, for example, are included in the VLIC, they carry no more "weight" in the index's computation than any other 30 issues. A 5 percent change in General Motors has the same impact on the index as a 5 percent change in Apple Computer. This property of the VLIC results in its being relatively more sensitive to the price movements of the less heavily capitalized stocks.

Second, the indicators considered previously are all averaged arithmetically (even when capitalization-weighted). In contrast, the VLIC is averaged geometrically. The geometric mean involves the *product* (not the sum) of *n* numbers and the *n*th root of that product; that *n*th root is the geometric average, or geometric mean.

It's really not as bad as it sounds in the abstract. For a simple example, if stock A's price were 2 and stock B's were 8, the geometric average would be the second root (commonly known as the square root) of the product (2 times 8 = 16, and its "second" root = 4). The arithmetic mean, or average, would be 2 + 8 = 10/2 = 5. The geometric mean is always less than the arithmetic mean of the same numbers. If we had considered three stocks, A, B, and C, the geometric mean would have been the third (or "cube") root of $P_a \times P_b \times P_c$. But since there are

Table 3.1 Comparison of Market Indicators

Indicator	Coverage	Weighting	Averaged	Estimated Capitalization (1982)
DJIA	30 large corporations	Price (implicit)	Arithmetically	$ 240 billion
S&P 500	500 major corporations	Capitalization	Arithmetically and indexed	$ 870 billion
NYSE	1520 listed corporations	Capitalization	Arithmetically and indexed	$1060 billion
VLIC	1700 selected corporations	Equal	Geometrically and indexed	$1100 billion

about 1700 stocks covered by Value Line, how, you may be wondering, do we extract the 1700th root? Computationally, it is very easy using logarithms and, of course, a computer. The virtue of geometric averaging is that it preserves the integrity of successive upward and downward percentage changes. "Arithmetic mean bias" creeps in otherwise. So much for the technicalities, for now. The interested reader can pursue more details in Appendix A.

The VLIC is referenced to a base value of June 30, 1961 = 100.00. Before 1983, the all-time high for the VLIC had occurred in 1968, a value of 188.64, and the record low in 1974 at 47.03. During 1982, the VLIC ranged between 112.0 and 161.0. However, in early 1983, the VLIC set new record highs near the 200 level.

A brief summary of the various characteristics of the DJIA, S&P 500, NYSE, and VLIC appears in Table 3.1.

CORRELATION

Table 3.2 displays the annual correlation coefficients (R) between all of the market indicators discussed in this chapter. The period covered in the table is from 1962 to 1982, and the data used to compute R for each pair of indicators was the weekly closing value of each. As suggested earlier, the correlation between the S&P 500 and the NYSE indexes is .99+ for almost every year. That is hardly surprising, since the two are virtually the same index with regard to the stocks of large corporations, and their

Table 3.2   Major Stock Market Indicators, Annual Correlation Coefficients,
Weekly Close, 1962–1982

Year	R(VLIC, DJIA)	R(VLIC, S&P)	R(VLIC, NYSE)	R(DJIA, S&P)	R(DJIA, NYSE)	R(S&P, NYSE)
1962	.974	.989	.987	.995	.997	.999
1963	.908	.938	.935	.983	.986	.999
1964	.982	.966	.991	.962	.990	.971
1965	.960	.955	.971	.992	.994	.995
1966	.972	.982	.984	.987	.985	.999
1967	.910	.968	.980	.909	.893	.996
1968	.933	.981	.988	.970	.963	.999
1969	.974	.937	.958	.978	.975	.992
1970	.489	.749	.830	.931	.879	.991
1971	.946	.866	.849	.950	.938	.997
1972	−.134	−.284	−.134	.973	.984	.987
1973	.960	.975	.986	.981	.986	.993
1974	.955	.983	.989	.982	.973	.999
1975	.908	.946	.964	.966	.961	.997
1976	.839	.846	.868	.799	.767	.995
1977	.299	.507	.610	.945	.913	.992
1978	.962	.966	.977	.989	.986	.999
1979	.581	.966	.979	.626	.563	.995
1980	.978	.965	.972	.966	.968	.999
1981	.909	.882	.919	.955	.944	.993
1982	.952	.977	.984	.958	.986	.999

Source: The Board of Trade of Kansas City, Missouri, Inc. (KCBT).

weighting by capitalization. In general, the DJIA tracks the NYSE and the S&P 500 fairly closely, except for 1979 when the Dow tended to rise rather more slowly than did the S&P 500 and the NYSE, as well as the VLIC. During 1979 the latter was highly correlated with the S&P 500 and NYSE, but not with the Dow Industrials ($R = .581$ for VLIC and DJIA). The interpretation is that, during that year, the rise in the market seemed to be led by less heavily capitalized companies, that is, those included in the S&P 500, NYSE, and even in the VLIC, while the Dow Jones Industrials remained rather flat (see Figure 3.1).

The only other year of mediocre correlation worth noting between the DJIA and each of the other indexes was 1976. In that year, there was not a pronounced strong direction for any of the indexes. All four moved within a fairly narrow range, and the differences in structure and method of computation would easily account for the divergent movements, and

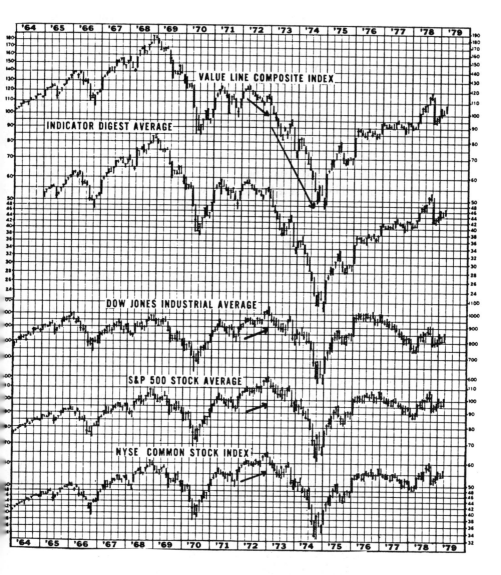

Figure 3.1 Major stock market indicators, graph of cycles and fluctuations, 1964 to 1979. Courtesy Securities Research Co., Boston, Massachusetts.

hence lower correlation (R) values for that year. With the exception of 1976 and 1979, the DJIA exhibits R values of at least .90 with the S&P and NYSE indexes, generally in the .95+ range, in Table 3.2.

With regard to the VLIC, it also correlates fairly well with the other indexes, except for 1977 and 1972. (As just mentioned, in 1979, the VLIC has high R values for S&P 500 and NYSE, but not for the DJIA.) During 1977, the DJIA, S&P 500, and NYSE exhibited a rather slow steady decline, while the VLIC remained rather flat: in Table 3.2, the R values for VLIC ranged between .299 and .610, with respect to the other indexes. In Table 3.3, during 1976 and 1977, the VLIC shows a barely perceptible 1.2 percent increase, while the NYSE, S&P 500, and DJIA exhibit declines of 10.9, 14.3, and 24.3 percent, respectively. Again, computation and structure would easily account for the differences, especially since the VLIC places relatively more weight on smaller, less heavily capitalized corporations.

The year 1972 provides the most interesting contrast of the VLIC with the DJIA, S&P 500, and NYSE. The R values shown in Table 3.2 indicate slight *negative* correlation. Recall that the VLIC is an equally weighted indicator. In that regard, James Lorie of the University of Chicago and Mary T. Hamilton commented that equal-weighted indexes may be more appropriate "for indicating movements in the prices of typical or average stocks" and "are better indicators of the expected change in the prices of stocks selected at random" (Lorie and Hamilton, 1973, p. 55).

They observed that, although the long run movements of the major market indicators are similar, the various indexes may differ markedly over short periods of time. That aspect seems well illustrated in Table 3.2. Lorie and Hamilton point out that such differences may be reflected in both turning points and index voltilities.

On one occasion there was a significant difference in the turning points of the market as a whole as measured by a comprehensive equal-weighted index and the Dow Jones Averages or the Standard and Poor's indexes. In 1929, the equal-weighted index reached its peak six months *before* the month-end peak in the other two. This suggests that the prices of stocks in relatively small companies turned down before the prices of stocks in large companies. In this instance at least, the use of the index giving greater weight to small companies could have had enormous value. The equal-weighted index also reached its trough in 1932, one month before either of

the other two indexes. All other turning points occurred in the same month."
(Lorie and Hamilton, 1973, p. 68)

That assessment appeared in Lorie and Hamilton's book, published in
1973, and obviously written a year or so before that. In more recent
retrospect, the equally weighted VLIC "peaked" in early 1972, equalling

Table 3.3 Comparison of Cyclical Percentage Changes: Major Stock Market
Indicators, 1962–1982[a]

Cycle Period	Percentage Change			
	VLIC	NYSE	S&P	DJIA
6/62 – 2/66	82.5	80.5	78.1	83.4
2/66 – 10/66	− 24.7	− 22.7	− 22.0	− 24.7
10/66 – 10/67	7.2	37.3	32.9	24.8
10/67 – 3/68	− 10.7	− 9.3	− 9.1	− 11.1
3/68 – 12/68	35.4	24.3	21.7	18.8
12/68 – 7/70	− 54.1	− 35.0	− 32.2	− 29.8
7/70 – 4/71	43.6	14.5	42.6	36.7
4/71 – 11/71	− 20.3	− 11.7	− 11.6	− 13.3
11/71 – 4/72	26.8	21.2	19.5	18.5
4/72 – 1/73	− 7.6	6.7	9.1	8.2
1/73 – 12/74	− 58.9	− 45.6	− 44.0	− 42.5
12/74 – 2/76	37.7	54.4	52.1	64.0
2/76 – 3/78	1.2	− 10.9	− 14.3	− 24.3
3/78 – 9/78	31.6	23.8	22.1	21.5
9/78 – 12/78	− 17.8	− 11.0	− 10.0	− 11.3
12/78 – 10/79	27.8	18.2	15.8	11.5
10/79 – 11/79	− 11.6	− 8.9	− 8.8	− 10.2
11/79 – 2/80	18.3	17.0	16.2	11.1
2/80 – 3/80	− 20.1	− 15.9	− 14.6	− 13.2
3/80 – 12/80	37.9	37.8	35.6	24.3
1/81 – 6/81	7.5	− 2.2	− 3.4	1.3
6/81 – 9/81	− 16.3	− 12.0	− 11.4	− 13.0
9/81 – 12/81	12.7	12.8	12.0	8.3
12/81 – 3/82	− 15.0	− 14.6	− 14.0	− 11.7
3/82 – 5/82	10.6	10.0	10.0	9.0
5/82 – 8/82	− 14.9	− 13.4	− 13.1	− 9.8
8/82 – 12/82	40.7	36.1	35.4	33.4

[a]Based on week-end closing values.

its 1971 high. But then the VLIC turned down fully 8–10 months before the Dow, S&P 500, and NYSE indicators began to reflect the bear market decline of 1973–1974 (cf. Figure 3.2). In that context, then, the slightly negative R values for the VLIC for 1972 seem to have a fairly well founded explanation.

FLUCTUATIONS AND CYCLES

The courses of the various stock market indicators and cycles are depicted graphically in Figures 3.1 and 3.2. The extent and length of the stock market cycles are presented in terms of percentage-change measures in Table 3.3.

All of the major indicators "peaked" in late 1968, and then fell to mid-1970 troughs. With the exception of the VLIC, which began to turn down in mid-1972, the other indexes reached or surpassed previous highs in the early part of 1973. From there all of the indicators, DJIA, S&P 500, NYSE, and VLIC, clearly display the 40–60 percent decline of the subsequent bear market of 1973–1974. In the following two years, the market rallied, so that by February 1976, the DJIA, NYSE, and S&P 500 had essentially returned to the levels attained in 1972. While the VLIC also recovered during this period, it did not reattain its pre-bear market levels of 1972.

From February 1976 through March 1978, the DJIA, NYSE, and S&P 500 all drifted downward on the order of 11–24 percent. During this two year period, the VLIC moved in a fairly narrow, "flat" range. From March 1978 through December 1980, all four indicators followed the same cyclical patterns, as is evident in Figure 3.2 and Table 3.3. Fourth quarter (October) declines of about 10–12 percent in 1978 and 1979 were followed by recoveries in the respective first quarters of 1979 and 1980. The February–March breaks of 15–20 percent in the indexes were followed by rallies of about 25–35 percent throughout the remainder of 1980.

During the first half of 1981, the various indicators moved in somewhat disparate patterns: the DJIA and VLIC increased slightly, while the NYSE and S&P 500 indexes declined about 2–3 percent. The sharp market break in the third quarter of 1981, ranging from -11 to -16 percent, was followed by a mild recovery of 8–13 percent during the September–December 1981 fourth quarter. A somewhat more intense seesaw pattern continued in the early part of 1982, with cycles of shorter duration;

Figure 3.2 Major stock market indicators, graph of cycles and fluctuations, 1979 to 1982. Based on weekly close data.

the 12–15 percent decline in March 1982 was followed by a 10 percent recovery into May 1982, which was followed by another decline of −10 to −15 percent into mid-August. After that the record-setting bull market move carried the indexes upward by 33–40 percent from August through year-end 1982.

The relatively higher volatility of the VLIC is readily apparent in Table 3.3. For almost every major cycle, the VLIC rose or declined by a greater percentage that the other three indexes: DJIA, S&P 500, and NYSE. The "drift" or relatively stable periods (February 1976–March 1978, and January 1981–June 1981) are obvious exceptions; these periods were characterized by the lack of a strong market direction. This higher volatility of the VLIC is, of course, a reflection of its different composition, computation, and equal weighting given to the stocks of relatively smaller companies.

From the weekly data used for Table 3.3's correlation coefficients, for the years 1981 and 1982, the mean values, standard deviations, and coefficients of variation appear in Table 3.4. Even though 1982 ended in a bull market episode, the deep decline in the forepart of the year resulted in the means of each respective index exhibiting a higher value for the entire year 1981. In every case the means of 1981 exceeded those for 1982, but just the reverse is true for the estimated standard deviations. Accordingly, the coefficients of variation are considerably higher for 1982: about 50

Table 3.4   Stock Market Indicators, 1981 and 1982, Weekly Observations

Index	Mean ($\bar{X}$)	Standard Deviation (s)	Coefficient of Variation ($s/\bar{X}$)
		1981	
DJIA	933.114	57.388	.062
VLIC	145.788	8.150	.056
S&P 500	128.126	5.748	.045
NYSE	74.089	3.238	.044
		1982	
DJIA	886.025	86.206	.097
VLIC	133.596	13.597	.102
S&P 500	119.562	11.131	.091
NYSE	69.078	6.541	.095

percent higher for the DJIA, and nearly double for the other stock market indexes, that is, the S&P 500, NYSE, and VLIC. In regression form, these changes from 1981 to 1982 reflect some interesting results as well.

REGRESSION ESTIMATES

From the weekly data used to generate Table 3.4, regression equations were fitted among the indicators. All combinations are displayed for 1981 and 1982, and are numbered 1a, 1b, . . . and 2a, 2b, . . ., respectively. These regression estimates appear in Table 3.5; the equations shown are in ordinary least squares linear form, and the estimated constant term ($\hat{A}$) is excluded. The estimates are shown for comparative and illustrative purposes. In 1981, for example, whenever the VLIC increased by 1.00, the DJIA increased, on the average, by 6.40; since the sign of $\hat{B}$ is positive, the same relationship applies for downward movements of both indexes. Note that this is not a cause and effect equation, but merely curve-fitting;

Table 3.5   Stock Market Indicators, Regression Estimates, Weekly Observations, 1981 and 1982

Dependent Variable (Y)	Regression Coefficient ($\hat{B}$)	Explanatory Variable (X)	R^2
1981			
1a DJIA	6.402	VLIC	.8211
1b DJIA	9.535	S&P 500	.9122
1c DJIA	16.730	NYSE	.8913
1d VLIC	1.250	S&P 500	.7774
1e VLIC	2.313	NYSE	.8446
1f S&P 500	1.764	NYSE	.9860
1982			
2a DJIA	6.036	VLIC	.9067
2b DJIA	7.421	S&P 500	.9181
2c DJIA	12.987	NYSE	.9712
2d VLIC	1.179	S&P 500	.9549
2e VLIC	2.044	NYSE	.9673
2f S&P 500	1.722	NYSE	.9986

either index could have been used as X or Y. For example, the S&P 500 is used on both sides of the equation (1d vs. 1f). Also shown are the R^2 statistics, which indicate in the first relationship 1a that the variation in the VLIC accounted for, or corresponded to, about 82 percent of the variation in the DJIA. Similarly, a 1.00 change in the S&P 500, on the average, corresponded to a change of 9.54 in the DJIA (1b), and the variation in the S&P 500 during 1981 "explained" about 91 percent of the variation in the DJIA. The interesting aspects of Table 3.5 are that, in every case, on the basis of the weekly data used for estimation:

1 The regression coefficient $\hat{B}$ decreased from 1981 in 1982 (e.g., $Y =$ DJIA, $X =$ VLIC) for the same dependent-explanatory variable pairs (i.e., 1a vs. 2a); for the S&P 500 and NYSE (2b and 2c vs. 1b and 1c), the decrease in $\hat{B}$ was about 23%, while the other $\hat{B}$'s changed by small amounts.

2 The explanatory power of the relationships all increased, from 1981 to 1982 (i.e., the R^2 values).

The regressions shown in Table 3.6 are in logarithmic-return form, so that we can interpret $\hat{B}$ as an estimated *percentage* change coefficient. The equations indicate that the VLIC was almost 23 percent more variable than the NYSE, in the period July 1973–June 1977; that is, if the NYSE increased (or decreased) 10 percent, the VLIC changed about 12.27 per-

Table 3.6   Return Form Regressions, VLIC and NYSE, Period: July 1973–June 1982, Monthly Observations in Logarithmic Specifications

5 Years, July 1973–June 1977

$$\log \left(\frac{\text{VLIC}_t}{\text{VLIC}_{t-1}} \right) = -.160 + 1.227 \log \left(\frac{\text{NYSE}_t}{\text{NYSE}_{t-1}} \right), \quad R^2 = .846$$

5 Years, July 1978–June 1982

$$\log \left(\frac{\text{VLIC}_t}{\text{VLIC}_{t-1}} \right) = .184 + 1.072 \log \left(\frac{\text{NYSE}_t}{\text{NYSE}_{t-1}} \right), \quad R^2 = .874$$

10 Years, July 1973–June 1982

$$\log \left(\frac{\text{VLIC}_t}{\text{VLIC}_{t-1}} \right) = -.016 + 1.154 \log \left(\frac{\text{NYSE}_t}{\text{NYSE}_{t-1}} \right), \quad R^2 = .853$$

cent in the same direction. During the latter 5 years ending 1982, the VLIC was about 7 percent more variable than NYSE, and for the whole 10 year period, about 15 percent more volatile. And since we know that the NYSE and S&P 500 are correlated at .99, the same approximation could logically be extended to the S&P 500 Index, as well.

THE VIEW FROM AFAR

From a longer run perspective, Professor Lorie has observed that the decade of the 1970s saw the *worst* stock market performance in a century. That is correct, worse than the Great Crash (and Great Depression) of the 1930s! Between 1969 and 1979, according to his calculations, which are in *real* terms, that is, adjusted for price level changes, "the average annual rate of return in constant dollars for a tax-exempt investor who invested in all stocks on the New York Stock Exchange in proportion to their initial value and reinvested the dividends was was about *minus 1.5 percent* (Lorie, 1980, p. 24, emphasis added). During the 1930s the comparable average annual rate of return was about 2 percent. And with the addition of income taxes in the later decade (due to higher rates of taxation of dividends), the 1970s compared even less favorably to the 1930s.

The cause of poor performance was evident in the 1930s, as GNP in constant dollars declined about 30 percent from 1929 to 1932, and was only 4 percent higher in 1939 than in 1929. But during the 1970s, there was substantial economic expansion. The culprits, in Professor Lorie's assessment, were the rate of inflation and the failure of corporate profits to rise sufficiently in the 1970s; in turn, he attributed those factors to the growing costs of government regulation and "a tax policy which heavily penalizes saving and investment and thus the sources of growing productivity" (Lorie, 1980, p. 24).

The peculiarity of the 1970s was not lost on other observers, either. John C. Bogle and Jan M. Twardowski (1980) remarked in an article on relative institutional investment performance that the period of their study (1967–1977) covered "a rather unusual period in stock market history." The 10 year compound rate of return on the S&P 500 was 3.6 percent per year, compared with 5.8 percent for U.S. Treasury Bills. "Thus a portfolio with a risk level lower than the market's . . . would have outperformed most equity portfolios" (Bogle and Twardowski, 1980, pp. 33–41).

In other words, the disparity in risk-reward terms for the stock market during the 1970s relates to the theoretical and empirical results we explore in the next chapter. Keep this oddity in mind, though, as it evidently was the source of empirical ammunition with which to shoot holes in the "capital asset pricing model" (CAPM). These various strands all come together in the following pages.

SUMMARY

The differences among the major stock market indicators are frequently not well understood. Even the preeminent DJIA possesses some properties and "limitations" that are not widely recognized. Although there is not presently a stock index futures contract based on the Dow, an examination of its history and characteristics seemed appropriate—due to the importance of explaining what the "Average" is all about, and due to the central role the DJIA has played in the approval process for the stock index futures contracts that do exist.

This chapter has explored the essential properties of construction, computation, and weighting for the three indexes that do underlie stock index futures: the S&P 500, the NYSE, and the VLIC. However, the basic features of *any* index—stock market or otherwise—are completely *arbitrary*. A more extensive survey of stock market indexes, their rationale, interpretation, and structures appears in Appendix A. Numerous variants have been proposed and "justified" as the *definitive* stock market indicator. The interested reader should find these "ultimate" indexes fascinating exercises in futility.

For most intents and purposes, the capitalization-weighted NYSE and S&P 500 indexes are both dominated by the same heavily capitalized U.S. corporations. Although the NYSE contains about 1000 more individual companies than the S&P 500, the latter accounts for about 80 percent of the total market value of the NYSE. Accordingly, it is not surprising to find correlation coefficients of .99+ for the two indexes for nearly every year, 1962–1982. In many respects, they can be regarded as almost the same.

The third stock index futures base, the VLIC, on the other hand, is somewhat distinctive. It is geometrically averaged and equally weighted. In particular, the VLIC is more sensitive to the stock price movements of smaller companies. These structural differences have on a few occasions resulted in the VLIC's movements diverging materially from those of the S&P 500 and NYSE. On the whole, however, all three of these indexes have moved in close concert, especially during strong market cycles. A thorough understanding and familiarity with the nature of these three indexes is an obvious crucial step toward the ultimate goal of mastering the futures contracts based on them.

Finally, from a longer run historical perspective, the decade of the 1970s was unique. Professor Lorie has argued that in many respects it was the *worst* stock market period of the last century. Yes, worse even than the "Great Crash" of the 1930s. In real terms, adjusting for price level changes and inflation, the average investor in New York Stock Exchange stocks would have fared worse than his or her counterpart during the 1930s. The failure of corporate profits to rise sufficiently in the 1970s in the face of substantial economic expansion and high inflation was due primarily to the growing costs of governmental regulation and "a tax policy which heavily penalized savings and investment, and thus the sources of growing productivity" (Lorie, 1980, p. 24). In the same vein, other authors have noted that a portfolio of just U.S. Treasury Bills would have yielded a higher return, with essentially no risk, than the 10 year (1967–1977) compound rate of return on the S&P 500 index.

4 Once over Lightly: Capital Market Theory

Thus far we have used comprehensive statistical instruments to conduct analytical autopsies on the major stock market indicators, especially those that are the underlying bases for existing stock index futures contracts. Now we are ready to explore the theoretical nature of "systematic risk"— the *raison d'être* of stock index futures. As promised, though, once over lightly.

The literature on capital market theory and related empirical testing is extensive. Although an exhaustive survey is beyond the scope of this book, some of the major developments and controversies are described briefly in this chapter. Intensive and technical summaries of some aspects appear in Appendix B. The evolution, however, is vital for understanding what stock index futures are all about.

Probably one of the best overviews about capital markets was that of Eugene Fama:

> The primary role of the capital market is allocation of ownership of the economy's capital stock. In general terms, the ideal is a market in which prices provide accurate signals for resource allocation: that is, a market in which firms can make production-investment decisions, and investors can choose among the securities that represent ownership of firms' activities under the assumption that security prices at any time "fully relfect" all available information. (Fama, 1970, p. 383)

THE RANDOM WALK HYPOTHESIS

Research into the movement of security prices is usually dated from Bachelier's contribution in 1900 (cf. Latane and Tuttle, 1970, p. 505). Several decades passed, however, before "Further study, particularly empirical investigations, was carried out. One reason was the lack of a sizable body of organized data to investigate" (Latane and Tuttle, 1970, p. 509). Another was the lack of electronic computers capable of making the extensive computations for statistical analysis.

The significance of the random walk hypothesis (RWH) is its role in initially focusing mathematical, statistical, and economic tools on stock price behavior. The RWH has been tested in a variety of forms. Basically, the RWH expresses a belief that changes in stock prices are completely unsystematic; this proposition has been tested in the form regarding price *changes,* asserting that there is no "serial (day-to-day) correlation between short-term stock price movements" (Latane and Tuttle, 1970, p. 505). That is, if on a given day a stock's price goes up 2 points, on the next day it is just as likely to go up as go down. Latane and Tuttle go on to quote the present-day author who calls himself Adam Smith: " 'Prices have no memory, and yesterday has nothing to do with tomorrow.' "

The RWH in its various forms of interpretation and testing incorporates implications about how fast information (e.g., earnings reports, cash flows, dividends) is reflected in the prices of securities. Further refinements relate to questions of market "efficiency." Fama has offered the definition that an efficient market is one in which prices fully reflect all available information (Fama, 1970).

Basically, the RWH holds that price change prediction cannot be based on past price changes. Houthakker has pointed out that the randomness in price changes can only be defined negatively, "as the absence of any systematic pattern. A particular (statistical) test can detect only a particular pattern or class of patterns, and complete randomness can therefore only be disproved, not proved" (Houthakker, 1961, p. 164). All this simply means that any systematic pattern in price changes remains undiscovered; if there is one, it is not likely to be obvious or simple.

The RWH is also important as a point of departure for Benjamin King, an extremely important researcher in this area. He noted that the trendist-RWH "controversy" had given rise to the (then, 1966) recent surge in the flow of literature on stock price behavior. His inquiry was to determine whether or not one could determine if there was a "togetherness" or "apartness" of a sufficiently "stationary nature to be compatible with a theory of common effects in the formation of price changes" (King, 1966, p. 142).

MODERN PORTFOLIO THEORY

Although the portfolio approach to money has been traced back to Keynes (ca. 1930) and Hicks (ca. 1935) as an explanation of liquidity preference, "modern portfolio theory" (MPT) is usually dated from the studies of Harry Markowitz (e.g., 1952). The investigation of the RWH can be classified as an exercise in *positive* methodology, that is, a description or explanation of security price fluctuations. In contrast, Markowitz's approach spelled out *normative* rules, that is, how an investor *should,* rather than necessarily does make rational choices under uncertainty.

This approach showed that an individual who maximizes "expected utility [i.e., "risk" preferences] inevitably chooses a portfolio which is *efficient* in terms of the mean and variances of the returns" (Sarnat, 1974, p. 1241). As we have already discovered, it is the dispersion of returns, typically measured as the variance or as the square root of the variance, the standard deviation, which has been employed to measure and characterize "risk."

The concept of "efficiency" relates to the choice among, say, portfolios with different *expected* returns and variances. For example, suppose the investor can choose any one of the three following portfolios:

Portfolio	Expected Return	Expected Variance
1	.18	3.25
2	.25	5.70
3	.11	7.45

Portfolio 3 is "inefficient" since it has a lower expected return than either 1 or 2, and also more *risk* (higher variance). Then the issue is reduced to a choice between 1 and 2; 1 has a lower return but also less risk then 2. It is the theoretical frontier of such portfolios as 1 and 2 that the investor "should" choose from, according to the "mean-variance" criteria. Note that these are expressed as *ex ante expected* characteristics of the portfolios. As noted in the last chapter, the 1970s in the aggregate provided the situation where a "riskless" portfolio (i.e., U.S. Treasury Bills) outperformed the stock market as a whole. The moral of this study is that *expectations,* no matter how extensive the data utilized to form them, sometimes go astray.

As mentioned previously, these theories and empirical testing of them are generally stated in "return" form. At this point, then, let us be more precise. For a single stock, the return, Y_t, during the holding period, t, is defined as

$$Y_t = \frac{P_t + D_t - P_{t-1}}{P_{t-1}} \tag{4.1}$$

where P_t = the price of the stock at the end of the holding period, t, D_t = dividends received during t, and P_{t-1} = the price of the stock at the end of the preceding period, $t - 1$, or, equivalently, the price of the stock at the beginning of the holding period, t. Since the dividend yield component (D_t/P_{t-1}) is usually fairly stable, the major variable component of Y_t, and hence var(Y_t), is the price change component $(P_t - P_{t-1})/P_{t-1}$. The holding period return for a single stock, Y_t, can be treated in "gross" return terms, which, neglecting dividends, reduces to simply P_t/P_{t-1}. For example, if the price, P_{t-1}, of the stock at the beginning of the holding period is \$20, and the price, P_t, at the end of the holding period is \$28, the return expressed in "gross" form would simply be 28/20 = 1.40. In net form, the only difference is to subtract 1.0 in percentage terms (or P_{t-1} in Eq. 4.1 above); then the net return would be expressed as .40 or 40 percent. In the case of a loss, if P_t = \$16, then Y_t = 16/20 = .80, and the corresponding net return would be stated as −.20 or −20 percent.

In order to implement the Markowitz technique, one requires a vector of estimated expected yields (Y_i's) for the stocks under consideration, and in addition a matrix of estimated variances and covariances. Thus, for example, if four securities were being considered (S1, S2, S3, S4), the vector of expected yields (returns), **Y,** and the variance-covariance matrix **V,** would consist of the following:

$$\mathbf{Y} = \begin{bmatrix} Y(S1) \\ Y(S2) \\ Y(S3) \\ Y(S4) \end{bmatrix}, \quad \text{and}$$

$$\mathbf{V} = \begin{bmatrix} \text{var}(S1) & \text{cov}(S1, S2) & \text{cov}(S1, S3) & \text{cov}(S1, S4) \\ \text{cov}(S2, S1) & \text{var}(S2) & \text{cov}(S2, S3) & \text{cov}(S2, S4) \\ \text{cov}(S3, S1) & \text{cov}(S3, S2) & \text{var}(S3) & \text{cov}(S3, S4) \\ \text{cov}(S4, S1) & \text{cov}(S4, S2) & \text{cov}(S4, S3) & \text{var}(S4) \end{bmatrix}$$

By convention the bold type refers to vectors, like $\mathbf{Y}$, or matrices, like $\mathbf{V}$. The time subscript, t, has been supressed above, also. Roughly, "Optimal portfolios are achieved by reducing the covariance term in the expression for the variance of the portfolio, i.e., through diversification" (King, 1966, p. 165).

Marshall Sarnat has observed that the essence of portfolio theory is that

> [The risk incurred] when a number of investments are combined in a portfolio is less, and often materially less, than the weighted average of the risks of the individual components; the degree of risk deduction being directly related to the size of the portfolio and inversely to the degree of correlation among the components. Hence, the covariances (correlation) among alternative investments' returns, and not just their own dispersions, are germane to the portfolio problem." (Sarnat, 1974, p. 1243)

Now for some of the practical problems in applying MPT. For one, if past data are relevant, historical estimation requires period by period yields for the J securities (here $J = 4$) "under consideration and the brute force calculation of sample estimates of the J means and variances and $J(J - 1)/2$ covariances" (King, 1966, p. 165). Although there are 20 elements detailed above, only 14 are unique, recalling that cov(S1, S2) = cov(S2, S1).

Nonetheless, the data requirements are not trivial. For instance, if 200 stocks are being considered, the number of estimates required for the candidate stocks, in the form analogous to the above, equals *20,300*. Even with modern computers, the combinations involved are prodigious. The following citation gives an insight into the enormity of the task: "The number of possible portfolios containing eight different stocks that could be selected from a list of 1000 stocks is more than *24 quintillion*" (Fisher and Lorie, 1970, p. 111). And that is only step one! The portfolio size is not predetermined. If the analyst wanted to consider portfolios of nine stocks, or maybe seven, ...

As a way out, Markowitz himself suggested that regression analysis of the yields on securities be regressed on some marketwide or industrywide index in order to shortcut the estimation of the $J(J - 1)/2$ covariances. Sharpe's contribution (in King, 1966, pp. 165–166) was the "diagonalization of the variance-covariance matrix V, such that off-diagonal elements (i.e., the covariances) take on values of zero":

$$V^* = \begin{bmatrix} \text{var(S1)} & 0 & 0 & 0 \\ 0 & \text{var(S2)} & 0 & 0 \\ 0 & 0 & \text{var(S3)} & 0 \\ 0 & 0 & 0 & \text{var(S4)} \end{bmatrix}$$

By regressing the returns of individual stocks on a single market index, each stock's yield is then decomposed into a common (i.e., market factor) component and a unique one. The market factor component is the basis of *systematic risk!* The unique components of each stock's "risk" are subject to reduction, and perhaps elimination, by diversification.

King cautioned, however, that Sharpe's model, with zeros in the off-diagonal elements of the covariance matrix "may be a dangerous simplification of the true relationships among residual yields" (1966, p. 166). King's results showed that the market effect accounts for about 50 percent of the variance of the stocks he studied; industry effects still accounted for about 10 percent.

King also warned about placing too much reliance on the estimates derived from historical data, and extrapolating from them into the future. His main objection was that changes "In the characteristics of firms may prevent historical behavior from being applicable to the future" (King, 1966, pp. 165–166).

THE MARKET-LINE MODEL

The methodology developed for the "zero off-diagonal" approximation to simplify Markowitz's portfolio model has been extended as an explanation of the pricing of capital assets. This theory has been dubbed the capital asset pricing model (CAPM). Developed somewhat independently by Sharpe and Lintner, the model is dependent upon the following assumptions (Friend and Blume, 1970, p. 562):

1   Every investor is a one-period expected utility maximizer and exhibits diminishing marginal utility of terminal wealth.
2   All investors have the same one-period time horizon.
3   Portfolios are evaluated solely in terms of the mean and variance of one-period returns.
4   There are no transactions or information costs; borrowing and lending rates are equal and the same for all investors, who will then select portfolios with optimal combinations of risk ("variance") and return.
5   All investors hold homogeneous expectations about the distributions of future returns.
6   The capital market is in equilibrium.

Then the expected return for asset (or portfolio) i, $E(Y_i)$, is expressed as

$$E(Y_i) - Y_f = \beta_i[E(Y_m) - Y_f] \tag{4.2}$$

where Y_f is the risk-free borrowing and lending rate, and β_i (beta) is defined as $\text{cov}(Y_i, Y_m)/\text{var}(Y_m)$, where Y_m is the return on the "market portfolio" which strictly speaking includes *all wealth* whose return is uncertain. As theoretically specified, Y_m is *not* just the return on the *stock market portfolio*.

Friend and Blume pointed out that if Eq. 4.2 held for all assets *ex ante* there would be no opportunity for abnormal profit, as all assets would be correctly priced. "Only if some of the above assumptions did not strictly hold for all securities and all investors could there be incorrectly priced securities" (Friend and Blume, 1970, p. 562).

The capital market theory of Sharpe and Lintner is, as any positive economic theory, an abstraction of reality. As such it seeks to capture the essential features of the complex realities of a competitive capital market equilibrium. Though the theory follows consistently from its assumptions, it cannot be judged on their reality. These assumptions are necessarily unrealistic, for they abstract the crucial elements from the mass of lesser important details. But in ignoring them the assumptions conflict with reality. The only proper evaluator of the theory is its ability to yield valid and meaningful predictions of the observed phenomena. For only by such a method can the power of the assumptions to abstract the crucial elements from the ever present mass of detail be tested (Bogue, 1973, p. 18).

Blume has also commented that a theoretical model "should not be judged by the accuracy of its assumptions, but rather by the accuracy of its predictions" (1971, p. 4).

Having observed Eq. 4.2, the reader can file it away for not much future reference. Strictly, that equation states the return relationships in "excess" form, that is, returns in *excess* of the "risk-free" (i.e., T Bills) borrowing and lending rate. For all practical purposes, the risk-free rate in Eq. 4.2 and the dividend return in Eq. 4.1 can be disregarded. Extensive testing has shown that the estimates of β_i, are essentially the same whether or not these other complicating aspects are included. For most purposes, the "market model" estimating equation that we need to be concerned with is of the following (and by now) familar form. For security i the return Y_i is expressed as

$$Y_i = \alpha_i + \beta_i M + u_i \qquad (4.3)$$

where Y_i is the one period holding return (Y_{it}/Y_{it-1}), α_i and β_i are constants, u_i is the spherical disturbance term, and in particular M is defined as a common "market factor" that affects the returns on *all* securities. In this form α_i represents the "constant" portion of the security's return *not* attributable to systematic risk.

A crucial distinction in this regard is between the market portfolio (m) and the market *factor* (M).* It is M, the market factor, that is germane to the systematic risk element, and hence the critical aspect for understanding stock index futures.

---

* Regarding the distinction between the "market factor" and the market portfolio: the two are not *identical*. The return on the market portfolio (Y_m) is then

$$Y_m = \sum_j x_{jm} (a_j + b_j M + u_j) \qquad (4.4)$$

where x_{jm} = the total market value of all outstanding shares in firm j divided by the total market value of all outstanding shares of all firms. Fama has shown (1971, p. 46) that even if a scale is chosen such that $\sum x_{jm} b_j = 1$, from Eq. 4.4

$$Y_m = \sum x_{jm} a_j + M + \sum x_{jm} u_j \qquad (4.5)$$

so that the return on the market portfolio (Y_m) is M *plus* the additional terms involving a_j and u_j.

The systematic risk of a portfolio (β_p) is equal to the average systematic risk of its component securities, weighted by their proportionate value in the portfolio:

$$\beta_p = \frac{\text{cov}(Y_p, Y_m)}{\text{var}(Y_m)} = \sum x_i \beta_i$$

where x_i is the proportion invested in security i and Y_p and Y_m are the returns on the particular portfolio and the market portfolio, respectively.

Writing his doctoral dissertation in 1973, Marcus Bogue asserted that empirical verification of the CAPM is generally considered to affirm that the theory is representative of the realities of modern securities markets. "The major contribution of the CAPM is a linear relationship between aggregate risk and return for well diversified portfolios" (Bogue, 1973, p. 1). The only component of a security's risk borne by an investor when that security is included in a well diversified portfolio is the *systematic, or market-related risk*.

The evidence suggests that systematic risk is "reasonably constant at the portfolio level, though exhibiting a marked tendency toward mean reversion. For individual securities, estimates of systematic risk appear to be volatile and far from constant over long periods. Little is known about the dynamic properties of systematic risk" (Bogue, 1973, p. 3).

Two important additional clarifications relate to Eq. 4.3. One is that the relationship portrayed is really two-dimensional. The regression estimate of beta (β) indicates the degree of responsiveness of the security's (or portfolio's) return to that of the market. Often interpreted as an "elasticity" parameter, a coefficient of 1.0 implies "systematic" return variability equal to the market's. Similarly, coefficients greater than 1.0 imply greater than proportional systematic returns, and those below 1.0 imply less.

The other dimension of Eq. 4.3, which has frequently been ignored, is the *extent* of market dependency, as measured by the R^2 statistic, the coefficient of determination. For individual securities, that proportion of return variability "explained" by the market generally ranges from about 2 to 76 percent, with 30 to 35 percent a fairly good average estimate. For portfolios, *if* they were efficiently diversified, the preceding discussion suggests that all of the return variability would be due to the market.

Recently, the R^2 dimension has been discovered. Camp and Eubank

(1981) have hypothesized a new measure, called the "beta quotient." They found that a number of mutual funds had portfolios with R^2 values of .85 or less. In those cases, where there remains a substantial amount of unsystematic or diversifiable risk, in their view, beta is no longer an "adequate" and proper risk measure. Instead, they have put forth an alternative measure, the "beta quotient," which is simply the portfolio's beta (β_p) divided by R_p (the square root of R_p^2); the beta quotient would be denoted as β'_p and

$$\beta'_p = \frac{\beta_p}{R_p} \qquad (4.6)$$

(Camp and Eubank, 1981, pp. 53–57).

In the mid-1970s, the analysts were convinced that beta told it all. The only risk an investor had to cope with was "systematic" risk, and it was sufficiently measured by the estimated regression coefficient, $\hat{\beta}$. This view, of course, really applied to portfolios with efficient diversification.

In even more comprehensive terms, a 1979 article by Bowman established a theoretical relationship between a firm's systematic risk, β_i, and its capital structure leverage (debt to equity ratio). Drawing upon the familiar linear formulation of the CAPM, Bowman added assumptions that firms are able to borrow and lend at the same risk-free interest rate as individual investors. If β_u is the systematic risk of an "unleveraged" firm, and β_L is the systematic risk for the same firm (in terms of physical assets, etc.) but "leveraged" with a debt (D) to equity (E) ratio of D/E, then

$$\beta_L = \left(1 + \frac{D}{E}\right)\beta_u$$

That is, since $(1 + D/E)$ is greater than 1.0, the β_L is hypothesized to be greater than β_U (Bowman, 1979, p. 621). Although this hypothesis is yet to be confirmed, it does offer an appealing explanation of why smaller firms, with presumably less secure capitalization structures, tend to be the "high" beta stocks, and also why a stock market index giving such firms relatively more weight (e.g., the VLIC) might tend to foreshadow significant market movements. However, the extent of β's credibility remains in question (see Appendix C).

THE "DEATH" OF BETA

The cover was black. And in compelling white lettering the question was posed: "Is Beta Dead?" Inside that July 1980 issue of the *Institutional Investor,* the cover story by Anise Wallace presented a Watergate-like exposé on the impending demise of the CAPM. Complete with an undercover financial analyst "mole" called "Deep Quant," the story disclosed a very entertaining tale of the growing numbers of doubters about the quantitative relevance and accuracy of betas and alphas, and their use in deriving "risk-adjusted" measures of fund managers' performances.

Unfortunately, such "investigative" reporting foundered a little on accuracy and chronological sequence. Maybe Deep Quant had misled her, but the "very foundation of MPT-based money management," as every reader here now knows, is *not* the CAPM (Wallace, 1980, p. 23). If anything, just the opposite is true. And supporters of the CAPM would not necessarily blindly endorse projecting past estimates of beta into the wild blue yonder. However, that a controversy exists is not to be denied. Here we briefly describe the points of contention and a few related side issues. The more interested reader is directed to Appendices B and C for more technical coverage.

Wallace identified the main protagonists of the "Beta Battle" as Barr Rosenberg (pro-CAPM), Professor of Finance at the University of California, Berkeley, Business School, and Richard Roll (con), Professor of Finance at the UCLA Graduate School of Management. Roll's 1977 article in the *Journal of Financial Economics,* "A Critique of the Asset Pricing Theory's Tests," was among the earliest to point out aloud that the emperor had no clothes on. As Wallace described the ensuing furor, Roll was nearly excommunicated by his colleagues. *The Journal of Financial Economics* would not publish the next two installments of Roll's paper— "reportedly because of the controversy it aroused" (Wallace, 1980, p. 26). Roll received abusive letters and phone calls. As the exposé article put it, Deep Quant "had underscored a furious controversy, until now relegated to the pages of academic journals. It could knock the struts out from under a multi-million dollar business in MPT-based products and services" (p. 23).

Much of the controversy, as reported by Wallace, revolved around the usefulness of beta estimates. As noted earlier, the CAPM really refers to all invested assets, and hence the S&P 500, for example, may be a poor proxy for "the market" in that expanded context. As Wallace told it, beta, therefore, was meaningless as a measure, and is a function of the index against which the stock's returns are measured, and not an intrinsic property of the stock itself. Other authors have noted this (e.g., Frankfurter and Frecka, 1979) but did not emphasize it, remarking only that the numerical estimates would be different if the index used as the market factor proxy was changed. For a given index, it is the relative betas that matter. (See Appendix E, where betas are shown for both the VLIC and NYSE; the decile range of a beta estimate is more significant than the beta's numerical value. Remember it's just a statistical *estimate*.)

Much of the debate about the validity and usefulness of the CAPM appeared in the Winter 1981 edition of the *Journal of Portfolio Management*, a companion quarterly published by the Institutional Investor, Inc. In his lead editorial, "Dead—or Alive and Well?," Peter L. Bernstein posed the issues, as he saw them:

1 The question of beta being dead was ridiculous, as long as securities vary with broad market movements, portfolio managers need to know about the sensitivity of their stocks to systematic influences, "and the accuracy of the measurement tools they employ."

2 The CAPM wasn't dead either; as long as investors are risk-averse, assets will tend to be priced so that expected risks and rewards will tend to be commensurate.

3 With regard to modern portfolio theory, "How ridiculous can you get?," asked Bernstein. "As long as the interaction of individual securities within a portfolio produces results that are different from the performance of a single security, the art of composing a portfolio will remain a different art from the skills employed in security selection as such" (Bernstein, 1981).

The "rub comes in" with regard to the market sensitivity of individual securities, their interactions with each other, and the degree of "rationality in investor expectations." The bottom line, as Bernstein saw it, was something to the effect that the theory and the models were robust descriptions about how free markets work under conditions of uncertainty, but that the quantitative tools readily lend themselves to improvement and revision.

Unfortunately, the contributing authors in that issue of the *Journal of Portfolio Management* weren't as eclectic as the editor. The proponents of beta's usefulness, for the most part, remained steadfast in their faith. In the lead article, Rosenberg (1981) dismissed the importance of the "market portfolio" definition as a phony issue. Since the market *factor* (different concept, remember?) is so prominent, and all widely based indexes are highly correlated, it is permissible to use any one of them to define "the market." As also indicated above, Rosenberg explained that the choice of index affects the *scale* of measured beta (e.g., Fahrenheit vs. Centigrade), but these matters are second order aspects. On the other hand, "Because the market factor is so much the most prominent, therefore, beta becomes a meaningful and *predictable* characteristic of a security" (Rosenberg, 1981, p. 10).

Sharpe (1982), in a somewhat later paper, retreated a bit, but altered the (now) "naive CAPM" by adding other factors to account for the differences in security returns. He found by studying the 1931–1979 period that stocks with high historic betas tended to outperform those with low ones. "The correlation between the beta factor and the excess return on the Standard and Poor's stock index was in fact .814 over the period." That indicated to him that the historic beta was a useful predictor of the future beta. But it can be improved upon "by incorporating the security specific attributes" (Sharpe, 1982, p. 16). [Didn't Benjamin King say that in 1966?] Sharpe's conclusions are somewhat qualified, and they deserve to be cited directly, so that nothing is added, or taken away, in the translation:

> The data may be completely consistent with the implications of an expanded Capital Asset Pricing Model, a joint hypothesis involving changes in expectations and risks over time, or the use of an alternative measure of the return on the market portfolio.
>
> Although these results do not confirm or reject the original Capital Asset Pricing Model as a description of reality, they do call into question naive applications in which expected returns are assumed to be related *only* to estimates of future betas based on past patterns of returns. (Sharpe, 1982, p. 18)

The ranks of the dissenters, nevertheless, seem to be growing. A frontal assault by Marc Reinganum (1981) is representative. In his paper "A New Empirical Perspective on the CAPM," he challenged even the current "consensus" that a security's beta is still an important economic determinant of equilibrium pricing, even though it may not be the sole determinant. His empirical test results demonstrated that

> Estimated betas are not systematically related to average returns across securities. The average returns of high beta stocks are not reliably different from the returns of low beta stocks. That is, portfolios with widely different estimated betas possess statistically indistinguishable average returns. Thus, estimated betas based on standard market indices do not appear to reliably measure a "risk which is priced in the market." These findings, along with evidence on empirical "anomalies," suggest that the CAPM may lack significant empirical content (Reinganum, 1981, p. 439).

Another doubter, Robert F. Vandell (1981), joined the chorus. His contribution appeared in the great "Beta Debate" issue of the *Journal of Portfolio Management*. In trying to employ beta estimates as good proxies for forecasting uncertainty, Vandell raised the possibility that perhaps such an exercise might be a search for the irrelevant. In particular, he contrasted the academic approach to more pragmatic conventional "street" wisdom. The latter he characterized by the security analysts' search for securities with low downside risk and high upside potential. In colorful terms Vandell described how betas only get in the way. "Skill and market efficiency are contradictory terms." In not distinguishing "good" risks (upside) from "bad" ones (downside), beta is

> [A] neutered risk measure. Beta treats good and bad risk as if they were the same. An analyst must be more venturesome in assessing risk. He must seek for the low downside, high upside play. That's where the action is! Only a eunuch can truly love a beta. (Vandell, 1981, p. 24)

THE BOTTOM LINE: THE MARKET FACTOR

Beta is under heavy fire. The recent barrange of empirical skepticism is perhaps the most vocal, but it is not the first. In Appendix C there is an extensive description of articles, dating as far back as a decade, that have questioned the "completeness" of beta as *the* measure of a security's risk, or even a portfolio's risk.

Is beta completely useless? Should it be discarded? Or has it been subjected to misguided abuse in the last few years? The truth, as the proverbial saying goes, probably lies somewhere in between. As we have seen, beta is a useful *historic* statistic—but it must be used with great caution, and often with other quantitative measures. The list of contortions that affect estimates of beta (length of data series, assumptions of holding periods, etc.) have been relegated to Appendix B. There are a number of "caveats" that should accompany any set of beta estimates. As is also so often the case, the qualifications are discarded and estimates treated as if they were gospel. That frequently leads to the type of difficulties that Anise Wallace found in her behind-the-portfolio exposé.

In any event, all of this "beta business" is a little beside the point. The empirical underpinning for stock index futures is the undisputed ubiquity of the *market factor*. Perhaps it is more faithfully represented by R^2 than by beta; no one knowns, or can test for sure. But *systematic risk* relates to the *market factor* of (modern) portfolio theory, and *not* the return on the market portfolio of the CAPM.

Unfortunately, systematic risk is never observable—even later. And it may well be the case that systematic risk is a dynamic, changing influence. That possibility may mean that the diversification of a given portfolio leaves it exposed to only systematic risk in one type of "market"—but not in a different type. For example, we have all heard of "interest rate" markets, "energy price" markets, and others. Pettit and Westerfield have speculated that there may be *two* market factors: one relating to an (expected) earnings stream for a stock, and the other relating to the capitalization rate at which those earnings are presently valued (Pettit and Westerfield, 1974, p. 951). That's yet another wrinkle we cannot hope to iron out here.

Finally, it seems appropriate to conclude this section with the thoughts of Benjamin King on the design of security price indexes. In his view, such measures could be seen as a problem in descriptive statistics:

> The construction of a number that will summarize the cross-section of prices or price changes and enable us somehow to see at a glance what is going on within the market. . . . Implicit in this proposed correlation study is the *isolation* of a market-wide impact on price changes and the estimation of the loadings (i.e., relative weights) of that effect in the changes for the various securities. If one is interested in an index of price change that shows what the market as a whole is doing, then a good index would be one that is highly correlated with that part of the changes in anticipation that is felt throughout the market; and it should be relatively *insensitive* to the noise

resulting from news that is pertinent only to individual firms. (King, 1966, p. 143)

That is, "It would be undesirable to allow securities with large components of unique variance to carry much weight in the index" (p. 161).

SUMMARY

This chapter has described the genesis of systematic risk, the focal element of uncertainty addressed by stock index futures. The origins of systematic risk are found in the attempts to apply Harry Markowitz's methodology of portfolio selection to the real world of almost infinite historical data about stock returns and their variances. Having garnered, organized, and assimilated that information, the analyst must then formulate expectations and decisions about future portfolio returns and risks. Even with modern computers, the possible combinations would fill many rooms with stacks of printouts.

William Sharpe's ingenuity cut through this Gordian knot by reducing the dimensionality of the problem to just two influences: a "systematic," market-related factor, and a (stock) "unique," unsystematic component. Like Alexander before him, however, Sharpe's solution may have been a bit too ingenious. Benjamin King in 1966 warned that such an approach might distort the *true* relationships among residual security yields by assuming away too much in the process.

Undaunted, the proponents of the capital asset pricing model (CAPM) simplified the matter even further by presuming that the entire spectrum of a security's or portfolio's, risk conveniently reduced to a single regression estimate: beta. This regression coefficient, generally estimated from "return form equations," indicates the degree of responsiveness of a given stock's or portfolio's returns to that of the "market" factor proxy, or index.

In this chapter, we may have covered the essential "lifetime" of beta—from its "birth" in the CAPM to its possible early demise under the onslaught of more recent empirical testing. Other investigators, cited in Appendix C, have suggested that less restrictive assumptions about investors' utility functions and risk preferences render beta an incomplete, measure of the true nature of portfolio risk (cf., Simonson, 1971, Cooley et al., 1977). Still other investigators have proposed modifications, such as the "beta quotient," to improve beta's usefulness. Finally, others, like Marc Reinganum, have come to even more extreme solutions, such as disregarding beta and the CAPM; these investigations have found little empirical validity to the CAPM at all. Here it seems premature to attempt to the decide the matter one way or the other. Additional quantitative studies, no doubt, will continue to appear in support of both sides.

For our purposes, the theoretical and statistical basis for justifying the risk reduction potential of stock index futures contracts requires less ambitious resolutions. The data are unequivocal about that: every stock has a *positive* correlation with the market. Other authors (e.g., Aber, 1973, and Blume, 1971) have noted that fact repeatedly. The reader can also observe the direction (positive) of the beta estimates for 1440 stocks in Appendix E.

The precision of beta estimates and R^2 statistics are not held to be sacrosanct or stationary over long periods of time. Studies involving 50 years of data seem to miss that point. Indeed, other econometric complications confound the estimated accuracy issue even further. The empirical validity of the CAPM—while providing useful insights and instructive implications—is *not* the *crucial* concern here. Stock index futures contracts depend only upon the existence of a *positive market factor* influence in the pricing of common stocks. That's all there is to it.

5 How Futures Markets Work

PRINCIPLES AND MECHANICS

Many people believe that futures trading is extremely complex or mysterious. To the contrary, the mechanics are fairly straightforward. Actually, if you know a little bit about how stocks are traded, you know much more than you realize about futures markets. In many respects, the two types of market are almost identical. In certain other respects, they differ. But for the moment let's concentrate on the similarities.

First, there is the futures transaction itself. Profits and losses are determined in the same way as they are for any stock market transaction: sales value minus purchase cost. If the sales value exceeds the purchase cost of a futures contract, there is a profit on the transaction. If the cost of purchase exceeds sales value, a loss occurs. There is nothing at all mysterious about that.

The same holds true for a stock market transaction. If you buy 100 shares of XYZ Company at $10 ($1000 purchase cost) and later sell them at $15 ($1500 sales value), you would realize a profit of $500. On the other hand, if the price of XYZ declined to $8 and you sold at that price, you would sustain a loss of $200 ($800-$1000), neglecting commissions.

There is no time limit on how long you might decide to hold your position (100 shares) of XYZ. One of the differentiating characteristics about futures trading is the "necessity" of completing a "round turn" within a specific time period; that is, before the last day of trading in the contract, when it "matures." A round turn is simply a sale offsetting a prior purchase, just as in the case of XYZ stock. That is, roughly speaking, every transaction (say, an initial purchase) in a given contract must be closed out by an eventual offsetting sale—sometime before the particular contract expires, that is, on or before its last day of trading. In contrast, many other assets (e.g., real estate, diamonds, common stocks) can be held indefinitely. Futures contracts require ultimate disposition within a given time period. Actually, "require" is a bit strong; because those positions not closed out, in other words, remaining "open" after the contract expires, result in delivery. (Delivery is discussed below.) But that is also ultimate disposition.

In futures markets, what are being bought and sold are futures *contracts*. These contracts are simply agreements to "perform" at a later date, that is, in the future. The "performance," strictly speaking, is to make or take delivery of the particular commodity in the delivery month. However, as indicated above, the obligation to perform is removed when the position is closed out, that is, when a "round turn" has been completed.

Traded only on authorized exchanges, futures contracts are highly standardized with regard to quantity of the underlying commodity, its quality (i.e., deliverable grades), and the delivery months (maturity months). For example, the soybean contract traded at the Chicago Board of Trade (CBT) is "sized" at 5000 bushels (quantity) of No. 2 Yellow (quality) soybeans. The delivery months are January, March, May, July, August, September, and November. The cocoa contract traded on the Coffee, Sugar and Cocoa Exchange in New York is sized at 10 metric tons; the delivery months are March, May, July, September, and December. The maturities of contracts authorized to trade can extend a year or more into the future; for example, in January 1983, some maturities of financial futures extended as far forward as June and September 1985. Since futures contracts are highly standardized with respect to quantity and quality (and points of delivery), the only variable that can then determine a contract's value is simply the *price*.

Just as in the stock market, the price is determined by supply and demand. Just as in the stock market, the quoted "bid" is the highest price buyers are willing to pay, at any given moment, and the "ask" is the lowest price sellers are willing to take, for a particular contract maturity. On many stock exchanges, there may be "specialists" for particular issues, located at designated places on the trading floor. On futures exchanges, there are designated "pits" for the trading of particular futures contracts. Stock exchange specialists are intermediaries who are supposed to maintain price continuity in their respective stocks, by buying and selling for their own accounts. On futures exchanges, trades are executed by open outcry in the pit. The particular details may differ somewhat between futures trading and the stock market, but the same principles underlie both.

Most of the confusion about understanding futures trading seems to revolve around the maturity aspect: "May" wheat, "July" soybeans, "September" gold. If today is March 6, what does it mean to speak about a price of $2.87 per bushel of *December* corn?

One way to look at it is the same way we might look at bonds (actual "cash market bonds," not the futures contracts). If the *price today* of U.S. Treasury Bonds, paying 9.75 percent, maturing in October 1984, face value $50,000, is 89.75, then the purchase cost is (.8975 × $50,000 =) $44,875.00. If that bond were purchased today but had to be sold next week at, say 87.25, the proceeds of sales value would be (.8725 × $50,000 =) $43,625.00, and a loss of $1,250.00 (= $44,875.00 − 43,625.00) would result. Alternatively, if the bond were sold for 95.00 (= .95 × $50,000), a sales value of $47,500.00 would be realized, and a gain on the bond of $2625.00 ($47,500 − 44,875) would occur, neglecting accrued interest and transactions costs. A third alternative is to just let the bond "mature", that is, hold it until October 1984, and the U.S. Government will pay $50,000 (face value) to redeem it.

That is where the crucial difference is: we know what the price of that bond will be at maturity, 100.00. *No one* knows what the last price for December corn will be! It will depend upon the harvest, foreign demand, competitive crops grown in other countries: a multitude of variables that are resolved into the demand and supply forces determining the price. There may be some fairly good "guesses" as to the last price (i.e., delivery price) of December corn, and those estimates will increase in accuracy as December approaches. But *everyone* knows *now* (or at least should) what the maturity "price" will be for the U.S. Treasury's 9.75 percent, October 1984 bonds. Common stocks, in contrast, never "mature" like bonds or futures contracts; they have a price today, and an uncertain price tomorrow, next week, next month. Think of a futures contract in much the same way, except at some point in time it will mature, and all contracts not closed out by a "round turn" go through the process of delivery. As a practical matter, only 1–2 percent of the futures contracts ever made result in actual delivery. That is because futures markets exist for risk transfer, and not principally as a means for acquiring the underlying commodity. More about that in a moment.

Another distinctive feature of futures trading is that it facilitates *reversing the sequence* of "normal" transactions. That is, one can *sell* initially, and execute a "round turn" by making an offsetting purchase at a later time to close out the position. This is precisely what an individual would do if he or she expected a *decline* in a particular contract's price; that is, if the trader expected the sales value *now* to exceed the purchase cost at a future (later) time, naturally prior to the contract's expiration. Profits and losses are determined in the same way as before. The difference is that an individual can profit from *falling* prices (sell first, buy later), as well as from *rising* prices (buy first, sell later). This "sell first" transaction is the procedure for most *hedging* operations in commodity futures markets. Hedging with stock index futures contracts appears in Chapter 7.

FUTURES TRANSACTIONS

Now let's treat ourselves to an example of actual futures trading. Suppose that on Tuesday, November 10, 1982, Trader A observes that the price of soybeans (January 1983 contract) is fluctuating between $5.70¼ and $5.79 (the actual trading range for that date). Trader A thinks that the price will rise, while another Trader, B, thinks that it will fall. Suppose further that Trader A buys and Trader B sells one contract at $5.75 on that day; the purchase cost to A = 5000 bushels × $5.75 = $28,750.00, neglecting commissions; that amount is the sales value for Trader B.

In the jargon of futures markets, Trader A is said to be "long" (bought first) and Trader B to be "short" (sold first). Until each completes a "round turn," they are both considered to have "open" positions. This view of pure price exposure, by the way, can be applied to any asset. (More about that later).

On December 15, 1982 the January 1983 contract for soybeans traded between $5.63 and $5.74; suppose both A and B decide to close out their positions at $5.65. The sales value to A would have been $28,250.00 and there would have been a loss of $500 ($28,250 − 28,750) on that side of the transaction, again further neglecting commissions. Similarly, the purchase cost for Trader B would have been $28,250, resulting in a gain of $500 on the transaction.

A number of principles about futures trading follow from this admittedly oversimplified, illustration. It would be extremely rare, for example, for Traders A and B to be the same transacting parties to open and close a given contract; but it is conceivably possible. First, the number of contracts bought always equals the number sold. Second, again neglecting commissions, total profits equal total losses. Futures trading per se (i.e., one of them might have been hedging) is a *zero sum* system. Third, futures contracts are created and destroyed through trading. The "round turn" aspect is important, too, because as a practical matter only 1–2 percent of the contracts ever made result in actual delivery. The major purposes and functions of futures markets are *not* for actual asset acquisition, but for price protection and risk transference.

One variation on the above example is to assume that Traders A and B closed out their respective positions on, say January 13, 1983, at the then prevailing price of $5.85. For January 13 Trader A would have realized a sales value of $29,250, and a *profit* of $500, instead of the loss incurred on December 15, 1982. Likewise, Trader B would have sustained a loss on January 13, 1983, of $500, if the transaction had been at $5.85.

As it turned out, the last pit price for January 1983 soybeans, on January 20, 1983, was $5.81, an opportunity for 6 cents more per bushel. But Trader B also could have had to settle for less than $5.75: not knowing for sure what that final price was going to be, Trader B "hedged." Trader B gave up the opportunity for additional gain on the cash market holdings of soybeans, to avoid the possibility of suffering a lesser price for the 5000 bushels. Approximately 123 contracts were delivered on the January 1983 contract (615,000 bushels). The option of whether or not to deliver the commodity typically is the "short's" prerogative. And since Trader B had not closed out the "short" position by an offsetting purchase for a round turn, there *had* to have been an offsetting "long" who was obliged to take delivery. Meanwhile, if Trader A had held the long position open past the December 15 dip in prices, there would have been an adequate reward for "bearing" the price risk that Trader B did not wish to bear. In this example, both parties might have been satisfied: Trader A recouped a "risk" premium for taking the long position to offset Trader B's *short hedge*. Trader B in effect "paid" some insurance (by not selling at $5.85 or higher), or just holding the soybeans "unhedged" until January 1983, when they could have been sold for $5.81 on the 20th. That "unhedged" strategy, by the way, is equivalent to having an outright "long" speculative position in the futures market. As hinted earlier, outright speculation is not confined to the futures market; just holding the cash crop unhedged is speculation also. However, it is frequently difficult (though possible) to have a "short" speculative position in the cash market.

DELIVERY

While we have set aside the delivery aspect, it is not unimportant. Delivery, or at least the threat of delivery, assures convergence of the futures price with the cash price of the commodity. "Such convergence is essential for futures contracts, as it provides a basis for their pricing, and allows them to serve as appropriate hedging vehicles for cash market participants" (Jones, 1982, p. 63). We explore how that convergence is achieved by delivery later, but for the moment let's explore the delivery mechanism itself.

In our example, going back to November 10, 1982, imagine that Trader B actually possessed 5000 bushels of deliverable grade soybeans and that they were located in an exchange-approved grain elevator. Trader B all along fully intended to deliver the actual commodity, rather than engage in a round turn. The price of $5.75 was satisfactory, because that price earned an adequate return on the investment in "cash" soybeans, and covered insurance and storage costs. By selling at $5.75, Trader B no longer had to worry about fluctuations in the price of soybeans. Yes, in retrospect, a higher price had been available on January 13, 1983 ($5.85), if the trader had remained unhedged and had waited until then to sell, but there also would have been the risk of having to sell at a lower price (e.g., $5.65 on December 15, 1982). Trader B's risk preferences were to settle for a "sure" $5.75, and let someone else (e.g., Trader A) worry about which way the price might go.

How does delivery assure convergence of the futures price with the cash market price? On this, let's hear Frank Jones:

> If convergence has not occurred during the delivery period [e.g., the "liquidation" month of January 1983], there will be an opportunity for arbitrage profits. For example, if the futures price is greater than the cash market price during the delivery period, arbitrageurs could buy the cash market commodity, sell the futures contract, and deliver the commodity at the higher (futures market) price. On the other hand, if the futures price is less than the cash market price, the arbitrageur could buy the futures contract

and short the cash market commodity, take delivery on the long futures contract at the lower (futures market) price, and repay the shorted cash market commodity. [That is, one might have to "borrow" the cash commodity to effectuate a "short" position; that is exactly what happens in the stock market when some one "sells short"; the stock is borrowed, frequently from the broker, in order to deliver the certificates sold to the buyer of the "short" sale.] Such arbitrage transactions which generate profits for the arbitrageur tend to make the futures price converge to the cash market price. Thus, the potential for delivery causes convergence (Jones, 1982, p. 64).

Historically, the delivery features of present day futures contracts appear to have evolved from the "to arrive" conditions of forward contracts in the pre-railroad era of the grain trade. As these "to arrive" contracts became more standardized, they grew to be more interesting to a greater number of traders. Merchants wishing to sell (contracted) wheat before it arrived from the outlying territories found it easier to locate a trading partner. The participation of these new traders—speculators, if you will—increased the volume of trading, thereby lowering the risks and transactions costs of engaging in "to arrive" forward contracts (cf., Houthakker, 1959, p. 148).

With the standardization of delivery terms and conditions, the identity of the buyers ceased to be important to the sellers, and conversely. The contracts accordingly became less and less personal, and the development of the Clearing House, a general intermediary between buyers and sellers, finally depersonalized them completely. Those who had bought contracts need no longer take delivery if they were not interested in actual merchandise, and they need not even approach the seller to annul the contract; all they had to do was sell the contract to someone else.

At this stage the original connection with "to arrive" dealings had become very faint indeed: the "to arrive" contract had evolved into the futures contract. This economic evolution had its counterpart in the realm of law. As the contracts became more remote from ordinary transactions in the cash markets, it became more dubious whether they were not mere gambling deals and legally unenforceable as such. The large-scale utilization by speculators made this question all the more acute. The courts established the rule that futures contracts were binding only when actual delivery was contemplated. [However,]. . . since traders can avoid delivery by buying or selling the contract before delivery is due, the presumption of intent to make or take delivery is largely a legal fiction. . . .

Although the possibility of delivery helped to maintain a relation between spot prices and futures prices it also led to abuses. Short sellers got into difficulties when they were unable to buy in their contracts before expiration or to obtain actual merchandise with which to meet their obligations. When deliverable stocks were small, large traders could exploit the plight of the shorts by operating "corners" or "squeezes," which are attempts to monopolize the long side.. . . The danger of corners and squeezes kept many potential traders from using the futures markets for speculation and hedging. The most effective weapon against this danger is extension of deliverability. The larger the variety of grades that can be tendered on futures contracts, the smaller the possibility that the deliverable stocks will be controlled by a corner. (Houthakker, 1959, pp. 148–149)

HEDGING AND THE "BASIS RISK"

The most important purpose served by futures markets is *hedging*. The essence of hedging is the shifting or transferring the price risks of inventory ownership from those who do not wish to bear such risks to those who are willing to accept them. In our previous numerical illustration with soybeans, Trader B was considered a possible hedger. There are some important aspects of hedging that need to be highlighted. First, a more extensive example, and then some philosophy about hedging.

Suppose yet another Trader, whom we call C, to protect his identity, is an extensive grain elevator owner, and in the course of the summer of 1982 has acquired *1 million bushels* of soybeans in his elevators. Temporarily, anyway, he owns that inventory, and with such extensive holdings he is exposed to considerable price risk. For every $.10 decline in the market price of his inventory, he would lose $100,000! If he had sold short 200 contracts (1 million bushels) of the January 1983 contract on July 13, 1982, at the closing price of $6.46, and if the "cash" price of soybeans had been $6.20, his respective market positions would have been as appears below:

July 13, 1982

Cash Market Inventory	Futures Market Position
1 million bushels, worth $6.20 per bushel = $6,200,000	"Short" 200 contracts, 1 million bushels at $6.46, sales proceeds: $6,460,000

Let's further suppose that he closed out his futures position on January 20, 1983, at the last price of $5.81, and by then he has sold his inventory of soybeans for $5.85 (due to location and transportation premiums). Then the respective accounts would look something like the display below:

January 20, 1983

Cash Market	Futures Market
Sold 1 million bushels at $5.85 = $5,850,000	Bought 1 million bushels at $5.81 = $5,810,000 purchase cost

Net Results from Hedging

Cash Market	Futures Market
Loss of $350,000 ($5,850,00 − $6,200,000)	Gain of $650,000 ($6,460,000 − 5,810,000)

$$-\$350,000 + \$650,000 = \text{net gain of } \$300,000$$

Even though elevator operator–Trader C "hedged" his inventory, he still came out ahead, way ahead with a "hedging profit" of $300,000. How could this happen? To hedge is supposed to mean giving up any chance for price gain, right? Not quite. What happened in this illustration is that the futures price fell by more than the "cash" price. The futures price fell $.65 = ($6.46 − $5.81) per bushel, and the cash price fell by *less*, $.35 = ($6.20 − $5.85).

By hedging, Trader C avoided a loss on his inventory of $350,000 (the change, decrease, in the cash price). So not only was he able to avoid that loss, but he made an additional $300,000 besides. Let's rearrange the prices, so that we can observe the "basis" aspect. The "basis" is defined as the difference between the cash price and the futures price: on July 13, 1982 the basis was ($6.20 − $6.46) = −$.26 and on January 20, 1983, the basis was ($5.85 − $5.81) = $.04, a net change in the hedger's favor of $.30 (× 1 million bushels) = $300,000. In contrast, suppose Trader C had closed out both his cash inventory and the futures positions when the futures price was $6.21 for the January 1983 contract, and the prevailing cash price was $5.90. The cash market and futures market results are shown below:

December XX, 1982

Cash Market		Futures Market	

Cash Market   Futures Market

Cost $6,200,000   Sale $6,460,000

Sale <u>$5,900,000</u>   Cost <u>6,210,000</u>

      −$ 300,000 loss $ 250,000 gain

     Net results from hedging: −$300,000 Cash market

                            <u>+$250,000</u> Futures market

                            −$ 50,000 Net loss from hedging

In this second example, Trader C avoided a loss of $300,000 on his cash market soybeans, but it cost him $50,000 to do so. (He might still feel all right about hedging.) Consider the terms of the basis aspect: on July 13, 1982, ($6.20 − $6.46) = −$.20 and on December XX, 1982, ($5.90 − $6.21) = −$.31; here the basis changed, weakened, against the hedger, but he was still protected from a much larger loss.

Now the philosophy. The point of all this is to demonstrate that hedging is not *riskless*. It is an operation that reduces risk but does not eliminate it. When someone can "lock in" a sure profit, that is called riskless *arbitrage* (as we cited in the delivery price convergence mechanism). Many textbooks and literature from futures exchanges often illustrate hedging with both the cash price and the futures price changing by the same amount, so that *all* of the price risk is transferred. True hedging doesn't operate that way.

In fact, the late Paul Cootner observed:

> In most circumstances, hedging is really a form of speculation—*speculation on the basis*. It has all the characteristics of speculation even though it is an essential normal aspect of doing business. It differs from the speculation of buying or selling futures only because the variance of the outcome is usually much less. In fact, in those cases where the basis is as volatile as the price of the spot commodity, the hedger moves naturally into holding inventories unhedged, i.e., into ordinary speculation, because there is no risk reduction from hedging (Cootner, 1967, p. 75).

Hedging, then is not "the elimination of risk, but its *specialization*: its decomposition into its components." By hedging, an inventory holder has passed on to the speculator "the risks of anticipating changes in absolute prices, but he still has basis risks to bear" (Cootner, 1967, p. 76).

Further, hedging is not viewed as merely risk avoidance, but rather as *profit maximization*, commensurate with the attendant uncertainty, or risk levels. With a presumed comparative advantage in basis speculation (i.e., in predicting the demand for inventory stocks), merchants can generally improve profitability by substituting hedged stocks for unhedged ones.

Basis changes are typically smaller than absolute price changes and entail less risk. What comparative advantage means, in this case, is that for a given level of risk, the merchant can earn more by holding inventories hedged than unhedged, but this may well mean holding a much larger volume of hedged inventory than he could hold unhedged. In fact, the evidence suggests that merchants do not hedge to reduce the absolute level of risk that they face but they hedge to increase their profits by being able to hold a *larger* volume of inventory (Cootner, 1967 p. 76).

The crucial nature of this interrelationship between spot and futures positions has also been emphasized by others. Houthakker has described the situation with clarity and eloquence:

Why does a trader hedge? The customary answer is: to reduce the risk of having a position in the cash market. If carefully interpreted, this answer is not incorrect, but stated without qualification it is highly misleading. Its defect is the suggestion that the cash position is primary, and the offsetting futures position no more than an afterthought. In an important paper Professor Holbrook Working has emphasized, on the contrary, that traders will normally consider cash and futures transactions in coordination and that the decision to engage in the one kind cannot be independent of the decision to engage in the other. According to Working, the decision to hedge is normally made in anticipation of a favorable change in the spot-futures price-spread, just as a decision to buy spot (without hedging) is motivated by an expected favorable change in the spot price. That this must be so is clear from the fact that the profit or loss on a hedging transaction equals the change over time in the "basis" (as the spread between spot and futures prices is often known) multiplied by the size of the commitment. (Houthakker, 1959, p. 153)

"LONG" HEDGING

The type of hedging considered above is called "short" hedging: the futures market initial position is a "short sale" to offset a "long" cash market position. Another brand of hedging is called "long" because the initiating transaction involves buying (first); also, since the cash market position is not to be established until some time in the future, in some instances, it is sometimes referred to as "anticipatory" hedging.

We need not belabor this. The cases most often cited as examples in the literature involve a miller who has committed to provide flour at a fixed price on a long term contract. His concern is with a rise in the price of wheat, his predominant cost, during the term of his obligation to deliver flour. In this instance, the miller "hedges" long by buying the appropriate number of wheat futures contracts. If the price increases, he will profit in the futures market and will offset the increased price he will have to pay for cash market wheat. Again, the miller could take delivery, but his milling facilities may be so far from the futures market delivery points, that he just acquires the wheat locally, but balances the pricing in the futures market. Like the short hedger, he also has to bear a basis risk, if he does not take delivery on the futures contract. He can limit his cost exposure by buying a forward maturity of the wheat contract closest to the quality of wheat he needs (there are three wheat contracts actively traded: one at the Chicago Board of Trade, another at the Kansas City Board of Trade, and still another at the Minneapolis Grain Exchange). As in short hedging, the miller passes up the possibility, if wheat prices decline, of benefiting from the windfall. His risk preferences are such that he is willing to forego any speculative gain in order to assure that his flour contract will earn the expected profit. In particular, he is more concerned about avoiding a decrease in his milling profit if the price of wheat increases.

PRICING AND PRICE DISCOVERY

Other functions that futures markets frequently perform are in the area of pricing. For some commodities, most notably agricultural products (e.g., grains), pricing in the cash markets is determined in relation to the "nearby" (earliest maturity) futures contract. The futures market is often the only location where buyers and sellers can interact for many products; cash market price quotations are often expressed as "10¢ under" or "15¢ over" (per bushel) the nearby contract's price. Those "overs" and "unders" are in fact the *basis* (the difference between the futures and spot prices).

For other commodities, such as precious metals, foreign currencies, or interest-bearing securities, the cash or spot prices are widely disseminated through a system of dealers or brokers, and those prices are determined principally by the contemporaneous forces of supply and demand. The spot price–futures price linkage is somewhat reversed in these latter cases. Where there is a well-developed, centralized "cash market" (as there is for common stocks) the futures markets do not affect pricing (that is, current pricing) per se very much.

Futures markets, on the other hand, do provide information in the capacity of *price discovery*. At any given time, all futures markets reveal an extant market consensus of expectations regarding the course of prices for the specific forward profile of maturities being traded. In effect, this time-shape profile of expectations revealed by the forward prices is generally interpreted to reflect the period to period time-differential carrying costs for tangible commodities. Similarly, for financial futures, some analysts feel that the time-shape of prices provides a market consensus about interest rate expectations. In all futures markets price movements reflect changes in the participants' expectations, transmitted by trading activity, given the information available and the respective risk preferences of the trading entities.

MARKET PARTICIPANTS

The focus of the preceding discussion was the mechanics of futures trading in general, and the risk-reduction aspects of hedging. Hedgers are typically depicted as willing to forego possible gains in order to reduce the risk of loss. A common analogy is the appeal to the "insurance" principle, whereby the risk is broken into numerous small parts that are "carried" by competent risk bearers. Sometimes the risk may be absorbed by other hedgers (e.g., "long hedgers"), but the lion's share of the normal inventory price risk transfer (short hedging) is borne by the *speculator*.

Again it should be stressed that futures markets are not principally arenas for asset acquisition, but provide the facility for risk transfer. Thus speculators are vital to the efficient functioning of any futures market. A speculator is a futures market participant who does not have a related position in the underlying cash market commodity. While the role of speculation in the economic system is still a matter of controversy, in popular parlance the word has acquired an unfavorable connotation; most economists would regard it at best as a necessary evil (cf. Houthakker, 1957, p. 143).

In terms of the realities of futures markets, however, speculators are crucial for providing price continuity and liquidity. Contrary to popular misconception, futures markets do not exist solely to furnish a speculative arena. Without adequate hedging participation, futures markets neither persist nor prosper. At the same time, hedgers will not utilize a futures market when there is insufficient speculative interest. In the absence of ample speculation, the price effects (and thus the "costs" of hedging) will discourage potential commercial interests from trading in such a market.

The key to the price effects inheres in the concept of market liquidity. The latter can be thought of as "the quantity of bids and offers flowing to a market; the more bids and offers there are competing with each other, the narrower will be the spread between them" (Melamed, 1981, p. 405). And the narrower the spread between the "bid" and "ask," the more viable and efficient the market.

Another subtle twist is that successful speculation, that is, profitable speculation, tends to serve the hedgers' interests.

> The role of the futures speculator, then, is to attempt to profit from skillful appraisal and accommodation of futures hedgers' demand and supply. If hedgers can buy and sell futures contracts without substantial transactions price effect . . . futures speculation may be said to be adequate (Gray, 1967, p. 181).

Successful speculation, in turn, depends on profitable anticipation of price movements. (For more discussion of technical trading systems, see Kaufman, 1978.)

So far we can regard long and short hedgers and speculators as being off of the trading floor. Their orders to buy and sell are executed through *futures commission merchants* (FCMs) who are analogous to stock brokerage firms. FCMs earn fees (i.e., commissions) for transacting their customers' orders at the best possible prices, just as in the stock market. (For more detail on the order execution flow, layout of pits, exchange memberships, and other aspects not covered here, see Powers and Vogel, 1981, and Chicago Mercantile Exchange, 1978.)

In addition to the (on the) floor brokers, who execute trades initiated off the floor, there are the floor traders who take positions in the market for their own account. These traders, sometimes called "scalpers," operate in very much the same manner as specialists do in the stock market.

However, they are not "obliged" to take positions against an imbalance of orders, as specialists are reported to be. Instead, the floor traders take positions in the anticipation of profit; they might maintain a given net long or short position for only a few minutes, measuring profits and losses in terms of fractional price changes. It is the combined interaction of all of these participants that results in the often hectic activity observed on the trading floors of the futures exchanges.

THE CLEARINGHOUSE

So far payment and "margins" have not appeared in our discussion, nor do they at this point ("margins" are considered in Chapter 9). However, the role of the clearinghouse needs to be mentioned. After a trade has been executed, the clearinghouse of an exchange becomes the intermediary to both buyer and seller. This interposition of the clearinghouse facilitates trading, transfers of contract positions, and ultimately settlement of all transactions.

The clearinghouse of an exchange deals only with its authorized clearing members. During each trading session, or in some cases only after the close of trading, clearing members submit confirmation records of trades executed during the session. These confirmations are "matched," usually by computer, so that an overall reconciliation of transactions is generated by the clearinghouse. "The brokers who executed the trades (buyers and sellers) are identified, along with the number of contracts, prices (of the trades), the commodity traded, and the delivery month" (Chicago Mercantile Exchange, 1978, p. 9).

By becoming the buyer to all sellers, and the seller to all buyers, the clearinghouse substitutes its financial strength for those of the actual traders (or their FCMs). The financial reliability of the opposite trading entity is not a matter of concern, once the trade has been verified by the daily matching and reconciliation procedure. The full faith and financial resources of the clearinghouse guarantee the validity of all "open" contracts. In turn, the financial viability of each exchange's clearinghouse is carefully safeguarded. Only members of the exchange who meet high standards of business integrity and financial condition are permitted to be "clearing members." Nonclearing members settle their transactions through the accounts of qualified clearing members (i.e., as if they were "customers"). All trades are settled daily.

SUMMARY

Contrary to many popular misconceptions, futures trading is neither extremely complex nor mysterious. For the most part, transactions executed on futures exchanges are similar to those in the stock market. True, in futures markets, the "stockbrokers" are called Futures Commission Merchants (FCMs), but most other basic aspects of trading are the same. At any given time, the maximum price buyers are willing to pay for a contract is called the "bid," and the minimum price sellers are willing to accept is the "ask." Profits and losses in both types of market are determined in the same manner: cost price versus selling price. If you buy at a price lower than you sell at, you realize a gain; if you sell at a price lower than the purchase price, a loss occurs. One difference in futures markets is that it is much more common to sell first (initially), and buy later to complete the transaction (a "round turn"). "Selling short" also exists in the stock market, but there are constraints on doing so, and it is much less common. In both cases, the expectation is to profit from a price decline.

Trading futures, in some other respects, is perhaps more akin to trading bonds. Both have maturity aspects that usually impel traders to take some action prior to expiry. In the case of bonds, the maturity price at par (100.0) is generally well known in advance with a high degree of confidence. On the other hand, in futures markets, the maturity price of expiring contracts is never known *a priori* with certainty. Those contract positions remaining "open" after the last day of trading are settled by "delivery." This aspect of futures trading tends to result in the convergence of the futures price of the underlying commodity with the cash or spot market price. Convergence is important in futures markets as it provides a basis for pricing the cash market commodity and furnishes a valid hedging instrument for cash market participants.

This chapter has provided some examples of typical futures transactions: various types of hedging as well as speculative trades. In addition, a bit of historical perspective on the evolution of delivery was covered also.

Mechanics aside, stock and bond markets are markets for actual asset acquisition. In contrast, futures markets exist to facilitate risk transfer. The predominant operation in this regard is known as hedging: a hedging transaction involves positions in both the cash market asset and the futures contract. The trader's profits or losses in the futures market, in these cases, are only part of the story. Offsetting gains or losses in cash market assets must also be taken into account.

Further, the type of risk management afforded by hedging in futures markets is risk specialization, or risk decomposition. Hedging is *not* risk elimination. It still involves the "basis risk," that is, the change in cash prices vis-à-vis the change in futures prices during the existence of the hedged position. Moreover, hedging is not merely risk *avoidance*, but profit *maximization* commensurate with the attendant levels of uncertainty.

The "risk bearers" in futures market are those without related cash market asset positions—the speculators. These market participants provide continuity to futures pricing and liquidity to facilitate transfering positions. Not generally recognized is that "speculation" is not confined to futures positions. Holding cash market assets without the opportunity to mitigate the full risks of inventory price changes is equivalent to holding a "long" speculative position in the futures markets. It is also the same risk exposure as holding an *unhedged portfolio* of common stocks.

Although the risk exposures are essentially equivalent, one position is said to be "investing" in stocks while the other is "speculating" in futures. Now we no longer need to split "semantic hairs." Stock index futures contracts provide the same type of opportunity for risk decomposition to the "outright investor" that has been available to cash market asset holders of commodities for over a century.

6 The Stock Index Futures Contracts

HISTORY AND LITIGATION

The exact origin of the stock index futures concept is difficult to pin down. Others have reported that in foreign countries, stocks regularly trade on both a cash and futures settlement basis (Figlewski and Kon, 1982, p. 3). And in Amsterdam, from 1973 to 1975, Arthur Lipper operated the Forward Contract Exchange Company. There primarily institutional clients traded forward contracts based on the Dow Jones Industrial Average (DJIA), the Financial Times Index of Ordinary Shares, and the Tokyo Dow Jones Index (Commodity Futures Trading Commission, 1978b, pp. 136–142).

In 1977, the Kansas City Board of Trade (KCBT) formed a special committee to explore potential new futures contracts. The committee retained Dr. Roger W. Gray of Stanford University as a consultant. After considerable research, the committee determined that a futures contract based on a stock index or average would offer the greatest economic utility. Due to the vast inventory of stocks that might be hedged (approximately $1.5 trillion) and the potential participation of 30 million stockholders, the expectations for the success of such a contract were high.

The first submission to the Commodity Futures Trading Commission (CFTC) of a proposal to trade a futures contract based on a stock index occurred in October 1977. The KCBT proposed a futures contract based on the DJIA. Public hearings on the stock index futures submission were held by the CFTC in Washington, D.C., during October 1978. Over 400 pages of testimony were presented by interested parties, who generally affirmed the positive public interest of the innovative proposal. However, final agreement was never reached with Dow Jones & Co. regarding the use of the DJIA. On April 20, 1979, the KCBT amended its proposal to the CFTC to base its futures contract on the Value Line Composite Index (VLIC).

Due to regulatory disagreement concerning jurisdiction of the new contract, CFTC action on the proposal was delayed for many months. However, with the appointments in 1981 of Philip M. Johnson as Chairman of the CFTC and John Shad as Chairman of the Securities and Exchange Commission, the bureaucratic logjam was finally broken. The new chairmen reached an accord with regard to the lines of jurisdiction for new financial products. The Shad-Johnson agreement was instrumental in the KCBT's proposal being approved on February 16, 1982—after a total delay of nearly 4 years.

The KCBT-VLIC futures contract's first day of trading occurred only 8 days later on February 24. Amid a euphoric atmosphere on the exchange's trading floor, the new stock index futures contract got off to a fairly robust start. The first day's trading volume amounted to nearly 1800 contracts.

Trading in two other stock index futures contracts followed soon thereafter. On April 20, 1982, the Chicago Mercantile Exchange (CME) received CFTC designation as a contract market for a stock index contract based on the Standard & Poor's (S&P) 500 Stock Index. The CME began trading one day after approval, on April 21. The initial volume totaled 3963 contracts. Two weeks later, on May 4, 1982, the New York Futures Exchange (NYFE) received CFTC approval to trade its stock index future based upon the New York Stock Exchange Composite Index (NYSE). The first day's trading volume on May 6 amounted to 6162 contracts. The comparative terms and conditions of the three contracts (KCBT, CME, NYFE) appear in this chapter. In addition, NYFE received approval and began trading a futures contract based on a sectoral index, the NYSE Financial Index; made up of 212 financial stocks listed on the big Big Board.

OTHER SUBMISSIONS AND LITIGATION

The extensive hedging potential and trading activity of stock index futures contracts have resulted in a virtual deluge of proposed index futures submissions to the CFTC. Competition among the various exchanges has been keen, active, and hard fought from the very beginning. Some of the participants have sought resolution in the courts. The number of combatants involved in various forms of litigation seems reminiscent of the simultaneous gladiator duels in the Coliseum of ancient Rome. These stock index legal battles are briefly described below.

KCBT v. CFTC (et al.)

During the week before the CFTC's scheduled approval of the CME-S&P contract, the KCBT sought to enjoin the CFTC from approving any other stock index futures contracts for a 1 year period. In a suit filed in Kansas City U.S. District Court, the KCBT argued that the inordinate (4 year) delay by the CFTC in approving its submission had eroded KCBT's competitive advantage. With neither copyright nor patent protections, the KCBT as innovator of the stock index futures concept asked that an adequate period be granted for exclusive trading in order to recoup its investment in development costs. The KCBT argued further that the longer term impacts would likely be a dilution of the incentives for the smaller futures exchanges to submit innovative proposals to the CFTC. Already rather highly concentrated in Chicago, the futures industry would not be as viable and competitive without the participation of the smaller exchanges in new product development.

The CME, in the role of intervenor in the proceedings, contended that there would be no provable damages if the CME-S&P contract were to trade the following week; and even if there were damages, the KCBT could litigate an appropriate suit at a later time. On the following Monday, April 19, 1982, Judge Joseph E. Stevens, Jr. denied the KCBT's petition, and the CFTC approved the CME-S&P contract for trading the next day.

Standard & Poor's Corporation v. Comex

On April 28, 1982, the CFTC approved the application of the New York Commodity Exchange (Comex) to trade a futures contract based on an index of 500 stocks, the "Comex 500." On the same day, in New York federal district court, Judge Milton Pollack granted Standard & Poor's a temporary restraining order that prevented Comex from actually trading the approved contract. The Standard & Poor's suit charged Comex with "misappropriation of proprietary information, unfair competition, and dilution of S&P's trademark."

Judge Pollack on May 13 granted a further preliminary injunction against Comex prohibiting trading of the Comex 500 contract. The judge said that Comex "intended improperly to link S&P with Comex as a commercial prop," thereby trading on Standard & Poor's name "without authorization and over S&P'S objections." Judge Pollack felt that Comex would have been "misappropriating the skill, expenditures, labor and reputation of S&P in generating and producing the S&P 500 index." In addition, he felt that Comex's promotional literature was somewhat misleading and confusing as to whether Standard & Poor's supported the Comex 500 contract (*Wall Street Journal, WSJ*), May 14, 1982, p. 15).

Comex filed an immediate appeal of that decision. Two weeks later, June 30, 1982, a federal appeals court unanimously upheld the lower court's ruling prohibiting Comex from trading the "500" stock index futures contract (*WSJ*, July 1, 1982, p. 26).

Dow Jones v. Chicago Board of Trade (et al.)

The most active and colorful of the stock index litigations involve the Dow Jones Averages. Originally the KCBT had intended to use a 30 industrial average (the DJIA, though not identified by name) as the basis for its stock index contract. As described above, when Dow Jones & Co. objected to even that passive arrangement, the KCBT established a formal agreement with Arnold Bernhard & Co., to use the VLIC and amended the application to the CFTC accordingly.

In its original stock index application, the Chicago Board of Trade (CBT) planned to employ "portfolio futures." The CBT proposed 10 industry indexes, each composed of about 5 stocks, and an eleventh portfolio future, the aggregate of the other 10 industry groups, a composite to represent "the market."

In March 1982, however, the CBT sought designation from the CFTC as a contract market for futures based on stock indexes remarkably similar to the Dow Jones Averages. Previously, the CBT had been refused use of the averages by Dow Jones & Co. Robert Wilmouth, then president of the CBT, described the industrial contract "as based on a stock market index, composed of 30 industrial stocks" (*WSJ*, March 1, 1982, p. 44).

Three separate court actions arose from the CBT's new submission to the CFTC.

CBT v. Dow Jones (Cook County, Illinois)

The initial legal action was filed by the CBT in Cook County court in March 1982. Claiming that its stock index proposal to the CFTC would not violate Dow Jones's rights, the CBT asked for a declaratory judgment to that effect. Dow Jones responded that the Cook County court did not have jurisdiction, and asked that the suit be dismissed.

Dow Jones v. CBT (New York)

Simultaneously with its response in Illinois, Dow Jones & Co. filed a suit in New York federal court to enjoin the CBT from trading the proposed stock index futures contract. Dow Jones contended:

> The proposed CBT stock indexes are in fact the Dow Jones Averages . . . and that the proposed trading by the CBT would constitute copyright and trademark infringement, false representation of goods and services, misappropriation of property, and injury to Dow Jones's business reputation.

[Dow Jones repeatedly objected to its name or product being associated with a "speculative trading device" (*WSJ*, April 1, 1982, p. 38).]

Dow Jones v. CFTC (Washington, D.C.)

The third legal action, in May 1982, was Dow Jones's request in federal court to enjoin the CFTC from approving the CBT's application to trade the disputed stock index futures contracts (*WSJ*, May 11, 1982, p. 10), claiming that the CBT "would cause severe and irreparable injury to Dow Jones's property interests." Judge Charles Richey dismissed the Dow Jones suit since the CBT had voluntarily pledged to delay trading until the Cook County, Illinois, suit had been decided. The CBT also stated that the Dow Jones name would not be used to promote the contracts. The CFTC approved the "Chicago Board of Trade Stock Market Index Contract." However, the Illinois and New York lawsuits remained pending.

Not finished yet, the venerable Dow Jones organization "threatened to alter or suspend publication of its stock averages" because of the dispute. In a letter to the CFTC, Dow Jones reiterated its contention that "use of the Dow Jones indexes as a trading vehicle posed a substantial threat to the company's reputation and value of its indexes" (*WSJ*, May 14, 1982, p. 15).

In New York federal court, those arguments were not persuasive. During July 1982 Judge Robert L. Carter denied Dow Jones's copyright infringement injunction request. He ruled that Dow Jones had "shown neither the probability of success on the merits nor possible irreparable harm." Judge Carter stressed "that the decision related solely to the alleged copyright infringement" (*WSJ*, July 19, 1982, p. 8).

In Illinois, the CBT also initially won the lawsuit against Dow Jones. State Judge James Murray ruled that trading in the CBT's stock index futures contracts would not be harmful to Dow Jones since the latter's name would not be used. Moreover, the CBT had said it would print a disclaimer of Dow Jones sponsorship in all advertising and promotional materials (*WSJ*, June 7, 1982, p. 10). That, in the opinion of the judge, differentiated the case from the Comex-S&P suit, partly because Comex had used Standard & Poor's name to promote its contract. However, the CBT victory turned out to be rather hollow: Judge Murray also granted a temporary stay of ruling to permit Dow Jones to appeal the decision.

An Illinois appellate court extended that stay indefinitely, until the New York copyright infringement case had been decided. The appeals court later reversed the earlier circuit court decision, and ruled in favor of Dow Jones & Co. The court did not issue its opinion, which was to be forthcoming at a future date. Until that opinion was issued no further legal action could have been undertaken.

The opinion of the three-judge appellate court was issued about 30 days later. In overturning the lower court's decision, in favor of Dow Jones, the opinion stated that the CBT would be misappropriating the averages, even if Dow Jones's name wasn't used in connection with the contract. The misappropriation did not relate to the name, but to "the property right of Dow Jones to its averages and the good will and public respect attendant to them" (*WSJ*, August 8, 1982, p. 25). The court further opined that "the strong correlation of the Dow Jones average to the general pattern of stock market activity is essential to the usefulness of the [Board of Trade's] index contract." There was no doubt in the court's mind that the name and reputation of Dow Jones figured heavily in the CBT's plans.

The CBT immediately appealed to the Illinois Supreme Court. In December 1982, that court agreed to review the appellate court's decision. That action remained pending as of the end of 1982.

TERMS AND CONDITIONS OF THE CONTRACTS

Basically the three stock index futures contracts, KCBT, CME, and NYFE, are very similar in their specifications. All three are "sized" at 500 times the futures prices, which in effect are the respective cash index values (identical at contract maturity).* The major differences among the contracts relate to the last trading day for each, and daily price change limits. (See comparative specifications in Table 6.1.)

Minimum customer margins are set by each exchange. The initial speculative margin, through informal suggestion by the Federal Reserve Board, was set at about 10 percent of each contract's value when trading began. Margins appear in Chapter 9.

INDEXES AS "COMMODITIES"

The "underlying commodities" for the three stock index futures contracts are the Value Line Composite Index (KCBT), the Standard & Poor's 500 (CME), and the New York Stock Exchange Composite Index (NYFE). The novelty of utilizing an index as the basis for a futures contract is more apparent than real. Learned students of futures markets have recognized that for some years that the bases of several existing futures contracts could have been interpreted as "indexes." The close correlation of price movements is utilized in "cross hedging". For example, the soybean oil contract has been characterized as an index representation for other oils hedged in that market, including cottonseed oil and palm oil. In addition, the GNMA and U.S. Treasury Bond futures contracts are more comprehensively viewed as representative of a wide range of long term debt instruments. Eurodollar futures contracts, approved in 1981, are explicitly based on an index.

---

*However, the NYFE's "Financial Index Futures Contract" is sized at 1000 times the NYSE Financial Index; also its minimum fluctuation is .01 (= $10). The volume and open interest of the Financial Index futures contract have been minimal. Therefore, this particular futures contract is not included in the subsequent discussions.

Table 6.1   Stock Index Futures Contracts—Contract Specifications[a]

Size of Contract and Price Quotations

All three contracts are sized at 500 times the respective index value:
KCBT: 130 × 500 = $65,000
CME: 115 × 500 = $57,500
NYFE: 70 × 500 = $35,000

Trading Hours (All Three Contracts)

10:00 A.M. to 4:15 P.M. (Eastern Time)
 9:00 A.M. to 3:15 P.M. (Central Time)

Minimum Price Change (All Three Contracts)

.05 × 500 = $25

Daily Price Change Limits

KCBT: None (changed to $5.00 in August 1982)
CME: $5.00 (changed from $3.00 on July 6, 1982)
NYFE: None

Delivery Months

March, June, September, December (plus two additional maturities, same cycle:
all contracts)

Last Day of Trading

KCBT: Last business day of delivery month
CME: Third Thursday of delivery month
NYFE: Next to last business day of delivery month

Delivery

All three contracts are settled in cash, marked to market at the closing value of
the respective underlying "spot" stock market index on the last day of trading

Settlement

Business day following last trading day, in U.S. funds. All contracts settled to
.01 ($5) in terms of the respective cash index.

Margins

Minimum customer margins are set by each exchange

[a]KCBT = Kansas City Board of Trade–Value Line Composite Index; CME = Chicago
Mercentile Exchange–Standard & Poor's 500 Index NYFE = New York Futures Exchange–New York Stock Exchange Composite Index.

CASH SETTLEMENT

Another innovation embodied in the stock index contracts was the provision for settlement at delivery by means of cash or of funds transfers.
Again, the Eurodollar contract of the International Monetary Market of
the CME, though proposed later, was the first futures contract to trade
with a full cash settlement provision.

During the four years of regulatory machinations about stock index futures, one of the concerns focused around the cash settlement aspect, especially with regard to state gaming laws. In some states, gambling statutes void futures contracts "where the seller and buyer intend to settle by cash payment rather than delivery" (Martell and Salzman, 1981, p. 294). On the other hand, many state gaming statutes also contain a provision exempting futures contracts that are entered into on a designated contract market. In any event, the "exclusive jurisdiction" provision of the Commodity Futures Trading Commission Act of 1975 provided ample legal justification for CFTC approval of the stock index futures contracts' applications, as far as the cash settlement feature was concerned.

In Chapter 5 we saw how futures prices and cash market prices converge, when physical delivery is called for by the futures contract. Most often, this provision is appropriate for agricultural commodities—especially when the "cash price" is apt to vary widely by locale and quality. For stock index futures, on the other hand, any sort of "physical delivery" for broad-based market indexes could imply enormous transactions costs. Fortunately, cash delivery is a very efficient mechanism—and wholly appropriate for these contracts.

With cash delivery, convergence of the futures price with the cash market "price" is assured in that the final settlement price is *imposed* from the cash market. That is, all contracts remaining open after the last day of trading are "closed out" or settled at the closing index value. That value is not determined in the futures trading pit, but by the closing prices of the index components in the cash market (i.e., the S&P 500, VLIC, and NYSE).

For cash settlement to work properly, there must be a "good" cash market *price*, or index value. This price should be uniform and freely available throughout the industry; further, it should be an accurate indicator of value, and immune to manipulation (cf. Jones, 1982, p. 68). For most agricultural commodities, those conditions do not exist. The heterogeneity of the cash market precludes the feasibility of cash settlement. In fact, as mentioned in Chapter 5, the situation is often the reverse: pricing in many agricultural cash markets is accomplished by using the "nearby" (earliest maturity) futures contract.

One of the advantages of cash settlement, when appropriate and feasible, is that the (quality or grade) basis risk is substantially reduced. Where setlement is specified by a cash market price index, the "average" grade is represented, not the cheapest.

Since the average price changes by less than the price of the cheapest deliverable grade due to the shifting among the various cheapest deliverable grades, cash settlement will reduce the grade basis risk in a futures contract under such circumstances. (Jones, 1982, p. 72)

More important, concern about market congestion, corners, and squeezes is eliminated. Traders can retain positions in a maturing contract through the last day of trading, if they so choose, without worrying about market liquidity. Similarly, exchange officials need not be concerned about "orderly liquidation" (as with physical delivery) since there cannot be any last minute squeezes in the trading pit.

Stock index futures contracts are settled to the closing values of broad-based stock market indicators: the VLIC, S&P 500, and NYSE. The contemporaneous values of these indexes are widely disseminated throughout each trading day, and are available to all actual and potential futures market participants. With this system of delivery, there is no incentive for the final pit price to differ from the closing cash price. That is the price each exchange's clearinghouse employs in closing out all open positions after the last day of trading. Convergence is guaranteed.

TRADING THE STOCK INDEX CONTRACTS

At this point we can illustrate some transactions in stock index futures, employing actual market data. All three contracts will be used in the examples. Suppose that "long" positions were initiated, on a given day: July 1, 1982, in the September 1982 maturities of each of the three contracts, at that day's closing price for each:

July 1, 1982

	CME- September 1982	NYFE- September 1982	KCBT- September 1982
Price	109.85	63.20	118.10
Contract value	$54,925	$31,600	$59,050
($P \times 500$)			

Since all were long positions, the dollar sums represent the "purchase cost" side of the transaction. If all were closed out at the July 22, 1982 closing prices three weeks later, then

July 22, 1982

	CME- September 1982	NYFE- September 1982	KCBT- September 1982
Price	113.55	65.25	123.10
($P \times 500$)	$56,775	$32,625	$61,550
Gain	$ 1,850	$ 1,025	$ 2,500

These particular transactions would have been profitable, since the price increased for our "long" positions. On the other hand, if we had thought the market was due for a downturn, those "gains" you see above would have been losses, if the initial positions taken had been "short."

Although the contracts are all "sized" at 500 times the futures (index) prices, and since the indexes are at different levels, the outright dollar "gains" are not comparable. However, if we calculate the percentage gains or "returns," (i.e., dollar gain/purchase cost), these are the respective percentages:

CME $1,850/$54,925 = 3.37%
NYFE $1,025/$31,600 = 3.24%
KCBT $2,500/$59,050 = 4.23%

These results are merely illustrative, and not intended to provoke any generalities. On different days, the percentage results could have shown entirely different orderings. We need more evidence, that is, a larger sample from which to draw any insights (coming up in Chapter 10).

CASH "DELIVERY" OR SETTLEMENT

To further illustrate the mechanics of these markets, again let's assume that "short" positions were initiated on September 1, 1982, and the positions were not "closed out" (i.e., round turns not accomplished), and all positions were left open through the last day of trading. Remember that each of these contracts has different delivery days, so the relative results are not strictly comparable. This example is just intended to illustrate the mechanics and the arithmetic.

September 1, 1982

	CME	NYFE	KCBT
Price	117.00	67.25	127.55
Sales value (short)	$58,500	$33,625	$63,775
Last day of trading (for September 1982 contract)	9/16	9/29	9/30
Settlement price	123.77	69.78	131.95
Cash index	S&P 500	NYSE	VLIC
Close on above date	123.77	69.78	131.95
"Purchase cost"	$61,885	$34,890	$65,975
Loss on trade	− $ 3,385	− $ 1,265	− $ 2,200

In this illustration, each contract was assumed to have remained "open" through the last day of trading. The settlement price was not determined in the trading pit but imposed by the clearinghouse on all open positions. And since for every open "short" there is an open "long," the respective settlement or "delivery" prices became the corresponding "sales" prices for the open long positions also. The clearing members forward the required sums to the clearinghouse. In turn, the funds are transferred to the appropriate other clearing members, and the contract is settled or delivered the day following the last day of trading for each, respectively. Actual cash flows are illustrated in Chapter 9 when "margins" are discussed.

SUMMARY

Although stock index futures contracts did not begin trading in the United States until February 1982, similar financial instruments previously had been in existence in other countries. The period of initial trading in the United States was one of robust action—both on and off the trading floors. As soon as the CFTC approved the stock index contracts, trading successes immediately followed: at the KCBT (February), the CME (April), and the NYFE (May). New contract record volumes marked the first year's trading for the total of these three contracts.

Meanwhile, off the trading floors, a variety of litigants lined up for concerted battles in the courts. The KCBT, as innovator, sought, unsuccessfully, to secure a period of exclusive designation as the sole market authorized to trade stock index futures. The New York Commodity Exchange (Comex) tried, also unsuccessfully, to trade a CFTC-approved futures contract based on an index of 500 stocks. The courts found that the "Comex 500" index's resemblance to the S&P 500 was too close to have occurred by sheer coincidence. Standard & Poor's Corp. was granted injunctive relief, which decision was upheld through Comex's appeal. That contract never traded.

The most widespread and colorful legal campaign pitted the CBT against Dow Jones & Co. Suits were filed in Chicago, New York, and Washington, D.C. In Cook County, Illinois, the CBT filed for a declaratory judgment, in March 1982, to the effect that its stock index proposal, then pending before the CFTC, would not violate Dow Jones's rights. Simultaneously, Dow Jones, claiming copyright and trademark infringement, filed in New York federal court to enjoin the CBT from trading the proposed stock index futures contract. And in Washington, D.C., Dow Jones sought to enjoin the CFTC from even approving the CBT's application. Because the CBT had pledged to delay trading pending the outcome of the suit in Cook County, Illinois, Dow Jones lost both the New York and Washington, D.C. court actions. Initially, Dow Jones also lost the Cook County suit, but won a reversal in appellate court. The CBT appealed that reversal to the Illinois Supreme Court, which agreed to review the lower court's decision. That action remained pending as of the end of 1982.

The structures of the three stock index futures contracts are very similar. All three (KCBT, CME, and NYFE) are "sized" at 500 times the respective underlying index's value or "price." Since the VLIC exhibits the largest index values, the KCBT contract represents the largest monetary magnitude, followed by the S&P-CME, and the NYSE-NYFE contracts.

All three contracts trade from 10:00 A.M. to 4:15 P.M. (Eastern time), have minimum price fluctuations of .05 ($25), and are settled to the underlying spot index close on the last day of trading by cash delivery.

The differences among the contracts are that: (1) the KCBT and CME have \$5.00 daily price change limits, while the NYFE has none; (2) while all three contracts mature on a March, June, September, December quarterly cycle, the last day of trading differs. The CME contract expires on the third Thursday of the maturity month; the NYFE contract on the next-to-the-last business or trading day of the maturity month, and the KCBT on the last trading day.

Two innovative features of these contracts seem to have confused many observers: the underlying commodity being a stock market index, and settlement by cash delivery. The "index" aspect is not really much of a novelty. For many years, the futures industry has recognized "cross-hedging" operations as bona fide risk reduction. In that context the underlying commodity of the particular futures contract acts as a surrogate index, for example the various types of vegetable oils that are hedged with the soybean oil contract.

The cash delivery feature has many virtues. When appropriate, cash settlement reduces the quality or grade "basis risk" since the average grade is represented by the cash market index. In other contracts, when physical delivery is called for, the cheapest qualifying grade is delivered. In any event, recall that these markets exist principally for risk transfer, and not for asset acquisition. The lack of a physical deliverable, in the eyes of many, seems to have confused the issue about the true nature of stock index futures in general. The reasoning actually is the converse; in most cases, the conditions necessary for cash settlement are not present, and physical delivery is the only alternative.

With cash settlement, convergence of the futures and cash prices is guaranteed. The closing price from the cash market on the last day of trading is imposed as the settlement price for all contracts remaining open. Finally, cash settlement is a regulator's dream come true. There can be no "corners," "squeezes," or other manipulations. And exchange officials need not worry about "orderly liquidation." When cash settlement is appropriate, the efficiency of the particular futures market is greatly enhanced.

7 Hedging with Stock Index Futures

The principal economic purpose of stock index futures contracts is to provide "price" or value protection for portfolios. The preceding examples of trading stock index contracts were intended to illustrate how gains and losses in these futures markets are determined. As we have seen, within futures trading per se, the sum of all profits equals the sum of all losses, when commissions are excluded. It is a "zero-sum" system. But that is only part of the picture. The true "net" economic value of utilizing stock index futures contracts must also take into account what happens to the values of related "cash market" holdings: associated portfolios of common stocks.

Due to the vast amounts of stock in the hands of the public, including institutions (approximately $1.5 trillion), the most natural type of hedging would be the "short hedge," the typical "inventory" hedge that we explored in the soybean illustration. Recall that a short hedge is accomplished through the "sell first" sequence of positioning in the futures market. A number of examples appear below.

HEDGING ONE STOCK

In order to keep this first illustration as concise as possible, let us consider an individual who has only one stock in the portfolio. (That situation is not so farfetched, by the way. See Appendix C on patterns of stock ownership.) Suppose the individual owned 2300 shares of Schering Plough on May 10, 1982; on that day the stock closed at 30½. The market value of this one-stock portfolio, then, was $70,150. In the futures markets on May 10, 1982, the June 1982 contracts closed at the following prices: Chicago Mercantile Exchange (CME) 118.50; New York Futures Exchange (NYFE) 68.40, and Kansas City Board of Trade (KCBT) 131.25. The investor could have hedged in any of the three markets; for purposes of comparison, we show all three hypothetical hedges (*Note* that two NYFE contracts are necessary to approximate portfolio value.):

May 10, 1982

	Cash Market (2300 shares of Schering Plough)	Futures Markets (June 1982 Contracts)		
		CME	NYFE (2)	KCBT
Price	30½	118.50	68.40	131.25
Value	$70,150	$59,250	$68,400	$65,625

If the hedged position had been maintained until June 15, 1982, when Schering Plough was selling at 28½, these would have been the respective results:

June 15, 1982

	Cash Market (2300 shares of Schering Plough)	Futures Markets (June 1982 Contracts)		
		CME	NYFE (2)	KCBT
Closing price	28¼	109.90	63.15	120.35
Value	$65,550	$54,950	$63,150	$60,175
Gain on futures transactions:		+$4,300	+$5,250	+$5,450
Loss in portfolio value:	−$4,600			
Net hedging results:		−$300	+$650	+$850

In all three futures markets, the individual would have avoided an outright $4600 loss in the value of his Schering Plough holdings. The net results differ by a few hundred dollars by futures market; the main point is that the "short hedge" helped the investor manage the risk of the position in the cash market.

One stock, while possessing a positive systematic risk component, still leaves the investor exposed to considerable unique or unsystematic risk. For example, if the stock had been Comsat (say 1100 shares roughly), the market price on May 10, 1982 was 61¼ and the market value $67,237.50; on June 15, the price of Comsat had declined to 50⅞, a market value of $55,962.50, and the loss sustained would have been −$11,275.00, about twice the amount gained from any of the contract hedges. *If* (and this is a risk preference decision for the investor) diversifiable risk is to be eliminated, most studies indicate that 8–15 stocks eliminate most of it. Further, with just one stock, it is not unlikely that the market could decline, and the single stock move in the opposite direction, resulting in either double profits (on both the futures and the cash asset), or double *losses*. However, even in the Comsat example, the investor's losses would have cut by nearly 50 percent by hedging.

Hedging generally involves smaller losses and smaller profits than those incurred with unhedged positions. That is precisely the price-risk-transferral function provided by stock index futures contracts. These are instruments for risk management for those who hold and trade common stocks.

HEDGING A PORTFOLIO

As indicated above, the most effective hedging results occur when the diversifiable risk is indeed diversified away; that is, by holding a portfolio of enough different stocks so that systematic "market risk" is the predominant uncertainty. To illustrate portfolio hedging, suppose that an investor held the example portfolio shown in Table 7.1, and that "short" hedges were established, for purposes of comparison, in the three contract markets. The September 1982 contracts of each stock index future are assumed sold on June 30, 1982, at the respective closing prices. (Again, two NYFE contracts are assumed, to approximate the initial portfolio value.)

June 30, 1982

	Cash Market (portfolio shown in Table 7.1)	Futures Markets (short positions initiated in the September 1982 Contracts, closing prices)		
		CME	NYFE (2)	KCBT
Price		111.50	64.05	119.50
Value	$71,412.50	$55,750	$64,050	$59,750

As of August 13, 1982, just prior to the bull market rally, the following would have been the results of the hedges as of that day (portfolio values for August 13, 1982 appear in Table 7.2):

August 13, 1982

	Cash Market (portfolio shown in Table 7.2)	Futures Markets (all September 1982 contracts purchased at closing prices)		
		CME	NYFE (2)	KCBT
Price		104.85	60.25	113.65
Value	$68,337.50	$52,425	$60,250	$56,825
Gain on futures transactions:		+ $3,325	+ $3,800	+ $2,925
Loss in portfolio value:	− $3,075			
Net hedging results:		+ $250	+ $725	− $150

As intended, the short hedge resulted in a negligible loss or small profit in the three markets. After August 13, 1982, everyone knows that the bull market continued almost unchecked throughout the remainder of 1982. But that is hindsight; this particular investor, looking forward on August

Table 7.1 Portfolio June 30, 1982

Stock	Number of Shares	Price	Market Value
Bausch & Lomb	100	$42\frac{1}{8}$	$ 4,212.50
Corning Glass	100	$43\frac{3}{8}$	$ 4,337.50
Dresser	200	$17\frac{7}{8}$	$ 3,575.00
duPont	100	33	$ 3,300.00
General Electric	100	$65\frac{3}{8}$	$ 6,362.00
Ingersoll Rand	100	$39\frac{1}{2}$	$ 3,950.00
International Paper	100	$36\frac{7}{8}$	$ 3,687.50
Loews	100	$86\frac{5}{8}$	$ 8,662.50
Martin Marietta	100	$25\frac{1}{2}$	$ 2,550.00
Merck	100	$67\frac{1}{2}$	$ 6,750.00
PPG	100	$33\frac{1}{4}$	$ 3,325.00
Squibb	100	$34\frac{3}{8}$	$ 3,437.50
Stauffer	200	$18\frac{1}{4}$	$ 3,650.00
Tenneco	200	$24\frac{3}{4}$	$ 4,950.00
Texas Instruments	100	$86\frac{5}{8}$	$ 8,662.50
Total portfolio value			$71,412.50

Table 7.2 Portfolio, August 13, 1982

Stock	Number of Shares	Price	Market Value
Bausch & Lomb	100	$38\frac{3}{8}$	$ 3,837.50
Corning Glass	100	44	$ 4,400.00
Dresser	200	$13\frac{3}{8}$	$ 2,775.00
duPont	100	31	$ 3,100.00
General Electric	100	64	$ 6,400.00
Ingersoll Rand	100	37	$ 3,700.00
International Paper	100	$37\frac{1}{8}$	$ 3,712.50
Loews	100	$82\frac{3}{8}$	$ 8,237.50
Martin Marietta	100	$24\frac{5}{8}$	$ 2,462.50
Merck	100	$64\frac{1}{4}$	$ 6,425.00
PPG	100	$33\frac{3}{4}$	$ 3,375.00
Squibb	100	$34\frac{1}{2}$	$ 3,450.00
Stauffer	200	$17\frac{3}{4}$	$ 3,550.00
Tenneco	200	$23\frac{1}{2}$	$ 4,700.00
Texas Instruments	100	$82\frac{1}{8}$	$ 8,212.50
Total portfolio value			$68,337.50

13, 1982, wasn't sure what the market was going to do. So as a cautious soul, our investor decided to "roll forward" the hedge positions on that day, that is, to reestablish short positions in the December 1982 contract(s). All markets are shown for another hedge evaluation on September 30, 1982. The portfolio values appear in Table 7.3.

September 30, 1982

	Cash Market (portfolio shown in Table 7.3)	Futures Markets (all December 1982 contracts shorted at the respective closing prices on August 13, 1982)		
		CME	NYFE (2)	KCBT
August 13 sales price:		105.30	60.70	113.20
August 13 value:	$68,337.50	$52,650	$60,700	$56,600
September 30 purchase price:		119.35	68.45	129.40
September 30 value:	$81,000.00	$59,675	$68,450	$64,700
Gain in portfolio value:	+$12,662.50			
Loss on futures transactions:		−$7,025	−$7,750	−$8,100
Net hedging results:		+$5637.50	+$4912.50	+$4562.50

Even in the face of a roaring bull market, our hedger still profited! True, losses on the futures contracts ranged from $7000 to $8000, but the portfolio gain was even more dramatic. Hindsight might still hamper us, but during the initial stages of the market's dramatic increase, there were a few hectic days when the Dow Jones Industrials declined by more than 10 points, four days during September 1982. On the 30th, our reference point, the Dow declined by 10.02, and by 13.06 on the 29th of September. By September 30, 1982 our investor, perhaps feeling *sure* the bull run

Table 7.3   Portfolio, September 30, 1982

Stock	Number of Shares	Price	Market Value
Bausch & Lomb	100	$38\frac{1}{4}$	$ 3,825.00
Corning Glass	100	$51\frac{3}{4}$	$ 5,175.00
Dresser	200	$14\frac{1}{4}$	$ 2,850.00
duPont	100	$34\frac{1}{2}$	$ 3,450.00
General Electric	100	$74\frac{3}{4}$	$ 7,475.00
Ingersoll Rand	100	$36\frac{3}{4}$	$ 3,675.00
International Paper	100	39	$ 3,900.00
Loews	100	$119\frac{3}{4}$	$11,975.00
Martin Marietta	100	$37\frac{1}{8}$	$ 3,712.50
Merck	100	$78\frac{1}{8}$	$ 7,812.50
PPG	100	$39\frac{3}{8}$	$ 3,937.50
Squibb	100	$40\frac{7}{8}$	$ 4,087.50
Stauffer	200	$19\frac{1}{2}$	$ 3,900.00
Tenneco	200	$29\frac{5}{8}$	$ 5,925.00
Texas Instruments	100	93	$ 9,300.00
Total portfolio value			$81,000.00

Table 7.4   Portfolio, December 31, 1982

Stock	Number of Shares	Price	Market Value
Bausch & Lomb	100	$45\frac{3}{4}$	$ 4,575.00
Corning Glass	100	$65\frac{7}{8}$	$ 6,587.50
Dresser	200	$19\frac{3}{4}$	$ 3,950.00
duPont	100	$35\frac{7}{8}$	$ 3,587.50
General Electric	100	$94\frac{7}{8}$	$ 9,487.50
Ingersoll Rand	100	$39\frac{1}{2}$	$ 3,950.00
International Paper	100	$48\frac{3}{8}$	$ 4,837.50
Loews	100	$143\frac{1}{2}$	$14,350.00
Martin Marietta	100	$43\frac{3}{4}$	$ 4,375.00
Merck	100	$84\frac{5}{8}$	$ 8,462.50
PPG	100	$51\frac{3}{4}$	$ 5,175.00
Squibb	100	$44\frac{1}{4}$	$ 4,425.00
Stauffer	200	$23\frac{1}{4}$	$ 4,650.00
Tenneco	200	$32\frac{3}{8}$	$ 6,475.00
Texas Instruments	100	$134\frac{5}{8}$	$13,462.50
Total portfolio value			$98,350.00

was over, might have, for one more example, again rolled the hedges forward in the March 1983 contracts for downside protection through December 31, 1982. The portfolio values are shown in Table 7.4.

December 31, 1982

	Cash Market (portfolio shown in Table 7.4)	Futures Markets (all March 1983 contracts shorted at the respective closing prices on September 30, 1982)		
		CME	NYFE (2)	KCBT
September 30 sales price:		119.80	68.80	129.70
September 30 value:	$81,000.00	$59,900	$68,800	$64,850
December 31 purchase price:		141.80	81.95	161.00
December 31 value:	$98,350.00	$70,900	$81,950	$80,500
Gain in portfolio value:	+$17,350.00			
Loss on futures transactions:		−$11,000	−$13,150	−$15,650
Net hedging results:		+$6,350	+$4,200	+$1,700

With regard to this extended example, a few words of explanation are in order. First, the portfolio was chosen much at random, to provide some diversification, and the issues selected were intended to be fairly recognizable corporations. For all except the December 31 period, the net hedging results were comparable among all the contracts. In this latter period, the KCBT hedge underperformed the other two, due perhaps to the VLIC's higher variability. Other portfolios might have shown different relative results. Second, the example may be a little skewed with regard to the NYFE, since two contracts were used for hedging protection. That results in the NYFE "hedge" moving at 1000 times the futures price, even though the basic contract is "sized" at 500 times the futures price (or index's value). The requirements for a bona fide hedge (according to the Commodity Futures Trading Commission, CFTC) specify that the value of the cash market assets equal or exceed the value of the futures position when the hedge is initiated. On those grounds, only one NYFE contract could have been employed, but that would have distorted the example in the other direction. In percentage terms, the NYFE contract is about as volatile as the CME's (see Chapter 10).

Third, and most important, throughout this example, a very "naive" hedging policy was employed. The investor executed the appropriate "short" in each contract, and incurred all of the offsets as insurance premiums. More sophisticated hedging practices might have lifted the hedges at various times so as not to continue to "drag down" the portfolio's performance as the market continued to escalate. Once lifted, however, a hedge can be easily reinstated, as these futures markets are fairly fast moving, and highly liquid. One could also make use of "stop" orders if the market moved downward enough to cause concern. With a less naive policy, the hedge protection might have been reestablished at higher and less costly price levels in terms of the futures contracts.

Fourth, the contracts employed in the hedges were not the "nearby" maturities. The reason for that minor variation is due to the different delivery date of the CME contract. In the delivery month it is closed on the third Thursday, and therefore, not open on the last business day of that month. Otherwise, the CME contract would have had to be rolled over when the other two did not, and that would have complicated the example.

HEDGING "LONG"

In contrast to the typical "inventory" or portfolio short hedge, stock index futures lend themselves to various situations where a "long" hedge is the risk reducing alternative. The most natural long hedge would be in a situation when someone is currently "short" stock. The natural form of hedging consists of equal and opposite positions in the cash and futures market. The stock market is one cash market where it is relatively easy to have a "short" cash asset position. The stock is "sold short" by borrowing it from someone else (usually one's broker) to deliver to the buyer. Just as in a speculative short futures position, the trader hopes to profit from a decline in the price of the stock by buying it back later at a lower price. However, if the price of the stock increases, the short position will be covered at a loss.

A short stock position can be hedged "long" by buying a forward maturity of a stock index contract; if the market rises, the stock or stocks shorted will probably also increase in price, but if the trader is hedged long, there will be an offsetting profit in the futures position. In order to simplify the illustration, an adequate number of shares of one stock are assumed sold short, and hedged by buying contracts in all three markets. Since we already have the futures results from September 30 to December 31, 1982 in our previous example, we "hedge" our short position in the stock market with the March 1983 contracts in all three futures markets. Again, due to the difference in the index values of the NYSE, two contracts are assumed executed in that market. For our stock to be sold short let's consider 1000 shares of Monsanto.

September 30, 1982

	Cash Market (sell 1000 shares of Monsanto)	Futures Markets (purchase "long" March 1983 contracts)		
		CME	NYFE (2)	KCBT
Price	72½	119.80	68.80	129.70
Sales value	$72,500			
Contract value		$59,900	$68,800	$64,850

December 31, 1982

	Cash Market (buy 1000 shares of Monsanto)	Futures Markets (sell March 1983 contracts to close out hedge position)		
		CME	NYFE (2)	KCBT
Price	76¼	141.80	81.95	161.00
Purchase cost	$76,250			
Sales value		$70,900	$81,950	$80,500

Net Results for Each Market

	Cash Market	Futures Markets		
		CME	NYFE (2)	KCBT
Sales value	$72,500	$70,900	$81,950	$80,500
Purchase cost	$76,250	$59,900	$68,800	$64,850
Totals	− $3,750	+ $11,000	+ $13,150	+ $15,650
Net hedging results		+ $ 7,250	+ $ 9,400	+ $ 11,900

In this particular instance, the investor would have profited substantially from the futures market positions, rather than from the cash market short position. In a sense, the rewards materialized from being "wrong" about the expectations of Monsanto declining. On the other hand, if the short position in the cash market had been in Data General, the following would have occurred:

September 30, 1982	December 31, 1982
Sold short 2800 shares of Data General at $24\frac{5}{8}$ = $68,950.00 (short) sales value	Bought 2800 shares of Data General at $39\frac{3}{4}$ = $111,300.00 purchase cost

Net cash market results: $ 68,950 Sales value
                         $111,300 Purchase cost
                       − $ 42,350 Loss on short sale

In this case, the net results even with hedging would have been disastrous, as the maximum futures market profit of $15,650 (KCBT) would still have left this trader *really* "short," on the order of about $27,000 to $33,000. As in the short hedging examples, the moral is the same. A single stock exposes the trader to substantial unsystematic risk—risk that can be diversified away. The appropriate procedure would be to create "a short portfolio," as was illustrated for short hedging. However, at this point too many numerical illustrations might be tiresome. The reader can easily imagine the mechanism: long positions in the futures markets to offset "portfolios" that are composed of a number of short positions in different stocks (à la Tables 7.1 through 7.4).

OTHER HEDGING USES OF THE CONTRACTS

In addition to the long and short hedging examples provided above, which are one or more stock portfolios, there are a number of other applications. Without dragging the reader through an excess of numerical examples, let us just list the possible risk reduction uses for stock index contracts in general. Short hedging situations still denote an initiating sale of a forward maturity to offset a long cash market position.

Short Hedges

1. Someone tendering stock, but not knowing whether the tender was accepted or not, might wish to guard against a market decline, in case the tender offer is called off.
2. Buyers of call options, and sellers of puts could use the contracts to mitigate risk.
3. Investment bankers and underwriters of stock flotations could use a short hedge to help stabilize risk during the period of distribution.
4. Executors of estates, who are "locked in" to a given portfolio during the period of probate, could use a short hedge to guard against heavy losses to the estate's value.
5. Specialists and brokers, "market-makers," who frequently have large inventories of stocks, could use the contracts to reduce their risks.

Long Hedges

The opposite positioning in the futures market, "long hedging", is appropriate for mitigating risk in a variety of circumstances. In addition to an investor hedging short stock positions, specialists and other "market-makers" may frequently find themselves in net "short" positions, in order to maintain orderly trading. Similarly, buyers of puts and sellers of "naked" call options might use a long hedge to reduce risk. (See Chapter 8 on utilizing the stock index contracts with individual stock options.)

The predominant uses of a long hedge in other futures markets involve "anticipatory" transactions, or positions to be established in the future. Some of the more common long hedges of this nature for stock index futures contracts are listed below.

1. Institutions that receive funds on a relatively regular basis might use the long hedge to improve the timing of establishing positions in stocks; also dealers who commit to provide future delivery of stocks to large institutional buyers.

2. A block-positioner might use a long (or short) hedge while completing the transition of positions.

3. Foreign investors in U.S. stocks, who have restrictions on the rate at which capital can be liberated from their countries, might use a long hedge.

4. A firm planning to grow by acquisitions could use a long hedge to offset the risk of a market rise in target company stocks; on the other side, the seller of a company whose transaction is fixed in dollar terms might wish to retain the future stock purchasing power of the sale proceeds by buying stock index futures.

PORTFOLIO MANAGEMENT

The hedging uses of stock index futures illustrated in this chapter have been directed to risk reduction. In that sense, these strategies imply a rather passive risk avoidance motivation. The flexibility of stock index contracts affords the capability for much more positive strategies. For example,

> A portfolio's systematic risk is usually adjusted by altering the proportion of high to low beta stocks in the portfolio and by adding or removing fixed-income securities. But the transaction costs associated with buying and selling individual securities in the cash market are high. Also, changing the composition of the portfolio can distort stock selectivity performance and hinder the diversification of unsystematic risk. Stock index futures could be used to accomplish the same adjustment both more simply and at much lower cost. (Figlewski and Kon, 1982, pp. 8–9)

If fund managers expect a bear market, they can fully reduce their exposure by hedging in the manner illustrated in the portfolio examples in this chapter. By "laying off" the entire market risk, a fund manager has essentially reduced the portfolio's beta to zero.

> If he is very confident of his prediction, he can even construct a portfolio with a *negative beta* by taking a short position in the futures market greater than the long position he holds in the spot market. A pension manager who predicts a bull market can construct a high beta portfolio by going *long* in the futures market. This is sometimes called, facetiously, a "Texas hedge." (Figlewski and Kon, 1982, pp. 9–10, emphasis added)

In a similar article, Dwight Grant demonstrated how an "optimal" portfolio can be selected. In essence, the portfolio was constructed of securities based solely on their unsystematic returns and risks, and then the portfolio manager achieved the preferred degree of systematic risk exposure by utilizing the futures market, that is, by taking the appropriate forward positions in the stock index contracts (Grant, 1982a, p. 35). The flexibility of the stock index futures contracts will allow fund managers to "fine tune" their portfolios to the risk-return profile they desire.

SUMMARY

Stock prices and portfolio values fluctuate due to systematic and unsystematic influences. The ultimate justification for stock index futures contracts inheres in their capability for managing systematic risk. Investors can reduce or control unsystematic risk through diversification. In this chapter, we have used some single stock illustrations to demonstrate the hedging mechanics of stock index futures. That alternative simplified the examples. And while Appendix C presents more technical explanations why investors might choose to hold relatively undiversified portfolios, that decision is a risk preference choice. It is *not* intended to be an implicit investment strategy recommendation here.

The basic hedging operation usually involves "equal and opposite" positions in cash market assets (e.g., "long" stocks) and futures (e.g., "short" stock index contracts). Hedged positions generally result in smaller losses and smaller profits than unhedged positions. That is the essence of hedging: the risk reduction choice of foregoing possible systematic speculative gains in order to avoid possible systematic portfolio losses. Due to the considerable holdings of common stock by the public, about $1.5 trillion, the most predominant hedge would be the typical "inventory" short hedge. However, stock index futures contracts are highly flexible instruments. They can mitigate risk for a wide variety of stock market participants: ranging from underwriters, dealers, and market-makers to firms planning to grow through acquisitions. The types of hedges in many instances could be either "long" or "short" with respect to the positioning in the futures markets. In addition, stock index futures contracts provide risk management potential for buyers and sellers of individual stock options. That topic appears in the next chapter.

Finally, hedging need not be merely a passive, risk-avoidance technique. Risk management with stock index futures can be as aggressive as the investor chooses. At very low transactions costs, the fund manager can alter a portfolio to a high systematic risk ("high beta") configuration, when confident of a strong upside market move. Further, a manager who expects a steep downside correction can create, in effect, a "negative beta" portfolio. In both cases, stock index futures contracts allow such risk posture adjustments without the necessity of actually buying or selling stocks themselves, or altering stock selection criteria, while at the same time avoiding the attendant high transactions costs. With less strongly held convictions about the market's future direction, the fund manager can "fine tune" the risk profile of the portfolio's market exposure to any intermediate posture desired with stock index futures. The actual portfolio's composition need not be disturbed. Stock index futures truly provide efficient *risk specialization*.

8 Hedging Stock Options Positions

In the preceding chapter, a few of the suggested applications of stock index futures for risk reduction involved the use of individual stock options. Before exploring how index futures contracts can be used in conjunction with various options' positions, the reader would be well-advised to obtain also the booklet "Understanding the Risks and Uses of Listed Options," a joint publication of the exchanges on which listed options are traded, and the Options Clearing Corporation. An associated document, the prospectus of the Options Clearing Corporation, is also recommended. These publications are intended to fulfill the risk disclosure requirements in conjunction with trading stock options, as promulgated by the Securities and Exchange Commission. In addition, Max G. Ansbacher's *The New Options Market* (1979) is highly recommended. Other related analytical sources appear in the references.

Frequently, the difference between individual stock options and stock index futures has been the subject of some confusion. Since both types of instruments can be used for "hedging" or mitigating the risks of portfolio holdings, they are often thought to be identical. In reality, stock index futures add yet another dimension of risk management potential for investors. This chapter, which emphasizes their complementarity, should help to make the distinction clear.

PUTS AND CALLS

While an extended journey into the intrigues of stock options is beyond the scope of this chapter, some brief definitions are not. A *call* option conveys to the buyer ("long") the right to purchase the particular stock

(XYZ Corp.) at a given price (e.g., $30 per share; this is referred to as the "strike" price) for a certain period of time. In other words, the call has an expiration date. A call option is not unlike an option that might exist in a real estate transaction: the buyer can exercise the option before a certain date, and after that the option is worthless. The seller of a real estate option must, therefore, hold the particular parcel off the market in case the option is exercised; after expiration, the parcel is no longer subject to sale under the terms of the option. The seller of a call option (the "short") may or may not actually hold the stock in question. If so, the option is referred to as a "covered call" and the seller of the option must hold the stock until expiration, or buy it back at some price (like a round turn). If the seller does not own the stock, referred to as a "naked call," the call seller must post margin to guarantee performance on the call if exercised.

For example, investor C pays $300 to call seller W (sometimes referred to as the option "writer") for the right to buy 100 shares of XYZ at $30, which let's assume is its current market price, until July 19, 1983, which is the expiration date. If the price of XYZ rises to $33, investor C could "call" the stock, sell it for $33 and just break even: C must pay W $3000 for the "called" stock, and has already paid $300 for the option. Investor C's proceeds from the sale at $33 = $3300. However, if the price of XYZ goes higher than $33 before the call is exercised, investor C will profit as long as the option has not expired.

If the price does not rise, however, and the call writer (W) owns the stock ("covered"), W has effectively lowered the investment cost in XYZ to $2700 ($3000 − $300 premium received for the call). The writer is "protected" down to a price of $27, but below that price W also sustains a loss. So writing calls against a portfolio provides some protection, but it is limited (see Merton et al., 1978). In effect, both C and W do not wish the price of XYZ to fall through the floor, since C's call will become worthless, and W will sustain net losses below $27. In this situation, Merton has suggested that both are basically, "bullish" on the stock but differ as to their estimates of the stock's variability.

A *put* is an option in the other direction; the buyer of a put (long) has the right to sell 100 shares of XYZ at the "strike" price until the date of expiration. The seller of the put (short) agrees to buy the stock at the strike price, and posts margin to guarantee performance as long as the option is outstanding. For example, if investor P expects the price of XYZ to decline rapidly, he might buy a put for 100 shares, at a strike price of

$30, and pay the seller Q $300 for the put option. If the price of XYZ instead increases above $30, the put option loses value as the price of XYZ increases, and also as the date of expiration approaches. On the other hand, if XYZ falls below $27 during the "life" of the put option, purchaser P will realize a profit. If the price of XYZ fell to $23, then investor P could buy the stock at $23, and immediately sell it to the put writer Q; P's profit is $400 ($2300 cost of the stock purchase + $300 premium paid to Q for the put option in the first place = $2600 costs, but sales price to Q = $3000, so the profit is $3000 − $2600). In the real world, neither investor C nor P would actually "exercise" his or her respective options. There are active markets for puts and calls on various exchanges: the Chicago Board Options Exchange, the American Stock Exchange, the Pacific Stock Exchange, and the Philadelphia Stock Exchange. The normal practice, if there were a profit in an option, would be to sell it to realize the gain, or to limit a loss, by executing such a transaction on the exchange that listed options for XYZ Corp. Options are generally exercised by brokers and dealers, for whom the costs of exercise, commissions, are minimal. Again, this description is very brief and intended only to define puts and calls. The reader is again referred to the literature mentioned above.

RISK DECOMPOSITION

As indicated earlier, stock options can be used for protecting portfolio values. For downside shelter, a portfolio manager might either sell *calls* or buy *puts*. However, the sale of call options against portfolio holdings only provides *limited* hedge protection. The price of the ("hedged") stocks can decline more than the option premium, and the seller of the calls would still lose.

On the other hand, a strategy of buying puts to shield portfolio holdings may provide more "protection" than the fund manager actually desires. Each put option is for a specific stock; accordingly, it provides downside protection for *both* systematic *and* unsystematic risks. But unsystematic risks are dealt with by portfolio *diversification*. Thus such a strategy would provide *excessive* protection, and at considerable cost. In contrast, stock index futures contracts allow the portfolio manager to isolate and deal with just the systematic risk component. These aspects are illustrated in Figure 8.1 for a single stock. The total risk of investing in a stock is

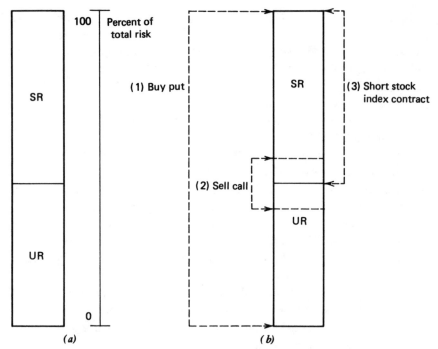

Figure 8.1 (*a*) Risk components of common stocks. (*b*) Hedging alternatives with individual stock options and stock index futures contracts. SR is systematic risk and UR is unsystematic risk.

represented vertically, and divided into systematic (SR) and unsystematic (UR) risk components. Figure 8.1*b* represents the extent of risk coverage afforded by (1) buying a put, (2) selling a call, and (3) "shorting" a stock index futures contract. Presumably, writing (selling) a covered call (2) involves some portion of both SR and UR components.

HEDGING A "LONG" CALL POSITION

Stock index futures mitigate the systematic risk portion inherent in any options position. Suppose an investor bought 13 call options (1300 shares) on AMP Corp. on May 12, 1982, August calls with a strike price of 55; AMP was at $55\frac{7}{8}$ on that day. The hedge position, in all three stock index futures contracts, would have been as follows:

May 12, 1982

AMP Call: $4\frac{1}{2}$ (August 55 strike) Options Position	AMP Stock: $55\frac{7}{8}$ Futures Markets Position		
Purchase calls: 1300 × $4\frac{1}{2}$ = $5,850.00	Sell September 1982: contract(s):		
		CME	NYFE(2)	KCBT
	Price	120.25	69.25	132.10
	Contracts values	$60,125	$69,250	$60,050

The number of call options to be purchased is determined by the values of the futures contracts, in relationship to the price of the underlying stock. Here 1300 shares of AMP at $55\frac{7}{8}$ = $72,637.50. This is, strictly speaking, a "cross hedge" and the value of AMP equals or exceeds the futures market contracts' values. A "short" position is initiated because a rapid decline in the market and AMP would result in a decline in the value of the AMP calls. On the other hand, if the market (and AMP) increase, losses on the futures positions would be sustained, but the AMP call should increase in price. Let's see what actually happened on August 13, 1982 when this hypothetical position was closed out.

August 13, 1982

AMP call: $\frac{1}{16}$ (August 55 strike) Options Position	AMP stock: $46\frac{1}{4}$ Futures Markets Position		
Sell 1300 AMP calls at $\frac{1}{16}$ = $81.25	Buy September 1982 contract(s):		
		CME	NYFE (2)	KCBT
	Price	104.85	60.25	113.65
	Contracts values	$52,425	$60,250	$56,825
	Gain in futures markets	+$ 7,700.00	$ 9,000.00	+$ 9,225.00
Loss on calls: $5,850 − $81.25		−$ 5,768.75	−$ 5,768.75	−$ 5,768.75
Net results from hedging options		+$ 1,931.25	+$ 3,231.25	+$ 3,456.25

In this particular case, the options premiums were essentially lost entirely; however, the short hedge in the futures market resulted in an overall net gain of nearly $2000–$3500, depending on the market used for hedging. Again, as before, the commission costs have been ignored, but would reduce the net profit in the futures market, and add to the loss on the options position. Also again, for simplicity of exposition, only one stock option is used in this example, which means that the unsystematic risk of the position was borne in its entirety by the investor.

As mentioned earlier, for short periods of time, some stocks may move contrary to the overall market's direction. For example, if our investor had been lucky (or wise) enough to buy calls on McDonald's, the following would have resulted:

May 12, 1982

McDonald's call: $4\frac{5}{8}$ (September 65 strike) Options Position	McDonald's stock: $65\frac{1}{4}$ Futures Markets Position
Buy 1100 McDonald's calls at $4\frac{5}{8}$ = $5,087.50	Same as in example above

August 13, 1982

McDonald's call: $5\frac{1}{2}$ Options Position	McDonald's stock: $69\frac{1}{2}$ Futures Markets Position		
Sell 1100 McDonald's at $5\frac{1}{2}$ = $6,050	Same as in example above		
	CME	NYFE(2)	KCBT
Gain on options: $6,050.00 (sell) −$5,087.50 (buy) = +$962.50	Gain on futures $7,700	$9,000	$ 9,225
	+$ 962.50	+$ 962.50	+$ 962.50
Overall net gain	+$8,662.50	+$9,962.50	+$10,187.50

The "unsystematic risk" can cut both ways; it would be easy to find examples of losses occurring on both the options and futures positions.

The obvious risk reducing strategy here would be to construct a "portfolio of calls" (that is, on four or five different stocks) to "diversify away" the unsystematic component of a single stock option position.

A poignant example of the risk exposure in one stock is the case of Warner Communications. On November 1, 1982, the stock was selling for 53¼, and the (55 strike price) February 1983 calls at 5⅛. An options hedge as we illustrated above would have involved about 15 Warner calls (1500 shares), and a premium cost of $7687.50. On November 1, the index futures, December 1982 maturities, closed at the following: CME 137.45, NYFE 79.05, and KCBT 150.70. Due to reports that the Christmas sales of Warner's Atari video games were not all that good the stock lost 19 points overnight during early December. On December 13, the stock dropped to 36, and the February 55 calls to ⁹⁄₁₆. The loss on the calls would have been $7687.50 − 843.75 = −$6843.75, and the short positions in the indexes would have lost also: on December 13, the CME was at 140.50 (loss on "hedging" short of $1525); the NYFE was at 80.75 (for two contracts, a loss of $1700); and KCBT had increased to 158.95, for a loss on a hedging short position of $4125, as of December 13, 1982. So in addition to the loss on the calls of $6843.75, the total loss including the futures hedge could have ranged from $8368.75 (CME contract) to $10,968.75 (KCBT contract).

HEDGING A "SHORT" CALL POSITION

Hindsight provides 20–20 vision. The "right" side of the illustration shown above for Warner Communications would have involved "writing" or selling the calls. Stock index futures can be used by both buyers and sellers of stock options. The correct positioning for a hedged option "writer" in the futures market entails a "long" futures postion. The principle is just the reverse of the long call positioning: the writer of the call option loses if the stock increases in price; therefore, to "hedge" the market risk, the writer of a call would undertake a long position in the futures. In the example for Warner Communications, the call writer ("short") would have profited from the decrease in the value of the options ($6843.75) plus the profits from the futures markets ($1525–$4125). In this case, the lack of diversification would have worked in favor of the writer; however, that is the most risky strategy, as emphasized previously. Generally, writers of calls hold the underlying stock in their portfolios so they are assured of its being available if actually "called," that is if the option is exercised. For less complication, we assume here that the writer is "naked" (does not own the stock), and assures performance by posting the required margin on "short" options with the stockbroker.

For a "somewhat" less dramatic example of hedging a short call position, consider call writer W who, on October 1, 1982, "shorted" calls on Teledyne, and hedged ("long") in the futures market(s):

October 1, 1982

Teledyne call 9¾ (January 90 strike) Options Position	Teledyne stock: 90⅜ Futures Market Position		
Sell eight calls (800 shares) at 9¾ = $7800	Purchase December 1982 futures		
	CME	NYFE(2)	KCBT
Price	120.15	69.05	130.35
Contract(s) value	$60,075	$69,050	$65,175

The "cross hedge" entails the underlying value of 800 shares of Teledyne = 800 × 90.75 = $72,600, which exceeds the values of the futures contracts. Let's suppose the hedge is lifted on December 1, 1982:

December 1, 1982

Teledyne calls: 47 (January 90 strike) Options Position	Teledyne stock: 135.00 Futures Market Position		
Buy eight Teledyne calls at 47 = $37,600	Sell Futures contract(s) to cover		
	CME	NYFE(2)	KCBT
Contract price	138.10	79.75	159.20
Loss on options: Contract(s) value	$69,050	$79,750	$79,600
Gain on futures	+ $8,975	+$10,700	+$14,425
$7,800 (sell) − $37,600 (buy) =	−$29,800	−$29,800	−$29,800
Net loss on hedge:	−$20,825	−$19,100	−$15,375

In this particular example, the hedger didn't fare so well; there were gains in the futures market to offset the loss on the options position, but Teledyne's increase during October and November of 1982 far outstripped the rise in the prices of the futures contract(s). Once again, this is a one-stock-only hedge to illustrate the principles. Diversification might have helped.

This example has another moral as well. The maximum gain available to a short options position (puts as well as calls), *if* the stock (and market) go in the "expected" direction, is simply the amount of premiums received for the options. If, as above, the stock, the option, and the market move in the "contrary" direction, the loss on the options position may exceed, or may be less than, offsetting futures results. Teledyne increased about 49 percent in the two month period considered here. A more restrained illustration for the months of October and November of 1982: a call writer on Pepsico would have experienced the following from October 1–December 1, 1982:

October 1, 1982

Pepsico call: $3\frac{3}{8}$ (January 45 strike) Options Position	Pepsico stock: $45\frac{5}{8}$ Futures Markets Position
Sell 16 Pepsico calls at $3\frac{3}{8}$ = $5,400.00	Same as in example above

December 1, 1982

Pepsico call: $1\frac{3}{8}$ Options Position	Pepsico stock: 42 Futures Markets Position		
Buy 16 Pepsico (January 55) at $1\frac{3}{8}$ = $2,200.00	Same as in example above		
	CME	NYFE(2)	KCBT
Gain on futures	+$ 8,975	+$10,700	+$14,425
Gain on options: $3,200 +$ 3,200	+$ 3,200	+$ 3,200	
Overall net gain	+$12,175	+$13,900	+$17,625

Here again, the unusual occurred: the market increased rather dramatically, from October 1 to December 1, but the price of Pepsico declined (from $45\frac{5}{8}$ to 42). The futures' profits are far out of proportion to the options gain, but that's what would have happened in those particular circumstances.

HEDGING A "LONG" PUT POSITION

The mechanics for hedging a "long" put position are straightforward. Since the buyer of a put hopes to gain if the stock declines in price, the risk-reducing hedge with stock index futures is a *long* position, in case the stock increases in price due to the market. For this illustration, let's use the May 12–August 13 period for a long put position in Honeywell:

May 12, 1982

Honeywell put: $4\frac{3}{8}$ (August 75 strike)   Honeywell stock: 74
Options Position

Buy 10 Honeywell puts (1000 shares) at $4\frac{3}{8}$ = $4,375.00

August 13, 1982

Honeywell put: $14\frac{1}{4}$ Honeywell stock: $60\frac{7}{8}$
Options Position

Sell 10 Honeywell puts at $14\frac{1}{4}$ = $14,250.00
Net gain on puts: $14,250.00(sell)
                                             $\underline{\$\ 4,375.00(buy)}$
            Gain: +$ 9,875.00

Since the hedging operation in the futures market would be a "long" hedge, that is a reversal of a long call position, we can reverse the results of the May 12–August 13 futures transactions from the AMP example above:

	CME	NYFE	KBCT
Loss on futures	− $7,700	− $9,000	− $9,225
Gain on options	+ $9,875	+ $9,875	+ $9,875
Net results from hedge	+ $2,175	+ $ 875	+ $ 650

HEDGING A "SHORT" PUT POSITION

The last case to be illustrated here is the hedge for a "short" put position; the put is sold by the writer, who hopes that it will decline in price. That will occur if the stock *increases* (puts are options to sell at a given price). To guard against a rapid decline in the stock's price due to market movements, the appropriate hedge position in the futures market is a "short" in the contracts. Here we again use the October 1–December 1 period; the investor sells puts on Merrill Lynch:

October 1, 1982

Merill puts: $3\frac{1}{2}$ (January 35 strike) Options Position	Merrill stock: $35\frac{1}{4}$
Sell 20 Merrill puts at $3\frac{1}{2}$ (2000 shares) = $7500	

December 1, 1982

Merrill puts: $\frac{1}{16}$ Options Position	Merrill stock: $65\frac{3}{4}$ Net Futures Contract Results (Short)		
Buy 20 puts at $\frac{1}{16}$ = $125.00. Net gain on puts: $7500 − $125 = $7,375		CME	NYFE	KCBT

		CME	NYFE	KCBT
	Loss on futures	− $8,975	− $10,700	− $14,425
		+ $7,375	+ $ 7,375	+ $ 7,375
Net hedging results:		− $1,600	− $ 3,325	− $ 7,050

HEDGING OPTIONS POSITIONS

In the preceding illustrations, rather naive assumptions were made to simplify the examples. The first bears repeating once again: options on only one stock expose the hedger to perhaps considerable unsystematic risk. This aspect cannot be overemphasized. The second "naive" assumption pertains to the hedging operation itself: once in place, the examples did not try to "time" the hedges by lifting them when it became obvious that the stock options positions no longer needed protection. In reality, once a short put or call had lost its value, it would be unnecessary to retain the futures contract position, since only further losses might be sustained. Accordingly, some of the "net results" amounts are exaggerated.

The array of various positions and outcomes are shown in Table 8.1. The presumption, as before, is that all "short" option positions are not covered by the underlying stock ("naked"). The position table details the various buying/selling ("writing") combinations for hedging such positions. The case A and B variants indicate the risk possibilities and outcomes when the market and the stock underlying the option move *with* and *contrary* to the expectations held when the hedge positions are initiated.

For all cases there are components of gain and loss, with the net results indeterminate. In some cases, however, the maximum extent of gain or loss is limited to the amount of premiums involved for "short" options positions, or "long" positions, as when they are "unhedged." For example, in Case IB (long calls/short futures), the limit of potential loss during an overall market decline would be the amount of call premiums invested. The net results, however, would depend upon the extent of the decline in the futures prices and the resulting gain on that short position. The latter might or might not exceed the loss of call premiums. Similarly, for Case IIB (short calls/long futures), the extent of gain is limited to the amount of option premiums received, while the extent of offsetting loss on the futures position is indeterminate.

As mentioned, in the numerical examples the assumption was that the options and futures contract positions were established and lifted simultaneously. On the hand, if a call were sold and the market declined subsequently (Case IIB), when the value of the call reached, say $\frac{1}{16}$, the writer could close out the futures and options positions without continuing to incur losses on the long futures position. Stock index futures afford considerable flexibility in timing and in various risk management strategies.

In a like manner, the buyer of a put (Case IIIA) and the seller of a put (Case IVA) can only lose or gain, respectively, in the amount of the premiums for the option positions during any subsequent market rise. The net results would again depend upon the extent of the offsetting movement in the futures' prices.

For cases IA, IIA, IIIB, and IVB, the value of the options gains or losses are not limited, nor is the extent of the offsetting futures transaction outcome. In all of these cases, the net results from hedging could yield

Table 8.1 Options Hedging with Index Futures: Positions and Outcomes

Case	Market Expectation	Position	Initial Funds Position	Actual Market/Stock Direction	Outcome Possibilities	Outcome Limits
IA	Market rise	Long calls, short contract	– Premiums, – margin	Rise	Gain on calls, loss on contract	± Net not limited
IB	Market rise	Long calls, short contract	– Premiums, – margin	Decline	Loss on calls, gain on contract	– Call premium, + not limited
IIA	Market decline	Short calls, long contract	+ Premiums, – margin	Rise	Loss on calls, gain on contract	± Net not limited
IIB	Market decline	Short calls, long contract	+ Premiums, – margin	Decline	Gain on calls, loss on contract	+ Call premium, – not limited
IIIA	Market decline	Long puts, long contract	– Premiums, – margin	Rise	Loss on puts, gain on contract	– Put premium, + not limited
IIIB	Market decline	Long puts, long contract	– Premiums, – margin	Decline	Gain on puts, loss on contract	± Net not limited
IVA	Market rise	Short puts, short contract	+ Premiums, – margin	Rise	Gain on puts, Loss on contract	+ Put premium, – not limited
IVB	Market rise	Short puts, short contract	+ Premiums, – margin	Decline	Loss on puts, gain on contract	± Net not limited

gains or losses as described above. But again, the extent of potential loss would be less than without the futures contracts hedging alternative. These futures contracts provide for those who trade in stock options an additional means for achieving risk efficiency.

SUMMARY

Puts and calls are options on specific stocks. Since their value at any given time derives from the price activity of the underlying security, they, too, contain an element of systematic risk. This chapter has explored the rudiments of hedging that risk component for options positions through the use of stock index futures contracts. These contracts can, of course, be employed in more complex option-investment alternatives, that is, for mitigating systematic risk in conjunction with covered writing strategies, or with a "portfolio" of options themselves.

As always, there is no "free lunch." Some potential gain must be sacrificed in order to reduce the potential loss that might be incurred in outright "long" or "short" positions in stock options. Stock index futures contracts can be utilized to recover option premiums if the market and stock move opposite to *a priori* expectations. And in the event that the market remains flat, the "insurance" against an adverse market move is relatively costless.

On the other hand, various basic truisms remain unchanged. The hedging potential of stock index futures contracts does not alter the desirability of long option positions in high ("beta") market-risk volatile stocks, and conversely of short positions in low beta stocks. If anything, the relative volatilities of the stocks vis-à-vis the futures contracts reinforce the asymmetry of the options mechanism.

9 Margins on the Stock Index Contracts

COMMODITY MARGINS

To this point, the perceptive reader may have noticed that "margins" for the stock index futures contracts have not been discussed. That was by design, not accident. The reason for postponing the topic until now was to stress that the costs, profits, and real risks of trading stock index futures are *independent*, at a first approximation, of the amount of margin involved. Look at any of the trading and hedging examples in the preceding chapters. All of the losses and gains are determined in terms of the *total values* of the transactions. The gains or losses would have been the *same*, whether $1000 or $100,000 had been the margin per contract.

Commodity margins assure the financial integrity of futures contracts. When a contract is traded on a futures exchange, *both* parties to the transaction (the "long" and the "short") post the required margins with their futures commission merchants (FCMs, i.e., brokers). In turn, these sums are deposited by the appropriate clearing members with the exchange's clearinghouse. If the FCM is not a clearing member, then some clearing member handles the transactions with the clearinghouse. But the net result is the same. The clearinghouse, who, remember, is the buyer to all sellers and seller to all buyers, requires margins from both sides. As such, these deposits or margins are guarantees of performance, earnest money: both the buyer and seller post margins to guarantee their performance to their respective FCMs, who must likewise guarantee that performance to the exchange's clearinghouse. Having these guarantees on deposit, the clearinghouse facilitates trading, transfers of contract positions, and ultimate settlement or "delivery." Both the buyer's and seller's margins remain on deposit with the clearing organizations (FCM and clearinghouse) until the open positions are closed out, by a "round turn" or until delivery is completed.

As performance guarantees, commodity margins differ substantially from *stock margins*. In futures markets, title does not pass from seller to buyer. Neither is there any credit extended, nor is interest paid. In the few instances when actual delivery does occur, payment must be made in full by the recipient. (Generally that party is the "long", but as we soon see, in the case of cash settlement, that is not always so.) Further, during the existence of an open contract, margins must be restored daily, if required, by both member firms to the clearinghouse, and by the customers to the clearing members.

The purpose and function of futures trading is *risk* transfer. In contrast, the stock market is a spot or cash market for asset acquisition. Title does change hands. For other than short sales, the seller does not post any funds; the seller's responsibility is to deliver the required stock certificates for transfer to the buyer. *Stock margins* are down payments for the purchase of securities, with the balance of the purchase amount borrowed from the stock brokerage, or from a bank. Powers and Vogel have observed:

> New purchases of stock on margin generate credit in a way that *adds* to the national *money supply*. . . . If the purchaser is buying stock on margin, the balance of the purchase price must be borrowed to make full payment. . . . The effect is to expand the national total of bank credit leading to an expansion of the national money supply by at least the amount borrowed. . . . [In contrast,] margin in commodities does not in and of itself involve the borrowing of money nor does it affect the money supply. (Powers and Vogel, 1981, pp. 27–28)

A further refinement that needs to be made here is the distinction between *leverage* and "risk." As every reader now recognizes, "risk" relates to price variability. Leverage, on the other hand, relates to the proportion of the total transaction value that the individual deposits as margin. Leverage itself does not create risk. Imagine a futures contract sized at, say, $1 million; suppose the "margin" were $1000. If the price never changed, it would be inconsequential whether the margin were $500,000 or $5. There would be no risk. But with price variation, "risk" can appear to be magnified by high leverage. That is the reason the conventional view holds futures trading to be "risky." But if a 100 percent margin were posted, that would not lessen the risk of *loss*; it would simply mean that there would never be a margin call! From the point of view of the individual, the profit or loss on the transaction would be the same as it was in Chapter 5: sales value minus purchase cost.

In some quarters, there seems to be the view that, *ceteris paribus*, larger margins afford more "protection." To the contrary, with "lesser" margins required, futures traders may be more acutely aware of their profits or losses in that all positions are "marked to the market" on a daily basis. Thus a smaller margin may indeed result in *more* protection for smaller traders than a large margin, since they will be called sooner, if the market is moving against their positions. This affords them the opportunity to become aware of the loss, and to make a decision whether or not to close out their positions.

Further, in the aggregate, excessive margin requirements for futures contracts can have mischievous effects. For one, margins required in excess of an amount necessary to guarantee performance can result in an uneconomic "sterilization" of capital. Finally, inappropriate margins can have price effects. Robert Bear has shown that margin levels can be set too high:

> To attract a volume of speculative services necessary for the maintenance of market balance. . . . If margins are set too high, a deficiency of speculative services will impede rapid adjustment of prices to new information. Thus, a positive dependency in day-to-day price changes will be evident. Conversely, excessive speculative interest, to the extent it promotes overadjustment of prices to the true economic value of new information, would provoke excessive variability characterized by a tendency toward reversal. (Bear, 1972, pp. 1911–1912).

THE SKIRMISH AT 20th AND CONSTITUTION, N.W.

Under the provisions of the Securities and Exchange Act of 1934, the Board of Governors of the Federal Reserve System was given the authority to establish the maximum amount of credit that can be provided to a customer for the purchase of stocks. This authority generally applies to exchange-listed securities, but the Federal Reserve Board (FRB) has approved some over-the-counter stocks as "marginable" also. The intent of this provision was to reduce the use of "excessive" credit in the stock market, and to reduce fluctuations in the stock market due to forced selling of securities when prices drop (cf. Moore, 1966). The Act was passed after the 1929 stock market "crash" in the belief that low margins, and under-margined accounts, had been a major cause of the financial debacle.

Since the Federal Reserve had also achieved margin-setting authority for stock options' transactions, the Board of Governors felt that the Act required them to establish margin requirements for futures contracts based on stock indexes. Stock options ("puts" and "calls") had been adjudicated to be "derivative" securities; that is, their value was "derived" from the prices of the underlying stocks. These puts and calls are those that apply to individual stocks.

The key assumptions surrounding the Fed's assertion of margin authority were: (1) that the SEC Act of 1934 superseded the "exclusive jurisdiction" provisions of the Commodity Exchange Act (et seq., the CFTC Act), which provided that the CFTC's regulatory role over futures markets was "exclusive"; and (2) that, somehow, a futures contract based on an arbitrarily defined and constructed index of stock prices was a "security" as intended under the SEC Act of 1934. Accordingly, an informal detente evolved: while neither granting nor denying that the Federal Reserve had margin authority, the three futures exchanges did set their initial speculative margins for the stock index contracts near the levels informally "suggested" by the Fed. The issue remains in doubt; when the stock index contracts began to trade in the spring of 1982, the FRB sought public comments on its proposed rulemaking for establishing margin requirements for stock index futures contracts, and an associated regulatory framework. Other studies and proposed legislation have been contemplated.

Some important differences exist with regard to the regulatory oversight of stock margins and futures "margins." The FRB sets only *initial* margin requirements for stocks; that is, the maximum amount that can be borrowed from the stockbroker (or a bank) to finance the purchase of securities. Maintenance margins, which we discuss shortly, are set by the respective exchanges on which the securities are traded.

In the futures markets, the Commodity Futures Trading Commission

(CFTC) ordinarily does not determine margins. As self-regulatory organizations, the exchanges themselves initiate the levels and changes of margins (performance guarantees). If these changes involve rulemaking by the exchanges, for example, in conjunction with changes in associated daily price limits, the latter are subject to CFTC approval. In general, so many different contracts and commodities exist that the futures industry has deemed that the expertise for margin control should be left at the exchange level. The exceptions to this generality are that: (1) for a new contract, the margins contemplated are included in the CFTC submission, the request for approval to trade; and (2) the CFTC does have emergency powers to set margins in extreme circumstances. Nonetheless, the delicate balance of market liquidity and safety of transactions, to the extent that margin changes might affect them, is the responsibility of exchange officials, the ones who are closest to the situation.

PERSPECTIVE ON STOCK MARKET MARGINS

Over the years, a number of studies about the effects and effectiveness of Fed-set margins for stocks have appeared in academic journals. Generally, the researchers have not been very impressed with the Federal Reserve's record in applying margin authority. Many have even questioned if the rationale behind the authorizing Securities and Exchange Act of 1934 was not somewhat misguided.

Thomas G. Moore, for one, contended that the data he analyzed "indicate that not one of the aims of the legislation establishing margin requirements has been accomplshed" (Moore, 1966, p. 158). Further, Moore recounted that margin requirements in 1929 were about 25–30 percent for large accounts and *higher* for smaller ones. The market decline actually started on Monday, October 26, 1929, with a drop of 12.5 percent and continued another 10.5 percent on "Black Tuesday." Somewhat surprisingly, as Moore has pointed out:

> [That was essentially] all the drop for that year. The market actually rallied and finished higher at the end of the year than it closed on "Black Tuesday." It seems possible that some of the fall on the second day might have been due to forced selling by those on margin. Thus, had there been higher requirements, it is possible that the fall might have been slower. (Note,

however, that *low* margins also made it easier for speculators to buy when the prices fell and hence might have prevented an even greater drop.) But considering the decline in corporate earnings of the next few years, it seems impossible to believe that, even if all sales on the exchange had been for *cash*, stock prices would not have declined to the same extent (Moore, 1966, p. 167, emphasis added).

In a later study, R. Corwin Grube and colleagues analyzed the "signal effects" to the market when the Fed *changed* margin requirements. Their study indicated asymmetric responses to margin changes: "The market responds differently to margin increases than to decreases." The authors found no significant responses when margins are increased: an absence of negative returns. However, "The market responded unambiguously in a positive manner when the Fed reduced margins." In effect, changes in margin requirements affect investor expectations, as the Fed is expressing its opinion about the level and/or activity of the market. The authors questioned whether this means of Fed intervention in the stock market was the most efficient way for the Fed to "send its signals," especially in view of the asymmetry of responses. Margin increases may "Reflect ambiguous signals or no signals at all" (Grube et al., 1979, p. 673).

ARE FUTURES MARGINS REALLY LOWER?

Michael Asay attempted to address this problem in the context of implied leverage in stock options. His analysis is helpful but not conclusive. His model showed that both "leverage and margin rates really depend upon interest rates, the time to maturity in the option" and other aspects about options that need not concern us here. In particular, he observed that the true degree of leverage in futures is not at all obvious. The contingent liability of daily marking-to-market means that the investor "will have to keep a ready reserve of liquid assets in order to avoid being sold out with every small adverse movement in price. This ready reserve also counts as "margin," although more latitude may exist in the form that the investor chooses to hold it" (Asay, 1981, p. 55).

From his assumptions and analysis about payoff structures of individual stock options, Asay commented that with "speculative margins of roughly 8 percent in the [then] proposed stock index futures, a call with less than nine months to maturity will contain *more* leverage (Asay, 1981, p. 57). However, with the initial speculative futures margins of roughly 10 percent, call options contain *even more* leverage than stock index futures.

MARGINS FOR THE STOCK INDEX CONTRACTS

Margins for futures contracts are generally determined in relationship to daily price limits. For example, both the Kansas City Board of Trade (KCBT) and the Chicago Mercantile Exchange (CME) have instituted a daily maximum price change for their respective contracts of $5.00, which equates to a $2500 change, up or down in the contract's value. At the same time, the initial hedge margin is $2500. That means that both the longs and shorts have deposited *in advance* the maximum amount their contracts can change in value in one day: that is "up front" assurance to the clearinghouse that every stock index contract is fully protected for the worst that could happen in one day to any trader's position. Therefore, the CME has characterized this correspondence of margins and daily price limits as a "no debt system" (CME, 1978, p. 10). If there is a "limit move," those in adverse positions must replenish their margins, or the positions are liquidated. (The New York Futures Exchange, NYFE, contract, however, does not have any daily price change limits.)

In addition, all speculative margins are higher than the $5.00 ($2500 per contract) daily limit. As indicated earlier, the speculative margins were set at about 10 percent of the contracts' values when trading began. The respective exchange minumum margins are shown in Table 9.1, as of year-end 1982. Note that FCM's and brokers can require *additional* margins, according to their internal policies; they cannot, however, accept less than the exchange-set margins for any respective position.

Although daily price change limits protect the FCMs and the clearinghouses, these limits prevent the market from reaching "equilibrium" prices. Accordingly, futures industry practice has evolved so that there are a couple of variants. One is that during the month of delivery, for "hard" commodities, there are no price limits applied to the maturing contract. Its price can change by any amount, so that an equilibrium price will be established as soon as possible. That also means that those in adverse (loss) positions are required to increase their margins substantially in order to maintain open positions.

TABLE 9.1   Stock Index Futures Contracts

	Exchange Minimum Margins		
	CME	NYFE	KCBT
Speculative			
Initial	$6000	$3500	$6500
Maintenance	$2500	$1500	$2000
Hedge			
Initial	$2500	$1500	$2500
Maintenance	$1500	$ 750	$1500
Spreads (intramarket)			
Initial	$ 400	$ 200	$ 400
Maintenance	$ 200	$ 100	$ 200
Spreads (intermarket), per one contract, one side only			
Initial	$ 600	$ 400	$ 500
Maintenance	$ 400	$ 300	$ 500

Another variant is "expanded" or "variable" price limits. For stock index futures, one such rule holds that after two consecutive days of limit moves, on the third day, the limit is increased from $5.00 to $7.50. On the fourth day, the limit is expanded to $10.00, and on the fifth day, all limits are removed. On the sixth day, the original $5.00 limits are reinstated.

HOW MARGINS WORK

In order to demonstrate how margins on stock index futures operate, let's assume Trader G initiated a long position in the CME December 1982 contract on December 6, 1982 at the closing price of 143.35 ($\times$ 500 =) $71,675. On the other side of this transaction is Trader H, the "short," and let's assume that for both these are speculative transactions. Both traders deposit the required $6000 "margin" with their respective FCMs.

December 6, 1982

Price: 143.35; Contract Value: $71,675

Trader G (Long)	Trader H (Short)
$6000 margin	$6000 margin

Not much happened the following day, but on December 8, the contract closed at 141.35, a loss of $1000 for Trader G and a gain of $1000 for Trader H (143.35 − 141.35 = 2.00 × 500 = $1000).

December 8, 1982

Price: 141.35

Trader G (Long)	Trader H (Short)
$6000	$6000
−$1000	+$1000
$5000	$7000

As of the close of business, December 8, Trader G's margin was reduced by $1000, as his position was marked to market, and Trader H's account reflected the $1000 gain. At this point is Trader G required to deposit $1000 to restore the full speculative margin? No. Look again at Table 9.1 where the CME speculative *maintenance* margin is shown as $2500. That means Trader G is not required to answer a "margin call" until the position erodes to the point where the margin is reduced to $2500; when that happens, however, Trader G must restore the balance to the *full* $6000. Although the margins are checked every day, let's cumulate them to December 15, when the contract closed at 135.80; the change from our last accounting on December 8 is a price decline of $5.55 (× 500) = $2,775, which we shall post:

December 15, 1982

Trader G (Long)	Trader H (Short)
$5000	$7000
−$2775	+$2775
$2225	$9775

At this point, Trader G does get a margin call, since the margin balance of $2225 is less than the $2500 maintenance requirement. (In the trade these are known as "variation" margin calls.) In order to maintain the position Trader G must put up additional margin of $3775.00 to restore the margin balance to $6000. Let's suppose that happens, so as of the close on December 15, 1982, after Trader G restores the margin balance, the respective accounts of Traders G and H appear as:

Trader G (Long)	Trader H (Short)
$2225	$9775
+$3775	
$6000	

CASH DELIVERY

Since the next day, December 16, was the last day of trading for the CME-December 1982 contract, let's suppose both of our traders do not engage in a round turn (we've done that before), but both go through the delivery process. On December 16, 1982, the Standard & Poor's index (S&P 500) closed at 135.30, the delivery price. First let's post the last price change to the accounts (135.80 − 135.30 = .50 × 500 = $250):

December 16, 1982

Trader G (Long)	Trader H (Short)
$6,000	$ 9,775
−$250	+$250
$5,750	$10,025

Before the last day of trading, Trader G had met the margin call; and Trader H had been credited for the gains through December 15. Delivery is achieved by transferring the last day's price change from Trader G to Trader H through the clearinghouse and all open contracts are effectively closed out at the S&P cash price of 135.30. Trader G gets the remaining $5750 returned, and Trader H can pick up a check for $10,025. Since all accounts are "marked to market" every day, going through cash delivery just means that all open contracts are closed out at the cash index price, and the appropriate amounts transferred through the clearinghouse. Let's see if it reconciles. For Trader G:

Purchase price on December 16: 143.35; contract value: $71,675
"Sales" price on December 16: 135.30; contract value: $67,650

Loss on contract: − $ 4,025

Trader G *reconciliation* is as follows:

Initial margin:	$6000
Variation margin:	+ $3775
	$9775
Less deposit returned after settlement:	$5750
Loss on trade:	− $4025

Trader H's situation is much simpler:

Gain on trade:	+ $ 4,025
Amount received:	$10,025
Less initial margin:	− $ 6,000
Gain on trade:	$ 4,025

That's all there really is to a cash settlement or delivery; it merely means that the last day's price change is posted and then the accounts are settled by actual funds delivery. Notice, however, as opposed to the *physical* delivery process where the underlying commodity always *flows* from *short to long*, with a cash settlement delivery, the flow *can* be, as here, from *long* (Trader G) to *short* (Trader H). All that really means, however, is that the "delivery" is of the losses to the profiting trader. The "flow of cash delivery" can be in either direction.

SUMMARY

In a heated moment, one exchange official in the futures industry vowed to have the term "margin" excised from all bylaws, rules, regulations, and promotional literature. For him, the confusion between stock margins and commodity performance guarantees (also called "margins") had become too frequent and too misleading. In futures markets, "margins" function as earnest money, posted by both the buyer and seller in a transaction. In contrast, stock market margins are down payments by only the buyer for the stock purchased, with the balance of the transaction amount borrowed from the stockbroker or a bank. The seller of the stock only delivers the required certificates. One crucial difference is that new purchases of stock on margin tend to generate credit in a way that *adds* to the national money supply. Commodity margins do not involve the borrowing of money nor do they affect the money supply. Futures markets function to facilitate risk transfer, not asset acquisition. The items being traded are simply promises to "perform" in the future.

On the other hand, margins in general tend to limit the size of a speculative position that any one trading entity might undertake. An individual with only $10,000 can not buy 500 shares of IBM nor take a position in five stock index futures contracts. Some regulators view this aspect of margins as a positive benefit: protecting the foolish from "excessive" risk exposure. In futures markets, however, margins greater than necessary to assure performance can result in an uneconomic sterilization of capital, and increase the costs of price protection for hedgers. Further, there is some evidence that inappropriate margin levels adversely affect the behavior of futures prices.

Another confusion about futures margins is that *leverage* creates risk. In reality, it is price variability that generates risk, which in turn may be magnified by leverage. When prices do not fluctuate, there is no more risk for a 2 percent margin level than for a 50 percent margin level. When prices do fluctuate, 100 percent margin levels do not decrease the risk; they simply eliminate (variation) margin calls. The risk of gain or loss is independent of the level of margin posted, for an individual.

Following the financial debacle of 1929, the Federal Reserve Board was empowered to set initial margins for purchases of stock. The intent of this provision of the Securities and Exchange Act of 1934 was to reduce the use of excessive credit in the stock market, and to reduce fluctuations in the stock market due to forced selling of securities when prices fall. Students of the FRB's margin setting authority have not been impressed with the record. One author contends that not *one* of the intended goals has ever been achieved. Another found that changes in FRB-set margins often sent ambiguous signals to the stock market. In futures markets, as self-regulatory organizations, the exchanges set and change various margins in accordance with particular market conditions. The Commodity Futures Trading Commission has margin-setting authority only in emergency situations.

In the case of stock index futures, the FRB had asserted margin authority from the very beginning. Contending that an arbitrarily defined and scaled stock market index was a "derivative type of security," like individual stock options, the FRB took the position that margins for the new index futures should be comparable to the leverage ratios for puts and calls. Careful analysis has shown, however, that a ready comparison is not so straightforward as it might at first appear. For stock options, the degree of leverage depends upon interest rates and the time to maturity of the option. In the case of futures, the true degree of leverage is not at all obvious, since daily marking-to-market means that investors have to keep a ready reserve of liquid assets in order to avoid being sold out with every small adverse price movement. This ready reserve also counts as margin. For all three stock index futures contracts, informal agreements with the FRB resulted in initial speculative margins being set at about 10 percent of the contract's value when each began trading.

Finally, with regard to the cash settlement delivery system for stock index futures, the mechanism is relatively uncomplicated. Daily marking-to-market prior to the last day of trading results in one additional entry for all contracts remaining open: settlement to the cash market index's closing price. Under this system final settlement is really a delivery of the losses to the profiting position holders. It is possible for "delivery" of cash settlement to flow from long to short, or vice versa. In the more "traditional" case, where there is a tangible delivery instrument (e.g., warehouse receipts or T-Bills), the delivery always flows from the short to the long. Payment in full for the delivered commodity, less margins already posted with the clearinghouse, then flow from the long to the short.

10 Market Performance: 1982 Statistics

Actual trading of stock index futures contracts began on February 24, 1982, at the Kansas City Board of Trade (KCBT). The Chicago Mercantile Exchange (CME) followed with the Standard & Poor's 500 contract on April 21, and the New York Futures Exchange (NYFE) began trading on May 6, 1982. Throughout the prolonged incubation period, while awaiting approval from the Commodity Futures Trading Commission (CFTC), a number of questions arose about the likely behavior of the futures prices of the contracts. The most frequently asked concerned the profile of the forward maturity prices: would the more forward prices show increasing premiums over the nearby contracts and the cash index? Or would the profile of forward maturities ever display discounts (or "inversions"), that is, reflect prices less than the cash index values? After two or three months of trading, the answer was both, and variants thereof.

PRICE PROFILES

In the tradition of never being always right, but never being in doubt, a number of analysts have expressed their views about the forward profile of stock index futures prices. One authority is on record to the effect that: "We've documented that the price of the future should always be at apremium to the market" (quoted in Putka, 1982). The arbitrage pricing model discussed in Cornell and French (1982) expressed about the same opinion. The model is a function of interest rates and dividend yields, and generally predicts that the futures prices should be at appropriate premiums to the cash or "spot" index. Unfortunately, the real world has not been very accommodating. For example, Cornell and French found that "the prices predicted by this model are significantly higher than the prices observed for stock index futures" (p. 2). They explored a number of possible explanations: short sale constraints (in the cash market), timing of capital gains—which seemed to reconcile their model a little closer, but not entirely, to reality. The "typical," or most common pattern, is indeed higher prices for more distant maturities. This type of profile is shown in Table 10.1.

On other days, the forward profiles have shown discounts to the cash price. These "inversions" should only occur, according to Cornell and French, if the dividend yield is larger than the interest rate. Frequently, these "inversions" are "V-shaped" with the more distant maturities reflecting higher premiums. The inversion profile was not uncommon in the period when trading of the stock index futures first began in the spring of 1982. However, a more recent example is shown in Table 10.2, for December 14, 1982. These profiles are also shown graphically in Figure 10.1 and 10.2.

Further, a word of caution about the contract prices more distant than the nearby and next maturity. As we see in our analysis of open interest, the more distant maturities have very low liquidity. On days when there are no transactions in a particular futures maturity, the exchange's "pit committee" artibrarily changes the settlement price so that it stays "in line" with the price changes in the more actively traded contracts. The reason for doing this is that, if there is a "limit move," the untraded maturities will continue to remain "in line" with the prices of the more actively traded contracts. In this regard the NYFE has a somewhat *peculiar* practice. Even though there are no price limits, the NYFE often

Table 10.1   Cash Index and Futures Prices: December 3, 1982

	CME	NYFE	KCBT
Cash market index	138.69	80.05	158.73
Futures prices (day's closing price)			
December 1982	139.15	80.30	159.35
March 1983	140.00	80.80	161.10
June 1983	140.80	81.30	161.70
September 1983	141.40	81.80	162.40

Table 10.2   Cash Indexes and Futures Prices: December 14, 1982

	CME	NYFE	KCBT
Cash market index	137.40	79.32	156.50
Futures prices (close)			
December 1982	136.45	78.75	154.25
March 1983	136.55	78.90	154.85
June 1983	137.05	79.40	155.60
September 1983	137.55	79.90	156.15

sets the settlement price *outside* of the day's trading range. For example, as recently as February 10, 1983, the NYFE's September 1983 contract traded between 86.20 and 87.20, yet the settlement price was arbitrarily set at *88.00*. That price kept the price change for the day "in line" with the other contracts, and maintained the maturity-to-maturity differential that the exchange deemed appropriate. In the absence of any transactions, that determination is questionable at best. But it is the *market's* function to determine those relative prices. If they are "out of line" (and at this point, it is uncertain what "in line" means), the market should quickly adjust the maturity profile according to the influence of trading. On that day, by the way, the September 1983 contract showed an open interest of 752 contracts. It would seem that this preemption of supply and demand forces would tend to discourage "spreading" activity (which is discussed later in this chapter). A committee or staff consensus seems a poor substitute for actual transactions.

Arbitrage models of stock index futures prices predict that the prices of the forward maturities should be close to an alternative portfolio of the cash asset valued in the future for the "cost of carry"—that is, the "risk-free" interest rate. Additional modifications involve dividend yields, short sale constraints in the cash market, and tax-timing aspects. So far the theorists have been puzzled by the actual futures prices, as they do not seem to behave as predicted.

In his analysis of inventories and futures, Scholes pointed out:

There are times when the price differential between the shorter term future and the longer term future does not appear to cover the carrying costs . . . In fact, . . . at times the carrying costs or the price appears to be negative. (Scholes, 1981, p. 269)

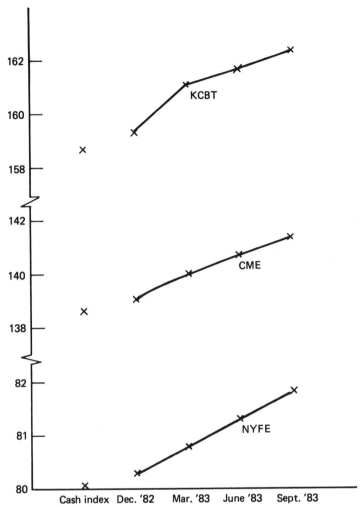

Figure 10.1 Cash indexes and futures prices premium profiles, December 3, 1982 (corresponds to Table 10.1).

At this point, the vagaries of the pricing of stock index futures contracts seem to be more consistent with an "expectational" hypothesis of the future values of the underlying cash indexes. However, as these markets mature and participation expands, the price behavior of stock index futures might reflect more closely the arbitrage pricing profile that the theorists expect.

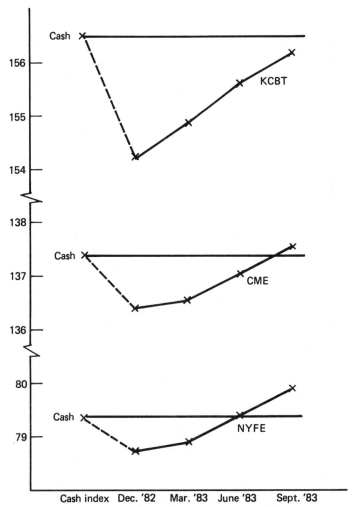

Figure 10.2 Cash indexes and futures prices inversion profiles, December 14, 1982 (corresponds to Table 10.2). Dashed lines represent negative basis to nearby contract.

At the 1978 CFTC hearings, Professor Richard Zeckhauser of Harvard University expressed an implicit sense of frustration:

It is not the least bit uncommon to read either the popular or more scholarly press and see discussions by one expert which suggest that the market will be going up dramatically and by another it will be going down dramatically and we do not have any convenient mechanism by which these individuals can test their expectations. . . . [The existence of stock index futures contracts] will provide once and for all an accurate prediction of what the *market* thinks about the market (CFTC 1978b, p. 333).

That may be overstating the case somewhat, but it does emphasize the crucial nature of expectations in futures markets and price formation.

CASH INDEXES: 1982

The initial year of actual trading of stock index futures contracts, 1982, was a year of fairly dramatic market movements and volatility. From the beginning of 1982 until mid-August, the stock market was in a rather unglamorous "free fall" in space—with but a minor respite during the early spring, March to May. On August 17th the market suddenly turned around as the Dow Jones Industrial Average (DJIA) gained 38.81 points that day, and stock prices rallied almost without interruption throughout the remainder of the year.

The statistics shown in Table 10.3 for the stock market indexes underlying the futures contracts have been segmented by periods conforming to the contracts' maturities. Period I, May 6 to June 17, is dated from the time when all three contracts were "up and trading" to the date of earliest delivery for the June 1982 maturity, the CME-S&P contract. The other two contracts, KCBT and NYFE, do not expire until about the month-end; unfortunately, this aspect distorts the comparisons somewhat. The CME contract converges to the cash index about 10 to 12 days before the other contracts mature. However, this distortion is not material, as we find out in the analysis of the daily price movements of the futures.

Period II, June 18 to September 16, covers the maturity of the September 1982 contracts, again pegged to the CME maturity date. In addition, Period II is divided into two subperiods: IIa, June 18 to August 16, the "tail" of the bear market, and IIb, August 17 to September 16, the beginning of the great bull market rally of 1982. Period III, September 17 to December 16, covers the maturity period for the December 1982 contracts. The data discussed in this chapter about futures prices, the basis, and other aspects of these markets are also generally segmented along the same lines.

Table 10.3   Spot Indexes, Stock Market Indicators Underlying Stock Index Futures Contracts, Daily Observations

Index	Mean ($\bar{X}$)	Standard Deviation (s)	Coefficient of Variation ($s/\bar{X}$)
Period I: May 6–June 17, 1982			
VLIC	126.021	4.766	.038
S&P	113.549	3.681	.032
NYSE	65.413	2.168	.033
Period IIa: June 18–August 16, 1982			
VLIC	118.626	2.792	.024
S&P	108.038	2.687	.025
NYSE	62.062	1.517	.024
Period IIb: August 17–September 16, 1982			
VLIC	128.196	5.319	.041
S&P	118.304	4.798	.041
NYSE	67.818	2.757	.041
Period II (overall): June 18–September 16, 1982			
VLIC	121.968	5.980	.049
S&P	111.623	6.066	.054
NYSE	64.072	3.422	.053
Period III: September 17–December 16, 1982 (III)			
VLIC	149.145	9.770	.066
S&P	134.140	6.712	.050
NYSE	77.209	3.975	.051

Now back to Table 10.3. As is apparent, the volatility of these indexes decreased both absolutely (standard deviations) and relatively (coefficients of variation) until August 17, at which time the turnaround in the market resulted in substantially higher measured volatility. Generally, the order of variability among the three indexes (the coefficients of variation) remained very close in all of the periods and subperiods. The minor exception was the Value Line Composite Index (VLIC) in Periods I and III, when the coefficient of variation measure showed some small increase over the other two. Also in Table 10.3, notice that the variability of the S&P and New York Stock Exchange (NYSE) indexes increased over the VLIC in Period II as a whole, suggesting that the heavier capitalized, larger company stocks became relatively more volatile in the early part of the market's rise (i.e., coefficients of variation in Period II were larger). However, as noted above, the VLIC caught up and passed the other two, in terms of variation in Period III.

Time out for a brief explanation. The alert reader might have wondered how the standard deviations and coefficients of variation for the entire Period II could exceed those of the component subperiods, IIa and IIb, for each of the indexes, respectively. This aspect is also noticeable in the other tables that follow, so we address the problem here. The answer is that the mean values for the entire Period II are *different* from the mean values for the subperiods, IIa and IIb. The observations themselves are the same, but the *mean* from which the deviations are calculated to obtain the variance and standard deviation is an intermediate value, and this leads to measures of greater overall dispersion for the entire Period II than for those in its subperiods IIa and IIb. This puzzle can be solved in the following example.

Period IIa

Observation	Deviation from Mean	(Deviation)^2
2	-2	4
2	-2	4
6	2	4
6	2	4
16		16

The total is 16, and the mean $= \frac{16}{4} = 4$. The sum of (deviations)$^2 = 16$, the variance $= \frac{16}{4} = 4$, and the standard deviation $= \sqrt{4} = 2$.

Period IIb

Observation	Deviation from Mean	(Deviation)^2
22	-2	4
22	-2	4
26	2	4
26	2	4
96		16

The total is 96, and the mean $= \frac{96}{4} = 24$. The sum of (deviations)$^2 = 16$, the variance $= \frac{16}{4} = 4$, and the standard deviation $= \sqrt{4} = 2$.

Periods IIa and IIb have identical variances and standard deviations. One might be tempted to expect that for the whole period II the variance would equal 4 and the standard deviation would equal 2, also. Right? No, wrong. Our intuition misleads us here. Watch below.

Period II (= IIa + IIb)

Observation	Deviation from Mean	(Deviation)²
2	− 12	144
2	− 12	144
6	− 8	64
6	− 8	64
22	8	64
22	8	64
26	12	144
26	12	144
112		832

The total is 112 and the mean $= \frac{112}{8} = 14$. The sum of (deviations)² $= 832$, the variance $= \frac{832}{8} = 104!$, and the standard deviation $= \sqrt{104} = 10.198!$ Q.E.D.

Table 10.4 shows the regression analysis among the cash indexes, on a daily observation basis. (Also daily observations in Table 10.3.) Recall that a $\hat{B}$ value means that on the average a 1.00 change in the S&P corresponds to a 1.284 index value change in the VLIC, for example in Period I. The $\hat{B}$ values for the VLIC - S&P, and VLIC - NYSE relationships correspond to the relatively higher variability of the VLIC in Periods I and III (also reflected by the coefficients of variation in Table 10.3). On the other hand the $\hat{B}$ values for the S&P-NYSE relationship hardly changed throughout the year, remaining at about 1.7. Since we know that the two are essentially the same indexes due to their capitalization-weighted construction, that finding is hardly surprising. The regression coefficients for Period II for the VLIC fell to less than 1.0 for the S&P, again reaffirming the greater volatility during the early phase of the bull market of the S&P stocks; a similar decrease holds for the $\hat{B}$ change of the VLIC-NYSE

Table 10.4   Cash Index Regressions, 1982 Contracts, Daily Observations

Dependent Variable (Y)	Regression Coefficient ($\hat{B}$)	Explanatory Variable (X)	R^2
Contract: June 1982; Period I: May 6–June 17, 1982			
VLIC	1.284	S&P	.984
VLIC	2.188	NYSE	.990
S&P	1.698	NYSE	.998
Contract: September 1982; Period IIa: June 18–August 16, 1982			
VLIC	1.020	S&P	.964
VLIC	1.818	NYSE	.975
S&P	1.770	NYSE	.998
Contract: September 1982; Period IIb: August 17–September 16, 1982			
VLIC	1.099	S&P	.982
VLIC	1.918	NYSE	.988
S&P	1.740	NYSE	.999
Contract: September 1982, Period II: June 18–September 16, 1982			
VLIC	.979	S&P	.985
VLIC	1.739	NYSE	.990
S&P	1.772	NYSE	.999
Contract: December 1982, Period III: September 17–December 16, 1982			
VLIC	1.373	S&P	.889
VLIC	2.297	NYSE	.926
S&P	1.685	NYSE	.995

regressions for Period I versus II. The R^2 values among all of the relationships shown imply very high correlation in the movement of the cash indexes. The only exception might be for the VLIC relationships in Period III, when the lower priced stocks moved with greater volatility relative to the S&P and NYSE capitalization-weighted components.

FUTURES PRICES

A similar analysis of relative variability (coefficient of variation) among the daily futures prices of the stock index contracts appears in Tables 10.5, 10.6, and 10.7. These tables are organized with respect to the June, September, and December 1982 maturities as before, again with subperiods IIa and IIb, shown in Table 10.6. In addition to the closing (settlement) futures prices, these tables include the correspondence relation-

Table 10.5 Futures Prices—June 1982 Contracts—Daily Observations, Period I: May 6–June 17, 1982

Futures Price	Mean ($\bar{X}$)	Standard Deviation	Coefficient of variation ($s/\bar{X}$)
KCBT—settlement	124.900	5.168	.041
KCBT—high	125.910	5.028	.040
KCBT—low	124.327	5.336	.043
CME—settlement	113.222	4.079	.036
CME—high	114.182	3.991	.035
CME—low	112.613	4.168	.037
NYFE—settlement	65.155	2.450	.038
NYFE—high	65.665	2.310	.035
NYFE—low	64.820	2.526	.039

Table 10.6 Futures Prices—September 1982 Contracts—Daily Observations

Futures Price	Mean ($\bar{X}$)	Standard Deviation(s)	Coefficient of Variation ($s/\bar{X}$)
Period IIa: June 18–August 16, 1982			
KCBT—settlement	118.407	3.863	.033
KCBT—high	119.623	3.655	.031
KCBT—low	117.196	3.864	.033
CME—settlement	109.161	3.707	.034
CME—high	110.306	3.481	.032
CME—low	107.912	3.656	.034
NYFE—settlement	62.734	2.175	.035
NYFE—high	63.415	2.057	.032
NYFE—low	62.026	2.164	.035
Period IIb: August 17–September 16, 1982			
KCBT—settlement	128.471	5.234	.041
KCBT—high	129.714	5.180	.040
KCBT—low	126.448	5.801	.046
CME—settlement	118.304	4.798	.041
CME—high	119.456	4.946	.041
CME—low	116.211	5.485	.047
NYFE—settlement	67.859	2.757	.041
NYFE—high	68.605	2.748	.040
NYFE—low	66.709	3.084	.046

Table 10.7 Futures Prices—September 1982 and December 1982 Contracts—Daily Observations

Futures Price	Mean $(\overline{X})$	Standard Deviation (s)	Coefficient of Variation $(s/\overline{X})$
	Period II: June 18–September 16, 1982		
KCBT—settlement	121.921	6.503	.053
KCBT—high	123.147	6.421	.052
KCBT—low	120.427	6.387	.053
CME—settlement	112.308	5.983	.053
CME—high	113.502	5.952	.052
CME—low	110.810	5.892	.053
NYFE—settlement	64.072	3.422	.053
NYFE—high	65.227	3.392	.052
NYFE—low	63.661	3.363	.053
	Period III: September 17–December 16, 1982		
KCBT—settlement	149.298	10.384	.070
KCBT—high	151.012	10.711	.071
KCBT—low	147.625	10.289	.070
CME—settlement	134.564	7.305	.054
CME—high	136.268	7.556	.055
CME—low	133.022	7.202	.054
NYFE—settlement	77.486	4.314	.056
NYFE—high	78.492	4.466	.057
NYFE—low	76.521	4.197	.055

ships among the daily high and low futures prices, as well. This additional dimension was included to investigate if the closing price relationships obscured some important range aspects (high-low). As the tables readily disclose, each contract's high and low variations are well reflected by the close-settlement prices. The sets of coefficients of variation differ only at the third decimal point, if at all.

Similarly, for each maturity set, and subperiod segmentation, the coefficients of variation of the CME-NYFE-KCBT contracts are nearly identical. The only exception appears in Table 10.7 for Period III. As noted for the VLIC cash index, the December 1982 KCBT contract exhibited higher relative variation (.07 vs. .05 for CME and NYFE). Figures 10.3a–g are the standard price charts that many analysts use to assess trends, support, and resistant price levels, and to formulate trading strategies (cf. Kaufman, 1978).

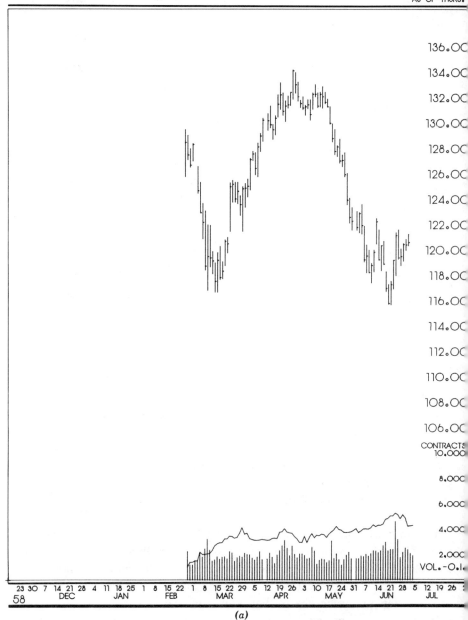

Figure 10.3 Price charts. (*a*) KCBT, June 1982 contract. (*b*) CME, June 1982 contract. (*c*) NYFE, June 1982 contract. (*d*) KCBT, September 1982 contract. (*e*) CME, September 1982 contract. (*f*) NYFE, September 1982 contract. (*g*) KCBT, December 1982 contract. (*h*) CME, December 1982 contract. (*i*) NYFE, December 1982 contract. Courtesy: Data Lab Corp., Chicago, Illinois.

CONTRACT HIGH - LOW
120.60-04/26/82
107.40-06/17/82
AS OF THURS.

126.00

124.00

122.00

120.00

118.00

116.00

114.00

112.00

110.00

108.00

106.00

104.00

102.00

100.00

98.00

96.00

CONTRACTS
25,000

20,000

15,000

10,000

5,000

VOL.-O.I.

23 30 7 14 21 28 4 11 18 25 1 8 15 22 1 8 15 22 29 5 12 19 26 3 10 17 24 31 7 14 21 28 5 12 19 26 2
4   DEC   JAN   FEB   MAR   APR   MAY   JUN   JUL

(b)

161

NYSE COMPOSITE
NYFE JUNE 82

CONTRACT HIGH - LOW
69.10-05/11/82
61.05-06/18/82
AS OF THURS.

72.00
71.00
70.00
69.00
68.00
67.00
66.00
65.00
64.00
63.00
62.00
61.00
60.00
59.00
58.00
57.00

CONTRACTS
25.000

20.000

15.000

10.000

5.000

VOL.-O.I.

23 30 7 14 21 28 4 11 18 25 1 8 15 22 1 8 15 22 29 5 12 19 26 3 10 17 24 31 7 14 21 28 5 12 19 26 2
56   DEC   JAN   FEB   MAR   APR   MAY   JUN   JUL

(c)

162

VALUE LINE STOCK INDEX
KCBT SEPTEMBER 82

CONTRACT HIGH – LOW
136.70–09/22/82
110.60–08/09/82
AS OF THURS.

140.00
138.00
136.00
134.00
132.00
130.00
128.00
126.00
124.00
122.00
120.00
118.00
116.00
114.00
112.00
110.00

CONTRACTS
10.000

8.000

6.000

4.000

2.000

VOL.–O.I.

1 8 15 22 29 5 12 19 26 3 10 17 24 31 7 14 21 28 5 12 19 26 2 9 16 23 30 6 13 20 27 4 11 18 25 1 8
8   MAR   APR   MAY   JUN   JUL   AUG   SEP   OCT

(d)

163

S AND P 500 INDEX
IOM   SEPTEMBER 82

CONTRACT HIGH - LOW
125.50-09/03/82
101.15-08/09/82
AS OF THURS.

130.00
128.00
126.00
124.00
122.00
120.00
118.00
116.00
114.00
112.00
110.00
108.00
106.00
104.00
102.00
100.00

CONTRACTS
25,000
20,000
15,000
10,000
5,000
VOL.-O.I.

1   8 15 22 29 5 12 19 26 3 10 17 24 31 7 14 21 28 5 12 19 26 2   9 16 23 30 6 13 20 27 4 11 18 25 1 6
54   MAR   APR   MAY   JUN   JUL   AUG   SEP   OCT

(e)

NYSE COMPOSITE
NYFE SEPTEMBER 82

CONTRACT HIGH - LOW
72.75-09/22/82
57.90-08/09/82
AS OF THURS.

74.00
73.00
72.00
71.00
70.00
69.00
68.00
67.00
66.00
65.00
64.00
63.00
62.00
61.00
60.00
59.00

CONTRACTS
25,000

20,000

15,000

10,000

5,000
VOL.-O.I.

8 15 22 29   5 12 19 26   3 10 17 24 31   7 14 21 28   5 12 19 26   2 9 16 23 30   6 13 20 27   4 11 18 25   1 8
MAR   APR   MAY   JUN   JUL   AUG   SEP   OCT

(f)

VALUE LINE STOCK INDEX
KCBT DECEMBER 82

CONTRACT HIGH - LOW
164.95-11/10/82
109.90-08/09/82
AS OF THURS.

185.00
180.00
175.00
170.00
165.00
160.00
155.00
150.00
145.00
140.00
135.00
130.00
125.00
120.00
115.00
110.00

CONTRACTS
10,000

8,000

6,000

4,000

2,000
VOL.-O.I.

24 31 7 14 21 28 5 12 19 26 2 9 16 23 30 6 13 20 27 4 11 18 25 1 8 15 22 29 6 13 20 27 3 10 17 24 31
58   JUN   JUL   AUG   SEP   OCT   NOV   DEC   JAN

(g)

166

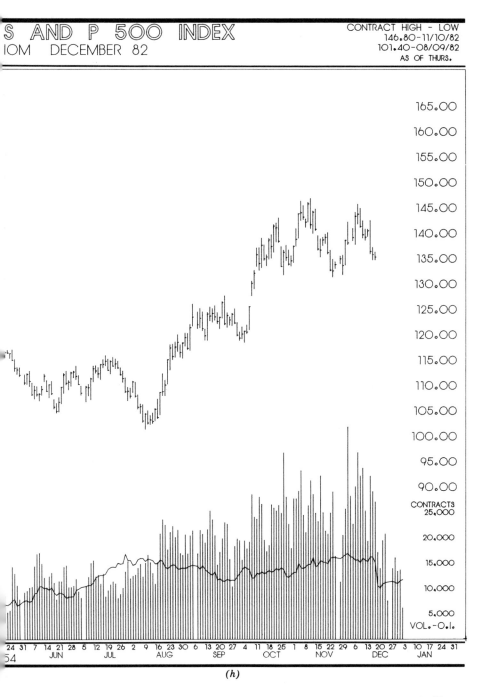

S AND P 500 INDEX
IOM   DECEMBER 82

CONTRACT HIGH - LOW
146.80-11/10/82
101.40-08/09/82
AS OF THURS.

165.00
160.00
155.00
150.00
145.00
140.00
135.00
130.00
125.00
120.00
115.00
110.00
105.00
100.00
95.00
90.00
CONTRACTS
25,000
20,000
15,000
10,000
5,000
VOL.-O.I.

24 31 7 14 21 28 5 12 19 26 2 9 16 23 30 6 13 20 27 4 11 18 25 1 8 15 22 29 6 13 20 27 3 10 17 24 31
54   JUN   JUL   AUG   SEP   OCT   NOV   DEC   JAN

(h)

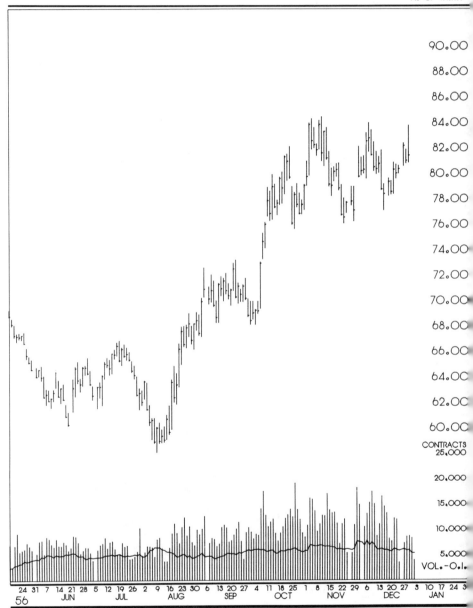

NYSE COMPOSITE
NYFE DECEMBER 82

CONTRACT HIGH - LOW
84.45-11/10/82
58.10-08/09/82
AS OF THURS.

90.00
88.00
86.00
84.00
82.00
80.00
78.00
76.00
74.00
72.00
70.00
68.00
66.00
64.00
62.00
60.00

CONTRACTS
25,000

20,000

15,000

10,000

5,000

VOL.-O.I.

24 31 7 14 21 28 5 12 19 26 2 9 16 23 30 6 13 20 27 4 11 18 25 1 8 15 22 29 6 13 20 27 3 10 17 24 3
56   JUN   JUL   AUG   SEP   OCT   NOV   DEC   JAN

(i)

Futures Prices: Regression Analysis

The regression equations fitted to the daily futures price data are summarized in Tables 10.8, 10.9, and 10.10. The estimates relate to the various corresponding maturities and subperiods IIa and IIb. Here again, the high and low relationships did not differ materially from the correlations and $\hat{B}$'s of the closing-settlement price equations. The higher variation in the KCBT June 1982 contract's coefficients (Period I) declined relative to the CME and NYFE September 1982 contracts in Period IIa ($\hat{B}$). That relative decrease seemed to hold throughout Period II, although in IIb, the KCBT-NYFE $\hat{B}$ regression coefficient increased slightly. As expected from the cash index regressions, and the coefficients of variation in Table 10.7, the KCBT December 1982 contract increased in price volatility, relative to the CME and NYFE (Period III). For the CME, $\hat{B}$ increased from around 1.08 in Period II to 1.34 in Period III for the KCBT maturity; relative to the NYFE, the KCBT $\hat{B}$ increased from 1.9 in Period II to over 2.3 in Period III.

The regression coefficients for the CME-NYFE price relationships, as in the case for the respective cash indexes, remained at about 1.7 for all 1982 maturities, and the subperiods. The R^2 values for the futures prices relationships also correspond closely to the cash index regressions, generally suggesting almost "perfect positive" correlation. Again, the only exception was the KCBT Period III change in volatility, which resulted in R^2 values for KCBT-NYFE and KCBT-CME relationships of about .90.

The percentage change correspondence among the stock index futures prices are more easily interpreted in logarithmic linear form. The period regressions for closing price/settlement data are shown in Table 10.11. The interpretation of $\hat{B}$ is as an "elasticity" estimate; thus the first $\hat{B}$ (Y = KCBT, X = CME) implies that during period I (June contract), for a given percentage change in the CME settlement price, the KCBT price changed by about 14 percent more (1.14), on the average.

For the same period (I), since $\hat{B}$ is less than 1.0, the CME settlement prices changed by only about 96 percent of the percentage change in the NYFE prices ($\hat{B}$ = .956). In general, these logarithmic regressions display coefficients fairly close to 1.0 for almost all combinations and periods. That suggests about equal percentage changes in prices among the contracts. Some estimated $\hat{B}$'s are under, and some over, 1.0. The notable

Table 10.8 Futures Price Regressions, Stock Index Contracts by Contract Maturity, Daily Observations

Dependent Variable (Y)	Regression Coefficient ($\hat{B}$)	Explanatory Variable (X)	R^2
Contract: June 1982; Period I: May 6–June 17, 1982			
KCBT—settlement	1.259	CME—settlement	.988
KCBT—high	1.252	CME—high	.986
KCBT—low	1.273	CME—low	.990
KCBT—settlement	2.102	NYFE—settlement	.992
KCBT—high	2.169	NYFE—high	.992
KCBT—low	2.105	NYFE—low	.994
CME—settlement	1.663	NYFE—settlement	.998
CME—high	1.724	NYFE—high	.996
CME—low	1.647	NYFE—low	.996
Contract: September 1982; Period IIa: June 18–August 16, 1982			
KCBT—settlement	1.029	CME—settlement	.993
KCBT—high	1.038	CME—high	.977
KCBT—low	1.043	CME—low	.974
KCBT—settlement	1.751	NYFE—settlement	.972
KCBT—high	1.749	NYFE—high	.968
KCBT—low	1.760	NYFE—low	.971
CME—settlement	1.702	NYFE—settlement	.997
CME—high	1.689	NYFE—high	.996
CME—low	1.687	NYFE—low	.997

exception, as previous data have also indicated, is for the KCBT coefficients in Period III. The percentage response increased to about 20 percent more volatility (i.e., 1.215 and 1.197) for the KCBT contract's price during this time period.

Futures Prices: Average Daily Changes

The average daily price changes for the stock index futures contracts are summarized in Table 10.12. The data are presented by month for the nearby contract (earliest maturity) and for the succeeding contract. As the Table shows, the largest daily changes (plus or minus), on the average, occurred in the KCBT contracts, which have the largest "size" due to the index values of the VLIC. All the changes indicated can be valued in money terms as the change in price × 500 (e.g., .78 × 500 = $390).

Table 10.9   Futures Price Regressions, Stock Index Contracts by Contract Maturity, Daily Observations

Dependent Variable (Y)	Regression Coefficient ($\hat{B}$)	Explanatory Variable (X)	R^2
Contract: September 1982; Period IIb: August 17–September 16			
KCBT—settlement	1.062	CME—settlement	.993
KCBT—high	1.044	CME—high	.993
KCBT—low	1.055	CME—low	.996
KCBT—settlement	1.911	NYFE—settlement	.992
KCBT—high	1.874	NYFE—high	.987
KCBT—low	1.879	NYFE—low	.997
CME—settlement	1.796	NYFE—settlement	.994
CME—high	1.790	NYFE—high	.990
CME—low	1.777	NYFE—low	.998
Contract: September 1982; Period II: June 18–September 16, 1982			
KCBT—settlement	1.082	CME—settlement	.991
KCBT—high	1.075	CME—high	.993
KCBT—low	1.080	CME—low	.992
KCBT—settlement	1.897	NYFE—settlement	.990
KCBT—high	1.882	NYFE—high	.989
KCBT—low	1.890	NYFE—low	.990
CME—settlement	1.752	NYFE—settlement	.997
CME—high	1.752	NYFE—high	.996
CME—low	1.751	NYFE—low	.998

Table 10.10   Futures Price Regressions, Stock Index Contracts by Contract Maturity, Daily Observations

Dependent Variable (Y)	Regression Coefficient ($\hat{B}$)	Explanatory Variable (X)	R^2
Contract: December 1982; Period III: September 17–December 16, 1982			
KCBT—settlement	1.339	CME—settlement	.888
KCBT—high	1.342	CME—high	.896
KCBT—low	1.351	CME—low	.895
KCBT—settlement	2.297	NYFE—settlement	.911
KCBT—high	2.295	NYFE—high	.916
KCBT—low	2.353	NYFE—low	.921
CME—settlement	1.687	NYFE—settlement	.993
CME—high	1.687	NYFE—high	.993
CME—low	1.709	NYFE—low	.992

Table 10.11   Futures Price Regressions, Stock Index Contracts, in Logarithmic Linear Form, Daily Observations, Settlement Prices, 1982

Dependent Variable (Y)	Regression Coefficent ($\hat{B}$)	Explanatory Variable (X)	R^2
Contract: June 1982; Period I: May 6–June 17, 1982			
KCBT	1.140	CME	.988
KCBT	1.098	NYFE	.992
CME	.956	NYFE	.997
Contract: September 1982: Period IIa: June 18–August 16, 1982			
KCBT	.947	CME	.976
KCBT	.925	NYFE	.972
CME	.978	NYFE	.997
Contract: September 1982; Period IIb: August 17–September 16, 1982			
KCBT	.976	CME	.993
KCBT	1.010	NYFE	.992
CME	1.033	NYFE	.994
Contract: September 1982; Period II: June 18–September 16, 1982			
KCBT-S	.995	CME-S	.991
KCBT-S	1.000	NYFE-S	.989
CME-S	1.005	NYFE-S	.997
Contract: December 1982; Period III: September 17–December 16, 1982			
KCBT	1.215	CME	.897
KCBT	1.197	NYFE	.918
CME	.971	NYFE	.993

However, as we have seen from our coefficient of variation and regression analyses, the percentage price volatility among all of the contracts was fairly close. Even during the December 1982 contracts' maturity period (III), when the KCBT's relative volatility was the largest, the price changes in absolute terms are not that much greater than for the CME and NYFE contracts. In October they are actually less, on the average, than the CME futures price changes. Table 10.12 also indicates larger average price changes for the more distant maturity; in general the nearby contract's average price changes are smaller for each exchange.

That generality seems confirmed in Table 10.13. The directly measured standard deviations of the respective maturities' futures prices are greater for the more distant maturities than for the "nearby" ones. The only exceptions occur for the CME contracts, due to the "splicing" effects discussed later. Part of the reason may be due to the differences in liquidity

Table 10.12 Futures Prices: Average Daily Price Changes, By Month, Positive and Negative Changes in Absolute Value (Positive), Period: May 6–December 31, 1982

	KCBT		CME		NYFE	
Contract:	June 1982	September 1982	June 1982	September 1982	June 1982	September 1982
May	.78	.81	.76	.73	.46	.48
June	1.27	1.78	1.30^a	1.54^a	.62	.88
Contract:	September 1982	December 1982	September 1982	December 1982	September 1982	December 1982
July	1.17	1.18	1.06	1.10	.61	.64
August	1.98	2.10	1.90	1.92	1.21	1.28
September	1.44	1.63	1.65^a	1.80^a	.92	1.04
Contract:	December 1982	March 1983	December 1982	March 1983	December 1982	March 1983
October	2.18	2.20	2.27	2.30	1.40	1.43
November	2.41	2.43	2.23	2.26	1.43	1.46
December	1.49	1.77	1.67^a	1.75^a	.85	1.00
Average Daily Price Change	Nearby Contract	Next Maturity	Nearby Contract	Next Maturity	Nearby Contract	Next Maturity
	1.59	1.74	1.61	1.68	.94	1.03

^{a}Denotes maturity month, and for CME price series requires "splicing" the next two earliest maturities.

at particular times. But more persuasive is the profile-shift effect, when one day the futures are at a premium to the cash index, and at a discount the next. For example, a typical change of this kind might be that the nearby contract is 1.10 over the cash index on one day, and .40 under on the next. The change for the nearby contract would thus be 1.50 in absolute terms. The corresponding changes for the next forward maturity might be from 1.60 over the cash index to .80 under, a net change of 2.40. Sequences of premium- discount-premium also occasionally were evident (see Figures 10.1 and 10.2).

Another facet of Tables 10.12 and 10.13 is the splicing effect caused by the mid-month maturity of the CME contracts. For example, when the CME September 1982 contract matured on the 16th, to continue the

Table 10.13   Futures Prices, 1982, Standard Deviations for Selected Contract Maturities, Daily Observations

Contract	Standard Deviation	Contract	Standard Deviation
Period I: May 6–June 17, 1982		**Period IIa: June 18–August 16, 1982**	
KCBT—June 1982	5.168	KCBT—September 1982	3.863
September 1982	6.023	December 1982	3.901
CME—June 1982	4.079	CME—September 1982	3.707
September 1982	4.657	December 1982	3.772
NYFE—June 1982	2.450	NYFE—September 1982	2.175
September 1982	2.890	December 1982	2.263
		Period IIb: August 17–September 16, 1982	
Period II: June 18–September 16			
KCBT—September 1982	6.503	KCBT—September 1982	5.234
December 1982	6.779	December 1982	5.399
CME—September 1982	5.983	CME—September 1982	4.798
December 1982	5.961[a]	December 1982	4.785[a]
NYFE—September 1982	3.422	NYFE—September 1982	2.757
December 1982	3.435	December 1982	2.634
Period III: September 17–December 16, 1982			
KCBT—December 1982	10.384		
March 1983	10.575		
CME—December 1982	7.305		
March 1983	7.271[a]		
NYFE—December 1982	4.314		
March 1983	4.371		

[a]Indicates higher standard deviation for nearby maturity.

series it was necessary to shift to the December 1982 and March 1983 contracts' price changes; for the NYFE and KCBT, the September–December 1982 futures prices were used throughout September 1982. This shift or splicing resulted in some minor distortion, since as we have noted the more distant maturities tend to have greater price volatility than the nearby contracts. That is especially so, as the current month contracts tend to converge with the underlying cash market index.

LIMIT MOVES

Daily price limit movements occurred 10 times during 1982 in the stock index futures prices. Such a limit move may have been the case for one or more contracts on one of the exchanges. It should be noted that the NYFE does not have any daily price movement limits, nor did the KCBT until late August 1982, when a $5.00 limit was implemented. The largest daily move occurred just prior to that, on August 17, when the December 1982 KCBT contract reflected a change of $6.60. The CME initially imposed a $3.00 daily price limit, but later increased it to $5.00. The days on which a limit move occurred in at least one contract are as follows: June 14(−), June 22(+), August 17(+), August 20(+), October 6(+), October 7(+), October 25(−), November 9(+), November 30(+), and December 14(−). Near-limit moves, over $4.00, occurred four times, three in September and one in November.

Since two of the exchanges (KCBT and CME) have daily limits and one (NYFE) does not, an interesting aspect to explore is the extent to which the "price pressure" flowed over to the NYFE on the days when limit moves occurred elsewhere. From our regression analysis, we know that the "average" correspondence between the CME and NYFE was about 1.7 throughout the year. If we invert that coefficient ($\frac{1}{1.7} = .588$), then on those limit days when the NYFE/CME price change exceeded .588, we might be tempted to conclude that indeed the equilibrium price was sought in the unconstrained market. The respective price-change ratios are shown below:

Date	NYFE/CME	Date	NYFE/CME
June 14	.683 +	October 7	.365
June 22	.583	October 25	.730 +
August 17	.790 +	November 7	.562
August 20	.560	November 30	.950 +
October 6	.760 +	December 14	.521

On 5 of the 10 limit days, the price change for the NYFE/CME contracts did not even change by the *average* amount. Those days that exceed the average of .588 are denoted with a " + " and, with the exception of June 14 (which is not much over .588), it would appear that traders attempted to protect their positions in the unconstrained NYFE contract. It might be surprising that this phenomenon appeared on only 4 days out of the 10, but recall that only one contract on one exchange had to exhibit a limit move in order to qualify as a "limit" day. On some occasions, not even all contracts on the limit-exchange were price constrained.

THE "BASIS"

In Chapter 5 one of the crucial elements emphasized in developing the concept of "hedging" was the *basis*. This component of the hedging calculus was defined as the difference between the futures price and the cash price at any given time. The basis in the context of stock index futures is computed in the same manner: the difference between the (nearby) futures price and the value of the underlying cash market index. For instance, on December 3, 1982, the CME December 1982 contract closed at 139.15, and the S&P index at 138.69; therefore, the basis for December 3 was (P_f-P_c) = 139.15 − 138.69 = .46. On that day the future closed at a .46 "premium" to the cash S&P index. In contrast, three trading sessions later on December 8, the CME December 1982 contract closed at 141.35 and the S&P at 141.82; for December 8 the basis was 141.35 − 141.82 = − .47; on that day the future closed at a "discount" to the cash index.

As indicated in Chapter 5, the differing movements and changes in the cash versus the futures prices constitute the "basis risk." It is the key element of uncertainty in hedging operations. Many market participants attempt to monitor the basis and establish their positions in the futures market with regard to it. "Trading the basis" is a common approach to positioning. Correct expectations about its movement underlie profitable hedging.

For the stock index contracts the basis appears in Tables 10.14 and 10.15. In all cases the basis is calculated as the price of the future minus the cash index value (P_f-P_c) so that positive values indicate premiums, and negative values denote "discounts"; in all cases the nearby maturity is P_f. Table 10.14 covers the "bear market" period, until August 13, 1982, and Table 10.15 the bull market rally through 1982 year-end. For each exchange, by week, the "high" and "low" basis values are shown. Sometimes the "high" is the smallest discount that week (e.g., KCBT for the week of June 4), and sometimes the "low" is the smallest premium for that week (e.g., NYFE, July 23). The algebraic sign is important.

One interesting aspect of Table 10.14 is that during this "bear market" the CME and NYFE show daily average basis values that on balance are premiums (positive); for KCBT, on the other hand, the daily average basis was a discount of − .48. In terms of relative volatility (coefficients of variation), the CME exhibits slightly higher basis variation. However, in this context, the CV ratios should not be taken too seriously. The mean,

Table 10.14   Index Futures Contracts: Range of Daily Basis (P_f-P_c), Nearby
Contract, Daily High and Low Basis Values for Each Week, Closing Prices,
Period: May 10–August 13, 1982

Week Ending	KCBT		CME		NYFE	
	High	Low	High	Low	High	Low
5/14/82	− .45	− .84	.38	.12	.21	.00
5/21	.07	− 1.23	.36	− .24	.16	− .17
5/28	− .57	− 2.58	.21	− .88	.08	− .84
6/4	− 1.24	− 2.91	− .49	− 1.99	− .45	− 1.22
6/11	.21	− 2.63	.21	− 1.13	.16	− .78
6/18	.07	− 2.20	.08	− 2.63	.10	− .69
6/25	.80	− 1.05	1.72	− .70	.56	− .04
7/2	.10	− 2.19	2.04	.65	1.03	.00[a]
7/9	2.56	− .42	3.87	2.08	2.11	1.27
7/16	2.78	1.44	3.11	2.35	2.13	1.35
7/23	2.19	.56	2.66	1.43	1.70	.95
7/30	.44	− 1.39	1.17	.25	.76	.24
8/6	.52	− 3.12	1.02	− 1.11	.71	− 1.04
8/13/82	.66	− 1.94	1.00	− .79	.71	− .05
Period	2.78	− 3.12	3.87	− 2.63	2.13	− 1.22
Daily average	− .481		.529		.257	
Standard Deviation	1.381		1.345		.818	
Coefficient of variation ($s/\overline{X}$)	− .348		.393		.314	

[a]Last day of trading for maturing contract.

$\overline{X}$, could be equal to zero, or near to zero, but the values around $\overline{X}$ could
be widely dispersed. In such a case the calculated CV, though, could be
extremely small, much less than the standard deviation itself. Here the
coefficient of variation could be highly misleading.

Tables 10.14 and 10.15 also indicate for the respective *period*, the
maximum "high" basis and minimum low basis values. In Table 10.14,
for NYFE, for example, the maximum high basis was 2.13 and minimum
low was − 1.22. In Table 10.15, all of the daily average basis values show
slight premiums of .21 to .38. However, even during the bull market rally,
daily discounts (− values) appear in almost every week, almost for every
contract. KCBT shows the highest premium for the period (3.96) and the
largest discount (− 2.55) as well.

Table 10.15　Index Futures Contracts: Range of Daily Basis (P_f-P_c), Nearby Contract, Daily High and Low Basis Values for Each Week, Closing Prices, Period: August 16–December 31, 1982

	KCBT		CME		NYFE	
Week Ending	High	Low	High	Low	High	Low
8/20/82	2.63	− 1.18	1.23	− .79	.85	.35
8/27	1.87	− 1.77	.39	− 1.21	.44	− .68
9/3	1.12	− 1.45	.62	− 1.25	.52	− .65
9/10	1.27	− 1.17	.45	− 1.32	.48	− 1.01
9/17	2.23	− .52	1.16	− .39	.92	− .40
9/24	.44	− 2.35	1.90	− 1.79	.56	− .90
10/1	.34	− 2.55	.43	− 1.82	.12	− .96
10/8	2.32	− 2.38	1.35	− 1.43	1.00	− .86
10/15	2.55	.05	1.97	− .39	1.20	− .10
10/22	2.61	− .91	2.23	− .38	1.50	.02
10/29	.93	− 2.06	1.77	− .09	1.24	− .55
11/5	.91	− .27	2.19	.98	1.80	.42
11/12	3.96	.87	2.78	.54	1.54	.17
11/19	1.95	− .90	1.29	− .82	.75	− .47
11/26	− .09	− 1.81	.07	− 1.52	.10	− 1.10
12/3	1.33	− .69	.46	− .62	1.70	− .63
12/10	2.91	− 1.36	1.58	− .47	.89	− .28
12/17	.63	− 2.25	1.06	− .95	.31	− .57
12/23	2.11	− .36	2.24	.60	.56	− .04
12/31/82	1.40	.27	2.53	.82	.92	.00[a]
Period	3.96	− 2.55	2.78	− 1.82	1.80	− 1.10
Daily average	.217		.384		.214	
Standard deviation	1.356		1.075		.636	
Coefficient of variation (s/X)	.160		.357		.336	

[a]Last day of trading for maturing contract.

BASIS REGRESSIONS

Regression estimates appear in Table 10.16, by contract maturity period, and by the subperiod segmentation IIa and IIb. These regressions are the nearby futures closing prices on the respective underlying cash indexes. A $\hat{B}$ less than 1.0 indicates that the futures price was less variable than the underlying index. This was the case for KCBT (.960) and NYFE (.972) in Period IIb, for example. However, the more common relationship was

Table 10.16 Basis Regressions 1982 Stock Index Contracts, Settlement Prices

Dependent Variable (Y)	Regression Coefficient ($\hat{B}$)	Explanatory Variable (X)	R^2
Contract: June 1982, Period I: May 6–June 17, 1982			
KCBT	1.072	VLIC	.976
CME	1.098	S & P	.982
NYFE	1.120	NYSE	.982
Contract: September 1982, Period IIa: June 18–August 16, 1982			
KCBT	1.262	VLIC	.832
CME	1.315	S & P	.909
NYFE	1.355	NYSE	.892
Contract: September 1982, Period IIb: August 17–September 16, 1982			
KCBT	.960	VLIC	.951
CME	1.012	S & P	.978
NYFE	.972	NYSE	.965
Contract: September 1982, Period II: June 18–September 16, 1982			
KCBT	1.057	VLIC	.944
CME	.962	S & P	.951
NYFE	.967	NYSE	.941
Contract: December 1982, Period III: September 17–December 16, 1982			
KCBT	1.055	VLIC	.980
CME	1.078	S & P	.982
NYFE	1.073	NYSE	.976

that the futures closing or settlement prices were more variable than the underlying cash index, for most of the 1982 contract maturities. The greatest basis volatility occurred in Period IIa for all three September 1982 futures contracts. In Period III, although previous evidence indicated that the KCBT futures contract was relatively more volatile than CME or NYFE, the $\hat{B}$ estimates suggest that KCBT was less variable in relation to the VLIC than the other two were relative to their underlying indexes. That implies that the KCBT appeared more volatile, relatively, but the reason was the variability of the underlying VLIC. In Period III both the NYFE and CME have regression coefficients that are almost equal but both exceed the $\hat{B}$ estimate for KCBT-VLIC. The R^2 values are all quite high, as the nearby futures prices tracked the underlying cash indexes very closely during 1982.

The final empirical basis examination appears in Table 10.17. This table shows basis vis-à-vis basis for the year, broken into two periods: the

Table 10.17 Basis Regressions, Daily Observations, Nearby Contracts,
Closing prices

Dependent Variable (Y)	Regression Coefficient ($\hat{B}$)	Explanatory Variable (X)	R^2
Period: May 10–August 13, 1982			
KCBT basis	.895	CME basis	.760
KCBT basis	1.507	NYFE basis	.797
CME basis	1.543	NYFE basis	.871
Period: August 16–December 31, 1982			
KCBT basis	.951	CME basis	.569
KCBT basis	1.689	NYFE basis	.616
CME basis	1.352	NYFE basis	.639

August 13 bear market, and the bull market for the remainder of the year.
The dependent Y variables are, for example, KCBT-VLIC, and X = CME-
S & P. That is, these regressions represent one contract's daily basis
values versus another's. As the estimates show (R^2), changes in the basis,
from one contract to another, were not particularly highly related. The
R^2 values are in the mediocre range of .62 to .87. The highest correlation
of basis changes appears to have been between CME and NYFE during
the market decline ending in August. During the subsequent upturn, the
statistics suggest that the correlation of basis changes fell off fairly sharply;
all three correlations fall within the .57 to .64 range. The divergence of
CME and NYFE is evident in the section on spreading.

SPREAD TRADING

Another technique used in futures trading is known as "spreading." The
basic principle involves taking opposite positions in two different futures
contracts (e.g., "long" December, "short" July) in order to profit from
apparent price discrepancies. When these price differentials "readjust,"
the nimble trader expects to profit. Since the prices of all contract maturities tend to move in the same direction (up or down), the rationale
behind speading includes a presumption of less risk than an outright long
or short position. That aspect is reflected in Table 9.1, where spread
margins are shown to be considerably less than those for hedging and
speculation. An "intramarket" spread involves the same commodity (i.e.,

long December wheat, short July wheat) in the same market (e.g, Chicago Board of Trade, CBT).

In order to demonstrate the mechanics, suppose on September 29, 1982, a trader expected the CME June 1983 stock index futures contract to increase in price more than the December 1982 maturity. Accordingly, the corresponding spread position would have been: long June 1983, short December 1982. For September 29, 1982:

CME Contracts Price	Contract Value
December 1982	119.95 (× 500) = $59,975 (short)
June 1983	121.30 (× 500) = $60,650 (long)
Price difference: +	1.35 (× 500) = +$675 difference in values.

If the position had been closed out on November 24, 1982, then the following would have been the results of the spread:

November 24, 1982

CME Contracts Price	Contract Value
December 1982 133.80 (× 500)	= $66,900 (buy)
June 1983 135.40 (× 500)	= $67,700 (sell)
Price difference + 1.60 (× 500)	= + $800 difference in values

The results of the spread were:

December 1982:	$59,975 (sale) − $66,900 (buy) =	− $6,925
June 1983:	$67,700 (sale) − 60,650 (buy) =	+ 7,050
	Net gain:	+ $ 125

A shorter way to arrive at the net results is just to calculate the change in the price differences:

$$(121.30 - 119.95) = 1.35$$
$$(135.40 - 133.80) = 1.60$$

and

$$(1.60 - 1.35) = .25 (\times 500) = \$125 \text{ gain (same as above)}$$

Again, this type of spreading is "intramarket" since both contracts were CME stock index maturities. Note that if the "spread" had nar-

rowed, say to 1.10, the trader would have lost $1.35 − 1.10 = .20 (×
500) = − $100. Alternatively, if the trader had shorted June 1983 and
bought December 1982, in the example above, the spread would have
resulted in a loss of $125.

Another brand of spreading is called the "intermarket" type. In the
same way, long and short positions are established in related contracts,
but in two different markets. Spreading operations are common between,
for example, CBT wheat and KCBT wheat. Again, the maturity months
may differ as well: CBT December 1982 wheat–KCBT May 1983 wheat.
In addition, there are "intercommodity" spreads, for example, hogs–cattle,
and commodity–product spreads: November soybeans–December soybean oil, or interest rate spreads: GNMAs–U.S. Treasury Bonds.

The actual positions undertaken by spreaders are not picked at random.
Implicit in the CME stock index spread above was a "bull spread" since
the premiums tend to widen when the prices rise, and we have seen that
forward maturities of the stock index contracts are more volatile. A "bear
spread" takes the opposite initial positioning: long December 1982, short
June 1983. The greater volatility of the forward maturities of stock index
futures contracts results in a situation that is slightly different from the
case for agricultural commodities. In the latter type of spreads, typically
the nearby maturities have the greater price variations. So a "bull spread"
in the expectation of a price increase would involve a long position in the
nearby and a short in the deferred maturity. However, for precious metal
and currencies, the more distant contract maturities tend to exhibit the
greater price variation due to interest rates and storage factors. Also, in
this regard, for stock index futures the greater price variation in the de-
ferreds can result from the "inversion to premium" shifts illustrated in
Figures 10.1 and 10.2. Powers and Vogel (1981) observed that a spread
position reveals the trader's expectations about future price movements:
that the market is expected to move either up or down, depending upon
the particular commodity and the long or short position in nearby versus
deferred maturities.

Scholes (1981) has commented that the theory of spreading in futures
markets is not well understood, and that it is often "artificially" distinguished from hedging. Schrock also noted that "while operations of this
nature frequently occur in the commodity futures market, little attention
has been devoted to providing a *rationale* for this form of speculative
activity" (Schrock, 1971, p. 270). Schrock further noted that spreading

represents a major portion of the commitments undertaken by large (reporting) speculators; yet the literature offers almost no theoretical consideration of spreading operations (p. 272). Schrock's model is basically a mean-variance (quadratic utility) formulation, and in it he shows

> There is no reason to expect the individual involved in straddle (spreading) operations for purposes of speculation to *choose matching quantities* of the *offsetting commodity* futures in preference to some other combination. The position taken in the commodity market by the individual trader will depend upon the nature of *anticipated changes in the prices of futures contracts.* If the speculator acts rationally on the basis of these expectations, he will generally take *unequal* positions, in terms of physical quantities, in the offsetting futures contracts. (p. 273, emphasis added)

In this regard, due to the smaller index scale of the NYFE contract, industry practice for an intermarket spread has been to equate two NYFE contracts to one KCBT or one CME. Recall that spreading attempts to extract profits from *changes* in price differences. Moreover, for the NYFE spreads, this imbalance is difficult to assess. For example, if one expects a market rise, then long one KCBT and short one NYFE seems unambiguous as a bull spread. But long one KCBT and short two NYFE contracts distorts the spread positioning, since a 1.00 change in two NYFE contracts results in a $1000 change in value, while for one KCBT contract, the change in value is only $500. For purposes of illustration, this latter spread is shown in Tables 10.18 and 10.19. But for the "reduced risk" speculative spreads illustrated below, all are evaluated on a one for one contract basis.

The most interesting spreads for stock index futures appear to be those that are the intermarket ones, for example, long KCBT, short CME. To see how such a spread might work, let's consider a trader who engaged in a KCBT–June 1982 short and CME–June 1982 long spread position on May 14, 1982 and lifted the spread on June 9.

May 14 Prices	June 9 Prices
KCBT–June 1982: 131.30(short)	KCBT–June 1982: 118.80(buy)
CME–June 1982: 118.35(long)	CME–June 1982: 108.60(sell)
Price difference: 12.95	Price difference: 10.20

Net gain: $(12.95 - 10.20) = 2.75 \ (\times \ 500) = \$1375$

Since the trader was short KCBT, the profitable price change was (131.30 − 118.80) = 12.50, and the loss on CME (108.60 − 118.35) = − 9.75, when combined with + 12.50 = 2.75 (× 500) = + $1375.

Our data have suggested that the VLIC and KCBT are more variable than the CME-S & P and NYFE-NYSE. Since the initial position involved a short in the KCBT and long CME, we can interpret the position as a "bear spread." For an example of a bull spread in the December 1982 contracts on September 1, consider the following:

Futures Market	September 1, 1982 Prices	October 1, 1982 Prices	Change
CME	117.30	120.15	+ 2.85
KCBT	127.80	130.35	+ 2.55
NYFE	67.45	69.05	+ 1.60

In this example, even though the KCBT contract is more volatile on the average, during September 1982 the CME price increased more. A "bull spread" with KCBT long and CME short would have lost (2.55 − 2.85) = − .30 (× 500) = − $150, and for KCBT-NYFE the spread results would have shown a gain (2.55 − 1.60) = .95 (× 500) = + $475. Note that for spreads, as opposed to our hedging examples, only one NYFE contract is utilized, since the price *changes* in all contracts are valued at $500. If the CME had been the initial long and NYFE the short, the spread would have gained (2.85 − 1.60) = 1.25 (× 500) = $625. However, during the month of October 1982, the results would have been quite different:

Futures Market	October 1, 1982 Prices	November 1, 1982 Prices	Change
CME	120.15	137.45	+ 17.30
KCBT	130.35	150.70	+ 20.35
NYFE	69.05	79.05	+ 10.00

A bull spread in KCBT-CME would have gained (20.35 − 17.30) = 3.05 (× 500) = $1525, in KCBT-NYFE (20.35 − 10.00) = 10.35 (× 500) = $5175, and for CME-NYFE (17.30 − 10.00) = 7.30 (× 500) = $3650. The corresponding "reverse" bear spreads would have lost the amounts shown above.

The statistics on the stock index price spreads are shown in Tables 10.18 and 10.19, and graphically in Figure 10.4. The data in Table 10-18 are for the bear market ending in mid-August 1982, and Table 10.19 for the bull market period through December 31, 1982. Daily figures do not exhibit much variation, so weekly averages for the spreads appear in the tables.

From Table 10.18 we can see that during the market's decline through August 13, 1982, the KCBT-CME spread narrowed by 3.67 (× 500) = $1835; a bear spread would have profited (short KCBT, long CME) and a bull spread (long KCBT, short CME) would have sustained a loss in the amount shown. Similarly, the KCBT-NYFE spread narrowed by − 10.12 (× 500 = $5060) and the CME-NYFE spread narrowed by − 6.44 (× 500 = $3220). The latter is a little surprising, given the essential similarity of the two underlying indexes.

Table 10.18 Stock Index Futures Contracts—Spreads Between Nearby Contracts, Weekly Averages; Period: May 10–August 13, 1982

Week Ending	KCBT-CME	KCBT-NYFE	CME-NYFE	KCBT–(2)NYFE
5/14/82	12.84	63.16	50.31	− 5.40
5/21	12.94	61.79	48.85	− 4.78
5/28	11.56	59.45	47.89	− 5.48
6/4	11.43	58.15	46.75	− 5.18
6/11	10.39	56.97	46.50	− 5.96
6/18	10.24	56.13	45.87	− 6.00
6/25	9.65	56.50	46.85	− 6.31
7/2	8.48	55.83	47.56	− 7.66
7/9	8.99	55.94	46.95	− 7.68
7/16	9.82	57.82	48.00	− 7.22
7/23	9.63	57.73	48.10	− 7.36
7/30	9.84	56.19	46.35	− 6.61
8/6	9.49	54.83	45.34	− 5.90
8/13	9.17	53.04	43.87	− 6.24
Change:				
5/14–8/13	− 3.67	− 10.12	− 6.44	− .84

Daily
Minima: KCBT(June 1982)-CME(September 1982), 6/29/82 = 8.15
   KCBT(September 1982)-NYFE(September 1982), 8/12/82 = 52.55
   CME(September 1982)-NYFE(September 1982), 8/10/82 = 43.40

Table 10.19   Weekly Average Spreads; Period: August 16–December 31, 1982

Week Ending	KCBT-CME	KCBT-NYFE	CME-NYFE	KCBT–(2)NYFE
8/20/82	9.74	55.84	46.10	− 6.71
8/27	9.77	59.40	49.63	− 7.49
9/3	10.49	61.39	50.90	− 7.28
9/10	10.89	62.58	51.69	− 6.99
9/17	10.55	63.21	52.66	− 7.54
9/24	10.04	63.00	52.96	− 7.79
10/1	11.13	62.56	51.43	− 7.17
10/8	10.17	63.57	53.40	− 8.84
10/15	10.22	68.04	57.82	− 9.69
10/22	11.39	70.73	59.34	− 9.35
10/29	12.01	69.40	57.39	− 7.88
11/5	13.79	73.78	59.99	− 7.71
11/12	18.58	79.15	60.57	− 3.21
11/19	19.55	77.59	58.04	− 1.91
11/26	20.13	76.43	56.30	− .78
12/3	20.64	78.54	57.88	− 1.26
12/10	19.01	79.03	59.97	− 2.48
12/17	17.58	75.81	58.23	− 3.28
12/23	16.61	76.41	59.80	− 3.39
12/31/82	16.27	77.39	61.12	− 3.85
Change:				
8/13–12/31	+ 7.10	+ 24.35	+ 17.25	+ 2.86

Daily Maxima: KCBT-CME(December 1982), 12/1/82 = 21.10
KCBT-NYFE(December 1982), 12/6/82 = 80.70
CME-NYFE(December 1982), 11/9/82 = 61.95

In Table 10.19 the spreads among all contracts opened as the market rallied. Again, most of the spread between KCBT-NYFE is accounted for by the CME-NYFE spread change: KCBT-NYFE = 24.35, which in turn is made up of the KCBT-CME change of 7.10 and the CME-NYFE spread change of 17.25. Not only is the extent of these spreads a bit surprising, but the timing is as well. The CME-NYFE spread change occurred mostly through October 1982, reaching a high in the first weeks of November. It was in this latter month that the KCBT contract widened from the other two.

Spreading, like hedging, is not a riskless operation. If one had been on the "wrong side" in either portion of the year, the losses could have been fairly substantial. The economic function of spreading is to "keep prices

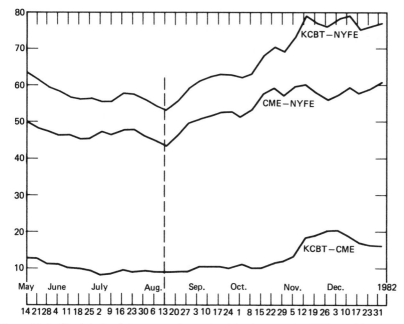

Figure 10.4   Stock index futures: nearby contracts' price spreads, 1982, weekly averages.

in line"—but it is difficult to determine whether an observed deviation is a temporary misalignment, or the result of a fundamental shift in the underlying forces. Floor traders and "scalpers" add to the markets' liquidity by spreading, especially in the deferred maturities. In general, spreads are less risky than outright positions, but for 1982, if held for substantial periods could have been very profitable, or disastrous, depending on which side the spreader took and at what time the position was initiated. The proverbial bottom line for profitable spreading is timing, especially with regard to the phase of the market, and which stock index is leading the market and in what direction.

VOLUME AND OPEN INTEREST

The data on 1982 trading activity and open interest for the stock index futures contracts are shown in Table 10.20 and in Figures 10.5(*a*) and (*b*). Open interest denotes those contracts that remain "open," that is, those that have not yet been closed out by a round turn. This item is important

Table 10.20   Stock Index Futures Contracts: Daily Average Volume and Open Interest, by Month, 1982, for Each Exchange Number of Contracts

Month	KCBT	CME	NYFE
	1982 Average Daily Volume		
March	1,906		
April	2,010	3,507	
May	1,822	6,186	6,602
June	2,306	11,958	7,053
July	2,351	11,284	6,219
August	2,863	16,835	7,418
September	2,903	19,847	8,799
October	2,650	22,544	10,766
November	2,837	24,499	11,797
December	2,758	22,401	11,230
	1982 Average Daily Open Interest		
March	2,643		
April	3,416	1,481	
May	3,651	4,753	2,771
June	4,413	8,893	4,848
July	4,706[a]	12,423	4,776
August	5,704[a]	14,904	5,365
September	4,697[a]	13,083	4,857
October	3,279	12,996	5,798
November	3,283	14,867	6,390
December	3,183	13,717	6,336

[a]May have resulted from reporting error.

to analysts and potential market participants, as it is generally interpreted as an indicator of liquidity.

The growth of trading in stock index futures has been impressive from the start. It would appear that the legal wars described in Chapter 6 were not fought for imaginary rewards. Reinforced by a dramatic turn around in the stock (cash) market in the latter half of 1982, trading activity in stock index futures has grown almost exponentially, for these markets as a whole.

In terms of market shares, the CME's S&P-based futures contract has been the dominant force. The CME accounted for about 62 percent of

Figure 10.5   Stock index futures contracts. (a) 1982 average daily volume for each week, by exchange. (b) 1982 average daily open interest for each week, by exchange.

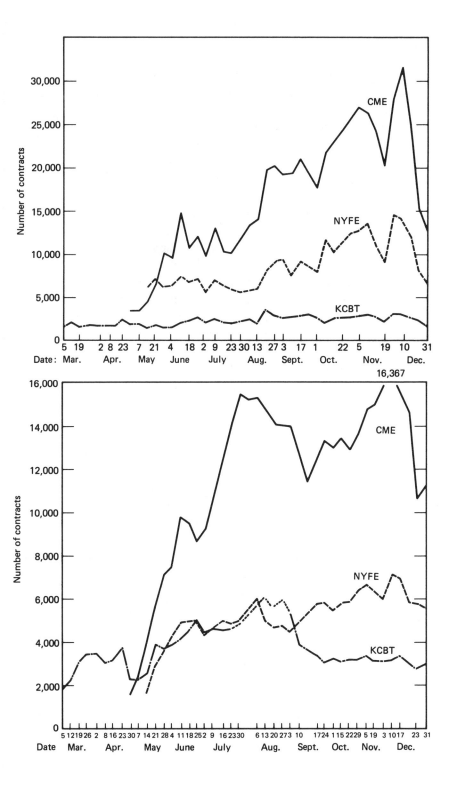

the volume and 61 percent of the open interest around the end of 1982. The NYFE's share, *not* adjusting for its contract's smaller size, was about 31 percent of volume, and 26 percent of open interest. The KCBT, pioneer and innovator of the stock index futures concept, shows the more disappointing results. Volume and open interest remained at levels attained three–four months after trading began in February.

The distributions of open interest by contract maturity, in Tables 10.21 and 10.22, are shown for the September 1982 and December 1982 contract maturity periods, respectively. For the September 1982 contract, about 70 percent of CME's open interest was concentrated in that maturity. As the reader can see from the table, a relative shifting took place into the December maturity, so that on September 9, 1982, 34 percent of total open interest remained in September 1982 and 64 percent had built up in the December 1982 maturity. The same shifting patterns, although not at the same rate, occurred in the NYFE and KCBT contracts as well. Table 10.22 exhibits the same general time shapes, for the December 1982 maturity. The cash settlement procedures for these contracts seem to function without difficulty: almost 3000 contracts for the CME went to cash delivery in December. Even with nearly 20 percent of its total open interest settling in this manner, liquidation appears to have been orderly, as designed.

SUMMARY

After nearly four years of regulatory review, stock index futures contracts at last began trading in February 1982. Throughout the regulatory approval process, many analysts had wondered about the likely shape of the profile of the contracts' forward maturity prices. Theoretical arbitrage models predicted that the futures prices should always be a premium to the cash indexes. However, actual market price behavior has not been very accommodating. Frequently, the futures prices traded and closed at discounts, or "inversions," to the cash indexes. Nevertheless, the most predominant pattern of futures price profiles reflected premiums for the forward maturities, though still not as high as the theoretical models predicted. A general expectations explanation appears to be more consistent with the observed behavior of stock index futures prices.

Table 10.21 Major Composition of Open Interest, By Maturity Month For Each Exchange, September 1982 Stock Index Futures Contracts (Approach to Maturity)

			Number of Contracts (Percent of Total Open Interest)			
Maturity Month	July 29	August 18	August 27	September 9	Sept. 16	Sept. 28
			CME			
September 1982	11,678(.70)	9,098(.60)	7,705(.53)	4,854(.34)	—	—
December 1982	4,888(.29)	5,829(.38)	6,393(.44)	9,196(.64)	11,389(.86)	10,686(.92)
March 1983						835(.07)
Total	16,745	15,254	14,471	14,431	13,203	11,569
			NYFE			
September 1982		3,432(.67)	2,661(.59)	1,109(.27)	561(.11)	239(.04)
December 1982		1,353(.27)	1,557(.35)	2,323(.56)	3,415(.65)	3,988(.70)
March 1983						836(.15)
Total		5,095	4,493	4,184	5,244	5,705
			KCBT			
September 1982			2,626(.48)	2,961(.45)	970(.26)	547(.17)
December 1982			2,452(.45)	3,290(.50)	2,356(.64)	2,156(.68)
March 1983						271(.09)
Total			5,437[a]	6,642[a]	3,694	3,158

[a]May involve a reporting error.

Table 10.22 Major Composition of Open Interest, By Maturity Month For Each Exchange, December, 1982 Stock Index Futures Contracts (Approach to Maturity)

		Number of Contracts (Percent of Total Open Interest)				
	October 15	November 15	December 1	December 16	December 29	
CME						
December 1982	11,736(.90)	11,486(.79)	11,564(.69)	2,929(.19)[a]	—	
March 1983	1,272(.09)	2866(.20)	5,080(.30)	11,667(.78)	10,863(.93)	
June 1983					693(.06)	
Total	13,101	14,625	16,811	15,037	11,681	
NYFE						
December 1982	3,597(.68)	4,466(.68)	4,494(.66)	942(.16)	—	
March 1983	871(.16)	1,275(.19)	1,751(.23)	3,958(.67)	4,073(.77)	
June 1983					709(.13)	
Total	5,300	6,611	7,527	5,942	5,273	
KCBT						
December 1982	2,709(.78)	2,756(.77)	1,845(.57)	1,122(.35)	—	
March 1983	532(.15)	561(.16)	1,063(.33)	1,713(.54)	1,738(.63)	
June 1983					332(.12)	
Total	3,451	3,561	3,224	3,165	2,777	

[a]Evidently the number of contracts for delivery.

From a statistician's viewpoint, 1982 was a fortuitous year for launching the trading of stock index futures. The stock market exhibited both robust bear and bull market movements. By the time all three contracts (CME, KCBT, NYFE) were "up and trading" (May 6), the market was in a general downward trend until August 16, 1982. But the next day a sudden turnaround occurred, and the stock market rallied almost uninterrupted through December 31: a gain of about 35 to 40 percent from the mid-August lows.

In terms of statistical measures, the three cash market indexes underlying the stock index futures contracts (S & P, VLIC, and NYSE) moved in close concert throughout the year. On the basis of daily observations, the indexes exhibited correlation coefficients with one another generally in excess of .95. With respect to relative variability, all three showed about the same degree, and all "shifted" together to comparable levels during the various market phases—with but the minor exception of the VLIC in the earliest period (May 6–June 17), and latest (September 17–December 16). Regression analysis of the indexes indicated a fairly stable relationship between the S & P and NYSE, which would be expected due to their very similar construction. The regression coefficients for the VLIC versus the S & P and NYSE did vary with the particular market phase.

Nearly the same correspondent patterns of correlation and relative volatility were apparent in the futures prices for the stock index contracts. Daily observations were tested for the three nearby (maturing) contracts of 1982: June, September, December. In addition, daily highs and lows were explored, but no material differences from the patterns of the closing prices were evident. The profiles of relative variability in the futures prices echoed those of the cash indexes: high correlation and stability of the CME and NYFE contracts, with the KCBT prices exhibiting noticeably higher volatility only after mid-October. Regressions in logarithmic linear form resulted in estimated elasticity coefficients very close to unity, among all futures prices; again, with the exception of the KCBT futures prices in the latter part of the year showing $\hat{B}$ values of 1.2 with respect to both the CME and NYFE.

Average daily price changes for the stock index futures contracts ranged from about .70 to 1.70 in May and June, to about 1.50 to 2.40 during the October–December period. In general, the nearby contracts exhibited less price volatility than the next forward maturities. That finding applies to all three contracts throughout the year, as reflected in higher average daily price changes, and in larger standard deviations.

Extreme daily price changes—limit moves—occurred on 10 trading days. However, not all contracts changed by the limit amount on those days. Only on 4 of the 10 days did the limits on the KCBT and CME contracts appear to divert the price pressure over to the unconstrained (NYFE, no daily limits) market.

Basis patterns (positive and negative) displayed wide variation among the contracts in terms of daily observations. Not infrequently one or two of the contracts would reflect discounts, while the other(s) would close at premiums. However, regressions of the futures prices on the cash indexes (daily close data) showed high correlations, by period, throughout the year. Not unexpectedly the regression coefficients ($\hat{B}$) indicated that the futures prices were more volatile than the respective cash indexes, by as much as 25 to 35 percent at the "tail" end of the bear market. Generally, the nearby contracts' prices appeared to be about 5 to 7 percent more volatile. And in 4 of the 15 regressions, the futures were less volatile than the respective cash indexes ($\hat{B}$ less than 1.0).

Other interesting aspects of the stock index futures contracts' price behavior in 1982 were the patterns of differentials that occurred at various stages of the bear and bull market moves. The differences among the prices of all three contracts narrowed from May to mid-August, and then widened throughout the remainder of the year. These differential price movements gave rise to spreading opportunities (short one contract, long another, intermarket), which in this context represent "reduced risk" speculative positions. Average weekly data indicated price spread changes ranging from -4.00 to -10.00 from May to August 13; these bear spreads would have yielded profits of $2000 to $5000. During the subsequent bull market phase of 1982, "bull" spreading could have resulted in profits of over $10,000 per position. However, the price movements were not evenly paced, and volatility "leadership" changed during the September–mid-November period. The timing of initiating and closing the positions would have been crucial elements in such trading strategies.

Finally, during 1982, open interest and especially volume increased at a record pace for these three contracts. At the year-end the CME-S & P contract was by far the dominant force, accounting for about 60 percent of both total volume for the year and open interest. The NYFE's share represented about 26–30 percent of the activity.

11 Summary and Synthesis

GRAINS AND COMMON STOCKS

Stock index futures have been viewed as vastly different from other futures contracts. The simple truth is just the contrary: They are very much like more familiar commodity futures. For holders of agricultural commodities, say grain merchants, the risk of an unhedged long position in the cash market is the possibility of a decline in the price of the commodity. That downside risk, of course, is offset by the possibility of "speculative" gain if the price of the commodity increases. For the unhedged investor in common stocks, the situation is obviously the same.

While the motivations for holding cash grain and common stocks may differ somewhat, the differences are in degree and not in kind. In most cases, cash grain is not viewed as a "capital asset" per se, a long term "investment," or a "wealth storage" vehicle. Those characteristics are frequently imputed to common stock holdings. When carefully analyzed, however, those characteristics simply describe a holding period horizon that is conceivably longer than one might usually infer for "commercial holders" of wheat. On the other hand, there are commercial holders of stocks (brokers-dealers), as well a "long term" holders (individual "investors" and institutions), just as there are in the case of U.S. Treasury Bonds and GNMAs. The time dimension differences among various "types" of asset holders is an insignificant distinction and illusory. For example, the holding periods for individual investors in common stocks, as shown in Appendix C, can be quite brief, in fact often less than a merchant might hold an inventory of grain.

Further, the "capital asset" nomenclature is not a meaningful distinction either, since it can be defined as a "title to future value"—which easily includes an inventory of grain as well as a share of common stock. Both wheat and common stocks have expected returns and risks attendant to holding them. The conceptual analogue applies in both cases under an inclusive theory of asset choice under uncertainty. The ability to hedge provides, in both cases, a means for achieving risk efficiency, as holders balance expected returns against the attendant risk exposure.

Richard Caves (1977–78) observed that the grain trade does not transform commodities *physically* (except by such ancillary services as cleaning, blending, and drying) but grain is changed in *value* by transforming it in *space* and *time*. Similarly, although the space dimension is not relevant, a holder of common stock realizes a change in value by carrying forward ownership in time. And just as a merchant attempts to earn a return on the spot commodity in excess of the costs of storage, so does an investor in common stocks attempt to realize a return in excess of the risk-free rate, the alternative "cost" inherent in any particular choice of stocks. In both cases, returns are realized (primarily) in the form of price appreciation of the cash market asset.

It is here that the "convenience yield" aspect of holding grain inventory is applicable in the context of a stock portfolio (see Appendix D). For grain the concept applies principally in terms of quantity, along with grade and location dimensions. In the grain trade, these are the variations which give rise to the greatest differential profits (i.e., from holding only futures grade and location inventories)—but also entail greater risk. The analogue to holding a "diversified" stock portfolio in terms of cash grain would be a position involving many different grades at a variety of locations, in the same way that an investor diversifies to reduce "nonsystematic risk."

Similarly, the opportunity for differential returns in the stock market inheres in holding specific stock issues as opposed to a general market surrogate, for example, an "index fund." This aspect for portfolios relates to the skewness dimension of return distributions (developed in Appendix C).

The nonstandard grade variations in common stocks are obviously the variety of issues available for "spot market" acquisition. Further, the past degree and nature of "off-standardness" of a given stock can be assessed in terms of market sensitivity, that is, relative beta values and degree of market dependency, R^2. Even at the level of individual securities, those relationships appear to have had some validity for short term prediction purposes. However, in both grains and stocks, past ("off-grade basis") relationships are not guaranteed to persist in the future.

For grains, the grade-quality variations from the standard futures grade are found in protein content, moisture content, degree of foreign material, damage, and so on. These variations give rise to a residual grade location "basis risk" which is unhedgeable, but which can also be substantial (see Appendix D).

At this point one can consider the use of an offsetting hedge position for a portfolio that is a "mirror image" of the futures contract's index base. That is, a so-called perfect hedge (i.e., a beta of 1.0 and an $R^2 \simeq 1.0$) in which gains of $X\%$ in the "indexed" portfolio would tend to be offset approximately by losses of $X\%$ in the futures market position, and vice versa. Any differences would be due to the time-dependent basis changes. Such a situation is exactly like the grain hedger who is exposed to only a similar "basis risk."

At the other extreme, a portfolio whose value was completely unrelated to the futures price variations would be of little relevance, since there would be no potential for risk reduction from hedging. The interesting cases are those which exist for R^2 between the extremes of 0 and 1.0. While well-diversified portfolios with respect to the futures index base will approach the 1.0 case (R^2), the evidence summarized in Appendix C suggests that well-diversified portfolios are not necessarily the rule, even for institutional investors. This aspect recognizes the limitations of the mean-variance criterion and that positive skewness of returns may be an appropriate property of risk-averse utility functions.

On the other hand, undiversified portfolios are subject to the vulnerability of returns to downside extremes. Under these circumstances, it would seem that a risk-adjustment alternative for hedging systematic variation would be a welcome addition to the alternatives now available to individuals and institutions holding common stocks.

To summarize, the risk components of a hedged position for grains and common stocks can be specified as follows. For grain, the variance of a hedged position would be the variance of the time-dependent basis of the futures grade *plus* the variance of the grade-location basis. For stocks, the variance of a hedged portfolio would be the variance of the time-dependent basis for a portfolio indexed to the futures contract's market indicator (index base) *plus* the variance of the actual portfolio held from that market index. In both cases, the total risk of an unhedged position can be reduced by selling a forward maturity of the relevant futures contract.

IN THE PUBLIC INTEREST

Stock index futures contracts fulfill a vital economic need. They provide a flexible financial instrument for protecting common stock portfolio values from the vagaries and fluctuations of the market as a whole. The public's exposure to that risk is substantial: on the order of $1.5 trillion.

These new futures contracts will not, of course, eliminate the risks of market fluctuations, but they do provide a means for *redistributing* those risks in a more economically optimal manner. Potential holders and traders of equities no longer have to be "polarized" in either high market risk or no market risk situations, the latter by remaining out of the stock market. Those investors who hold common stocks will no longer be forced into outright speculative positions, that is, holding an asset with no opportunity to hedge or reduce the risks. Stock index futures contracts allow investors to equilibrate their positions along the dimension of systematic uncertainty, and more closely achieve "risk efficiency." Nothing about these contracts impedes those who wish to continue to function as speculators in equities. These are free markets and participation is voluntary.

The implications for portfolio composition are substantial. In effect, what will eventually be created will be a "risk-adjusted" price for stocks. Particular issues that had been avoided previously by portfolio managers could now be included in appropriately hedged portfolios. The results of reducing "prudent" concentration in a limited number of stocks should provide a new market-determined realignment of relative stock prices and returns throughout the entire spectrum of equities. Finally, in this regard, portfolio managers will be able to "fine tune" their positions to the desired balance of yield, liquidity, and asset price variability.

From a wider perspective, stock index futures have the potential for dampening overall stock market behavior. A number of empirical studies on tangible commodities show that the introduction of futures trading is associated with a decrease in the volatility of "spot" or cash prices. The theoretical explanation is found in terms of efficient markets, as information and expectations are economically reflected in the profiles of the futures contracts' prices. Other studies of interest-rate futures characterize those markets as useful arenas for observing interest rate expectations. Stock index contracts are still in their infancy; those important overtones lie further in the future.

By reducing the risk of "short sellers," stock index contracts will help provide a cushion for downside movements of the cash market. The contracts can be used as substitutes for "stop-loss" orders for large blocks, when there is marginal uncertainty. Frequently, the large "stops" trigger other stops at slightly lower prices. With stock index futures contracts available to hedge against sudden market downturns, large scale liquidations should no longer be necessary to preserve, or just rescue, portfolio values. Zeckhauser has suggested that instability in the stock market has been attributable to the participation of individuals with expectations well out of the mainstream. The sets of forward prices will provide, at any time, a clear indication of how "the market" feels about the future course of the market. At times, this extant *price discovery* feature should be useful for economic decision makers, both public and private.

THE CAPITAL FORMATION ISSUE

The stock index futures contracts have frequently been attacked as possibly diverting funds from the capital formation process. In truth, just the opposite is the case. Hedging is an operation in risk management. In particular, hedging in both agricultural commodities and common stocks is timing optimization under uncertainty with assets of differing maturities. In particular, hedging behavior, appropriately viewed, emphasizes that cash market and futures positions are not undertaken independently. The implications for *real* capital formation relate to stock index futures contracts in this context of cash market positions and futures positions being intimately entwined.

First, hedging by underwriters should reduce the risks, and hence costs, of floating new stock issues in the capital markets. More important, however, is the effect of risk reduction on the prices of equities *relative* to other assets.

Why does a trader hedge? The customary answer is: to reduce the risk of having a position in the cash market. If carefully interpreted, this answer is not incorrect, but stated without qualification it is highly misleading. Its defect is the suggestion that the cash position is primary, and the offsetting futures position no more than an afterthought. In an important paper Professor Holbrook Working has emphasized, on the contrary, that traders will normally consider cash and futures transactions in coordination and that the decision to engage in the one kind cannot be independent of the decision to engage in the other. (Houthakker, 1959, p. 153)

For another link in this chain of reasoning, Cootner commented:

Thus, a merchant carrying unhedged stocks can generally improve his profitability by substituting hedged stocks for unhedged ones. This does not mean that the improvement takes place by simply hedging existing stocks. Basis changes are typically smaller than absolute price changes and entail less risk. What comparative advantage means in this case is that for a given level of risk, the merchant can earn more by holding inventories hedged than unhedged, but this may well mean holding a *much larger volume* of hedged inventory than he could hold unhedged. In fact, the evidence suggests that merchants do not hedge to reduce the absolute level of risk that they face but they hedge to increase their profits by being able to hold a *larger volume of* inventory. (Cootner, 1967, p. 76)

That is, with less risk attendant to holding stocks, in the aggregate, more investors will be willing to devote their funds to equities. As a result, the prices of stocks, relative to other alternative forms of holding wealth, should rise. How does this all tie into real capital formation?

Malkiel pointed out that the inducement for private investment depends on the relationship between the *market value* of a company and the replacement value of its assets (Tobin's q ratio).

If for example, assets are valued in the market at, say one and one-quarter times their replacement cost, corporations will be encouraged to invest in new equipment. On the other hand, if assets sell for less [market value] than their replacement value, corporations who sell new securities to buy new capital goods will be creating capital losses for their security holders. . . . Why invest in real capital assets? the corporate treasurer may say, when he can buy claims on these assets in the market place [i.e., through *mergers*] at 75 cents on the dollar. (Malkiel, 1979, p. 301)

The merger wave of early 1982 is evidence of this phenomenon. When the market value (via stock prices) of a company is considerably less than the cost of duplicating its assets, and a merger occurs, no *new* capital is formed. Its ownership is merely transferred to the new conglomerate. No new capital formation, no increase in potential supply, and no advances in productivity are *inflationary*.

On the other hand, if the market value of the company exceeds the (real asset) replacement cost, the corporate treasurer will be induced to undertake the purchase of new assets. The linchpin to this whole conundrum is the *market value of the company*. That is obviously a direct result of the price of its stock. Again, reducing the risks of holding stocks will increase their relative prices. *That* is where the impact on capital formation occurs.

To be sure, at the margin, an individual may choose to participate in the stock index futures markets, and not buy common stocks directly. But the compositional effects of creating a risk-transfer market should induce other investors to buy stocks, when they might otherwise have sought gold, paintings, or undeveloped land. Stock index futures contracts are *beneficial* and *not harmful* to the process of real capital formation.

Another criticism of stock index futures inheres in the cash settlement mechanism. Somehow, the critics assert, this changes the economic purpose of these contracts. As we have seen, cash settlement is just an efficient means for closing out open positions, after the last day of trading. True, it is not appropriate in every circumstance, but since physical delivery in agricultural markets is minimal, that innuendo is a "red herring" at best. Cash delivery eliminates the other problems that frequently plague futures contracts: the potential for manipulation and squeezes. What is it we said in the introduction? "A little knowledge. . . ."

In any event, the market knows better. The booming success in the first year of trading is unquestioned. As more investors become knowledgeable and can penetrate the shibboleths of the half-informed, the outlook for continued growth and useage of these instruments is rosy indeed. After four years of regulatory delay, at last stock index futures will be able to serve the wide variety of positive economic and public interest functions for which they are intended.

A More on Stock Indexes

Indexes have fascinated economists for decades. The technical difficulties of selecting the appropriate construction, weights, and base period have led to the perplexing theoretical and practical conundrum known as the *index-number problem*. However, Professor Gerschenkron tells us,

> Up to a point the index-number problem is not dissimilar to problems encountered in descriptive geometry. In either case, the attempt is to define an object by its projection; in either case, the result varies with the direction of the projection or the position of the observer. What is seen as a square in one perspective appears as a triangle in another. Index numbers of (for example) output are essentially projections of changes in physical quantities against the screens of weights. Beyond this, however, the geometric analogy fails. Unlike the case in geometry, the individual projections cannot be meaningfully combined to reveal the "true" shape of the object of study. Nor can we walk around the pyramid of output and measure its base and sides directly. This is so because the *aggregation* of output has no independent existence except in terms of the *individual* projections. (Gerschenkron, 1962, p. 250)

Any index, then, is ultimately a subjective entity. While there are some conventional, and generally acknowledged, desired properties of indexes, the precise form an index may take depends upon the decisions of the index's creator. As we have seen in Chapter 3, various stock market performance measures can differ with respect to construction and computation: (1) weighting (e.g., value-weighted, equal-weighted, or some other method); (2) composition (number and type of stocks in the index); and (3) calculation procedure (generally, either arithmetic or geometric averaging).

Numerous authors have been concerned about the structural differences among stock market indicators. For example, William Balch recounted a number of "shortcomings" in the popular indexes: for one, the Dow Jones Averages being implicitly weighted by the price level of component stocks. In addition, Balch also described the Dow Jones Industrial Average's (DJIA's) so-called splitting bias. Yet he concluded that the "Dow, if properly understood, is a fairly good measure of the market" (Balch, 1966).

With regard to value-weighted indexes (i.e., Standard & Poor's, S&P's, and the New York Stock Exchange, NYSE, indexes), Balch's concern focused on the disproportionate weight of the most heavily capitalized companies. On December 31, 1965, five stocks (AT&T, General Motors, Exxon, IBM, and Texaco) accounted for over 20 percent of the NYSE's total market value, as well as accounting for more than 30 percent of the weight in the S&P 425 Industrial Index. As of September 29, 1978, the top five stocks accounted for 20 percent of the S&P 500; the top 15 stocks (3 percent of 500) accounted for over 32 percent of the S&P 500 index weight. "One questions whether the remaining stocks are so relatively unimportant" (Balch, 1966).

Balch did champion the Value Line Composite Index (VLIC), calculated as a geometric average. "This method provides a distortion-free measure of percentage change in stock prices. It gives equal weight to the fluctuations in the prices of all stocks, regardless of price (level), or total market value" (Balch, 1966).

Cootner, on the other hand, did not agree. Granted that arithmetic averages suffer from an upward bias, he felt that the downward bias of the geometric averaging procedure was more objectionable. (Cootner, 1966) These issues, it seems clear, cannot be resolved (if at all) by appeal to rhetoric.

IMPLICIT PORTFOLIOS

Latane, Tuttle, and Young took a slightly more objective view: "Selection of the appropriate market average or index can be an important consideration if it is likely that *significantly* different results will be obtained from different computational procedures." In their view, market indexes could be thought of as portfolios of stocks (Latane et al., 1971, p. 75).

In addition, the "portfolio" interpretation of market indexes carried with it implications about internal reallocation among the component stocks.

For example, the DJIA, the S&P 500 Index, and the NYSE were considered as "buy-and-hold" portfolios, whereas the VLIC, due to its geometric averaging calculation, was classified as a "continuously reallocated" portfolio.

An intermediate case between buy-and-hold and continuous reallocation was that of "periodic reallocation." Examples of the latter were the United Press International (UPI) Market Indicator (now discontinued), which involved *daily* equal dollar reallocation; and the "Average Investment Performance Index" (AIPI), developed by Cohen and Fitch (1966), involving *annual* equal dollar reallocation. The AIPI is discussed below.

The interpretation of a geometric mean index as a "continuously reallocated" portfolio was given more rigorous treatment by Rothstein, and contrasted with periodic reallocation types of indexes (i.e., UPI, AIPI). *Periodic* reallocation, $U(t)$, "refers to a policy wherein all N securities are purchased in equal dollar amounts at time 0. At the end of each period $(t - 1, t)$, the portfolio is liquidated and the proceeds are reinvested instantaneously (at the latest prices, P_{it}) among N securities in equal dollar amounts" (Rothstein, 1972, p. 1984).

A geometrically averaged index, $V(t)$, also refers "to a policy wherein all N securities are purchased in equal dollar amounts at time 0. In this policy, however, it is imagined that the prices P_{it} are known at each instant of time and that the portfolio is *continuously* liquidated and reinvested in equal amounts" (Rothstein, 1972, p. 1985). The value of $U(t)$ is affected by the choice of the time interval between computations. On the other hand, $V(t)$ is *not* affected by the choice of this interval. Rothstein showed that both arithmetic and geometric averages were special cases of the power mean, and demonstrated the application to security indexes.

Extensive analyses, illustrated by numerical examples for the different "portfolio" interpretations of stock market indexes, appeared in Latane and Tuttle (1970, pp. 162–181) and in Latane et al. (1971, pp. 77–80). With regard to the geometric average (continuous reallocation interpretation), one conclusion of the authors was that such an average appears to be

sensitive to the distribution of price changes in the securities making up the index. If the distribution is very narrow (all price changes closely bunched), the geometric average of compounded price changes will closely approximate the arithmetic average; but if it is very wide, the geometric average will be substantially smaller than the arithmetic average (Latane et al., 1971, p. 80).

This latter observation stems from a mathematical proposition suggested in Yule and Kendall (1965, p. 150). If A represents the expected portfolio return (arithmetic mean) and S^2, the variance, then one approximation to the geometric mean, G, is as follows:

$$G^2 \simeq A^2 - S^2$$

For a given value of A, G becomes smaller as S (and S^2) increases. Other forms of the geometric mean approximations appeared in Young and Trent (1969).

Latane and his coauthors (1971) summarized and contrasted the different portfolio-reallocation interpretations as follows:

> In general, a periodic reallocation index reflects the potentially beneficial effects of diversification of the portfolio over time, by preventing the portfolio investment from becoming concentrated in a few securities, while a buy-and-hold index reflects the potentially beneficial effects of the divergence of two or more time series with different growth rates. The performance of the two policies is basically a function of: (1) differences in the price trends of individual stocks and (2) the variance and covariance of percentage price changes or price ratios in the component securities.
>
> If upward-trending stocks in a buy-and-hold index continue to perform that way *indefinitely,* the value of that type of index will ultimately be accounted for by those such stocks. On the other hand if the *random* element is the predominant factor in security price movements relative to sustained growth rates, the reallocation policy, which redistributes portfolio net worth each period to maintain a constant proportion invested in each stock, is superior (Latane, et al., 1971, p. 81).

In concluding their discussion about the "latent-portfolio" characteristics of existing stock market indexes, Latane and Tuttle take the following position:

> Just as one writer's cautions against the use of the Dow Jones Industrial Average may not be appropriate for an investor who buys and holds industrial blue chips (except that he reallocates when one of them splits), so another writer's warnings against the use of the Value Line Average may not be applicable to an investor who is constantly reassessing and restructuring his portfolio, selling off stocks that have gone up in price, and adding to those that have not.
>
> Rather than worry about all the warnings, the individual investor should choose the market performance measure that most nearly approximates his own portfolio strategy as his standard for comparison. (Latane and Tuttle, 1970, p. 191)

THE INVESTMENT PERFORMANCE APPROACH

At about the same time as King's, Balch's, and Cootner's studies (1966), other stock market index-construction analyses appeared in the literature. Lawrence Fisher presented an "investment performance index" to serve as a benchmark for the evaluation of any particular portfolio of stocks. His overall index consisted of all New York Stock Exchange common stocks (January 1926–December 1960). Fisher's construction included cash dividends and gave *equal weights* to the percentage change in the price of each stock. "The bench mark provided is one that, given the prices set by investors in the market place, assumes naive, random selection" (Fisher, 1966, p. 191).

Fisher formulated three index configurations: an arithmetic, geometric, and combination (weighted average of the arithmetic and geometric "link relatives"). Finding that the arithmetic index of price relatives possessed an upward bias exemplified by negative serial correlation, Fisher corrected for this problem by combining a geometric mean specification with the arithmetic mean.

Fisher compared his combination investment "link" index with the DJIA and the S&P Index, month-end values, 1926–1960. The Fisher combination link relative is denoted by L^*. The correlation coefficients from the regressions were as follows (Fisher, 1966, p. 207):

$$R(L^*, S\&P) = .9191$$
$$R(L^*, DJIA) = .9852$$
$$R(S\&P, DJIA) = .9754$$

The Average Investment Performance Index (AIPI) of Cohen and Fitch also appeared in 1966. The AIPI's purpose was to provide a benchmark against which any actual managed investment portfolio could be measured. The AIPI is the "expected (or average) percentage rate of return obtainable from investing in a randomly selected portfolio of stocks from the universe during a specified time period." This index is an arithmetic average performance of portfolios composed of equal dollar amounts of all N stocks in the universe. The AIPI included a periodic reallocation (in equal dollar amounts) at the beginning of each "investment performance period" (Cohen and Fitch, 1966, p. B-197).

Cohen and Fitch interpreted their index as an annually compounded, and therefore annually reallocated, measure. The UPI Market Indicator, linked to an April 1, 1966, base of 100, was an equivalent type of index but differed in that the reallocation occurred *daily*. The UPI market indicator was subsequently discontinued.

The AIPI was also contrasted to both the DJIA and the S&P indicators. Cohen and Fitch found that, using *first differences* (which emphasize price *movements* rather than price *levels*), the correlation of the AIPI and the S&P 425-Stock Industrial Index was .9861, and the AIPI-DJIA correlation was .9828.

INDEX WEIGHTING

The rationale for choosing any particular weighting scheme depends on the purpose of the index. Lorie and Hamilton suggested that an index should be value-weighted for *indicating changes* in the *aggregate market value* of stocks. Thus, "changes in general market value are more important for studies of relationships between stock prices and other things in the national economy" (Lorie and Hamilton, 1973, p. 55). Value-weighted indexes are also "macro-consistent" with the total aggregate value of stock holdings. As is well known, value-weighted indexes attach great importance to a relatively few large companies.

Equal-weighted indexes, on the other hand, are "more appropriate for indicating movements in the prices of typical or average stocks," and "are better indicators of the *expected* change in prices of stocks selected at random" (Lorie and Hamilton, 1973, p. 55).

Although long-run movements are similar, indexes may differ *markedly over short periods of time*. This is reflected both in turning points and volatility. On one occasion, there was a significant difference in the turning points of the market as a whole as measured by a comprehensive equal-weighted index and the Dow Jones Averages or Standard & Poor's Indexes. In 1929, the equal-weighted index reached its peak six months before the month-end peak in the other two. This suggests that the prices of stocks in relatively small companies turned down before the prices of stocks in large companies. In this instance at least, the use of the index giving greater weight to small companies could have had enormous value. The equal-weighted index also reached its trough in 1932, one month before either of the other two indexes. All other turning points occurred in the same month. (Lorie and Hamilton, 1973, p. 68)

With regard to the use of stock market indicators as a yardstick for portfolio performance, Latane and Tuttle have also suggested that a value-weighted construction is not necessarily appropriate.

> Questions have been raised from time to time as to how rational it is to compare portfolio performance with value-weighted measures. It has been argued that investors do not consciously attempt to invest in an individual stock in an amount proportionate to its aggregate market value relative to that of all other stocks in the portfolio. They would be more likely to distribute their net worth in approximately equal dollar amounts in industries with highly favorable expected returns relative to expected risk. . . . But they would not concentrate their investments in IBM, AT&T, GM, and Jersey Standard simply because these stocks have large common stock capitalizations. (Latane and Tuttle, 1970, p. 170)

Similarly, Fisher's comments about index weighting are worth noting:

> Although holders of common stocks as a whole (including corporations whose own stocks are listed) must have their holdings distributed proportionally to the market value of all shares outstanding, there is no need for any particular investor to distribute his own holdings in this manner or any reason to believe that those shares in existing portfolios that were acquired during any particular period of time are so distributed. . . . In the indexes presented here a given relative change in the price of one stock has the same effect on the index as an equal relative change in the price of any other common stock on the New York Stock Exchange. Thus an increase of 10 per cent in the price of the stock of any company has an effect on the index that is independent of either the size of the company that issued the stock or the absolute price of the stock.
>   This is the method of allocation in our previously published studies. Its justification may be summarized by pointing out that the individual investor may allocate his resources any way he pleases. If the resources used to own common stock listed on the New York Stock Exchange were distributed at random among the stocks by the individual investor, the number of dollars' worth of each stock held would be expected to be equal independent of the number of shares a company had outstanding or of the price of each share. (Fisher, 1966, p. 195)

Finally, in this regard, Bogue's approach to quantifying "the market return" is also instructive, Throughout his thesis:

The *equally weighted average return* of all common stocks listed on the New York Stock Exchange has been taken as the return on the market. This, of course, represents only a *surrogate for the true market return*. For there are many securities not listed on the New York Exchange, and there are other assets available to investors not represented by any securities, certain real estate for example. Furthermore, in the true market portfolio securities are weighted in proportion to their total value outstanding. However, it has been repeatedly shown that all extremely well diversified portfolios are very highly correlated and represent a good surrogate for the market. (Bogue, 1973, p. 168, emphasis added)

(Interestingly, Bogue's thesis advisers at Standford, 1973, were William F. Sharpe, William H. Beaver, and Paul H. Cootner.)

NORMATIVE ASPECTS OF EQUAL WEIGHTING

Approaching this issue from another direction, Latane and Tuttle explicitly confronted the question of the optimal weighting aspect in the context of portfolio building. Three portfolio allocation policies were tested: (1) where the portfolio was equally allocated among n stocks, with w_i being the proportion of the portfolio invested in stock i, $n = 4, 8, 16$, and 32 (number of stocks in the portfolios), and

$$w_i = \frac{l}{n}$$

(2) where the relative weights w_i were determined so that *total* portfolio risk (SD) was minimized, that is,

$$w_i = \frac{1/SD_i}{\Sigma(1/SD_i)}$$

where SD_i was the standard deviation of stock i's holding period returns; and (3) where the w_i were chosen to minimize *residual* portfolio risk, that is,

$$w_i = \frac{1/DS_i}{\Sigma(1/DS_i)}$$

where DS_i was the standard error for security i's holding period returns regressed on the market index.

Alternatives (2) and (3) also affected the expected value of the portfolio returns as well as the risk, and thus the portfolios were comparable only within a given size class ($n = 4, 8, \ldots$).

It was found that *equal allocation* gave the best results, on average, for the various portfolio size classes.

> This means that minimizing the portfolio risk and residual risk also led to a disproportionate reduction in the portfolio mean return. . . . The reduction in variance through the use of the min SD and min DS led to higher long-run returns for all portfolios selected on the basis of expected value. But with this exception, the method of equal *allocation proved superior.* (Latane and Tuttle, 1970, pp. 704–705)

B The Capital Asset Pricing Model: Estimating Systematic Risk

QUANTIFYING THE MARKET FACTOR

The discussion in Chapter 4 indicated that the *market factor* and *market portfolio* are different theoretical concepts. Strictly speaking, the "return on the market portfolio" of the capital asset pricing model (CAPM) refers to an "all wealth" perspective. Indeed, some investigators have found evidence of market imperfections, or perhaps institutional segmentations, which have persisted over significantly long periods of time, with respect to the risks and returns of common stocks vis-à-vis both government and corporate bonds (Sarnat, 1974). This result also seems to account for the observed differences in the "market price of risk" among various asset types reported by Friend and Blume (1975). Even within the narrower context of stocks only, the market factor and market portfolio remain two different and distinct concepts, as demonstrated by Fama (1971).

In this regard, King's approach to the (normative) design of an index number of security prices is enlightening:

> Most of the discussion of the adequacy and appropriateness of such measures has been in terms of a problem in *descriptive statistics,* i.e., the construction of a number that will summarize the cross-section of prices or price changes and enable us somehow to see at a glance what is going on

within the market. . . . Few builders of index numbers have explicitly viewed these measures as functions on a set of jointly distributed random variables, making possible the *contemplation of a statistical distribution* for the index number itself. . . . Implicit in this proposed correlation study is the isolation of a market-wide impact on price changes and the estimation of the loadings of that effect in the changes for the various securities. If one is interested in an index of price change that shows what the market as a whole is doing, then a good index would be one that is highly correlated with that part of the changes in anticipation that is felt throughout the market; and it should be relatively *insensitive* to the noise resulting from news that is pertinent only to *individual* firms. (King, 1966, p. 143)

Further, King commented on the design of such an optimal index number:

One should aim for an index number or average that is maximally correlated with the part of each security's movement that results from a market-wide change. Furthermore, it would be undesirable to allow securities with large components of unique variance to carry much weight in the index. (King, 1966, p. 161)

With regard to isolating this "market-wide" impact statistically, Pettit and Westerfield hypothesized that there may in fact be more than *one* market factor. If a security's price represents the discounted future stream of expected earnings, "Two market-wide factors will determine asset returns; namely, an earnings factor and a capitalization rate factor" (Pettit and Westerfield, 1974, p. 590). The beta coefficient, β_i, can then be seen as a weighted average of the security's earnings beta, b_{ei}, and the respective capitalization rate beta, b_{ci}, or

$$\beta_i = xb_{ei} + (1 - x) b_{ci}.$$

King's model specified that the first difference in the logarithm of a stock's price change was functionally related as a linear combination of factors. The basic random variable for the security, j, was defined as

$$Y_{jt} = \log \frac{\text{price}_{jt}}{\text{price}_{jt-1}} = \log(P_{jt}) - \log(P_{jt-1})$$

that is, "the first difference in the logarithm of the price of security j, observed at time t" (King, 1966, pp. 143–144). Using the Guttman-Harris method of factor analysis, his methodology provided a view such that each change in log price consisted of two main parts, a *common* part of the covariance matrix, and a *unique* one. This quantification led to an estimated market factor expressed as a column of normalized eigenvectors.

King found a high degree of correlation between his series and the log-transformed S&P 90/500 series: the lowest value being .9072 for the fourth subperiod of August 1952–December 1960. His analysis showed

> how it is possible to estimate the market factor and employ this quantity as an indicator of the direction and magnitude of change in log price that affects *all securities* to some degree. . . . Although our conclusions are only tentative, it appears that a large number of stocks is unnecessary for an index of market change *if* one can weight the component stocks according to their association with the appropriate factor or factors that we choose to call the market. (King, 1966, p. 167)

Extensive empirical testing of the CAPM has resulted in a wide variety of comments and qualifications. Most obvious is the fact that the model is postulated in *ex ante* terms, but the data available for testing are *ex post*. There remains the question regarding the use of *ex post* returns and dispersions to represent *ex ante* expectations (cf. Friend and Blume, 1970). Other aspects that have been investigated, qualified, attacked and defended, include: (1) the assumption regarding the equality of the borrowing and lending rate (the "riskless asset" with return Y_f); (2) the bias caused by the lack of a viable short-selling alternative; (3) the distortion resulting from constraints on the number of securities that can be held by an investor; (4) the various conditions under which Y_i as a one-parameter measure can replace the two dimensions of mean and variance; and (5) the homogeneity of and specification of investors' utility functions. An exhaustive journey into the various controversies is well beyond the scope of this brief survey. Nonetheless, some of the major strands have important implications and are mentioned in passing. (The interested reader can pursue numerous other sources, many of which are listed in the references at the end of the book.)

One of the most sensitive assumptions empirically relates to the market horizon problem. This assumption states that all investors have identical planning horizons over which all parameters are measured.

> In such a market, trading would occur only at the beginning and end of each planning period. But in reality trading takes place almost continuously

in security markets. What then is the relevant holding period over which the market parameters should be measured and what effect does the use of some other holding period have? . . .

The market horizon interval in an active, continuous auction market is likely to be quite short (less than a trading day). In a perfect continuous market, void of transactions and evaluation costs, the horizon would be instantaneous, since nothing would prevent investors from having instantaneous planning horizons. The introduction of market costs makes it impractical for investors to evaluate and revise their portfolios instantaneously. However, if a sufficient number of investors are making portfolio decisions at every instant, then one might suspect that the market would behave as though it had an instantaneous (or quite short) horizon interval. (Bogue, 1973, pp. 15–17)

Michael Jensen, in his landmark study of mutual fund performance, noted that it was the lack of a well-developed multiperiod theory of choice under uncertainty that has resulted in the single period investment horizon formulation (Jensen, 1969, p. 171). Also, recognizing that the conditions of perfect liquidity (i.e., zero transactions costs) were not met in the real world, Jensen postulated that "at every instant of time a large number of investors are making portfolio decisions and trading in the market." If the market is to be in equilibrium at each instant, the resulting "market horizon" is instantaneous. Under these conditions, it is appropriate to measure investment relatives in logarithmic form (Jensen, 1969, p. 188).

In addition to King (1966) and Jensen (1969), Klemkowsky and Martin (1975) also measured asset returns in logarithmic form. They employed that particular specification "to approximate monthly percentage price changes in an attempt to improve the normality of the price changes and to approximate monthly prices under continuous compounding" (Klemkowsky and Martin, 1975, p. 149).

Latane has advocated the related geometric mean (i.e., the average of logarithms) as a rational criterion for choice among risky ventures. In the context of Markowitz's mean-variance-expected utility framework for portfolio selection, Latane has shown that the portfolio having the greatest probability of being more valuable than any other specified portfolio at the end of n periods is also the portfolio having a probability distribution of returns with the largest *geometric* mean (cf. Latane and Tuttle, 1970). Young and Trent (1969, p. 186) note that the geometric mean criterion specifies the same "types of investor risks" for variance and absolute skewness, as shown elsewhere, using the principle of expected utility maximization of a type of function that is solely dependent on the sum of wealth and income. They also note that the geometric mean shows that absolute kurtosis is important. The significance of these higher distributional moments (e.g., skewness and kurtosis) are pursued in Appendix C.

ESTIMATING SYSTEMATIC RISK

By far, simple regression techniques have had the widest application in estimating CAPM specifications. Arguments against ordinary least squares

center on its inapplicability because (1) security systematic risk is not constant over time and (2) the distributions of security returns appear to have infinite variances. Objections on the second point have been considered, and investigations have shown that regression estimates are appropriate even if the underlying distributions of security returns have infinite variances (Bogue, 1973, p. 20).

Such regression estimates are subject, of course, to all the classical measurement error problems and in particular the errors-in-variables problem. Bogue found, however, that inclusion of the riskless rate was not important. "Whether returns are stated in excess of the measured riskless rate or not, apparently has little if any effect on the resulting risk (Beta) estimates" (p. 105). Correlation between the differently specified estimators of systematic risk was found to be "virtually perfect."

It should therefore be unnecessary for most uses to calculate the least-square regression estimates with return stated in excess of the riskless rate, thus alleviating the need for its collection.

Though certainly having more effect than the riskless rate assumption, the inclusion or omission of dividends in calculation of the returns also makes little difference in the resulting estimates. And least-square estimation of both systematic and unsystematic risk from price appreciation data only should also be sufficient for most any purpose, alleviating the collection of dividend data. Of the three variations the assumed length of the market horizon period has the most effect on the resulting estimates (Bogue, 1973, p. 122).

With regard to the choice of estimators, some evaluation criterion must be chosen:

"In general, estimators are evaluated in terms of the size of their estimation error, with mean-squared error often taken as an inverse measure of goodness. For systematic risk estimates this *error is never directly determinable,* since the *true value is never observable,* even later. Measurement of the estimation error can only be accomplished in some indirect manner. Moreover, it is not always true that evaluation by the size of the mean-squared estimation error is appropriate, since this approach implicitly assumes that the appropriate loss function is quadratic. It depends on the use to which the estimates are being put. Systematic risk estimates are useful basically in decisions concerned with evaluation of past estimation of future portfolio performance. A useful criterion must take into account the decisions being made" (Bogue, 1973, p. 114, emphasis added).

Bogue found that the fluctuation of systematic risk over time behaves approximately as a first order autoregressive process. When the capital structure remains fixed, the process constants are related to the firm's real asset depletion rate, growth rate, and capital budgeting policies:

Since major capital structure changes occur rarely and somewhat randomly, actual firm systematic risk should approximate a first order autoregressive process in its dynamics. The tendency of systematic risk estimates to revert toward their mean, noted by Blume, is completely consistent with autoregressive behavior. But such results are inconsistent with the limiting case of random walk behavior. The suggestion by Fisher (1970) that firm systematic risk follows a random walk must therefore be rejected. Instead, it must be that the behavior is governed by some other process. The individual security tests, tend to confirm that the process is first order autoregressive as the theoretical investigations suggest. But the discriminatory power of the tests conducted was relatively weak. Although the first order autoregressive model derived theoretically was found to be consistent with observed results, its parameterization proved to be extremely difficult (Bogue, 1973, pp. 164–165).

Bogue's empirical estimates suggested that systematic risk changes slowly. According to his autoregressive model's parameters, it reverts toward its long run average somewhere on the order of 1–2 percent per month for a security. (Bogue, 1973, p. 143).

To the extent that stock market movements reflect anticipations about general economic conditions, the link to increased profitability in expansions, and increased risk of insolvency or bankruptcy in recessions through each firm's systematic risk (beta coefficient) should be quite clear. Bowman's model (1979) incorporated a clear connection of beta to the firm's capital structure.

THE ECONOMETRICS: SUMMARY

Various regression problems inherent in estimating the parameters of the linear CAPM specification have been alluded to in the preceding discussion. The significance of these statistical difficulties is that estimators ($\hat{\beta}$) of beta (β) must be interpreted with some caution. The extent and implications of these problems are summarized below.

First, the true "market factor" (μ) is never observable, even later. The use of the "return on the market portfolio" (Y_m) introduces a proxy variable, with all of the accompanying errors-in-variables complications. This consideration relates to the choice of an appropriate index regressor for the CAPM. One of the regression models typically specified is of the following form:

$$Y_j = A_j + B_j M + u_j$$

where Y_j is the return on security j, M is a market indicator, and A_j and B_j are estimated coefficients, and A_j is the "non-systematic" return of j.

The required "spherical" assumptions about the error term, u_j, include the condition that $E(M, u_j) = 0$. Jensen noted that, when M is represented by an average of security returns or as returns on the "market portfolio," an overspecification results. "That is, if M is some average of security returns, then the assumption that u_j is uncorrelated with M cannot hold, since M contains u_j" (Jensen, 1969, p. 179). Most empirical investigators have consequently employed equal-weighted index regressors to minimize this misspecification.

On the other hand, if M is a value-weighted market indicator, the Y_j's comprising significant weights in M (e.g., IBM, AT&T, and GM) will generate biased estimates of B_j, since in such instances Y_j would be a substantial portion of the variables on *both sides of the equation*. The application of ordinary least squares yields biased and inconsistent estimates of alpha and beta, for individual securities.

Second, the error components do not "average out" in calculating portfolio risk levels. It has been shown that, when portfolios are formed on the basis of estimated security beta coefficients, portfolio betas ("risk levels") contain a systematic bias, "Even if the estimation functions for the individual securities are unbiased." It should be added that "Bias alone, of course, does not invalidate an estimator." But appropriate caveats should accompany such estimates. (Frankfurter et al., 1974, p. 412).

Third, the econometric problems are compounded when both errors in variables and autocorrelated disturbance terms are present. Scott and Brown showed that under these conditions application of ordinary least squares produces instable and biased estimates of beta. More important, the instability can be observed in the regression coefficients "Even if the *true* Betas are *constant* over time (Scott and Brown, 1980, p. 55, emphasis added).

C Investment Behavior in Common Stocks: Beyond the Mean-Variance Criterion

PATTERNS OF STOCK OWNERSHIP

Although somewhat dated, one of the more recent published analyses of stock ownership patterns is that of Blume et al. (1974). Contrary to the assumptions of the capital asset pricing model (CAPM), the authors found that in tax year 1971 individuals held highly undiversified portfolios. Imputations were made for 17,056 individual income tax returns on the basis of cash dividends reported. The findings were that 34 percent of the individuals held only one such stock; 50 percent held no more than two different stocks, and only about 11 percent held more than ten stocks (cf. Levy, 1978).

The authors stated the following:

> In 1971, a surprisingly high proportion of the portfolios held by individuals was dominated by a very small number of issues; thus, the portfolios were not well diversified. This finding applies to all income groups. Since there is ample evidence that investors are risk-averse, the lack of *effective diversification* strongly suggests that two of the basic assumptions typically made in capital asset pricing theory cannot both be valid: namely, that investors measure risk by the volatility of the rate of return on the entire portfolio, and that investors hold homogeneous expectations about rates of return and risk. The lack of effective diversification also has important social

implications since, in a major downturn in the stock market, a *high pro-portion of investors will do very much worse than the market.* Thus, since early last year (1973–4), when the market value of NYSE stock as a whole dropped nearly 40 percent from its high point, millions of investors—including many with moderate means—must have experienced catastrophic losses. (Blume et al., 1974, pp. 17–18)

In general, Blume et al. found that lower income groups tended to hold somewhat less risky stock than did upper income groups. In terms of employment status, managers tended to hold the riskier stock, and retired individuals the least risky stock (p. 17). Sharpe and Cooper have also suggested that corporate officers do not, and perhaps cannot, hold well-diversified portfolios (Sharpe and Cooper, p. 52).

Why do individuals hold undiversified portfolios? Blume et al. offer a number of explanations:

One reason why a person might hold an undiversified portfolio is to be able to realize *the potential returns from superior security analysis.* (In this connection, it might be noted that there is no evidence that any substantial group of investors, except for exchange specialists and, to some extent, corporate insiders, has outperformed the market consistently over long periods of time.) A second reason is that an individual may have a large *holding in a particular security in order to maintain effective control over the company.* A third reason is that, over time, the one or two securities with the highest returns will tend to dominate a portfolio if, because of tax considerations or other reasons, no adjustments are made. A fourth reason is that some investors do not understand the principles of diversification; therefore, the standard deviation of returns on a portfolio is not the appropriate measure of risk in explaining their behavior. The explanation for such poorly diversified portfolios must await further research. (Blume et al., 1974, p. 32, emphasis added)

In a later paper, Blume and Friend explored the utility function implications of undiversified portfolio holdings. Using a measure of the sum of squared deviations from the market portfolio, they found that only 5.2 percent of the tax forms filed had values less than 0.14—"roughly consistent with the level of diversification achieved in an equally weighted portfolio of seven securities." Further testing led the authors to conclude that "at all levels of adjusted gross income, a substantial number of portfolios appear to be highly undiversified (Blume and Friend, 1975, p. 586).

Additional evidence on this matter appeared in Cohn et al. The authors commented that while "*theories* of portfolio selection have been developed, very little is known about how individuals *actually* go about constructing their asset portfolios" (Cohn et al., 1975, p. 605). The data for their analysis was obtained from a mail questionnaire survey of customers (2506 accounts) of a large nation-wide retail brokerage firm. In particular, the study investigated the effect of wealth on the proportions of individual portfolios allocated to risky assets. Employing a variety of econometric tests, the authors concluded that the data suggested a strong pattern of (decreasing relative) risk aversion. As wealth increases, "A higher proportion of the total is committed by the individual involved to risky assets" (Cohn et al., 1975, p. 618).

Some qualifications, however, were mentioned. First, risky human wealth was omitted from the analysis. Second, the tests presented were cross-sectional; that is, the data reflected wealth differences among individuals rather than wealth *changes* for the same individual. Third, "The capital gains tax may serve to lock individuals into (risky) assets which have appreciated in value, thereby imposing some constraints on portfolio design" (Cohn et al., 1975, p. 618).

In a later study, Schlarbaum et al. employed a longitudinal analysis, based upon the same sample data described above. This particular effort was intended to provide some "hard empirical data" on individual-investor portfolio experiences. The analysis focused on an actual securities transactions history of some 2500 individual brokerage house customers during the period January 1964–December 1970. Rates of return realized by that group from direct investments in common stocks—both before and after transactions costs—were constrasted with those that could have been attained "By investing instead in several broadbased market portfolios or a representative collection of mutual funds, as performance benchmarks" (Schlarbaum et al., 1978, p. 300).

With regard to holding periods, trading pattern data suggested a mean investment cycle duration of approximately $8\frac{1}{2}$ months and a median of 4 months, both surprisingly short. Whether this particular finding has broad generality must be questioned, as the authors did, recognizing that external market conditions can be expected to have an influence on holding periods. However, they concluded that the market movements during the six–seven years investigated were cyclical, "But not severely so, around a moderate uptrend," and therefore fairly representative of the era (Schlarbaum et al., 1978, pp. 305–306).

In addition, a broad range of trading styles among investors was evident: the most active 10 percent accounted for 57 percent of all the round trips, and less than 1 percent of the total came from the least active 10 percent. In terms of "position days," the degree of concentration was less pronounced, but nonetheless substantial heterogeneity was apparent.

With regard to performance, by "annualizing" short term returns, the authors calculated a mean rate of return of 9.9 percent before transactions costs, and 5.5 percent after those costs were taken into account. Distributional data indicated the highest percentage returns in the 0–30 day category (122 percent), which returns declined *pari passu* with the length of holding period to 6.1 percent for durations over one year.

Casting these results into a relative benchmark context, the authors compared the investment experience of the sampled individual accounts with a number of different market measures and indexes of mutual fund types.

> While the findings—perhaps not surprisingly—admit of some discretion in interpretation, they portray a reasonably favorable picture of the security-selection abilities of the individual investor. In the aggregate, pretransactions-costs rates of return better than those available from most passive investment strategies were realized by the sample. (Schlarbaum et al., 1978, p. 300).

However, the most favorable results tended to be concentrated in the short duration cycle of holding periods. Another observation was:

> The observed round trips took place, on balance, at times of marginally less favorable market moves than the 7 year average. The performance of the investor sample, therefore, does not seem to be attributable to any skill in *investment timing*, but instead to skill in individual security selection (Schlarbaum et al., 1978, p. 315).

One explanation offered in view of this fact was that individuals may be able "to engage in prompt trading responses to many temporary securities price disequilibria immediately, and on average to turn a profit before they disappear, whereas large-bloc institutional trading pursuit of the same discrepancies would be self-defeating" (Schlarbaum et al., 1978, p. 322).

INSTITUTIONAL INVESTMENT PERFORMANCE

The landmark study of mutual fund performance appeared in the *Journal of Business*. Michael Jensen, drawing upon a number of theoretical and empirical aspects of the Sharpe-Lintner model of capital asset pricing, developed a methodology for evaluating the performance of risky-asset portfolios. Jensen presented a model that explicitly allowed for the effects of differential degrees of "risk" on the returns of portfolios.

> A measure of portfolio performance was defined as the difference between the actual returns on a portfolio in any particular holding period and the expected returns on that portfolio conditional on the riskless rate, its level of systematic risk, and the actual returns on the market portfolio (Jensen, 1969, p. 241).

Jensen further established criteria for judging neutral, superior, or inferior portfolio performance.

On the basis of his model and its empirical results for 115 funds, Jensen concluded that on the average the mutual funds provided investors with inferior and inefficient portfolios (pp. 242–243).

> Thus, on the basis of these results (net and gross), we conclude that in the ten year period 1955–64 mutual fund managers in general showed no evidence of an ability to predict the future performance of securities. That is, they did not as a whole show evidence of superior analytical or forecasting ability in spite of the considerable resources devoted to these activities. (Jensen, 1969, pp. 228–229).

Subsequent articles have taken some exception to Jensen's rather strong conclusions. Mains, for example, seemed to find that Jensen's principal empirical results were biased due to an understatement of the mutual fund rates of return and an overstatement of systematic risk levels (Mains, 1977, pp. 382–384). He concluded that "Rather than being 'inferior' performers on a net return basis, the mutual funds were approximately neutral performers" (p. 384).

In a more recent study, Kon and Jen pointed out that the condition of *stationary* systematic risk may be in direct conflict with the notion of a "managed" portfolio. "If a manager can make better-than-average forecasts of future realizations on market factors, he is expected to adjust portfolio risk in anticipation of market changes. The level of systematic risk can be changed substantially in either direction by altering the proportions of high- and low-risk securities in the portfolio (Kon and Jen, 1979, p. 264).

The authors formulated an econometric model to explicitly distinguish between an investment manager's portfolio activity: when the focus was on forecasting the prices of individual securities and when forecasting future realizations on market factors. Their investment performance model provided separable measures of timing and selectivity. "The methodology is essentially the Quandt switching regression model with an identifiability condition. Simulation results permit confidence in the methodology" (Kon and Jen, 1979, p. 287).

Tests of the model's specification on a sample of 49 mutual funds indicated that for many individual funds it was more likely that the data were generated by a mixture of two or three regression equations than by that of the standard linear model. Given a specification for each fund, determined by the likelihood-ratio test, the null hypothesis of risk level stationarity was rejected for many individual funds. The null hypotheses of constant selectivity performance or constant portfolio diversification strategies were also rejected for many individual funds.

> We provide evidence that is not inconsistent with the joint hypothesis that the Black (1972b) model is empirically valid and that mutual fund managers individually and on average are unable to consistently forecast the future prices on individual securities well enough to recover their research expenses, management fees, and commission expenses. (Kon and Jen, 1979, p. 288).

Most historical studies of managed portfolio performance, because of data availability, have been directed at mutual funds. However, with more comprehensive data, Bogle and Twardowski (1980) compared the investment performance of banks, investment counselors, insurance companies, and mutual funds. The authors found that mutual funds rather consistently outperformed the other three categories, during the 1968–1977 period.

Although their analysis was highly aggregative, some of their findings remain of interest. One, for example, was the heavier relative concentration of bank-administered portfolios in large capitalized companies, an approach that the authors termed "index oriented." Mutual fund holdings, on the other hand, were reported to be considerably less concentrated in such stocks.

Other aspects of their analysis raised—but left unanswered—a number of issues. For one, Bogle and Twardowski, seemed unable to explain the superior performance of mutual funds for the entire period in terms of a comparison with the Value Line Composite Index (VLIC). This lack of year-to-year correspondence led them to reject the position that "mutual fund results were due solely to a concentration in secondary stocks" (p. 37). This conclusion may or may not have been true, but it abstracted from the possibility of differing investment policies over the period. In fact, the authors seemed to be in search of some decade-long generalizations to explain the observed differences in performance.

The results of Kon and Jen (1979), cited above, indicated investment policy variability—both within a given fund over time, and among funds. Beyond that, not very much is known about the switching activities and policies of mutual funds or other institutional investors.

Bogle and Twardowski also recognized the degree of variation buried in the broad aggregates. For example, they distinguish among fund objectives ("growth" vs. "growth and income") as well as size:

> The smaller mutual funds diversified well beyond the largest stocks, and it is possible that a part of their superiority may be accounted for by use of this greater flexibility in the investment selection and supervision process—i.e., by more imaginative portfolio management. (Bogle and Twardowski, 1980, p. 38)

The authors also underscored the *ex ante* nature of capital asset pricing theory:

> The 10-year period of this study covers a rather unusual period in stock market history, in that the absolute returns of the equity markets were generally less than the risk-free rate of return, with the S&P 500 having a 10-year compound rate of return of 3.6 per cent, compared with 5.8 per cent for Treasury bills. Thus a portfolio with a risk level lower than the market's (resulting, for example, from holding a significant cash position) would have outperformed most equity portfolios. Do differences in the risk levels assumed by the various manager classes provide an explanation for some of the divergence in performance? (Bogle and Twardowski, 1980, p. 39).

The mean betas for the institutional groups, however, appeared to be in the "wrong" direction. Bogle and Twardowski concluded that the differing risk levels did not satisfactorily explain the observed performance differentials. The inability to account for mutual fund superiority in terms of market-related risk remained a significant puzzle. As developed below, however, it may be that beta levels are poor proxy measures for other relevant dimensions of portfolio behavior.

BEYOND THE MEAN-VARIANCE CRITERION

Investment decisions, or portfolio selection, can be regarded "As choices among alternative probability distributions of returns, where the optimal choice is determined by maximization of the expected value of an investor's utility function" (Hanoch and Levy, 1970, p. 181). Modern portfolio theory has been developed solely in terms of the first two moments of investment return distributions. It is well known that the only mathematical form of a utility function applicable to just the mean and variance parameters of a distribution is of the quadratic, or second order form:

$$U(X) = a + bx + cx^2.$$

Arrow, among many others, has shown that this particular functional form is unacceptable since it violates certain risk aversion principles and implies negative marginal utility of wealth (X) for some values of X (Arrow, 1971, pp. 97–98). The only other conditions where the mean and variance parameters apply would be if investment returns were normally distributed. However, it is has been demonstrated a number of times that such normality conditions do not hold either (see, for example, Fama and Roll, 1968).

Recognition of these theoretical and empirical limitations of the mean-variance criterion has led a number of investigators to search elsewhere for explanations of observed investment behavior. "In the real world, investors' utility functions and investment probability distributions may assume highly complex or irregular forms" (Hanoch and Levy, 1970, p. 181). In general, if the utility function can be expressed as an nth degree polynomial, then the first n moments of the probability distribution are relevant (Hadar and Russell, 1969, p. 25). That is, if $U(X)$ is a third degree polynomial ("cubic utility"), then, in addition to the mean and variance (the first two distributional moments), the third moment, skewness, must also be considered. A fourth degree polynomial function would involve consideration of kurtosis (the fourth moment) as well.

Tsiang (1972) mentioned, however, that polynomials are generally not suitable functions for the utility of wealth, since they do not exhibit reasonable risk-aversion properties as suggested by Arrow. Utility functions that are better behaved with respect to the desired conditions are the negative exponential functions, for example, $U(X) = B(1 - e^{-ax})$, the family of constant elasticity functions, and the logarithmic utility function (cf., especially, Rubinstein, 1977).

These nonpolynomials can generally be expanded into a Taylor's series. Using the negative exponential function, Tsiang showed that for most practical purposes terms with higher moments than the third or fourth may safely be neglected. Further, he demonstrated:

> [The influence of skewness (the third moment)] on the expected utility is positive. That is to say, a positive skewness of the distribution is a desirable feature, and, other things being equal, a greater skewness would increase the expected utility. This is not a result peculiar to the assumption of a negative exponential utility function, but may be shown to be a general pattern of behavior towards uncertainty on the part of all risk-avert individuals with decreasing or constant absolute risk-aversion with respect to increases in wealth. . . .
>
> Thus if we regard the phenomenon of increasing absolute risk aversion as absurd, we must acknowledge that a normal risk-avert individual would have a preference for skewness, in addition to an aversion to dispersion (variance) of the probability distribution of returns. It is interesting to note that Harry Markowitz once remarked that "the third moment of the probability distribution of returns from the portfolio may be connected with a propensity to gamble." Nevertheless, as we have shown above, skewness preference is certainly not necessarily a mark of an inveterate gambler, but a common trait of a risk-avert person with decreasing or constant absolute risk-aversion. I cannot, therefore, go along with Markowitz in taking the view that since gambling is to be avoided, the third moment need not be considered in portfolio analysis. . . .
>
> Anyway, skewness preference must be a fairly prevalent pattern of investor's behavior, for modern financial institutions provide a number of devices for investors to increase the positive skewness of the returns of their investments, for example, the organization of limited liability joint stock companies, prearranged stop-loss sales on the stock and commodity markets, puts and calls in stocks, etc., which otherwise would perhaps not have been developed. (Tsiang, 1972, pp. 358–360)

A more extended journal into the analytics of utility functions, other candidate forms, and their implicit risk aversion properties are not appropriate here. The interested reader is again directed to the references (e.g., Arrow, 1971; Friend and Blume, 1975; Rubinstein, 1977; Tsaing, 1972).

The concept of return distribution skewness has also been applied to the assessment of mutual fund behavior. Simonson noted a concern about the "speculative investment policies," attributed to fund managers, during the latter half of the 1960s. Subjectively measured as (1) a dramatic increase in portfolio turnover, and (2) a rise in holdings of letter stock and "small, less seasoned corporations generally," Simonson pointed out that this concern stemmed from the risk borne by fund managers as they "strive for quick gains from short-term, extrinsic increases in the price-earnings ratios of securities. The risk derives from the *vulnerability* of such securities to a severe fall in price which may result from a loss of institutional partisanship or a *downturn* in market prices generally" (Simonson, 1972, p. 381).

Simonson suggested that a more rigorous treatment should incorporate the third moment of the distribution of portfolio returns as a potentially useful measure. Extending mean-variance analysis, he proposed to think in terms of two quantifiable kinds of risk: one, the variability or instability per se of portfolio returns;

> [The other] is speculative risk which is associated with the third moment or the *vulnerability of returns to downside extremes* and derives from the assumption that investors' utility is positively related to the third moment of returns. . . . [In these terms,] speculative risk exists because investors regard with *disutility the negative third moment or negative skewness of distribution of investment returns.* (Simonson, 1972, p. 382, emphasis added)

LIMITATIONS OF BETA

The analytics of portfolio skewness have been derived by Simkowitz and Beedles (1978) from the following formulation of the excess return of any asset:

$$Y_i - Y_f = a_i + S_i + e_i \qquad (C.1)$$

where Y_i is the asset's total return, Y_f is the return on risk-free assets, a_i is a unique return portion, S_i represents a systematic return portion, and

e_i is an error term with the usual spherical assumptions. For mean-variance analysis, substracting the *expectation* of Eq. C.1 from C.1, squaring and taking expectations yields

$$\text{var}(Y_i) = \text{var}(S_i) + \text{var}(e_i) \qquad (C.2)$$

This representation is simply the familiar generalization that "Asset return variance can be divided into systematic risk (variance) and unsystematic risk (variance) (Simkowitz and Beedles, 1978, p. 929). Analogously, subtracting the *expectation* of Eq. C.1 from C.1, *cubing,* and taking expectations yields an equation for the third moment of Y_i that consists of four terms: (1) systematic skew, (2) unsystematic skew, (3) and (4): two cross product terms involving the cross expectations between the error term and the systematic deviations. When the model is properly specified, the cross product terms will equal zero (cf. pp. 929–931, for a more detailed development of the derivation). With regard to portfolio composition, Simkowitz and Beedles showed "That diversification will decrease skew as long as the errors are less than perfectly correlated" (p. 931).

The authors computed monthly holding period returns for 549 common stocks continuously listed on the New York Stock Exchange (NYSE) from January 1945 to December 1965. For the 252 month period for 549 securities, Simkowitz and Beedles investigated the distribution of the 138,348 resulting error terms. They found that the regression errors were "Markedly right skewed around the mean of zero" (p. 932). The noteworthy implication of their analysis was that *positively* skewed errors from Eq. C.1 imply *decreasing* portfolio skew with *diversification.*

To confirm this, Simkowitz and Beedles constructed randomly drawn portfolios ranging in size from 1 to 50 stocks, and 1 portfolio containing all 549 stocks. In accordance with previous studies, the authors found that nearly 80 percent of the unsystematic risk, var(e), was diversified away by the five stock level portfolios. Furthermore, skew is diversified away rapidly, as well. Over 92 percent of *diversifiable* skew was eliminated by the five stock level (p. 938).

In their concluding commentary the authors stated:

Many investors hold less than perfectly diversified portfolios, a phenomenon in contradiction with frequently offered advice. The results reported in this essay may be interpreted as suggesting that the contradiction may be the result of the inadequacy of the traditional two-parameter normative framework. In particular, if positive skewness is a desirable characteristic of return distributions, then the fact that the simple act of diversification *destroys skew is a likely explanation of observed behavior.* Moreover, the results presented herein suggest that even in a perfect, frictionless market, some investors should hold a limited number of assets in their portfolios, the exact number being a function of each individual's skewness/variance awareness. Those who are most concerned with skew should hold a relatively small number of assets in their portfolios. (p. 939)

Simonson's (1972) analysis of the "speculative" behavior of mutual funds, like that of Simkowitz and Beedles (1978), focused on the measure of *systematic skewness.* This measure is essentially defined as the ratio of two parameters: Z_{im}/Z_m^3, where Z_{im} is a measure of curvilinear interaction between the returns of the asset or portfolio i, and the market portfolio, and Z_m^3 is the third moment of market returns. Simonson identified this ratio, systematic skewness, as Γ_i. This latter measure seemed to pick up changes in fund investment behavior that beta did not.

A striking feature is the comparison of average β_i and Γ_i values for the periods 1961–65 and 1966–70. The average Γ_i value rose from 0.964 in 1961–65 to 1.233 in 1966–70, an increase of 28 percent, while the average β_i rose only 5.5 per cent from 0.947 to 0.998. This evidence seems to support qualitative comment from the investment industry to the effect that mutual funds shifted toward more highly "risky" or speculative investment policies in the late 1960's.

It is interesting to note that in this latter period the allegedly exhaustive measure of risk generally applied in the studies of investment performance, i.e., variability risk, does not exceed the market's risk level which has a value of one. The implication from the more traditional capital market theory that this sample of mutual funds incurred no greater risk during 1966–70 than the risk inherent in the market as a whole is strongly challenged by the measure of speculative risk and, as noted earlier with respect to the whole universe of mutual funds, by commentary from the investment community.

The variances of β_i for the two subperiods indicate little change in the spread of variability risk over the sample funds. On the other hand, the variance of Γ_i for the subperiod 1966–70 is significantly greater than that for the subperiod 1961–65. This suggests far less uniformity of investment policies with respect to speculative risk-taking in the later subperiod than in the earlier.

The quantification of *speculative risk* appears to be a useful and even necessary extension of the measurement of risk in diversified portfolios.

Thus, the measure of systematic skewness appears to explain the alleged shift among mutual funds toward more highly aggressive investment policies and the apparent increase in the diversity of investment policies from fund to fund. The failure of the mean-variance view of portfolio analysis and capital market theory to detect any change in the policies of growth funds between 1961–65 and 1966–70 raises the *question of the exhaustiveness of this measure.* [i.e., beta] (Simonson, 1972, pp. 388–389)

A related study by Cooley et al. (1977) presented evidence to demonstrate the redundancy of certain risk surrogates. For 943 firms, using month-end price data from January 1966 to January 1974, the authors showed that 6 of 11 suggested risk measures tended to cluster and convey essentially the same information. Additionally, two subperiods, 1966–69 and 1970–73, were explored to permit analysis of "intertemporal stability among the risk measures" (Cooley et al., 1977, p. 356).

The six measures—(1) range (2) semivariance, (3) semi-interquartile deviation, (4) mean absolute deviation, (5) standard deviation, and (6) lower confidence limit, "join to form a single homogeneous cluster at levels of similarity equaling or exceeding 0.94. . . . These six risk measures apparently capture similar facets of risk, although small differences between risk surrogates might admittedly lead to different portfolio selection (Cooley et al., 1977, p. 362).

Skewness (7) and kurtosis (8), on the other hand, tended to form a cluster at lower levels of similarity (.63, .26, and .48), and tended not to be correlated with other measures. Similarly, (9) coefficient of variation, and (10) coefficient of quartile variation formed a cluster at levels of similarity of .32, .37, and .21.

This reflects their higher correlations with each other than with other risk measures. (11) Beta consistently joins the cluster of six measures at levels of similarity between .42 and .40. This results from its low significant correlations with the group of six measures. Beta also exhibits nonsignificant correlations with coefficient of quartile variation, skewness, and kurtosis in each of the three periods. (Cooley et al., 1977, p. 362).

The authors concluded that the interrelationships between risk measures tended to be stable over time. "Note that this does not address the question of whether a risk measure is *stationary* over time; only the relative position among risk measures is evaluated" (p. 363).

The initial six measures, forming a homogeneous group at a significantly high level of association, have a high degree of substitutability for the purpose of assessing relative riskiness of assets.

The remaining five measures form clusters by themselves at this level and thus may provide additional risk information by capturing *other dimensions of risk*. Skewness and kurtosis join a separate group at much lower levels of association. To the extent that they are behaviorally important, each one has the potential of providing additional risk information. Previous work by Alderfer and Bierman and by Arditti indicates that higher order moments may be behaviorally important to investors for decision making. *Beta also forms a relatively independent group by itself and thus may possess unique risk information*. Due to their association with other risk measures at consistently low levels, coefficient of variation and coefficient of quartile variation appear to capture distributional information different from that provided by other risk measures. (Cooley et al., 1977, p. 363, emphasis added)

D Hedging Theory in Depth, and A Portfolio Model of Hedging

HEDGING THEORY REVISITED*

Louis Ederington observed that there is less than perfect unanimity "in the futures market literature as to what *hedging is or why it is undertaken*" (1979, p. 158). In view of that assessment, it seems that a useful starting point is a restatement of hedging theory. The formulations by both Cootner (1967) and Ederington (1979) are worth summarizing in some detail: the former for its development in familiar economic concepts of supply curves and motivational interpretations, and the latter because of its clarity and precision. Of further relevance here, an interesting aspect of both developments is the appeal to the structure and tenets of "portfolio theory."

The "Basis," Hedging, and Arbitrage

Following Ederington's notation, let X represent the number of commodity units, and let P_s^1 and P_s^2 represent the cash or spot prices at times t_1 and t_2, respectively. Then the gain or loss of an unhedged position, U, is $X(P_s^2 - P_s^1)$, and the gain or loss on a hedged position, H, is $X(P_s^2 - P_s^1) - X(P_f^2 - P_f^1)$, where P_f are the *futures* prices at t_2 and t_1, respectively (Ederington, 1979, p. 159).

First, both Cootner and Ederington reject the "traditional" hedging

---

*All quotations in this section are from Cootner, 1967, unless otherwise noted.

exposition as oversimplified and erroneous. This naive presentation is the familiar "perfect hedge" example, wherein the price movements of hedged inventory and relevant futures contracts are represented to be exactly offsetting, thereby eliminating the risks of price fluctuations.

The simplified "perfect" hedge alluded to previously implies that $E(H)$ = 0, and that var (H) = 0. Cootner commented that: "Both of these ideas are incorrect. In normal hedging practice (futures and cash market) price changes are not *expected* to be offsetting, and while risks will be reduced, they will not be *eliminated*" (p. 66).

Ederington also observed that, according to the theory of adaptive expectations, "If futures prices reflect market expectations they should not normally match changes in cash prices" (1979, p. 160). That is, the traditional exposition of the "perfect" hedge and the implications of adaptive expectations theory are mutually inconsistent. (See Ederington, 1979, p. 160, for a mathematical derivation of these contradictions.)

This relationship between spot and futures prices is the "basis," namely the difference between the two $(P_s - P_f)$, and a change in the basis equals $(P_f^2 - P_s^2) - (P_f^1 - P_s^1)$ or $(P_s^2 - P_s^1) - (P_f^2 - P_f^1)$. As the notation specifies, what is referred to as the "basis" is strictly a time-dependent, dynamic relationship. The behavior of the spot price (P_s) relative to the futures price (P_f) is the critical dimension of hedging operations.

Further, it is important to recognize that *hedging,* as opposed to arbitrage, differs from speculation, not in kind, but only in degree. Hedging is *not* risk *elimination,* but rather risk reduction, or risk specialization.

> In most circumstances, hedging is really a form of speculation—speculation on the basis. It has all the characteristics of speculation even though it is an essential normal aspect of doing business. It differs from the speculation of buying or selling futures only because the variance of the outcome is usually much less. In fact, in those cases where the basis is as volatile as the price of the spot commodity, the hedger moves naturally into holding inventories unhedged, i.e., into ordinary speculation, because there is no risk reduction from hedging. (p. 75)

Houthakker has stated a similar proposition in terms of the variance (risk) per unit of inventory. The key factor is the correlation between the spot and futures prices:

More particularly, short selling to offset a long position completely will reduce the variance per unit of the long position if the regression coefficient of the spot price on the futures price is positive and exceeds one-half. . . . Reduction in the unit variance, it should be added, is only a necessary and not a sufficient condition for the profitability of hedging (Houthakker, 1959, p. 156).

Other factors need to be examined; especially, the cost of hedging, which consists of the "transaction costs of futures trading and probably more important—the risk premium paid to speculators" (Houthakker, 1959, p. 156).

Another clarification in Cootner's development relates to terminology. *Hedging,* as opposed to *arbitrage,* is not riskless. The latter is the type of transaction using the futures markets to "lock-in" differentials that assure minimum profits.

The gains and losses arising from errors in forecasting the demand for the inventory are among the residual, unavoidable, risks involved in hedging. While better forecasts could eliminate any particular error, the basic risk will remain, since no hedging policy and no future contract maturity can assure a merchant that he will receive the opportunity rate of return on his inventory. It is for this reason that *hedging cannot properly be described as arbitrage.* It is arbitrage only in the extreme case when the *basis exceeds* the actual *costs* of carrying inventory with no allowance for any convenience yield, since only in that circumstance is the profit a certain one. (pp. 74–75, emphasis added)

By a similar line of reasoning, it is possible to analyze the choice among three alternatives: hedging, long cash speculation (that is, the holding of an unhedged long position in the cash market), and long futures speculation. After the elimination of long hedging and short futures speculation, these are the principal alternatives to be considered. Clearly, the choice among them depends on the total profit obtainable, given the resources with which the trader operates. (Houthakker, 1959, p. 153)

The Inventory Model

Cootner further pointed out that another problem with the standard definition of hedging is that it does not properly take into account the cost of, and motivations for, the holding of inventory.

[A merchant's] willingness to carry the asset must depend on his ability to recoup the net costs of storage. Since in selling a futures contract as a hedge, the merchant is setting the return he will earn on the spot commodity if he holds it until the futures contract matures, the relation between the spot and futures prices is of utmost importance to the hedge transaction. *It is not a subsidiary matter which can be ignored without essential concern.* Like the finance company that borrows at one rate to lend at another, a merchant normally earns his profits from reaping a *return on his inventory* greater than the costs of storage. This is equally true whether or not he hedges. To say that a merchant hedges in anticipation of profit does not necessarily mean that he will not settle for a smaller profit if accompanied by lower risk, but he measures the profit as carefully as the risk reduction. (p. 66, emphasis added)

Now, "No rational person will hold inventories unless he expects the benefits from such inventories to at least equal their costs." The latter are classified as being either direct or indirect. And it is the direct costs of holding inventory that are the most straightforward. "They are the marginal costs of warehouse space, interest charges, and insurance against physical damage, theft or deterioration" (p. 68).

The indirect cost is more interesting: it is the threat, if any, posed to the capital position of the holder.

It is, of course, possible that a merchant will cool-headedly value inventory without any allowance for the disutility of capital variance, but if he is averse to risk, he will count it as a real cost of doing business. Furthermore, while the risk itself is not a money cost of doing business, the risk-averse merchant will stand ready to pay to avoid the risk, just as he buys insurance against fire damage for a larger premium than justified by the expected cost of fire. And if he cannot buy insurance directly, he will refuse many opportunities to profit rather than incur incremental risk, thus paying for "insurance" indirectly. For any individual merchant, the marginal payment he is willing to make to reduce the risk associated with carrying another bushel of inventory doubtless rises with the level of inventory he is already carrying (p. 68).

On the benefit side, Cootner found that it was the indirect aspects of inventory holding that have been least carefully spelled out. For a merchant:

Inventories are the "liquidity stocks" of his profession. Out of such holdings he can meet importunate demands of customers for immediately available supplies. If such supplies are restricted, he will be able to derive revenues

somewhat greater than normal in addition to securing business that would
go elsewhere if he did not have the goods available. (pp. 68–69)

For example, transportation costs of alternative supplies can give the
merchant an economic rent on the last supplies available in an area. In
general,

> The merchant knows that the lower his inventories in terms of the level and
> variability of demand, the more likely it is that he will have to forego some
> lucrative business. Since these foregone revenues increase as inventories
> decline, we can attribute to each marginal unit of inventories a return or
> yield which increases as the level of inventory decreases. This is what
> Working, Brennan, Kaldor, and Telser call the "convenience yield" of
> inventory. (pp. 68–69)

Moreover, the convenience yield of an inventory is an expected value
concept: namely, the present value of an increased income stream expected as a result of a "conveniently" large inventory. The convenience
yield concept is

> quite independent of any attitudes the inventory holder may have toward
> risk. This is important to recognize, because the fact that a convenience
> yield would not exist in the absence of uncertainty or transaction costs
> sometimes leads to the erroneous conclusion that such a yield arises out of
> an attitude toward risk.
>   There is, however, an analogue to capital risk which can arise out of
> income variability. Just as increasing inventory increases the holder's ex-
> posure to the risk of price fluctuation, decreases in inventory holdings in-
> crease the prospect of income variability. When inventories are quite low
> the prospect of such income variability may very well induce the holder to
> carry somewhat more stocks when the level is low than could be justified
> on the basis of present value in much the same way that he might carry
> somewhat less inventory when stocks were already high. Such an attitude
> of aversion to income variability would produce an income risk premium,
> analogous to the capital risk premium, which would be large when inven-
> tories were low, but decreased monotonically with stocks. (p. 69)

Hedging Alternatives

Hedgers, Cootner aptly observed, do not behave as if they were autom-
atons. As indicated above, it is in the expectation of realizing convenience

yields that inventories are held and carrying costs incurred. As indicated above,

> These yields arise from the ability to use the holdings at the owner's discretion, for non-storage purposes. . . . The convenience yield arises because of the "spot" nature of the commodity—because of its immediate usefulness and availability.
>
> The futures contract, on the other hand, has a fixed maturity; it calls for delivery during a specific period. Now, the sale of a future for a short hedge does not *commit* the merchant to holding the inventory until the maturity of the futures contract. In fact, he will customarily plan on using his inventory prior to the maturity of the hedge: if he holds the inventory to maturity it can generally be assumed that expected commercial opportunities *did not* develop. He is likely to hedge in the full knowledge that the quoted difference between spot and futures will not provide returns in excess of costs *unless* he gets an opportunity to sell or use the inventory prior to the maturity of the futures contract. He hedges in the *expectation* that he will get such an opportunity. It is the expected value of that selling opportunity which comprises the convenience yield. Once the possibility arises of *not* holding the hedge to maturity, the hedge is no longer a riskless alternative to holding inventories unhedged, but merely a less risky one. (p. 68)

There is another way to see the complexity inherent in hedging:

> Examine the rational behavior of a merchant in the face of an expected decline in prices. Under most circumstances, the rational action would be the sale of the *actual* inventories held rather than the sale of futures to a speculator as a hedge. In fact, a merchant who is *already* short hedged and foresees a price decline would better off to *sell* his spot inventories and *lift* his hedge. If the foreseen decline in price is due to an expected reduction in demand below previously expected levels, spot prices will be expected to decline more than futures because inventories would be less valuable and the costs of storage higher. . . . To the extent that merchants can forecast price changes, it is most likely that they would foresee events just ahead and in those circumstances the sale of spot would be the preferable option. Where price rises are forecast, the situation is quite symmetrical. . . .
>
> The prevalence of this pattern of behavior depends on an empirical, rather than a logical, proposition. If the spot price is positively correlated with the basis, it will prove unprofitable to hold inventories either *hedged* or *unhedged* if declines are expected. Working has shown that this correlation does exist in the case of wheat and that it is most likely to be true when inventories are greatest, i.e., when hedging is most widespread. (pp. 75–76)

The introduction of risk premia (imbedded in the futures prices) adds further decision alternatives for the hedger to consider. One is how much of a given spot inventory should be hedged.

> If inventory holding was a constant cost of industry in terms of risk, this argument would call for merchants to always remain completely hedged. But the premise clearly does not hold. When inventory levels are low, the marginal unit may increase risk negligibly (or, as indicated above, actually reduce income variability). However, increases in inventory increase the risk of the marginal unit, so it is quite normal to expect some relatively constant amount of inventory to be held unhedged, with hedging only beginning once the marginal risk "cost" to the hedger begins to exceed the premium demanded by speculators. If no risk premium is demanded, hedging should be universal. Of course, since the size of the premium is subjective, it is quite conceivable that we would observe merchants changing their fraction of inventories hedged as their expectations change due to changes in either futures prices or exogeneous conditions. Hedgers will certainly try to hedge as cheaply as possible and take advantage of whatever errors speculators may make. All the theory requires is that they will continue to hedge even if their net cost is positive. (p. 77)

As inventories grow, so do the risk premiums. If there is an insurance at some fixed premium, then merchants would hold inventories unhedged until their "demand" for insurance rose to that level. They would "self-insure" until that point.

> Beyond that level of inventory, speculators would be willing to write insurance more cheaply than merchants could self-insure. Since speculative participation reduces costs of this insurance, futures markets have grown up largely to facilitate speculative entry. The fact that merchants are not always hedged, or if hedged, are often not fully hedged is often taken as evidence that they *only* hedge when prices are expected to fall rather than to avert risk with the subsidiary implication that since they are more knowledgeable than speculators they are likely to outwit them. The conclusion may be valid, but it is certainly not a defensible deduction from the premise. In fact, the reverse hypothesis is much more defensible. If speculative services are provided free or at a loss, then we should expect hedging to be universal, since the hedger reduces his risk at no cost to himself (or perhaps even a profit). (pp. 70–71)

Another decision variable facing the hedger is the choice of futures maturity. The risk associated with hedging arises:

From the difference in maturity between the spot asset and the future sold as a hedge. We have also shown that, as expected, the spot price is positively correlated with the basis. Under these conditions, the more distant is the maturity of the futures contract relative to the expected duration of inventory holding, the more of any expected increase in spot prices will be reflected in changes in the basis and the greater will be the variance of changes in the basis. As a result of this, hedgers can take a more or less aggressive policy with regard to price expectations depending on their confidence about their expectations. While the unconditional variance of the basis with respect to distant futures is greater than with respect to near futures, an increased confidence in the expectation of a price rise may reduce the conditional variance of the distant basis to a level low enough to make it more attractive than the safer hedge.

Putting it another way, every hedger can choose among a series of possible hedges yielding larger prospective gain at the expense of greater risk. At any particular time one of these hedges seems most attractive in light of his attitudes toward risk. However, as expectations about gains and risks change, his choices include shifting to longer or shorter hedges as well as deciding simply to hedge or not to hedge. Since not hedging usually involves a substantial increase in risk, there may be an intermediate alternative which involves shifting hedges to more distant futures. A merchant who confidently foresees an increase in demand under present conditions but who does not want to completely expose himself to the risks of legislation, regulatory activity, foreign policy, and weather may prefer to shift his hedge forward rather than lift it altogether.

In discussing the decision to hedge or not to hedge, the critical variable was the risk premium the merchant was willing to pay and the premium demanded by the speculator. Whatever the level of those premiums, the decision of the hedger to shift hedges forward depends critically not only on the merchant's comparison of the risks of hedging in futures of different maturities, but also the speculator's comparison of the risks of speculation in futures of different maturities. If the variance of futures prices decreases with the maturity and if speculators are risk-averters and measure risk in terms of variance, they will require a smaller premium per unit time on the more distant futures. Thus hedgers should be expected to be able to hedge more cheaply, but with greater risk, in more distant maturities. (pp. 77–78)

The Grade-Location "Basis"

To this point the "basis" has been dealt with strictly in terms of the *time* dimension: that is, the difference between the spot and futures prices ($P_s - P_f$), and their correlation as a given contract approaches maturity. The profits or returns discussed above are those obtained from holding a commodity, say wheat, of a standard grade and location (e.g., futures grade: No. 2 Hard Red Winter, ordinary protein content, Kansas City). This operation is usually intensely competitive, since all participants in the futures market are potential suppliers.

It is the off-standard grade and locational variations, however, that give rise to most profit potential for merchants. (The locational returns and economic "rents" were alluded to in the discussion of convenience yields.)

> Regardless of the degree to which the grade-location basis is predictable it is generally *unhedgeable*. The merchant does not usually have any way of avoiding that risk. And so a merchant who hedges off-standard (non-futures grade) grain may gain or lose on his hedges even if the (time dimension) basis of the standard grade behaves exactly as expected. (p. 80)

The latter off-grade variation can be illustrated by a real world example. Consider an individual holding grade 13 protein spot wheat (Kansas City location) on January 3, 1980, and hedged in the March 1980 contract. As of January 3 the spot-futures prices per bushel were as follows:

	Cash Price (13 Pro)	March 1980 Futures Price (Ordinary)
1/3/80	$454\frac{3}{4}$	$444\frac{3}{4}$
1/9/80	$422\frac{1}{4}$	$419\frac{1}{4}$
Change	$-32\frac{1}{2}$	$-25\frac{1}{2}$

This period encompassed the announcement of the Russian grain embargo, but nonetheless, only 78.5% of the price change was hedgeable in the futures market. The illustration can be considered further, say on January 30, 1980, when the futures price had *more* than recovered:

	Cash Price (13 Pro)	March 1980 Futures Price (Ordinary)
1/30/80	446	447
Change from 1/3/80	$-8\frac{3}{4}$	$+2\frac{1}{4}$

In addition, holders of the standard grade would not have been fully protected either. The cash price of No. 2 ordinary was 444¾ on January 3, and 442 on January 30, reflecting a basis change loss of 2¾ cents per bushel. Moreover, on the interim date of 1/9/80, the cash price of ordinary protein wheat had changed from 444¾ on January 3 to 407¼, reflecting a change of −37½ cents per bushel, only 68% of which (25½ cents) was hedgeable in the March 1980 contract.

As the above illustration highlights, hedging can hardly be considered a "riskless" operation. Since the basis reflects not only current inventories, but the time pattern of expected demand for those inventories as well, "it can be expected to fluctuate in response to revisions in those expectations. Furthermore, since changes in the basis affect the profitability of the hedge, this uncertainty about future demand introduces riskiness into the hedge, and the ability to profit from more accurate predictions about basis changes" (p. 72).

When the grade-location variance is quite large, and when speculative interest is sufficiently strong, more than one market can exist.

> The three U.S. wheat markets are one obvious example. . . . Given the advantages of liquidity in markets, the existence of separate markets implies that the basis risks are large enough to render the markets imperfect substitutes for price insurance, the price that hedgers are willing to pay to avoid that grade-location risk is large enough to attract enough speculators to support both markets. (p. 80)

Finally, it seems appropriate to conclude Cootner's exposition with his own summary and comparison of merchant-hedgers to bankers.

> With this discussion behind us, we can once more point up the analogy between hedging and the portfolio policies of financial institutions. In both cases, the firms involved handle portfolios of assets and liabilities in such a way as to maximize return for a given risk or minimize risk for a given return. In both cases the main tool for accomplishing this result is varying the maturity of assets or liabilities to alter the opportunities for gain at the expense of increasing exposure to risk. In the limiting case, both kinds of institutions can keep their positions unhedged—either by holding inventories unhedged or by holding cash, but in each situation the extreme position is not normal business practice. In each case, the firms generally pursue their portfolio adjustments in a specialized market that is much more liquid than the market in which the central business of the firm is conducted. Thus

the futures market and the U.S. government securities market are the main arenas for adjusting portfolios, although it is the cash commodity market and business loan which are the central business of the firm. (p. 79)

Accordingly, the theory of hedging can be seen to be a rich theory, admitting of adjustments along a variety of dimensions. In particular, the hedger–risk manager can choose among a variety of maturities, and proportions of inventory to hedge. This latter aspect is developed more fully in Ederington's portfolio model in the next section.

A PORTFOLIO MODEL OF HEDGING*

Ederington's portfolio model of hedging behavior explicitly provides a rationale for understanding why hedgers behave as they do. On the one hand, traditional theory suggests that hedgers should always be completely hedged, while earlier developments of Holbrook Working indicated that hedgers would be completely hedged or unhedged. The more general portfolio model includes these as special (but possible) outcomes.

The model (pp. 161 ff.) takes spot market holdings, X_s, as given exogenously. Letting U denote the return on an unhedged position,

$$E(U) = X_s E(P_s^2 - P_s^1) \tag{D.1}$$

$$\text{var}(U) = X_s^2 \, \sigma_s^2 \tag{D.2}$$

Let Y represent the return on a portfolio that includes both spot market holdings, X_s, and futures market holdings, X_f.

$$E(Y) = X_s E(P_s^2 - P_s^1) + X_f E(P_f^2 - P_f^1) - K(X_f) \tag{D.3}$$

$$\text{var}(Y) = X_s^2 \sigma_s^2 + X_f^2 \sigma_f^2 + 2X_s X_f \sigma_{sf} \tag{D.4}$$

where X_s and X_f represent spot and futures market holdings.

$K(X_f)$ represents brokerage and other costs of engaging in futures transactions including the cost of providing margin.

σ_s^2, σ_f^2, and σ_{sf} represent the subjective variances and the covariance of possible price changes from time 1 to time 2.

*All quotations in this section are from Ederington, 1979.

Note that the portfolio, whose returns are represented by Y, may be a portfolio that is either completely or partially hedged. There is no presumption, as in traditional theory, that $X_f = -X_s$ (in which case $Y = H$). Indeed cash and futures market holdings may even have the same sign (i.e., a "Texas" or "reverse" hedge).

If the proportion of the spot position that is hedged is denoted by $b = -X_f/X_s$, and since in a hedge X_s and X_f usually have opposite signs, b is usually (but not necessarily) positive. Ederington's model provides a means for determining the risk-minimizing $b = b^*$, that is, in terms of the proportion of X_s to be hedged.

If the expected change in the basis is zero, then clearly the expected gain or loss is reduced as b approaches 1. It is also obvious that expected changes in the basis may add to or subtract from the gain or loss that would have been expected on an unhedged portfolio $[E(U) = X_s E(S)]$, where $E(S) = E(P_s^2 - P_s^1)$ is the expected price change on one unit of the spot commodity. (See Ederington, p. 162, for the mathematical derivation.)

Holding X_s constant, Ederington considers the effect of a change in b, the proportion hedged, on the expected return and variance of the portfolio Y. "Since $E(\Delta B)$ and $E(S)$ may be either positive or negative, the opportunity locus of the possible combinations of $E(Y)$ and var(Y) may lie in first or second quadrant or both" (p. 162). The optimal $b = b'$ will be the usual point of tangency to the highest indifference curve.

> Not only need b' not equal one as traditional hedging theory presumed, but b' may be greater than one, in which case one takes a greater position in the futures than in the cash market, or b' may be less than zero, in which case one takes the same position (either short or long) in *both the spot and futures markets*. . . .
>
> While traditional theory indicates that the risk reduction to be achieved by hedging can be measured by comparing the variance of the change in the basis to the variance of the change in the cash price, this presumes that $b = 1$ which as shown above may not be the case. Fortunately, portfolio theory also provides a measure of hedging effectiveness. While the risk reduction achieved by any one hedger depends on the chosen b, the futures markets' potential for risk reduction can be measured by comparing the risk on an unhedged portfolio with the minimum risk that can be obtained on a portfolio containing both spot and forward positions. (pp. 162–163)

The measure of effectiveness is ϵ, where

$$\epsilon = 1 - \frac{\text{var}(Y^*)}{\text{var}(U)}$$

and var(Y^*) denotes the minimum variance (determined by b^*) on a portfolio containing futures. Consequently, Ederington shows that the ϵ can be expressed as

$$\epsilon = \frac{\sigma_{sf}^2}{\sigma_s^2 \sigma_f^2} = \rho^2$$

where ρ^2 is the population coefficient of determination between the changes in the cash price and the changes in the futures price (p. 164).

Ederington empirically tested this model for four-week hedges in 8 percent GNMA's, 90 day T-Bills, wheat, and corn.

> Of most interest here is that b^* was estimated for all hypothetical hedges. Since traditional theory implies that $b^* = 1$ . . . in most cases b^* was significantly different from 1, and in general was less than 1. The hypothesis that $b^* = 1$ is therefore rejected. (p. 166)

Three of Ederington's conclusions and observations are noteworthy for a variety of reasons. The most germane may be summarized as follows:

1. "The decision to hedge a cash or forward market position in the futures market is not different from any other investment decision— investors hedge to obtain the best combination of risk and return. Basic portfolio theory, which best explains when and how much holders of financial portfolios will wish to hedge, encompasses both the traditional hedging theory and Working's theory as special cases." (p. 169)

2. Standard hedging simplifications, which suggest that hedges are (supposed to be) "perfect" because cash and futures prices change by equal amounts are "completely indefensible."

3. "Contrary to traditional hedging theory (but consistent with the theory of adaptive expectations), our empirical results indicate that even pure risk-minimizers may wish to hedge only a *portion* of their portfolios" (p. 169). In most cases, the estimated value of the minimum risk parameter, b^*, was less than one.

E Individual Stock Statistics, Estimated Betas, Standard Deviations, and R^2 with VLIC and NYSE as Market Factors, 1978–1982 and 1973–1977

This appendix displays systematic risk estimates for over 1400 stocks. It is a somewhat rare compilation, as the estimates shown relate the variability of each stock, in logarithmic return form, to *two* different market factor proxies for the *same* time periods. Each stock's returns (P_t/P_{t-1}) were regressed on the VLIC and NYSE indexes for two 5 year periods: January 1978 to December 1982 and January 1973 to December 1977.

Although the S&P 500 index was not used as a market factor proxy in these estimations, the high correlation of the NYSE with the S&P 500 ($R = .99+$) indicates the NYSE estimates are probably close approximations to those that would have resulted for the S&P 500. That, admittedly, is an inference without any direct testing. However, for the same time periods (1978–1982 and 1973–1977) the estimates from the NYSE regressions correspond closely to those estimates of the VLIC regressions, on a stock by stock basis. Given the lower levels of correlation between the VLIC and NYSE ($R = .883$, 1973–1977; $R = .966$, 1978–1982, on the average), the conjecture about such S&P 500 estimates is probably not too fanciful.

ECONOMETRIC SPECIFICATION

Since two market factors were utilized for two different time periods, there were four equations estimated for each stock, as follows.

Period: January 1978–December 1982

$$\log\left[\frac{P_{jt}}{P_{jt-1}}\right] = \log A + B \log\left[\frac{(VLIC)_t}{(VLIC)_{t-1}}\right] \qquad (E.1)$$

$$\log\left[\frac{P_{jt}}{P_{jt-1}}\right] = \log A + B \log\left[\frac{(NYSE)_t}{(NYSE)_{t-1}}\right] \qquad (E.2)$$

Period: January 1973–December 1977

$$\log\left[\frac{P_{jt}}{P_{jt-1}}\right] = \log A + B \log\left[\frac{(VLIC)_t}{(VLIC)_{t-1}}\right] \qquad (E.3)$$

$$\log\left[\frac{P_{jt}}{P_{jt-1}}\right] = \log A + B \log\left[\frac{(NYSE)_t}{(NYSE)_{t-1}}\right] \qquad (E.4)$$

The j subscript simply refers to the particular individual stock; that is, j = 1 for ACF Indus., j = 2 for AMF Inc., j = 3 for AMR Corp., and so on, for all of the stocks shown below.

STANDARD DEVIATION

The data for the left-hand sides of Eq. E.1 and Eq. E.2 are the same; for example, ACF's price returns for 1978–1982. Similarly, for j = 1, the left-hand sides of Eq. E.3 and Eq. E.4 are also the same; that is, the price returns for ACF during 1973–1977. Thus the log standard deviation (SD) of ACF in Eq. E.1 equals the log(SD) for Eq. E.2. Therefore, there is only one log(SD) shown for each period for each stock: log SD(ACF) in (E.3) equals log SD(ACF) in (E.4). The data file from which these estimates were extracted are compiled on a weekly basis. Rather than identifying each observation's date, every fourth week's observation was selected to approximate "monthly" holding periods. However, that procedure resulted in 64 "monthly" observations, instead of 60 for both five-year time periods. Further, every log(SD) is multiplied by 100, so that the SDs shown can roughly be interpreted as a "monthly" (average) percentage deviation for the respective five-year period. The monthly standard deviation for ACF during 1978–1982 was 6.692 percent; it was 8.156 percent for 1973–1977.

ESTIMATED BETA ($\hat{\beta}$) and R^2

The systematic risk estimates across the row follow from (E.1) to (E.4): ACF's estimated $\hat{\beta}$ with VLIC as the market factor proxy is 1.00 for 1978–1982; when the VLIC changed (up or down) by 10 percent, ACF did also, on the average during the period. For R^2, the interpretation is that the variations in VLIC "explained" about 59 percent (.590) of the variation in ACF, on a logarithmic return basis. When NYSE was the market factor, ACF's $\hat{\beta}$ was 1.12, so that if the NYSE index increased 10 percent, ACF increased 11.2 percent on the average during the 1978–1982 period. Similarly, the R^2 statistic means that during that period, the variations in the NYSE index accounted for an estimated 56.2 percent (.562) of the variation in ACF, on a monthly return basis.

The estimates of the constant term, log A, are not shown. In addition, it is customary in econometric work to display the standard error of the estimated coefficient ($\hat{\beta}$), or its t-ratio. The critical t value for "testing" the statistical significance of an estimate is approximately 2.0. Almost every $\hat{\beta}$ shown below has a t-ratio well in excess of 2.0, frequently as high as 6 or 7. Only those $\hat{\beta}$ estimates at the very low end of the spectrum— .40 or less—occasionally showed t-ratios less than 2.0. However, such stocks exhibited low market dependency also (R^2). Accordingly, the t statistics have been omitted here, as they do not add much information and only complicate the display. My apologies to the econometricians, but rarely have other studies of stocks' betas shown t-ratios, or even R^2 values for that matter.

Finally, the regression form utilized here is a "gross return" specification. That is, the "risk-free" rate and cash dividends have been omitted, since others have pointed out that their inclusion does not affect the estimates in a material way. However, the length of the holding period assumed, here monthly, is important. Also, the length of the data series employed has significant effects on the estimates. Accordingly, stocks with *less* than 40 observations do not appear in the display. For those in the intermediate range ("incomplete" data series) the estimates are shown, but the number of observations is noted in the far right columns, and the applicable period is identified (i.e., 40–63 observations). All other estimates shown imply a full series of 64 observations.

INTERPRETIVE PRECAUTIONS

The estimated coefficients, which may be close in numerical value for the VLIC and NYSE, should be kept in relative perspective also. Accordingly, Table E.1 shows the approximate decile ranges for the VLIC and NYSE estimated betas. Similarly, Table E.2 (a repeat of Table 2.7, for

Table E.1 Estimated Betas for Individual Stocks, Approximate Decile Ranges by Market Index, 1978–1982 and 1973–1977

Market Index: VLIC	Decile	Market Index: NYSE
	1978–1982	
2.47 – 1.60	I	2.65 – 1.75
1.59 – 1.38	II	1.74 – 1.50
1.37 – 1.22	III	1.49 – 1.33
1.21 – 1.13	IV	1.32 – 1.19
1.12 – 1.00	V	1.18 – 1.08
.99 – .90	VI	1.07 – .97
.89 – .81	VII	.96 – .87
.80 – .70	VIII	.86 – .73
.69 – .50	IX	.72 – .54
.49 – .01	X	.53 – .09
	1973–1977	
2.46 – 1.60	I	2.92 – 1.84
1.59 – 1.36	II	1.83 – 1.55
1.35 – 1.19	III	1.54 – 1.39
1.18 – 1.05	IV	1.38 – 1.26
1.04 – .96	V	1.25 – 1.16
.95 – .87	VI	1.15 – 1.05
.86 – .77	VII	1.04 – .94
.76 – .68	VIII	.93 – .82
.67 – .58	IX	.81 – .67
.57 – .21	X	.66 – .20

Table E.2 Stock Price Standard Deviations, in Logarithmic Return Form, Stocks Comprising the VLIC, Ranked by Deciles from Highest Standard Deviations to Lowest, Monthly Observations

| | July 1977–June 1982 | | July 1972–June 1977 | |
Decile	Number of Stocks	Standard Deviations	Number of Stocks	Standard Deviations
I	166	26.472 – 13.957	144	36.411 – 15.896
II	167	13.929 – 12.235	144	15.820 – 13.799
III	167	12.225 – 11.055	144	13.701 – 12.210
IV	167	11.044 – 10.034	144	12.207 – 11.103
V	167	10.032 – 9.173	144	11.101 – 10.145
VI	167	9.172 – 8.278	144	10.139 – 9.407
VII	167	8.274 – 7.652	144	9.406 – 8.473
VIII	167	7.644 – 6.874	144	8.465 – 7.708
IX	167	6.872 – 5.834	144	7.705 – 6.716
X	167	5.825 – 3.463	144	6.706 – 4.063
	1669		1440	
	Median Standard Deviations: 9.17		10.14	
	Standard Deviations of VLIC: 5.25		6.46	
	NYSE: 4.57		4.84	

the reader's convenience) shows the relative respective decile ranges for the log standard deviation measures. The periods covered in Table E.2 do not conform exactly with the individual stock estimates but differ by only six months (June–December 1982).

Further, our previous analyses suggest that the estimates of β and R^2 tend to be positively correlated but only at a moderate level of association, .625; and R^2 has an average value, across individual stocks, of about .30–.35.

Finally, we repeat again that the following statistics are *estimates,* and not "gospel." The beta controversy reported in Chapter 4 should still be kept in mind. What we have in the following display are *historical* estimates. For some stocks estimates of beta show dramatic shifts, from 1973–1977 to 1978–1982, for example, PSA, Inc., and Hecla Mining.

These estimates have been generously provided by the Statistics Department of Arnold Bernhard & Co.

Stock	Jan 1978–Dec 1982 Log (%) Std. Dev.	Jan 1978–Dec 1982 VLIC Est. Beta	Jan 1978–Dec 1982 VLIC R²	Jan 1978–Dec 1982 NYSE Est. Beta	Jan 1978–Dec 1982 NYSE R²	Jan 1973–Dec 1977 Log (%) Std. Dev.	Jan 1973–Dec 1977 VLIC Est. Beta	Jan 1973–Dec 1977 VLIC R²	Jan 1973–Dec 1977 NYSE Est. Beta	Jan 1973–Dec 1977 NYSE R²	Incomplete Data Series Number of Obs.	Incomplete Data Series Period
Abbott Labs.	7.050	.85	.392	.92	.343	9.372	.71	.272	1.09	.422		
ACF Indus.	6.692	1.00	.590	1.12	.562	8.156	.75	.396	.76	.273		
Acme-Cleveland	10.248	1.32	.443	1.46	.408	8.728	.76	.362	.72	.215		
Adams Drug	9.976	1.22	.399	1.19	.284	14.564	1.35	.400	1.28	.267	52	1973–77
Adams Express	5.217	.68	.456	.79	.459	5.066	.48	.432	.54	.362		
Adams-Millis	10.821	.93	.195	.75	.095	12.607	.95	.269	.79	.123		
Advanced Micro-Dev.	13.823	1.60	.372	1.89	.389	—	—	—	—	—	61	1978–82
Aetna Life & Casual.	7.226	.77	.307	.89	.306	10.309	.75	.251	1.23	.447	51	1973–77
Ahmanson & Co.	12.475	1.37	.321	1.48	.281	12.668	1.24	.449	1.23	.330		
Aileen, Inc.	12.872	1.40	.316	1.41	.240	15.456	1.58	.494	1.40	.256		
Air Florida Sys.	18.275	1.75	.266	1.92	.257	—	—	—	—	—	45	1978–82
Air Products & Chem.	8.372	1.19	.537	1.26	.451	8.674	.81	.414	1.07	.480		
Airborne Freight	11.321	1.24	.319	1.27	.251	10.785	1.06	.478	1.05	.353	47	1973–77
Alagasco Inc.	4.655	.45	.245	.46	.192	7.814	.53	.216	.44	.099		
Alaska Airlines	12.087	1.56	.484	1.58	.397	—	—	—	—	—	45	1978–82
Albany Int'l.	11.115	1.19	.305	1.13	.208	14.678	1.19	.421	1.37	.274		
Alberto-Culver	11.562	1.40	.388	1.47	.322	7.430	1.38	.254	.76	.327		
Albertson's, Inc.	7.014	.82	.361	.86	.297	8.226	.54	.161	.59	.159		
Alcan Aluminium, Ltd.	8.492	.88	.288	.99	.272	8.657	.48	.684	1.15	.550		
Alco Standard	6.992	.75	.310	.78	.251	9.820	1.04	.274	.99	.320		
Alexander & Alex Sv.	8.577	.94	.320	1.05	.297	15.672	.75	.570	1.75	.391		
Alexander & Baldwin	9.894	1.31	.467	1.33	.362		1.72					
Alexander's, Inc.	12.056	1.10	.222	1.18	.191		.60					
Algoma Steel	7.771	.60	.161	.57	.109							
Alleghany Corp.	9.834	1.38	.523	1.52	.478	10.892	1.16	.538	1.24	.404		
Allegheny Int'l.	10.584	1.45	.500	1.60	.458	8.636	.79	.401	.85	.303		
Allegheny Power Sys.	5.479	.34	.105	.41	.110	7.633	.66	.356	.89	.423		
Allen Group	7.042	.93	.468	.96	.370	12.375	1.17	.423	1.31	.352		
Allied Bancshares	8.440	1.01	.428	1.04	.361	—	—	—	—	—	44	1978–82
Allied Corp.	7.995	.95	.380	1.16	.420	9.201	.86	.414	1.15	.486		

| | January 1978–December 1982 | | | | | January 1973–December 1977 | | | | | Incomplete Data Series | |
| | | VLIC | | NYSE | | | VLIC | | NYSE | | | |
Stock	Log (%) Std. Dev.	Est. Beta	R²	Est. Beta	R²	Log (%) Std. Dev.	Est. Beta	R²	Est. Beta	R²	Number of Obs.	Period
Allied Products	8.348	.61	.143	.51	.076	9.436	.84	.374	.76	.204		
Allied Stores	6.496	.70	.306	.72	.243	9.187	.87	.424	.93	.323		
Allied Supermarkets	23.538	1.29	.080	1.53	.084	18.055	1.10	.177	1.16	.130		
Allis-Chalmers	9.804	1.02	.286	1.14	.270	10.496	1.05	.472	1.11	.348		
Alpha Portland Ind.	9.545	1.08	.342	1.06	.246	11.889	1.04	.361	1.03	.234		
Aluminum Co. of Amer.	7.718	.90	.363	1.06	.376	9.296	.59	.188	.71	.182		
Amax Inc.	11.408	1.36	.376	1.65	.419	8.346	.46	.141	.63	.177		
Amdahl Corp.	14.117	1.51	.307	1.75	.308	—	—	—	—	—		
Amerace Corp.	8.144	1.00	.402	1.05	.334	8.533	.87	.488	.90	.345		
Amerada Hess	11.942	1.48	.409	2.00	.558	10.814	.91	.339	.94	.237		
Amer. Bakeries	10.924	1.20	.320	1.42	.340	12.997	.82	.189	.90	.151		
Amer. Bankers Ins. Gr.	10.381	.77	.146	.70	.091	14.545	1.21	.338	1.29	.258	60	1973–77
Amer. Brands	6.448	.73	.343	.83	.329	5.010	.51	.499	.57	.399		
Amer. Broadcasting	8.053	.97	.384	1.06	.345	12.065	1.25	.508	1.24	.332		
Amer. Bldg. Mainten.	7.577	.82	.311	.83	.243	15.400	1.28	.326	1.13	.167		
Amer. Can	7.555	.75	.265	.84	.249	5.741	.47	.314	.56	.296		
Amer. Century Tr.	14.408	1.34	.230	1.55	.230	20.987	1.99	.426	1.73	.213		
Amer. Cyanamid	7.418	.71	.242	.86	.269	7.678	.81	.525	.91	.436		
Amer. District Teleg.	8.581	1.19	.515	1.27	.436	11.126	1.23	.581	1.47	.546		
Amer. Electric Pwr.	4.561	.24	.073	.26	.065	6.739	.59	.369	.63	.272		
Amer. Express	8.176	1.00	.397	1.05	.331	11.459	1.17	.493	1.66	.660		
Amer. Family	8.060	.64	.170	.55	.092	13.084	1.30	.475	1.48	.413		
Amer. Gen. Bond Fd.	5.349	.37	.138	.40	.117	—	—	—	—	—	62	1973–77
Amer. General	7.768	.89	.353	.90	.270	9.478	.96	.485	1.16	.473	54	1978–82
Amer. Greetings A	7.761	.97	.417	1.09	.393	15.606	1.34	.351	1.84	.435		
Amer. Heritage Life	8.043	.75	.230	.75	.174	—	—	—	—	—		
Amer. Hoist/Derrick	9.894	1.29	.454	1.60	.522	9.452	1.00	.525	.99	.344		
Amer. Home Products	5.776	.63	.314	.69	.283	8.275	.60	.246	.97	.432		
Amer. Hospital Sup.	7.638	.94	.401	1.08	.399	9.705	.87	.377	1.32	.578		
Amer. Int'l Group	6.483	.80	.408	.86	.355	—	—	—	—	—		

Amer. Maize-Prod.	11.436	1.22	.301	1.33	.269	11.364	.91	.318	1.19	.447
Amer. Medical Int'l.	11.279	1.46	.448	1.54	.373	18.552	1.84	.466	1.98	.356
Amer. Motors	11.334	1.24	.319	1.28	.256	11.315	.93	.318	.79	.154
Amer. Natural Res.	6.682	.76	.342	.99	.435	5.800	.44	.271	.49	.225
Amer. Quasar Petrol'm	13.265	1.00	.152	1.39	.221	—	—	—	—	—
Amer. Ship Bldg.	10.117	1.30	.440	1.40	.382	12.989	1.02	.291	1.21	.270
Amer. Standard	9.039	1.25	.512	1.39	.475	10.342	1.14	.576	1.19	.415
Amer. Sterilizer	9.746	1.17	.387	1.32	.366	10.939	.99	.392	.96	.241
Amer. Stores	8.239	.79	.245	.96	.272	12.511	1.24	.469	1.33	.356
Amer. Tel. & Tel.	3.621	.32	.207	.32	.154	4.557	.43	.414	.58	.513
Amer. Water Works	5.436	.44	.174	.45	.137	6.878	.73	.529	.67	.300
AmeriTrust Corp.	6.194	.83	.483	.84	.364	7.591	.84	.585	.87	.413
Ameron, Inc.	7.954	1.04	.453	.98	.306	7.624	.68	.377	.75	.302
Ames Dept. Stores	10.141	1.16	.354	1.10	.237	—	—	—	—	—
Ametek, Inc.	7.453	.94	.424	.94	.318	8.323	.97	.638	1.06	.512
AMF Inc.	8.085	.97	.387	1.04	.331	12.133	1.31	.553	1.41	.426
Amfac Inc.	8.962	1.18	.460	1.27	.403	10.032	.94	.416	.97	.292
Ampco-Pittsburgh	8.963	.77	.196	.93	.217	9.124	.76	.332	.83	.259
AMP Inc.	6.964	.82	.366	.97	.388	8.790	.71	.311	1.07	.467
AMR Corp.	13.408	1.22	.222	1.15	.146	13.780	1.32	.434	1.52	.381
AMREP Corp.	14.103	1.57	.332	1.45	.211	17.995	1.39	.285	1.35	.175
Amstar Corp.	9.839	1.24	.426	1.35	.374	8.087	.67	.321	.65	.205
Amsted Indus.	7.977	1.08	.487	1.13	.404	8.532	.92	.549	1.05	.476
Analog Devices	11.224	.97	.222	1.11	.233	—	—	—	—	—
Anchor Hocking	6.005	.69	.356	.75	.309	7.912	.81	.501	.92	.425
Anderson Clayton	6.682	.80	.384	.92	.379	9.670	.97	.477	1.24	.516
Angelica Corp.	10.278	1.21	.371	1.23	.286	11.051	1.10	.473	1.06	.285
Anglo-Amer. So. Afr. ADR	11.842	1.01	.194	1.14	.186	—	—	—	—	—
Anglo Amer. Gold Inv. ADR	12.062	.94	.161	1.14	.178	—	—	—	—	—
Anglo Energy Ltd.	13.941	1.70	.396	1.87	.360	—	—	—	—	—
Anheuser-Busch Cos.	7.353	.75	.274	.73	.195	9.713	.71	.256	1.05	.363
Anixter Brothers	12.357	1.80	.569	2.04	.544	—	—	—	—	—
Apache Corp.	12.396	1.42	.349	1.77	.409	11.484	1.00	.360	1.09	.280
Applied Magnetics	13.629	1.16	.192	1.25	.167	15.547	1.46	.419	1.41	.257
ARA Services	6.821	.70	.280	.77	.256	10.756	.96	.381	1.32	.473
Archer-Daniels-Midl.	9.067	1.19	.463	1.42	.487	12.356	.78	.189	1.03	.216

Stock	January 1978–December 1982					January 1973–December 1977					Incomplete Data Series	
	Log (%) Std. Dev.	VLIC Est. Beta	VLIC R^2	NYSE Est. Beta	NYSE R^2	Log (%) Std. Dev.	VLIC Est. Beta	VLIC R^2	NYSE Est. Beta	NYSE R^2	Number of Obs.	Period
Arden Group	14.519	1.57	.312	1.73	.283	16.486	1.15	.229	1.03	.122		
Arizona Public Serv.	5.173	.30	.091	.34	.087	6.482	.73	.602	.80	.476		
Arkansas Best	11.097	1.18	.304	1.06	.184	13.401	1.09	.316	1.12	.220		
Arkla Inc.	7.733	.81	.290	1.07	.384	7.265	.74	.489	.80	.382		
Arlen Realty & Dev.	19.238	1.46	.154	1.22	.080	17.014	1.59	.416	1.46	.231		
Armada Corp.	9.647	.78	.173	.85	.155	10.000	.38	.070	.25	.020		
Armco Inc.	8.375	.97	.361	1.11	.353	7.074	.61	.354	.69	.299		
Armstrong Rubber	10.144	1.01	.263	1.01	.198	9.823	.88	.378	.78	.196		
Armstrong World Indus.	7.445	1.03	.513	1.20	.519	9.051	.68	.270	.86	.285		
Aro Corp.	5.656	.56	.259	.54	.184	8.104	.73	.381	.81	.316		
Arrow Electronics	12.578	1.35	.307	1.35	.231	—	—	—	—	—		
Artra Group	11.115	1.34	.387	1.48	.357	—	—	—	—	—		
Arvin Indus.	8.275	1.11	.482	1.11	.358	13.565	1.21	.377	1.12	.215		
Asamera Inc.	11.477	1.46	.443	1.64	.441	—	—	—	—	—	49	1978–82
ASA Ltd.	12.889	1.08	.187	1.33	.212	12.412	.15	.007	.36	.026		
ASARCO Inc.	13.176	1.49	.340	1.65	.312	9.800	.93	.423	.99	.317		
Ashland Oil	9.899	.79	.171	1.05	.227	7.332	.82	.598	.94	.515		
Associated Dry Gds.	8.134	.85	.292	.87	.228	10.623	.77	.251	1.03	.293		
Athlone Indus.	7.297	.72	.259	.67	.168	10.738	.77	.245	.69	.129		
Atlanta Gas Light	4.235	.46	.313	.50	.277	6.765	.70	.503	.70	.333		
Atlantic City Elec.	5.196	.36	.131	.41	.125	6.792	.71	.520	.84	.474		
Atlantic Metropolitan	16.145	1.74	.310	1.57	.188	18.189	1.77	.449	1.83	.318		
Atlantic Richfield	8.696	.67	.160	1.14	.341	6.187	.20	.051	.46	.175		
Atlas Con. Mining/Dev. "B"	16.333	1.36	.186	1.30	.126	13.981	1.13	.246	1.21	.188		
Atlas Corp.	12.315	1.44	.367	1.48	.288	14.113	1.08	.278	1.25	.244		
Augat, Inc.	9.371	1.36	.561	1.53	.535	—	—	—	—	—	60	1973–77
Automatic Data Proc.	7.868	.95	.385	1.02	.333	15.844	1.70	.543	2.05	.526		
Avco Corp.	11.839	1.68	.536	1.93	.529	16.361	1.92	.651	1.98	.461		
Avery Int'l.	8.392	1.10	.460	1.25	.441	11.461	1.03	.383	1.47	.517		
Avnet Inc.	9.685	1.47	.617	1.74	.643	12.618	1.52	.688	1.66	.544		

Avon Products	6.677	.83	.416	.91	.375	12.851	1.11	.352	1.57	.468	44	1978–82
AVX Corp.	15.909	1.67	.327	1.69	.268	9.083	—	—	—	.307		
AXIA Inc.	7.191	.79	.325	.76	.224	—	.92	.485	.90	—	48	1978–82
Aydin Corp.	12.437	1.34	.323	1.50	.324	16.385	1.93	.659	1.81	.382		
Bairnco Corp.	8.715	.99	.345	.93	.229	10.273	.50	.112	.85	.217		
Baker Int'l.	9.435	1.11	.369	1.47	.484	—	—	—	—	—	48	1978–82
Baldor Electric	10.230	1.02	.280	1.03	.224	9.977	—	—	—	—		
Baldwin-United	10.872	1.31	.388	1.30	.284	19.426	.72	.249	.66	.152	51	1973–77
Ball Corp.	7.391	.98	.471	1.06	.414	7.019	2.01	.500	2.07	.408	50	1973–77
Bally Mfg.	15.331	1.54	.270	1.56	.206	8.482	.68	.450	.73	.338		
Baltimore Gas & El.	5.140	.38	.143	.38	.107	12.130	.68	.304	.78	.265		
BanCal Tri-State	10.336	.81	.165	.73	.099	15.623	.95	.288	1.25	.331		
Bandag, Inc.	8.104	1.22	.600	1.29	.503	8.304	1.49	.429	1.41	.255		
Bangor Punta	11.996	1.53	.433	1.61	.358	—	.82	.458	1.02	.473		
BankAmerica Corp.	6.193	.56	.216	.61	.194	8.882	—	—	—	—		
BankAmer. Realty Inv.	9.421	1.23	.455	1.25	.354	6.993	.99	.595	1.08	.459		
Bankers Trust NY	7.088	.87	.402	.98	.382	10.727	.76	.555	.74	.350		
Bank of New York	6.804	.81	.382	.97	.409	—	1.00	.408	1.12	.342		
Bank of Virginia	6.571	.88	.480	.93	.402	—	—	—	—	—		
Banner Indus.	15.532	1.30	.187	1.41	.164	12.240	—	—	—	—	57	1978–82
Barber-Greene	11.986	1.17	.270	1.11	.179	7.822	1.37	.591	1.76	.645		
Bard (C.R.)	9.088	1.21	.474	1.33	.429	—	.68	.361	.85	.368		
Barnes Group	8.349	.91	.316	1.00	.288	—	—	—	—	—		
Barnett Banks of Fla.	8.099	1.13	.518	1.10	.367	15.378	—	—	—	—		
Barry (R. G.)	14.659	1.37	.232	1.17	.126	9.781	—	—	—	—		
Barry Wright	10.121	1.33	.459	1.48	.427	7.344	—	—	—	—		
Bausch & Lomb	8.715	.73	.186	.86	.193	—	1.30	.339	1.44	.276		
Baxter Travenol Lab.	6.630	.67	.268	.70	.224	7.835	.83	.343	1.29	.547		
Bay State Gas	5.882	.66	.331	.71	.288	7.295	—	—	—	—		
BBDO Int'l.	6.627	.81	.397	.79	.283	11.832	.66	.382	.72	.348	50	1973–77
Bearings, Inc.	7.188	.59	.177	.56	.121	—	—	—	—	—		
Beatrice Foods	6.047	.67	.330	.73	.294	—	.66	.339	.82	.340		
Becton, Dickinson	6.204	.69	.327	.75	.291	—	.66	.384	.94	.525		
Beker Indus.	16.207	1.87	.353	2.18	.360	—	.66	.144	.80	.157		
Bekins Co.	15.861	1.73	.346	1.71	.270	—	—	—	—	—	52	1973–77
Belco Petroleum	10.554	.98	.228	1.33	.315	11.264	.94	.333	1.02	.258	45	1978–82

Stock	January 1978–December 1982 Log (%) Std. Dev.	VLIC Est. Beta	VLIC R²	NYSE Est. Beta	NYSE R²	January 1973–December 1977 Log (%) Std. Dev.	VLIC Est. Beta	VLIC R²	NYSE Est. Beta	NYSE R²	Incomplete Data Series Number of Obs.	Period
Belding Hemingway	8.044	.60	.149	.44	.059	9.990	.86	.353	.88	.242		
Bell & Howell	9.794	1.33	.493	1.46	.446	11.846	1.17	.461	1.13	.283		
Bell Industries	11.878	1.57	.466	1.61	.369	—	—	—	—	—		
Bell Tel. of Canada	4.838	.36	.145	.42	.149	—	—	—	—	—		
Bemis Co.	6.892	.56	.179	.68	.196	8.551	.95	.589	1.00	.429		
Bendix Corp.	8.307	1.04	.421	1.22	.429	8.068	.91	.602	.95	.432		
Beneficial Corp.	8.533	.96	.341	1.08	.319	10.593	1.06	.472	1.18	.390		
Benguet Corp.	20.159	1.72	.194	1.89	.175	15.996	.93	.161	1.04	.132		
Berkey Photo	15.518	1.20	.159	.99	.082	17.700	1.97	.588	2.01	.405		
Best Products	11.993	.98	.179	.88	.108	16.138	1.47	.409	1.64	.388	47	1973–77
Bethlehem Steel	8.247	1.07	.448	1.18	.412	8.642	.76	.365	.89	.334		
Betz Laboratories	8.090	.94	.364	1.04	.332	12.006	1.09	.407	1.65	.618	60	1973–77
Beverly Enterprises	12.016	1.90	.664	2.03	.570	—	—	—	—	—		
BIC Corp.	10.292	1.27	.406	1.26	.302	—	—	—	—	—		
Big Three Indus.	8.418	1.16	.506	1.31	.485	9.954	1.04	.520	1.27	.511		
Binney & Smith	12.484	1.36	.314	1.50	.289	—	—	—	—	—		
Bird & Son	11.254	1.38	.401	1.64	.424	—	—	—	—	—		
Black & Decker Mfg.	7.495	1.05	.523	1.12	.449	10.131	.91	.382	1.33	.539		
Blair (John)	9.831	1.09	.328	1.18	.287	12.084	1.29	.541	1.24	.332		
Block (H & R)	7.128	.99	.516	1.16	.525	14.649	1.39	.424	1.45	.306		
Blue Bell	8.199	.86	.295	.97	.277	11.938	1.24	.510	1.25	.345		
Blyvoor Gold Mng. ADR	15.183	1.13	.147	1.52	.199	—	—	—	—	—		
Bob Evans Farms	8.074	.79	.261	.82	.222	—	—	—	—	—	49	1978–82
Boeing Co.	11.025	1.28	.361	1.42	.330	10.170	.82	.305	.92	.258		
Bohemia Inc.	11.407	1.54	.483	1.79	.490	—	—	—	—	—		
Boise Cascade	9.206	1.45	.664	1.60	.603	12.090	1.28	.528	1.48	.470		
Borden, Inc.	5.107	.41	.169	.42	.134	7.139	.62	.356	.72	.323		
Borg-Warner	7.171	1.05	.567	1.19	.550	8.890	1.00	.594	1.05	.433		
Borman's Inc.	14.054	1.16	.182	.96	.093	14.265	1.47	.506	1.41	.308		
Boston Edison	4.809	.17	.033	.16	.022	8.228	.66	.301	.62	.181		

Brascan Ltd.	8.785	.89	.273	.97	.245	7.094	.66	.424	.66	.281	60	1973–77
Brigadier Indus.	13.252	1.50	.343	1.50	.255	19.910	1.76	.370	1.59	.200		
Briggs & Stratton	6.399	.70	.316	.77	.291	8.365	.69	.324	.90	.360		
Bristol-Myers	6.348	.80	.421	.91	.408	8.881	.70	.290	1.15	.525		
British Petroleum	9.068	.51	.086	.87	.182	9.393	.68	.249	.87	.266		
Brockway Inc.	6.140	.61	.261	.63	.208	10.184	1.06	.511	1.10	.365		
Broken Hill Prop. ADR	8.907	.92	.283	1.02	.278	—	—	—	—	—	52	1978–82
Brooklyn Union Gas	5.588	.40	.137	.32	.066	5.536	.58	.521	.57	.335		
Brooks Fashion Stores	11.603	1.28	.323	1.22	.221	—	—	—	—	—		
Brown & Sharpe Mfg.	11.077	1.31	.371	1.32	.285	11.840	1.23	.510	1.08	.262		
Brown-Forman Dist.	7.466	1.01	.490	1.12	.448	9.246	.79	.349	.77	.218		
Brown Group	7.381	.95	.441	.94	.325	8.242	.69	.331	.69	.218		
Browning-Ferris Ind.	9.657	1.47	.620	1.64	.579	13.489	1.18	.363	1.22	.257		
Brown (Tom) Inc.	16.623	1.61	.250	2.09	.316	8.692	.08	.004	.02	.001	44	1973–77
Brunswick Corp.	11.464	1.26	.323	1.30	.257	14.936	1.68	.601	1.82	.464		
Brush Wellman	9.234	1.28	.514	1.34	.418	12.150	1.26	.508	1.31	.365		
Bucyrus-Erie	9.194	.88	.245	1.00	.236	10.256	.62	.173	.85	.217		
Burlington Indus.	7.470	.86	.351	.88	.279	9.102	.86	.428	1.00	.379		
Burlington-Northern	10.502	1.32	.424	1.64	.488	10.015	.74	.256	1.08	.361		
Burndy Corp.	7.561	1.02	.498	1.08	.407	11.935	1.22	.497	1.36	.409		
Burroughs Corp.	7.263	.70	.248	.79	.237	9.319	.78	.330	1.23	.549		
Butler Int'l.	11.153	1.54	.510	1.61	.415	—	—	—	—	—		
Butler Mfg.	6.615	.50	.155	.44	.087	8.927	.47	.103	.44	.063	41	1973–77
Buttes Gas & Oil	12.325	1.25	.276	1.49	.293	13.597	1.26	.421	1.63	.469	60	1973–77
Cabot Corp.	10.012	1.34	.478	1.59	.506	9.910	.99	.472	1.01	.324		
Cadence Indus.	14.898	1.23	.182	1.09	.107	17.868	1.48	.323	1.19	.140		
Caesars World	19.649	1.73	.206	1.89	.185	13.735	1.08	.296	1.10	.200		
Callahan Mining	13.247	1.03	.161	1.24	.175	13.488	.91	.216	.99	.170		
Cameron Iron Works	11.285	.97	.196	1.28	.258	—	—	—	—	—		
Campbell Red Lake	13.026	1.17	.215	1.42	.238	12.405	.11	.004	.39	.032		
Campbell Soup	5.587	.55	.262	.57	.208	6.494	.61	.421	.77	.446		
Canadian Pac. Enter.	9.336	.92	.279	.97	.248	—	—	—	—	—	46	1978–82
Canadian Pacific	8.737	.96	.321	1.05	.290	6.212	.46	.265	.58	.274		
Canal-Randolph	11.125	.58	.072	.67	.073	7.498	.49	.203	.53	.154		
Canon Inc. ADR	10.515	.70	.120	.74	.098	—	—	—	—	—		
Capital Cities Comm.	6.742	.96	.543	.99	.434	10.549	1.06	.483	1.38	.533		

| Stock | January 1978–December 1982 | | | | | January 1973–December 1977 | | | | | Incomplete Data Series | |
	Log (%) Std. Dev.	VLIC Est. Beta	VLIC R²	NYSE Est. Beta	NYSE R²	Log (%) Std. Dev.	VLIC Est. Beta	VLIC R²	NYSE Est. Beta	NYSE R²	Number of Obs.	Period
Capital Holding	6.851	.70	.280	.70	.211	9.331	.78	.330	1.04	.393		
Carling O'Keefe Ltd.	10.554	1.20	.344	1.26	.286	10.266	.80	.291	.67	.134		
Carlisle Corp.	12.336	1.48	.382	1.59	.334	10.357	1.12	.553	1.19	.412		
Carnation Co.	6.066	.71	.364	.74	.295	7.485	.60	.301	.80	.359		
Carolina Freight Carrier	11.629	1.14	.257	1.19	.210	9.843	.94	.434	.94	.286		
Carolina Pwr. & Lt.	5.768	.17	.022	.12	.009	7.035	.60	.341	.66	.275		
Carpenter Technology	8.545	.89	.291	1.04	.297	9.145	.95	.514	1.00	.376		
Carson Pirie Scott	8.914	.80	.213	.89	.201	—	—	—	—	—		
Carter Hawley Hale	7.583	.89	.367	.99	.343	10.681	1.04	.446	1.06	.309		
Carter-Wallace	9.026	1.11	.406	1.00	.244	10.797	1.20	.585	1.34	.481		
Cascade Natural Gas	5.191	.35	.119	.36	.095	—	—	—	—	—		
Castle & Cooke	7.283	.92	.430	.99	.367	7.681	.60	.285	.79	.332		
Caterpillar Tractor	6.074	.73	.386	.84	.378	7.633	.77	.487	1.03	.575		
CBI Indus.	8.657	.80	.227	1.09	.314	9.056	.63	.174	.76	.185	41	1973–77
CBS Inc.	7.474	.94	.423	1.03	.378	9.179	1.05	.625	1.26	.586		
CCI Corp.	13.917	1.93	.513	2.11	.459	19.301	1.44	.263	1.14	.110		
CCX Inc.	10.833	1.05	.252	1.05	.187	12.568	.87	.228	.90	.162		
Ceco Corp.	8.429	1.11	.466	1.20	.406	7.806	.62	.303	.63	.205		
Celanese Corp.	7.068	.92	.453	1.00	.401	8.052	.63	.288	.68	.224		
Centel Corp.	5.674	.45	.167	.46	.132	7.262	.61	.340	.82	.396		
Centerre Bancorp.	5.869	.72	.402	.77	.343	7.643	.71	.407	.73	.286		
Centex Corp.	10.913	1.53	.524	1.80	.544	15.332	1.70	.581	1.92	.493		
Central & So. West	4.673	.20	.051	.21	.040	8.396	.76	.392	1.05	.489		
Central Hudson Gas & El.	4.880	.35	.141	.39	.127	6.301	.44	.236	.37	.106		
Central Illinois Lt.	5.062	.37	.146	.38	.115	7.287	.74	.483	.78	.363		
Central Ill. Pub. Ser.	4.731	.27	.090	.25	.056	6.611	.63	.429	.66	.309		
Central Maine Power	5.089	.41	.170	.48	.180	5.121	.44	.353	.38	.169		
Central Soya	10.593	1.37	.448	1.67	.498	10.146	.95	.416	1.22	.456		
Centronics Data	17.423	1.51	.201	1.57	.161	17.329	1.53	.382	1.93	.405	60	1973–77
Certain-teed Corp.	8.935	.97	.315	1.14	.326	12.381	1.01	.315	1.11	.250		

Company											
Cessna Aircraft	1.30	.304	1.33	.242	14.943	1.49	.473	1.46	.299	41	1978–82
CFS Continental	1.09	.443	1.04	.323	—	—	—	—	.501		
Champion Home Bldrs.	1.46	.251	1.57	.217	16.122	1.79	.587	2.04	.456		
Champion Int'l.	1.33	.541	1.51	.521	10.885	1.21	.583	1.31	.369		
Champion Spark Plug	.81	.333	.86	.276	8.739	.82	.419	.95	—		
Charming Shoppes	1.41	.376	1.51	.327	—	—	—	—	.383		
Charter Co.	1.31	.153	1.62	.176	13.619	1.21	.373	1.51	.422		
Chart House	1.25	.412	1.34	.356	11.598	1.14	.378	1.27	.393	51	1973–77
Chase Manhattan	.76	.276	.83	.247	8.312	.88	.527	.93	.154		
Chelsea Indus.	1.12	.352	1.03	.222	12.230	1.00	.318	.86	.344		
Chemical New York	.81	.394	.83	.313	7.851	.83	.528	.82	.371		
Chesapeake Corp. Va.	.95	.261	.91	.181	6.902	.72	.520	.75	.523		
Chesebrough-Pond's	.64	.312	.69	.272	10.477	.89	.345	1.35	.262		
Chicago Milwaukee	1.63	.166	1.68	.131	15.081	1.30	.354	1.38	—		
Chicago & N.W. Tran.	1.43	.237	1.75	.282	—	—	—	—	.329	49	1978–82
Chicago Pneum. Tool	1.13	.485	1.14	.373	8.375	.84	.471	.86	—		
Chieftain Develop.	1.37	.269	1.37	.202	—	—	—	—	.167		
Chock Full O' Nuts	1.20	.300	1.25	.245	17.391	1.28	.256	1.27	.185		
Chris-Craft Indus.	1.18	.304	1.28	.267	17.076	1.28	.267	1.31	.366		
Chromalloy American	1.50	.547	1.58	.455	8.405	.95	.611	.91	.233		
Chrysler Corp.	1.18	.231	1.08	.145	11.491	1.07	.411	.99	.203		
Chubb Corp.	.43	.085	.46	.074	9.231	.50	.144	.73	.499	60	1973–77
Church's Fried Chicken	1.31	.514	1.42	.447	12.703	1.39	.566	1.51	.481	51	1973–77
CIGNA Corp.	.92	.347	1.04	.332	9.694	.77	.297	1.20	.365		
Cincinnati Bell	.39	.217	.44	.211	4.036	.39	.436	.44	.176		
Cincinnati Gas & El.	.32	.084	.39	.093	6.594	.48	.251	.49	.201		
Cincinnati Milacron	1.38	.501	1.49	.435	11.434	1.03	.384	.92	.529		
Citicorp	.80	.286	.91	.278	10.367	.98	.426	1.35	.385		
Citizens & Sthn. Ga.	.99	.415	.94	.276	9.823	.76	.286	1.09	—		
Citizens Util. B	.73	.354	.76	.307	—	—	—	—	.347		
City Investing	1.27	.442	1.36	.383	12.862	1.41	.573	1.35	.553	44	1978–82
Clark Equipment	.78	.335	.76	.240	11.067	1.29	.640	1.47	—		
Clark (J.L.) Mfg.	.85	.349	.88	.281	—	—	—	—	—		
CLC of America	1.24	.287	1.39	.270	11.314	1.09	.438	1.15	.321		
Cleveland-Cliffs	.88	.412	.97	.371	8.381	.75	.383	.99	.434		
Cleveland Elec. Ill.	.33	.091	.33	.068	5.296	.47	.368	.46	.238		

Stock	Jan 1978–Dec 1982 Log (%) Std. Dev.	VLIC Est. Beta	VLIC R²	NYSE Est. Beta	NYSE R²	Jan 1973–Dec 1977 Log (%) Std. Dev.	VLIC Est. Beta	VLIC R²	NYSE Est. Beta	NYSE R²	Incomplete Data Series Number of Obs.	Period
Clevepak Corp.	10.322	1.35	.456	1.27	.302	—	—	—	—	—		
Clorox Co.	7.642	.80	.293	.89	.270	15.959	1.46	.396	1.72	.362		
Cluett, Peabody	9.693	1.10	.347	1.29	.356	11.907	1.03	.353	1.02	.228		
CNA Financial	9.937	1.21	.394	1.31	.349	17.549	1.80	.501	1.73	.303		
Coachmen Indus.	15.294	1.91	.418	1.90	.308	16.615	1.29	.281	1.62	.341	50	1973–77
Coastal Corp.	14.730	1.44	.256	1.79	.296	17.883	1.38	.283	1.39	.188		
Cobe Laboratories	10.196	.94	.226	1.02	.201	—	—	—	—	—		
Coca-Cola	5.719	.64	.331	.66	.266	9.595	.92	.562	1.42	.683		
Coherent, Inc.	12.932	.99	.173	1.00	.140	—	—	—	—	—	45	1978–82
Coleco Indus.	19.329	1.77	.223	1.84	.180	17.435	1.59	.396	1.70	.296		
Coleman Co.	8.251	.89	.311	.95	.263	11.971	1.22	.495	1.26	.346		
Colgate-Palmolive	6.598	.66	.266	.68	.211	8.129	.67	.323	1.03	.502		
Collins & Aikman	8.101	1.11	.496	1.22	.455	11.041	1.11	.479	1.16	.344		
Collins Foods Int'l	11.721	1.53	.456	1.43	.299	16.054	1.80	.617	1.88	.447	60	1973–77
Colonial Penn Group	9.992	1.08	.312	1.06	.223	16.204	1.34	.324	2.05	.499		
Color Tile	13.023	1.02	.175	1.25	.195	—	—	—	—	—	54	1978–82
Colt Indus.	9.973	.89	.210	1.03	.213	10.526	1.03	.458	1.09	.336		
Columbia Gas System	6.152	.59	.242	.78	.324	6.277	.59	.419	.67	.362		
Combined Int'l.	6.441	.71	.321	.81	.313	11.690	1.26	.548	1.32	.400		
Combustion Eng.	9.316	1.08	.359	1.32	.404	12.128	.84	.228	.95	.192		
Cominco Ltd.	9.076	.85	.234	1.08	.283	6.387	.42	.203	.52	.206		
Commerce Clear House	9.019	.68	.153	.86	.181	11.732	.79	.223	.84	.167	60	1973–77
Commercial Metals	11.576	1.15	.287	1.33	.306	—	—	—	—	—	45	1978–82
Commodore Int'l.	18.828	2.07	.354	2.25	.332	—	—	—	—	—	45	1978–82
Commonwealth Edison	5.094	.32	.103	.35	.097	6.483	.54	.326	.76	.431		
Commonwealth Energy Sys.	5.813	.45	.160	.48	.138	7.000	.64	.390	.64	.262		
Communic. Satellite	9.159	1.20	.461	1.38	.451	10.516	.90	.346	1.02	.296		
Community Psych. Ctrs.	10.684	1.53	.550	1.60	.447	—	—	—	—	—		
Compugraphic Corp.	13.975	1.31	.233	1.43	.208	15.520	1.82	.673	2.09	.592	60	1973–77
Computer Sciences	12.636	1.52	.387	1.47	.269	13.941	1.45	.515	1.39	.311		

Computervision Corp.	14.519	1.98	.494	2.24	.476	—	—	—	—	—	
ConAgra Inc.	8.654	.88	.273	.97	.251	12.174	.84	.174	.72	.090	41 1973–77
Conair Corp.	16.226	1.77	.365	1.59	.236	9.781	.82	.336	.86	.243	42 1978–82
Cone Mills	7.945	.96	.390	1.12	.394	—	—	—	—	—	
Connecticut Nat. Gas	5.982	.43	.121	.48	.128	12.161	1.23	.487	1.42	.428	
Conrac Corp.	10.685	1.47	.506	1.66	.482	14.474	1.17	.312	1.20	.217	
Consolidated Edison	5.244	.24	.054	.28	.058	9.759	.96	.460	1.09	.388	
Consolidated Foods	6.355	.63	.259	.62	.193	13.197	1.25	.426	1.36	.332	
Consol. Freightways	9.566	1.22	.436	1.27	.353	5.512	.49	.372	.46	.220	
Consol. Natural Gas	6.923	.69	.265	.90	.336	—	—	—	—	—	
Consol. Oil & Gas	14.222	1.73	.397	2.05	.414	—	—	—	—	—	
Consolidated Papers	8.710	1.07	.405	1.16	.356	7.878	.62	.291	.50	.125	
Consumers Power	5.216	.34	.111	.31	.069	6.829	.48	.230	.76	.385	
Continental Corp.	6.449	.66	.280	.82	.321	7.271	.58	.298	.61	.221	
Cont'l Group Inc.	6.140	.82	.478	.95	.476	10.896	1.12	.502	1.31	.370	
Cont'l Illinois Corp.	9.187	.98	.301	1.02	.245	8.104	.86	.539	1.08	.558	
Cont'l Telecom Inc.	5.355	.52	.250	.52	.190	13.837	1.64	.666	2.00	.651	
Control Data	9.530	1.37	.550	1.49	.487	6.020	.58	.446	.70	.420	
Conwood Corp.	6.971	.85	.399	.95	.373	18.016	1.91	.533	1.91	.351	
Cook United	13.834	1.42	.279	1.26	.165	10.906	1.14	.516	1.50	.592	
Cooper Indus.	8.923	1.00	.336	1.35	.455	19.862	1.69	.342	1.67	.222	
Cooper Laboratories	11.996	1.12	.234	1.08	.163	13.791	1.35	.454	1.29	.272	
Cooper Tire & Rubber	11.218	.80	.135	.90	.129	—	—	—	—	—	
Coors (Adolph)	9.613	1.16	.391	1.26	.341	10.327	.85	.324	.95	.263	
Copperweld Corp.	8.772	.67	.154	.73	.140	—	—	—	—	—	
Cordis Corp.	15.371	1.91	.412	2.04	.353	17.633	1.48	.332	1.32	.175	
Cordura Corp.	12.090	1.13	.232	1.30	.231	10.352	1.17	.608	1.11	.360	
Core Indus.	8.358	1.07	.438	1.13	.363	—	—	—	—	—	
Core Laboratories	13.817	1.65	.448	2.00	.523	10.629	1.06	.467	1.31	.477	41 1978–82
Corning Glass Works	7.175	.92	.442	1.08	.452	8.794	.80	.405	.79	.261	60 1973–77
Corroon & Black	7.850	.89	.346	.81	.214	11.512	1.31	.617	1.36	.439	
Cowles Communications	8.600	1.19	.514	1.30	.460	12.648	1.33	.525	1.42	.395	
Cox Communications	7.466	.83	.331	.93	.313	6.870	.59	.350	.81	.440	
CPC Int'l	5.201	.65	.414	.70	.366	—	—	—	—	—	
CP National	5.875	.47	.168	.50	.144	—	—	—	—	—	
Craig Corp.	9.582	.82	.196	.81	.144	—	—	—	—	—	

| Stock | January 1978–December 1982 | | | | | January 1973–December 1977 | | | | | Incomplete Data Series | |
	Log (%) Std. Dev.	VLIC Est. Beta	VLIC R^2	NYSE Est. Beta	NYSE R^2	Log (%) Std. Dev.	VLIC Est. Beta	VLIC R^2	NYSE Est. Beta	NYSE R^2	Number of Obs.	Period
Crane Co.	10.124	1.25	.408	1.52	.448	10.206	.90	.370	1.07	.345		
Crawford & Co.	8.646	.96	.331	1.04	.291	—	—	—	—	—	50	1978–82
Cray Research	12.808	1.59	.413	1.84	.442	—	—	—	—	—		
Crocker National	7.134	.76	.302	.80	.254	9.086	1.08	.672	1.20	.550		
Crompton & Knowles	7.794	.87	.333	.89	.258	10.427	1.19	.614	1.23	.435		
Cross & Trecker	11.597	1.36	.366	1.42	.301	14.382	1.58	.573	1.62	.397		
Cross (A.T.)	7.568	.88	.357	.91	.288	—	—	—	—	—		
Crown Cork & Seal	7.306	.96	.458	1.03	.396	8.283	.83	.479	1.01	.463		
Crown Zellerbach	9.411	1.25	.468	1.43	.462	8.215	.82	.476	1.06	.524		
Crum & Forster	10.443	.99	.239	1.09	.216	8.983	.76	.340	1.01	.394		
CSX Corp.	8.478	1.20	.537	1.41	.554	7.466	.56	.262	.81	.368		
CTS Corp.	9.543	1.31	.502	1.37	.412	11.336	1.21	.540	1.32	.425		
Cubic Corp.	12.254	1.63	.489	1.66	.380	—	—	—	—	—	61	1978–82
Culbro Corp.	11.812	1.08	.223	1.04	.154	8.173	.79	.444	.71	.238		
Cummins Engine	9.421	1.25	.471	1.29	.375	12.058	1.07	.376	1.18	.302		
Curtiss-Wright	11.157	1.02	.221	1.10	.196	14.637	1.40	.435	1.43	.301		
Cyclops Corp.	10.399	1.30	.415	1.31	.319	10.757	.98	.394	.99	.263		
Damon Corp.	15.014	1.84	.402	2.02	.363	22.631	1.98	.363	2.82	.487		
Dana Corp.	7.325	.62	.189	.63	.148	10.132	1.08	.540	1.14	.398		
Daniel Indus.	11.316	1.24	.320	1.51	.354	—	—	—	—	—		
Dan River	10.098	.91	.216	.83	.136	10.658	.94	.371	.82	.186		
Dart & Kraft	4.613	.49	.301	.55	.280	6.588	.45	.217	.55	.215		
Data General	13.161	1.38	.294	1.52	.267	15.526	1.30	.331	1.85	.446		
Datapoint Corp.	15.197	1.51	.263	1.71	.252	15.587	1.81	.492	2.11	.475		
Dataproducts Corp.	13.177	1.89	.550	2.15	.534	—	—	—	—	—	41	1973–77
Data Terminal Sys.	14.959	1.06	.134	1.03	.094	—	—	—	—	—		
Dayco Corp.	8.821	.99	.338	.96	.238	7.854	.70	.377	.76	.295		
Dayton-Hudson	7.480	.90	.387	.99	.347	11.909	1.05	.369	1.22	.331		
Dayton Power & Lt.	5.291	.39	.143	.39	.111	6.654	.63	.426	.73	.374		
DeBeers Cons. Mns. ADR	10.982	1.13	.283	1.34	.298	—	—	—	—	—		

Company												
Deere & Co.	6.483	.82	.426	1.00	.474	8.868	.60	.220	.87	.300		
DEKALB AgResearch	10.810	1.23	.343	1.58	.429	10.414	.71	.227	.97	.286	60	1973–77
Delmarva Pwr. & Lt.	5.305	.35	.118	.42	.128	6.700	.72	.547	.83	.481		
Delta Air Lines	9.268	.95	.280	.95	.211	10.559	1.04	.462	1.40	.554		
Deltona Corp.	15.901	2.29	.555	2.50	.548	16.830	1.50	.375	1.21	.162		
De Luxe Check Print	7.654	.87	.347	.97	.322	8.406	.51	.178	.64	.189	60	1973–77
Denison Mines Ltd.	10.329	1.02	.259	1.15	.246	8.423	.57	.224	.63	.177	62	1973–77
Dennison Mfg.	7.232	.78	.314	.84	.267	9.405	.97	.504	.93	.309		
Denny's Inc.	9.336	.90	.249	.89	.180	15.678	1.91	.703	2.33	.700		
DeSoto, Inc.	8.572	1.07	.412	1.20	.395	12.910	.99	.280	.95	.170		
Detroit Edison	4.258	.31	.139	.32	.113	8.635	.82	.423	.86	.311		
Dexter Corp.	7.933	.68	.199	.81	.210	12.329	1.24	.483	1.36	.382		
Diamond Shamrock	10.085	1.28	.429	1.64	.529	8.359	.87	.515	.99	.442		
Diebold, Inc.	10.116	1.01	.268	1.13	.248	12.512	1.06	.339	1.30	.338		
DiGiorgio Corp.	10.037	.96	.244	1.00	.199	11.251	1.11	.462	1.01	.254		
Digital Equipment	8.206	1.12	.493	1.30	.503	10.204	.87	.342	1.15	.397		
Dillon Cos.	8.072	.64	.168	.50	.076	7.253	.47	.203	.50	.148		
Disney (Walt) Prod.	8.484	1.00	.371	1.14	.363	13.392	1.60	.675	2.01	.704		
Diversified Energies	5.142	.52	.268	.47	.164	—	—	—	—	—		
Diversified Indus.	16.199	1.45	.215	1.30	.129	16.338	.84	.124	.75	.067		
DMG Inc.	14.567	1.64	.337	1.72	.278	26.159	2.46	.418	2.20	.221		
Dr. Pepper	8.135	1.00	.403	1.02	.315	12.841	1.20	.415	1.75	.579		
Dollar General	10.589	1.21	.369	1.30	.316	—	—	—	—	—	57	1978–82
Dome Mines, Ltd.	13.921	1.30	.233	1.58	.259	10.126	.20	.018	.41	.052	60	1973–77
Dome Petroleum Ltd.	14.645	.69	.059	.52	.025	12.711	1.07	.347	1.33	.361		
Dominion Stores Ltd.	6.416	.64	.265	.71	.246	—	—	—	—	—		
Dominion Textile	7.989	.78	.254	.85	.228	—	—	—	—	—		
Domtar, Inc.	8.213	.87	.297	.91	.245	8.708	.62	.245	.74	.237		
Donaldson Co.	9.226	1.10	.382	1.12	.297	14.775	1.37	.430	1.66	.414		
Donaldson, Lufkin & Jen.	13.878	1.92	.508	2.02	.421	14.433	1.37	.428	1.65	.410		
Donnelley (RR) & Sons	6.379	.85	.474	.96	.455	7.252	.52	.248	.58	.200		
Dorchester Gas	11.804	1.21	.280	1.57	.354	—	—	—	—	—		
Dorsey Corp.	10.315	1.17	.346	1.21	.275	14.516	1.61	.586	1.55	.355		
Dover Corp.	7.426	.98	.468	1.23	.552	10.247	1.09	.533	1.08	.350	60	1973–77
Dow Chemical	7.531	1.05	.515	1.31	.605	8.460	.79	.415	1.20	.625	60	1973–77
Dow Jones & Co.	7.462	.94	.423	1.07	.413	—	—	—	—	—		

| | January 1978–December 1982 | | | | | January 1973–December 1977 | | | | | Incomplete Data Series | |
| | Log (%) Std. Dev. | VLIC | | NYSE | | Log (%) Std. Dev. | VLIC | | NYSE | | Number of Obs. | Period |
Stock		Est. Beta	R²	Est. Beta	R²		Est. Beta	R²	Est. Beta	R²		
Doyle Dane Bernbach Int'l.	7.725	.70	.221	.79	.207	10.920	1.11	.494	1.26	.419		
Dravo Corp.	8.438	.81	.248	1.01	.284	8.873	.70	.295	.75	.224		
Dresser Indus.	9.781	1.05	.306	1.40	.409	9.317	.69	.263	1.03	.385		
Drexel Bond Deb. Tr. Fd.	4.717	.39	.182	.43	.165	5.560	.40	.243	.38	.148		
Dreyfus Corp.	12.331	1.05	.195	1.11	.161	11.706	1.21	.503	1.25	.358		
Driefontein Consol. ADR	12.877	.91	.133	1.17	.164	—	—	—	—	—		
Duke Power	5.436	.18	.029	.13	.012	6.836	.65	.429	.67	.299		
Dun & Bradstreet	6.098	.81	.476	.90	.435	9.678	.89	.400	1.23	.504		
Dunkin' Donuts	11.497	1.50	.453	1.46	.320	—	—	—	—	—		
du Pont (E.I.) de Nemours	7.392	1.00	.490	1.12	.456	8.156	.73	.377	.95	.427		
Duquesne Light	5.407	.40	.147	.46	.144	6.489	.70	.549	.75	.419		
Duriron Co.	8.734	.83	.249	.82	.181	—	—	—	—	—	61	1978–82
DWG Corp.	12.360	1.18	.243	1.30	.220	15.409	.80	.130	.59	.054	49	1973–77
Dynalectron Corp.	16.118	1.71	.320	1.93	.303	—	—	—	—	—	54	1978–82
Dynamics Corp. Amer.	11.098	1.35	.394	1.42	.327	20.243	1.75	.354	2.01	.344	51	1973–77
E-Systems	10.127	1.31	.445	1.49	.430	11.950	1.05	.357	1.08	.282	52	1973–77
Eagle-Picher Indus.	8.834	.77	.205	.79	.158	8.149	.87	.542	.99	.458		
Easco Corp.	7.923	1.08	.492	1.11	.139	12.458	1.19	.433	1.27	.328		
Eastern Air Lines	12.498	1.49	.381	1.53	.300	13.470	1.51	.595	1.61	.446		
Eastern Gas & Fuel	10.091	1.45	.552	1.71	.575	14.101	1.17	.328	1.53	.366		
Eastern Util. Assoc.	4.699	.28	.094	.33	.098	8.730	.81	.410	.78	.252		
Eastman Kodak	6.890	.73	.301	.87	.320	8.031	.69	.355	1.09	.573		
Eastmet Corp.	11.071	1.11	.266	1.05	.179	14.421	1.00	.228	.98	.148		
Eaton Corp.	7.131	.97	.497	1.11	.480	8.359	.95	.608	.99	.444	63	1973–77
Echlin Inc.	8.967	.86	.247	.93	.213	11.419	1.07	.418	1.25	.374		
Eckerd (Jack)	8.276	.97	.366	1.03	.309	11.701	1.15	.458	1.39	.444		
Economics Lab.	8.710	1.06	.398	1.21	.388	13.184	1.15	.372	1.66	.589	48	1973–77
Edison Bros. Stores	7.472	.90	.384	.90	.288	9.520	.98	.504	1.21	.504		
Edwards (A.G.) & Sons	12.721	1.80	.535	2.04	.513	11.810	1.27	.545	1.23	.341		
E G & G Inc.	9.819	1.39	.533	1.66	.571	12.908	.87	.217	1.34	.337		

55

1978-82

61 1973–77
57 1978–82

Elcor Corp.	10.402	1.07	.296	1.25	.302	—	—	—	—	—
Electronic Assoc.	16.108	2.06	.435	2.11	.342	18.636	1.93	.509	1.75	.276
Electronic Data Systems	9.872	1.42	.555	1.56	.501	14.518	.93	.196	1.17	.204
Electronic Mem. & Mag.	12.633	1.78	.528	2.00	.502	18.017	2.08	.630	2.09	.423
Elgin National Indus.	10.787	1.37	.431	1.49	.381	14.851	1.07	.247	1.00	.142
El Paso Co.	9.127	1.05	.356	1.26	.379	8.296	.94	.607	.85	.332
El Paso Electric	4.441	.28	.104	.28	.082	—	—	—	—	—
Emerson Electric	6.067	.76	.418	.87	.415	8.933	.94	.521	1.29	.655
Emery Air Freight	8.685	.90	.289	.92	.224	11.070	.92	.325	1.25	.398
Emhart Corp.	7.946	1.17	.578	1.21	.462	9.637	1.07	.579	1.14	.435
Empire Dist. Elec.	4.845	.31	.110	.32	.085	5.589	.48	.348	.48	.229
Empire Inc.	14.410	1.11	.157	1.33	.170	13.194	1.27	.436	1.51	.413
Ennis Business Forms	10.136	1.26	.415	1.24	.299	10.502	.90	.347	.99	.280
ENSERCH Corp.	9.300	1.04	.333	1.41	.460	7.910	.65	.320	.77	.294
ENSTAR Corp.	10.724	1.03	.247	1.38	.332	15.303	1.67	.567	1.99	.527
Entex, Inc.	8.346	1.15	.504	1.30	.487	9.070	.73	.304	.88	.292
Equifax Inc.	6.738	.62	.227	.67	.198	8.425	.72	.344	.70	.214
Equimark Corp.	9.226	.85	.225	.84	.165	8.240	.63	.274	.48	.105
Equitable Gas	8.909	.97	.313	1.12	.318	5.233	.57	.567	.61	.422
Esmark Inc.	9.295	.99	.302	1.22	.342	8.956	.66	.259	.78	.240
Esquire Inc.	9.762	1.20	.403	1.22	.314	12.219	.99	.311	1.06	.234
Essex Chemical	9.808	.88	.217	1.00	.209	—	—	—	—	—
Esterline Corp.	13.874	1.80	.449	1.84	.352	11.608	1.23	.531	1.17	.320
Ethyl Corp.	7.818	.85	.317	.92	.275	10.682	1.08	.480	1.10	.333
Evans Products	10.775	1.13	.295	1.38	.329	16.575	1.96	.660	2.04	.475
Ex-Cell-O	9.745	1.22	.415	1.29	.350	8.954	.95	.528	1.02	.404
Exxon Corp.	5.588	.54	.250	.79	.398	6.749	.60	.376	.91	.569
Faberge Inc.	10.942	1.11	.273	1.29	.276	12.971	1.48	.614	1.62	.486
Fabri-Centers Amer.	10.421	1.08	.284	1.17	.250	—	—	—	—	—
Facet Enterprises	10.810	.98	.219	1.01	.175	—	—	—	—	.310
Fairchild Indus.	10.928	1.22	.330	1.30	.283	12.877	1.35	.520	1.28	.291
Falconbridge Ltd.	13.850	1.46	.298	1.65	.283	10.326	.80	.288	.98	—
Family Dollar Stores	10.039	1.14	.363	1.23	.316	—	—	—	—	.066
Farah Mfg.	15.269	1.41	.226	1.58	.213	17.271	1.16	.215	.80	—
Farmers Group	7.912	.90	.348	1.02	.333	—	—	—	—	.078
Far West Financial	12.578	1.40	.333	1.57	.313	12.647	.89	.233	.63	—

Stock	January 1978–December 1982 Log (%) Std. Dev.	VLIC Est. Beta	VLIC R²	NYSE Est. Beta	NYSE R²	January 1973–December 1977 Log (%) Std. Dev.	VLIC Est. Beta	VLIC R²	NYSE Est. Beta	NYSE R²	Incomplete Data Series Number of Obs.	Period
Fedders Corp.	13.425	1.44	.308	1.31	.188	17.686	1.58	.378	1.24	.154		
Federal Co.	7.233	.79	.314	.85	.276	10.046	.92	.400	.99	.303		
Federal Express	11.930	1.48	.424	1.70	.427	—	—	—	—	—	56	1978–82
Federal-Mogul	7.308	.71	.248	.63	.150	9.637	.96	.469	.88	.260		
Federal Nat. Mtg.	10.213	.84	.180	.87	.144	10.803	.85	.299	1.10	.326		
Federal Paper Board	9.641	1.02	.298	1.06	.243	9.628	.83	.351	.89	.268		
Federal Signal	8.194	.80	.256	.74	.163	12.233	1.19	.444	1.16	.279		
Federated Dept. Strs.	7.006	.76	.318	.81	.264	8.690	.80	.400	.98	.396		
Ferro Corp.	9.437	1.08	.352	1.12	.281	11.766	1.16	.457	1.34	.403		
Fidelcor, Inc.	11.707	1.14	.254	1.22	.216	7.907	.79	.472	.87	.380		
Fidelity Union Banc.	4.944	.53	.312	.52	.222	5.761	.61	.535	.70	.456		
Fieldcrest Mills	8.831	.84	.239	.79	.159	10.592	1.05	.462	1.09	.329		
Figgie Int'l.	9.443	1.34	.536	1.48	.492	12.014	1.29	.549	1.23	.326		
Financial Corp. Amer.	15.598	1.83	.368	2.12	.370	13.487	.94	.228	1.09	.204		
Finan. Corp. St. Barbara	12.934	1.33	.282	1.43	.244	—	—	—	—	—	60	1973–77
Financial Federation	13.354	1.28	.246	1.46	.239	13.762	1.44	.521	1.46	.352		
Firestone Tire/Rub.	8.247	.74	.217	.74	.159	8.611	.88	.489	.99	.416		
First Bank System	6.133	.74	.393	.81	.352	9.286	.81	.359	1.02	.376		
First Boston	10.611	1.39	.460	1.54	.418	12.701	1.38	.563	1.54	.460		
First Charter Fin'l.	11.983	1.21	.274	1.30	.234	13.557	1.07	.293	1.26	.272		
First Chicago	8.773	1.10	.416	1.23	.394	11.665	1.11	.428	1.42	.464		
First City Banc. Tex.	7.787	.87	.330	1.00	.328	9.337	.99	.548	1.19	.530		
First City Prop.	9.465	1.17	.404	1.34	.403	21.512	1.40	.200	1.42	.136		
First Interstate Bancorp.	8.026	.91	.344	.96	.288	9.817	1.09	.583	1.18	.455		
First Mississippi	13.657	1.29	.238	1.51	.245	12.421	.41	.053	.61	.089	47	1973–77
First Nat'l Boston	6.788	.74	.320	.74	.239	9.875	1.04	.526	1.23	.482		
First Nat'l St. Bancorp.	6.156	.76	.406	.78	.318	6.174	.65	.528	.67	.365		
First Pennsylvania	10.187	1.03	.273	1.05	.213	10.058	1.05	.519	1.16	.419		
First Union Real Est.	6.271	.74	.375	.79	.317	8.294	.89	.548	.94	.404		
First Va. Banks.	6.994	.67	.246	.63	.163	9.086	.70	.282	.72	.196		

First Wisconsin	6.595	.75	.349	.87	.344	9.728	.85	.365	.96	.302		
Fischbach Corp.	7.499	.96	.450	1.05	.394	12.925	1.17	.391	1.55	.448		
Fischer & Porter	11.808	1.46	.409	1.52	.332	14.693	1.56	.530	1.49	.320		
Fisher Foods	10.149	.79	.162	.73	.104	11.795	1.25	.536	1.40	.438		
Fleet Financial Gr.	6.303	.82	.448	.86	.374	9.640	.97	.480	.82	.227		
Fleetwood Enterpr.	11.372	1.51	.472	1.59	.392	19.695	1.66	.336	1.85	.275		
Fleming Cos.	6.450	.83	.438	.96	.438	5.835	.52	.376	.61	.336		
Flexi-Van	13.416	1.42	.296	1.52	.255	15.530	1.78	.625	1.92	.481		
Flightsafety Int'l.	11.310	1.42	.422	1.66	.433	—	—	—	—	—		
Florida EastCoast Ry.	9.030	.95	.293	.97	.233	11.635	1.06	.395	.95	.209		
Florida Power & Lt.	4.918	.41	.184	.44	.162	8.361	.79	.428	.91	.368		
Florida Progress	5.890	.48	.180	.53	.163	10.590	.95	.379	.97	.261		
Florida Steel	12.550	1.44	.353	1.59	.322	8.576	.80	.408	.89	.338		
Flow General	17.484	2.16	.408	2.36	.388	—	—	—	—	—	50	1978–82
Fluke (John) Mfg.	9.936	.94	.238	.93	.174	—	—	—	—	—		
Fluor Corp.	10.658	1.03	.250	1.43	.360	12.443	1.08	.353	1.41	.402		
FMC Corp.	6.975	.97	.520	1.18	.568	9.891	1.18	.678	1.29	.533		
Foote, Cone & Belding	7.886	.76	.245	.77	.189	9.082	.80	.372	.81	.248		
Ford Motor	8.201	.76	.230	.75	.167	7.789	.66	.336	.71	.258		
Foremost-McKesson	6.544	.69	.298	.77	.278	8.107	.89	.571	.90	.382		
Forest Labs.	15.295	1.42	.253	1.43	.203	—	—	—	—	—	45	1978–82
Forest Oil	11.553	1.29	.333	1.60	.384	10.751	.89	.326	.91	.182		
Fort Howard Paper	6.670	.95	.541	1.07	.518	13.934	1.24	.374	1.55	.387		
Foster Wheeler	10.860	1.32	.395	1.59	.428	—	—	—	—	—		
Fotomat Corp.	16.226	1.09	.119	.87	.058	—	—	—	—	—		
Foxboro Co.	8.944	.95	.303	1.05	.273	11.795	1.09	.406	1.45	.476		
Franklin Electric	9.365	.58	.103	.56	.070	—	—	—	—	—		
Freeport-McMoran	10.804	1.19	.323	1.37	.319	8.490	.67	.295	.86	.320		
Free State Geduld ADR	16.371	1.11	.124	1.25	.116	—	—	—	—	—		
Fremont Gen'l.	12.954	1.29	.288	1.11	.172	—	—	—	—	—		
Frigitronics Inc.	12.157	1.18	.250	1.18	.186	—	—	—	—	—		
Frontier Holdings	13.589	1.68	.405	1.71	.315	—	—	—	—	—		
Fruehauf Corp.	7.622	.82	.309	.78	.211	8.049	.89	.585	.95	.439		
Fuji Photo Film ADR	9.210	.56	.100	.52	.064	—	—	—	—	—	45	1978–82
Fuller (H.B.)	8.724	.98	.339	.96	.240	—	—	—	—	—		
Fuqua Indus.	10.068	1.15	.347	1.07	.226	15.328	1.67	.562	1.45	.283		

Stock	January 1978–December 1982					January 1973–December 1977					Incomplete Data Series	
	Log (%) Std. Dev.	VLIC Est. Beta	VLIC R²	NYSE Est. Beta	NYSE R²	Log (%) Std. Dev.	VLIC Est. Beta	VLIC R²	NYSE Est. Beta	NYSE R²	Number of Obs.	Period
GAF Corp.	12.248	1.35	.322	1.30	.226	10.487	1.19	.609	1.15	.375		
Gannett Co.	6.853	.94	.507	1.03	.453	7.741	.80	.508	.96	.477		
Gap Stores	13.392	1.52	.342	1.68	.315	—	—	—	—	—	61	1978–82
Gas Service	6.770	.57	.191	.59	.152	6.033	.66	.569	.66	.379		
Gates Learjet	12.542	1.35	.324	1.42	.267	—	—	—	—	—		
GATX Corp.	7.709	1.08	.522	1.23	.509	9.415	.97	.498	1.26	.565		
GCA Corp.	16.367	1.93	.370	1.92	.276	16.644	1.80	.554	1.73	.339		
Gearhart Indus.	12.496	1.00	.171	1.42	.259	—	—	—	—	—		
GEICO Corp.	9.972	1.35	.489	1.48	.443	22.124	.44	.019	.86	.047		
Gelco Corp.	11.854	1.43	.388	1.57	.351	—	—	—	—	—		
Gemini Fund	6.305	1.04	.726	1.14	.657	11.600	1.51	.804	1.56	.568		
General Amer. Inv.	7.879	.92	.362	1.08	.378	6.583	.56	.342	.68	.331		
General Amer. Oil Tex.	11.303	.95	.189	1.27	.252	8.341	.23	.037	.14	.009		
General Bancshares	5.711	.60	.298	.59	.216	6.481	.51	.290	.49	.179		
General Cinema	8.448	1.04	.406	1.09	.332	17.060	1.85	.574	1.74	.340	60	1973–77
General Dynamics	11.308	1.07	.240	1.34	.279	13.411	.99	.256	.87	.131		
General Electric	5.278	.75	.543	.87	.541	7.608	.87	.619	1.07	.624		
General Foods	5.961	.57	.245	.66	.246	8.231	.83	.487	1.00	.464		
General Host	8.454	1.04	.400	1.09	.331	12.657	.85	.216	.68	.089		
General Instrument	10.795	1.56	.559	1.72	.505	15.045	1.80	.675	1.95	.528		
General Mills	7.453	.60	.173	.64	.148	8.701	.71	.313	1.07	.470		
General Motors	6.415	.64	.270	.59	.171	7.470	.78	.513	.86	.416		
General Public Util.	10.152	.47	.057	.42	.034	7.218	.66	.391	.67	.273		
General Re Corp.	7.785	.79	.277	.89	.259	9.805	.50	.123	.85	.236		
General Refractories	12.899	1.48	.350	1.48	.263	11.264	1.04	.406	1.00	.246		
General Signal	7.226	.92	.428	1.02	.397	10.424	1.18	.602	1.39	.553		
General Tire & Rubber	9.464	1.00	.295	.95	.203	9.385	1.05	.596	1.08	.417		
Genesco Inc.	13.061	1.43	.320	1.44	.244	14.306	1.14	.299	1.05	.168		
Genstar Corp.	11.449	1.16	.274	1.20	.219	5.784	.59	.497	.60	.341		
Genuine Parts	6.421	.57	.211	.66	.210	10.812	1.11	.496	1.53	.625		

Georgia-Pacific	8.952	1.29	.544	1.48	.548	8.914	.97	.559	1.24	.601	
Gerber Products	7.908	.76	.244	.80	.203	10.118	.67	.209	.78	.184	
Getty Oil	9.505	.99	.288	1.46	.473	6.722	.19	.039	.37	.096	
GF Business Equip.	12.356	1.14	.226	.93	.114	10.545	.89	.341	.78	.171	
Giant Portland Cement	10.913	1.02	.233	.95	.151	8.123	.78	.436	.91	.396	
Gibraltar Financial Cal.	15.481	1.88	.394	2.13	.377	13.646	1.12	.320	1.12	.210	
Gifford-Hill	10.812	1.23	.344	1.36	.316	11.007	1.08	.459	1.13	.331	
Gilbert Assoc.	9.744	1.03	.300	1.15	.277	—	—	—	—	—	
Gillette Co.	6.915	.86	.410	.82	.284	9.355	.76	.309	1.06	.406	
Girard Co.	7.571	.86	.345	1.03	.372	6.131	.65	.531	.70	.402	
Gleason Works	11.445	1.44	.424	1.33	.271	12.069	1.13	.419	1.15	.283	
Global Marine	15.717	2.05	.455	2.53	.519	13.892	1.19	.349	1.44	.334	
Golden Nugget	13.571	1.04	.176	.98	.123	—	—	—	—	—	1978–82 44
Golden West Financial	12.454	1.26	.273	1.33	.226	14.652	1.31	.379	1.34	.261	
Goodrich (B.F.)	7.922	1.02	.440	1.12	.396	11.088	1.08	.453	1.15	.337	
Goodyear Tire & Rub.	6.294	.60	.244	.59	.173	8.249	.85	.505	.91	.382	
Gordon Jewelry	9.851	.93	.238	.89	.164	14.405	1.39	.439	1.61	.389	
Gould Inc.	8.458	.91	.307	1.06	.311	11.053	1.24	.599	1.42	.517	
Goulds Pumps	7.570	.89	.370	.95	.316	—	—	—	—	—	
Grace (W.R.)	7.373	.90	.396	1.14	.479	7.784	.85	.569	1.00	.521	
Grainger (W.W.)	6.725	.94	.522	1.09	.525	6.717	.57	.263	.39	.089	1973–77 41
Graniteville Co.	7.451	.78	.290	.75	.200	9.711	1.03	.537	1.27	.538	
Graphic Scanning	18.066	1.86	.301	1.87	.241	—	—	—	—	—	1978–82 47
Great Atl. & Pac. Tea	11.398	.89	.162	.77	.092	10.820	.79	.251	.71	.136	
Great Lakes Chemical	8.410	.95	.343	.96	.261	10.554	1.25	.509	1.60	.601	1973–77 41
Great Lakes Int'l.	10.302	.76	.144	.86	.138	10.460	.70	.214	.72	.149	
Great Northern Iron Ore	8.425	.38	.054	.22	.013	8.960	.36	.076	.37	.054	
Great Northern Nekoosa	7.184	.95	.464	1.03	.409	8.581	.92	.547	.97	.400	
Great Western Financial	10.508	1.12	.304	1.25	.285	15.400	1.26	.319	1.54	.311	
Greyhound Corp.	7.920	.90	.343	.93	.278	7.278	.59	.308	.51	.155	
Grolier, Inc.	22.968	.38	.007	.22	.002	21.232	1.73	.314	1.89	.248	
Grow Group	10.008	.68	.124	.86	.148	—	—	—	—	—	
Grumman Corp.	11.646	1.03	.209	1.01	.152	10.932	.88	.306	.79	.165	
GTE Corp.	5.686	.57	.272	.67	.274	6.433	.69	.548	.79	.473	
Guardian Indus.	11.896	1.40	.371	1.43	.290	15.731	1.54	.456	1.72	.376	
Gulf Canada Ltd.	12.341	.67	.079	.70	.065	9.054	.63	.233	.83	.265	

269

Stock	January 1978–December 1982					January 1973–December 1977					Incomplete Data Series	
	Log (%) Std. Dev.	VLIC Est. Beta	VLIC R²	NYSE Est. Beta	NYSE R²	Log (%) Std. Dev.	VLIC Est. Beta	VLIC R²	NYSE Est. Beta	NYSE R²	Number of Obs.	Period
Gulf Oil	8.220	.54	.114	.89	.236	5.724	.60	.526	.70	.467		
Gulf Resources/Chem.	14.088	1.26	.212	1.63	.266	12.808	1.10	.352	1.46	.404		
Gulf States Util.	5.131	.31	.095	.35	.092	7.922	.81	.497	1.00	.497		
Gulf United	8.953	.93	.291	1.00	.247	10.492	1.09	.514	1.25	.442		
Gulf & Western Indus.	8.243	1.22	.580	1.43	.598	8.757	.82	.416	.97	.383		
Gulton Indus.	10.371	1.40	.488	1.61	.480	15.976	1.67	.515	1.47	.267		
Hackensack Water	6.606	.40	.099	.39	.071	4.673	.45	.442	.47	.311		
Hall (Frank B.)	7.158	.74	.286	.66	.172	9.811	.53	.145	.77	.203	60	1973–77
Halliburton Co.	8.924	1.11	.412	1.51	.575	8.057	.37	.097	.80	.309		
Hammermill Paper	8.049	.92	.345	.88	.241	10.048	.95	.428	1.07	.357		
Handleman Co.	12.031	1.36	.342	1.51	.314	14.336	1.50	.519	1.65	.414		
Handy & Harman	14.348	1.51	.296	1.65	.264	8.426	.28	.054	.37	.060		
Hanna Mining	9.791	.99	.274	1.19	.296	10.652	.64	.169	.86	.205		
Harcourt Brace	9.062	1.06	.363	1.10	.295	9.277	.89	.437	.93	.315		
Harland (John H.)	8.346	1.06	.434	1.17	.391	—	—	—	—	—		
Harnischfeger Corp.	12.209	1.10	.215	1.18	.186	9.719	.90	.403	1.03	.349		
Harris Bankcorp	7.485	.83	.326	.86	.261	7.786	.80	.496	.93	.449		
Harris Corp.	8.985	1.15	.434	1.31	.424	12.672	1.44	.609	1.61	.508		
Harsco Corp.	5.306	.52	.257	.51	.185	8.003	.75	.411	.82	.332		
Harte-Hanks Commun.	10.102	1.19	.370	1.38	.371	12.982	1.18	.397	1.27	.309	61	1973–77
Hart Schaffner Marx	8.216	1.08	.457	1.11	.364	11.060	1.14	.506	1.12	.323		
Hawaiian Electric	4.848	.26	.078	.25	.051	6.740	.61	.391	.69	.332		
Hayes-Albion	9.739	1.08	.325	1.04	.229	8.460	.89	.528	.83	.303		
Hazeltine Corp.	9.856	1.18	.381	1.28	.337	15.775	1.49	.421	1.34	.227		
Heck's Inc.	9.290	1.39	.599	1.48	.505	14.036	1.42	.486	1.44	.370	51	1973–77
Hecla Mining	17.918	1.59	.210	1.77	.195	13.508	.72	.134	.84	.122		
Heileman (G.) Brewing	8.255	1.10	.474	1.09	.349	9.254	.65	.232	.70	.177		
Heinz (H.J.)	6.088	.56	.227	.69	.258	7.942	.68	.345	.99	.486		
Helene Curtis Indus.	13.506	1.43	.298	1.50	.246	15.136	1.32	.360	1.25	.215		
Heller (W.E.) Int'l	12.563	1.61	.439	1.71	.369	10.017	.76	.273	.93	.269		

Helmerich & Payne	10.767	1.26	.365	1.69	.492	11.110	.78	.236	1.16	.342		
Hemisphere Fund	9.033	1.11	.401	1.26	.392	11.492	.73	.193	.59	.083		
Hercules, Inc.	9.472	1.42	.602	1.60	.573	8.870	.76	.347	1.05	.439		
Hershey Foods	6.848	.57	.182	.47	.096	9.125	.86	.421	.92	.319		
Hesston Corp.	11.860	.91	.158	.85	.103	13.478	.97	.255	1.06	.204	60	1973–77
Hewlett-Packard	7.685	.97	.423	1.21	.495	9.342	.91	.446	1.22	.534	48	1978–82
Hexcel Corp.	12.085	1.73	.576	1.87	.533	—	—	—	—	—		
High Voltage Engr.	13.240	1.82	.503	1.72	.335	16.626	2.00	.685	2.15	.525	41	1973–77
Hillenbrand Indus.	6.927	.88	.431	.92	.355	7.584	.78	.382	.86	.333	61	1978–82
Hilton Hotels	10.823	1.47	.495	1.64	.461	13.657	1.39	.494	1.53	.393	62	1973–77
Hi-Shear Indus.	12.125	1.22	.281	1.39	.273	—	.25	.034	.27	.027		
Hitachi, Ltd. ADR	9.526	.58	.010	.59	.076	9.343	1.41	.443	1.61	.385		
HMW Industries	13.811	1.55	.337	1.51	.239	14.557	1.76	.604	1.90	.463		
Holiday Inns	10.445	1.45	.517	1.50	.413	15.618	.59	.130	.65	.106		
Holly Sugar	15.268	.61	.043	.65	.036	11.219	.20	.012	.41	.033		
Homestake Mining	14.208	1.44	.272	1.81	.325	12.591	1.37	—	—	—		
Honda Motor ADR	9.756	.73	.150	.61	.078	—	1.37	.548	1.59	.487		
Honeywell, Inc.	7.828	.94	.387	1.04	.353	12.752	—	—	—	—		
Hoover Co.	10.458	.82	.166	.85	.133	—	1.20	.648	1.38	.564		
Hoover Universal	8.572	1.09	.434	1.06	.304	10.256	1.50	.349	1.14	.132		
Horizon Corp.	17.739	1.90	.306	2.03	.263	17.495	.25	.070	.25	.045		
Hormel (Geo. A.)	8.129	.73	.217	.70	.148	6.517	1.60	.349	1.52	.208		
Horn & Hardart	14.735	1.32	.213	1.52	.211	18.671	1.65	.475	1.85	.395		
Hospital Corp. Amer.	9.207	1.32	.549	1.45	.499	16.443	.92	.396	.96	.286		
Houghton Mifflin	7.534	.61	.175	.67	.156	10.080	1.22	.594	1.47	.572		
Household Int'l.	6.644	.57	.194	.62	.175	10.867	1.53	.569	1.66	.442		
House of Fabrics	10.059	1.06	.296	1.19	.280	13.927	.76	.351	.96	.374		
Houston Indus.	4.960	.32	.111	.31	.079	8.779	1.07	.400	1.30	.392		
Houston Natural Gas	9.387	1.23	.459	1.51	.516	11.652	—	—	—	—		
HRT Industries	12.270	.98	.171	1.04	.142	—	.78	.388	.83	.291		
Hubbard Real Est. Inv.	4.240	.45	.296	.47	.246	8.619	—	—	—	—		
Hubbell (Harvey) B	6.638	.89	.499	.93	.437	—	.53	.154	.59	.127	48	1978–82
Hudson Bay Mining	10.598	1.09	.284	1.21	.259	9.295	—	—	—	—		
Hudson's Bay Co.	8.056	.50	.102	.48	.071	—	—	—	—	—		
Huffy Corp.	9.725	.26	.020	.13	.003	—	—	—	—	—		
Hughes Tool	10.094	1.06	.297	1.46	.416	10.549	.44	.084	.89	.227	62	1973–77

271

Stock	January 1978–December 1982 Log (%) Std. Dev.	January 1978–December 1982 VLIC Est. Beta	January 1978–December 1982 VLIC R²	January 1978–December 1982 NYSE Est. Beta	January 1978–December 1982 NYSE R²	January 1973–December 1977 Log (%) Std. Dev.	January 1973–December 1977 VLIC Est. Beta	January 1973–December 1977 VLIC R²	January 1973–December 1977 NYSE Est. Beta	January 1973–December 1977 NYSE R²	Incomplete Data Series Number of Obs.	Incomplete Data Series Period
Humana Inc.	10.955	1.43	.457	1.48	.365	14.087	1.50	.534	1.60	.404		
Hunt (Philip A.) Chemical	8.973	1.05	.364	1.13	.315	14.608	.97	.207	1.40	.286		
Husky Oil Ltd.	10.328	.96	.231	1.13	.241	10.798	.76	.244	.84	.196	60	1973–77
Hutton (E.F.) Group	13.401	1.95	.567	2.32	.598	14.891	1.74	.650	2.02	.578		
Hyster Co.	7.891	.86	.318	.87	.245	12.597	1.25	.473	1.56	.488		
IC Indus.	7.496	.96	.440	1.04	.381	9.257	1.02	.579	1.14	.474	63	1973–77
ICN Pharmaceuticals	15.614	1.57	.269	1.36	.151	20.353	2.16	.533	2.17	.355		
Idaho Power	4.589	.28	.098	.28	.075	5.111	.40	.296	.48	.278		
Ideal Basic Indus.	9.900	1.21	.396	1.25	.317	9.167	.92	.479	1.08	.431		
Illinois Power	5.795	.30	.072	.34	.070	6.350	.62	.451	.65	.329		
Illinois Tool Works	6.060	.82	.488	.86	.400	10.335	1.07	.517	1.16	.409	61	1973–77
Imperial Corp. Amer.	16.028	1.88	.366	2.07	.334	13.222	1.11	.336	1.18	.248		
Imperial Group ADR	8.797	.36	.046	.43	.048	—	—	—	—	—		
Imperial Oil Ltd. A	9.393	.68	.141	.74	.124	8.393	.70	.328	.82	.300	62	1978–82
I.M.S. Int'l.	9.877	1.05	.302	1.14	.266	—	—	—	—	—		
Inco Ltd.	9.751	1.14	.362	1.27	.337	8.028	.72	.381	.80	.314		
Indiana Gas	6.327	.71	.339	.71	.249	6.370	.70	.565	.73	.413		
Indianapolis Pwr. & Lt.	4.918	.25	.070	.30	.073	7.179	.71	.457	.80	.385		
Inexco Oil	12.179	1.30	.302	1.74	.408	15.427	1.19	.291	1.17	.189	60	1973–77
Ingersoll-Rand	7.822	.99	.424	1.14	.424	8.519	.63	.262	.99	.426		
Ingredient Technology	10.578	1.05	.262	.96	.164	15.021	.82	.142	.83	.096		
Inland Steel	6.569	.66	.273	.74	.255	6.693	.49	.249	.61	.256		
Insilco Corp.	8.673	1.15	.468	1.32	.464	8.143	.86	.531	.96	.435		
Intel Corp.	9.491	1.16	.401	1.30	.374	18.213	1.75	.442	2.37	.545		
INTERCO, Inc.	5.824	.86	.578	.94	.519	9.776	1.06	.555	1.05	.364	62	1973–77
InterFirst Corp.	7.658	.93	.392	1.06	.385	8.460	.84	.478	1.10	.550	60	1973–77
Interlake, Inc.	8.201	1.00	.397	1.11	.363	7.654	.73	.432	.85	.386		
Intermedics Inc.	13.315	1.03	.161	1.01	.120	—	—	—	—	—		
Int'l. Aluminum	12.340	1.79	.561	1.92	.485	—	—	—	—	—	52	1978–82
Int'l. Banknote	12.382	1.23	.264	1.17	.180	18.311	.93	.123	.89	.074		

Int'l. Bus. Machines	5.522	.66	.375	.76	.378	7.549	.61	309	.99	.533	48 1978–82
Int'l. Controls	13.945	1.69	.414	1.84	.387	—	—	—	—	—	
Int'l. Flavors/Frag.	7.020	.57	.177	.59	.141	8.759	.81	406	1.19	.575	
Int'l. Harvester	11.605	1.42	.398	1.54	.353	8.648	.90	508	1.04	.452	
Int'l. Minerals/Chem.	8.482	.91	.306	1.11	.341	9.215	.46	119	.55	.110	
Int'l. Multifoods	6.838	.74	.314	.66	.184	8.496	.90	537	1.00	.436	
Int'l. Paper	7.622	1.08	.536	1.23	.518	9.107	.81	378	1.07	.434	
Int'l. Rectifier	14.069	1.57	.332	1.56	.244	12.537	1.08	352	1.09	.235	
Int'l. Tel. & Tel.	6.448	.93	.552	1.10	.582	9.903	1.16	655	1.20	.457	
InterNorth Inc.	7.976	.69	.200	1.04	.337	8.078	.75	404	.99	.473	
Interpace Corp.	6.925	.71	.282	.76	.238	8.634	.93	553	.95	.375	
Interpublic Group Cos.	6.898	.89	.440	.93	.363	10.624	1.20	600	1.22	.411	
Interstate Bakeries	11.728	1.36	.356	1.34	.262	13.355	1.09	313	1.14	.228	
Interstate Power	5.462	.33	.099	.38	.096	5.254	.45	353	.40	.181	
Iowa Elec. Lt. & Pwr.	5.502	.39	.134	.43	.122	7.215	.76	527	.84	.420	
Iowa-Ill. Gas & Elec.	4.778	.29	.097	.36	.113	6.383	.59	408	.54	.228	
Iowa Public Service	4.440	.38	.191	.36	.128	4.221	.33	289	.32	.177	
Iowa Resources	5.036	.38	.151	.46	.164	4.630	.42	385	.52	.391	
Iowa Southern Util.	5.564	.46	.179	.49	.158	6.702	.69	500	.79	.434	
IPCO Corp.	11.069	1.30	.370	1.35	.296	15.777	1.86	662	2.27	.646	
Iroquois Brands Ltd.	12.617	1.42	.398	1.46	.335	—	—	—	—	—	41 1978–82
Irving Bank	5.494	.65	.375	.73	.352	6.275	.73	643	.78	.487	
Itek Corp.	13.304	1.88	.533	1.92	.416	17.025	1.83	549	1.79	.345	
Itel Corp.	22.462	.97	.050	.85	.028	16.657	2.08	739	2.33	.614	
IU Int'l.	10.299	1.09	.301	1.19	.269	9.885	1.08	568	1.18	.449	
James River	11.912	1.31	.341	1.25	.230	—	—	—	—	—	54 1978–82
Jamesway Corp.	10.934	1.59	.566	1.65	.456	8.801	.65	260	.78	.244	
Japan Fund	6.912	.59	.195	.52	.114	8.001	.74	407	.99	.476	
Jefferson-Pilot	6.375	.73	.351	.86	.360	15.625	1.12	242	1.40	.280	
Jerrico, Inc.	11.277	1.39	.403	1.56	.383	9.892	1.00	486	1.05	.350	51 1973–77
Jewel Co's.	6.910	.84	.392	.86	.308	5.433	.45	320	.46	.226	
John Hancock Inv.	4.931	.34	.131	.37	.115	—	—	—	—	—	
Johnson (E.F.)	14.454	2.00	.511	2.16	.446	6.468	.37	154	.69	.352	
Johnson & Johnson	6.269	.66	.297	.77	.298	11.894	1.18	465	1.08	.259	
Johnson Controls	9.057	1.16	.438	1.12	.304	11.131	.98	380	1.16	.356	
Johnson Products	12.232	1.51	.404	1.42	.268						60 1973–77

| | January 1978–December 1982 | | | | | January 1973–December 1977 | | | | | Incomplete Data Series | |
| | Log (%) | VLIC | | NYSE | | Log (%) | VLIC | | NYSE | | Number | Period |
Stock	Std. Dev.	Est. Beta	R²	Est. Beta	R²	Std. Dev.	Est. Beta	R²	Est. Beta	R²	of Obs.	
Jonathan Logan	10.261	1.27	.408	1.41	.375	16.814	1.76	.518	1.75	.341		
Jorgensen (E.M.)	6.305	.74	.370	.73	.270	7.649	.59	.278	.54	.155		
Jostens Inc.	6.404	.67	.292	.60	.176	11.047	.96	.356	1.03	.270		
Joy Mfg.	8.338	1.16	.514	1.28	.473	10.594	.61	.158	.81	.184		
Justin Indus.	13.641	1.76	.469	1.98	.441	—	—	—	—	—	57	1978–82
JWT Group	7.665	.94	.401	.96	.316	12.139	1.29	.532	1.36	.391		
Kaiser Alum. & Chem.	7.966	.91	.347	.93	.274	12.325	1.13	.399	1.30	.349		
Kaiser Cement	10.608	1.50	.532	1.48	.388	10.344	1.03	.474	.94	.258		
Kaiser Steel	11.048	.58	.074	.64	.068	12.297	1.02	.327	1.15	.274		
Kane-Miller	9.191	.79	.195	.68	.109	12.290	.72	.161	.77	.123		
Kaneb-Services	10.711	1.21	.339	1.60	.443	—	—	—	—	—		
Kansas City Pwr. & Lt.	5.431	.36	.119	.37	.090	5.903	.64	.555	.71	.453		
Kansas City So. Indus.	9.453	1.09	.353	1.24	.346	10.762	1.05	.455	1.13	.344		
Kansas Gas & Elec.	4.800	.35	.142	.38	.127	6.127	.55	.380	.63	.327		
Kansas-Neb. Nat. Gas	8.130	.58	.137	.78	.183	5.355	.31	.161	.31	.106		
Kansas Power & Lt.	4.762	.39	.181	.44	.172	4.657	.32	.228	.34	.166		
Katy Indus.	11.418	1.41	.409	1.43	.314	15.635	1.75	.590	1.74	.386		
Kaufman & Broad	13.638	1.91	.525	2.05	.451	21.710	2.38	.571	2.83	.532		
Keller Indus.	14.033	1.69	.389	1.77	.319	13.409	1.38	.503	1.27	.279		
Kellogg Co.	6.400	.63	.255	.63	.193	7.383	.58	.289	.78	.353		
Kellwood Co.	8.808	.83	.239	.83	.175	—	—	—	—	—		
Kelly Services	8.586	1.09	.433	1.14	.351	—	—	—	—	—		
Kemper Corp.	9.328	1.08	.374	1.05	.279	—	—	—	—	—	48	1978–82
Kennametal, Inc.	8.978	1.07	.378	1.20	.359	9.463	.57	.174	.62	.132		
Kentucky Util.	4.656	.30	.111	.29	.075	5.807	.50	.354	.41	.159		
Kerr Glass Mfg.	8.471	1.17	.513	1.20	.404	—	—	—	—	—		
Kerr-McGee	8.812	.80	.221	1.08	.297	9.346	.44	.103	.81	.232		
Keystone Consol. Indus.	12.028	1.01	.188	.97	.130	9.005	.78	.359	.83	.266		
Kidde Inc.	7.177	.97	.485	1.13	.495	12.385	1.45	.653	1.71	.594		
Kimberly-Clark	5.516	.69	.422	.79	.409	8.935	.81	.388	1.01	.404		

KLM Royal Dutch Air	10.190	.92	.218	.84	.135	11.730	.89	.274	.89	.178		
Kloof Gold Mining	14.091	1.06	.152	1.34	.181	—	—	—	—	—		
K Mart	8.246	.91	.327	.85	.212	8.518	.76	.375	1.14	.558	53	1978–82
Knight-Ridder News	7.298	.99	.494	1.03	.398	12.808	1.20	.418	1.22	.283	61	1978–82
Kollmorgen Corp.	10.924	1.50	.501	1.66	.463	—	—	—	—	—		
Koppers Co.	8.477	1.04	.400	1.20	.401	11.164	1.08	.446	1.26	.397		
Kroehler Mfg.	13.788	.71	.071	.65	.045	9.611	.94	.454	1.10	.407		
Kroger Co.	7.158	.58	.176	.65	.166	8.956	.90	.481	.94	.345		
Kubota, Ltd. ADR	4.683	.14	.025	.06	.003	—	—	—	—	—		
Kyocera Corp. ADR	7.419	.63	.193	.58	.127	—	—	—	—	—		
Kysor Ind'l.	8.615	1.01	.363	.96	.250	—	—	—	—	—		
Labatt (John) Cv A	5.501	.64	.374	.78	.415	—	—	—	—	—		
Laclede Gas	6.519	.32	.062	.41	.079	6.125	.59	.444	.60	.298	49	1978–82
Lamson & Sessions	11.606	1.16	.267	1.18	.208	8.508	.63	.262	.68	.201		
Lancaster Colony	11.783	1.21	.281	1.48	.315	—	—	—	—	—		
Lanier Business Prod.	9.235	1.10	.375	1.12	.296	—	—	—	—	—		
La Quinta Motor Inns	9.678	.98	.272	1.05	.234	—	—	—	—	—		
Lawter Int'l.	8.002	.96	.385	.92	.262	—	—	—	—	—		
Lear Petroleum	15.974	1.64	.287	2.04	.355	—	—	—	—	—		
Lear Siegler	10.269	1.41	.506	1.64	.509	10.638	1.25	.653	1.20	.396		
Leaseway Transport	7.718	.78	.274	.86	.249	14.174	1.54	.562	1.69	.445		
Lehman Corp.	6.980	.92	.462	1.07	.466	6.860	.81	.663	.95	.597		
Lennar Corp.	14.842	1.92	.446	2.12	.409	20.286	2.21	.563	2.26	.390		
Lenox, Inc.	7.604	1.07	.529	1.05	.382	10.679	1.12	.521	1.34	.491		
Leucadia National	15.815	1.50	.239	1.51	.182	17.895	1.22	.221	1.20	.140		
Levi Strauss	9.583	1.01	.296	1.15	.286	12.521	1.17	.413	1.12	.251		
Levitz Furniture	10.851	1.18	.316	1.15	.223	16.538	1.85	.592	1.74	.345		
LFE Corp.	14.182	1.94	.498	2.03	.408	13.911	1.43	.503	1.57	.401		
Libbey-Owens-Ford	5.326	.55	.286	.53	.196	9.839	1.10	.590	1.17	.440		
Liberty Corp.	8.733	1.04	.380	1.07	.302	8.543	.90	.531	.91	.353		
Lifemark Corp.	10.852	1.51	.519	1.67	.475	—	—	—	—	—		
Lilly (Eli)	6.345	.74	.359	.79	.307	8.690	.56	.195	.90	.337		
Limited Inc.	14.357	1.52	.298	1.74	.295	—	—	—	—	—		
LIN Broadcasting	8.886	.89	.317	.91	.260	—	—	—	—	—		
Lincoln First Banks	7.851	.80	.278	.77	.190	7.675	.76	.470	.86	.389		
Lincoln National	6.039	.86	.540	.87	.419	9.034	.96	.532	1.18	.538	41	1978–82

| Stock | January 1978–December 1982 | | | | | January 1973–December 1977 | | | | | Incomplete Data Series | |
	Log (%) Std. Dev.	VLIC Est. Beta	VLIC R²	NYSE Est. Beta	NYSE R²	Log (%) Std. Dev.	VLIC Est. Beta	VLIC R²	NYSE Est. Beta	NYSE R²	Number of Obs.	Period
Litton Indus.	8.898	1.16	.452	1.34	.454	14.922	1.30	.358	1.19	.199		
LLC Corp.	14.605	1.21	.182	.95	.085	20.197	2.18	.551	2.25	.390		
Lockheed Corp.	15.836	2.07	.458	2.11	.355	14.847	1.15	.282	1.24	.218		
Loctite Corp.	11.618	1.14	.258	1.36	.274	—	—	—	—	—		
Loews Corp.	8.508	1.19	.520	1.32	.479	11.774	1.37	.644	1.53	.529		
Lomas & Nettleton Fin.	9.493	1.32	.517	1.30	.373	14.442	1.46	.482	1.53	.352		
Lomas/Nettleton Mtg.	7.471	.89	.382	.98	.344	11.486	1.11	.439	1.18	.331		
Lone Star Indus.	8.642	1.20	.512	1.36	.492	11.240	1.16	.501	1.16	.332		
Long Island Ltg.	4.360	.27	.100	.30	.097	6.572	.59	.379	.68	.339		
Longs Drug Stores	7.297	.76	.290	.77	.221	9.597	.90	.421	1.13	.438		
Loral Corp.	9.234	1.10	.380	1.28	.382	15.852	1.43	.385	1.44	.258		
Louisiana Land/Exp.	9.288	.82	.210	1.02	.240	10.106	.83	.318	1.06	.344		
Louisiana Pacific	9.617	1.39	.560	1.56	.526	14.252	1.48	.517	1.64	.426	62	1973–77
Louisville Gas & Elec.	4.629	.27	.089	.29	.078	6.492	.47	.252	.52	.200		
Lowenstein (M.)	14.387	.99	.127	1.02	.101	10.642	1.02	.439	1.20	.399		
Lowe's Cos.	9.138	.99	.314	1.14	.311	10.680	1.03	.438	1.30	.520	51	1973–77
LTV Corp.	13.947	1.73	.408	1.97	.400	11.884	1.24	.516	1.43	.451		
Lubrizol Corp.	7.736	.97	.418	1.08	.390	9.184	.78	.343	1.06	.419		
Lucky Stores	6.342	.69	.318	.80	.319	7.566	.68	.381	.73	.290		
Lukens Inc.	8.957	.93	.287	.99	.244	10.693	.93	.361	1.10	.333		
Lynch Commun. Sys.	10.016	.63	.104	.57	.064	13.401	1.25	.411	1.19	.246		
M/A-Com. Inc.	12.049	1.73	.553	1.98	.540	13.098	1.49	.555	1.47	.423	44	1973–77
MacMillan Inc.	10.751	1.20	.330	1.27	.281	13.643	1.37	.480	1.38	.319		
Macy (R.H.)	7.194	.86	.381	.88	.296	11.619	1.15	.465	1.29	.386		
Magic Chef	10.611	1.26	.375	1.25	.278	13.636	1.57	.624	1.62	.443		
Malone & Hyde	7.499	.86	.354	.99	.351	10.621	1.11	.518	1.30	.469		
Management Assist.	17.175	.54	.027	.58	.024	—	—	—	—	—	52	1978–82
Manhattan Indus.	11.110	1.02	.227	1.02	.167	14.541	1.43	.455	1.51	.338		
Manitowoc Co.	10.739	1.14	.299	1.28	.284	—	—	—	—	—		
Manufacturers Hanover	6.739	.71	.296	.78	.265	11.358	1.13	.465	1.36	.447		

Company	1978–82 (55)					1973–77 (41)				
Manville Corp.	11.060	.87	.165	.70	.079	9.450	.99	.525	1.11	.429
MAPCO, Inc.	8.696	1.05	.387	1.20	.378	12.287	.77	.185	1.05	.229
Marine Midland Banks	10.041	1.22	.394	1.22	.297	9.734	.82	.340	.70	.163
Marion Laboratories	9.548	.98	.278	1.00	.218	14.225	1.16	.313	1.48	.341
Mark Controls	11.757	1.49	.427	1.50	.323	—	—	—	—	—
Marriott Corp.	9.369	1.23	.463	1.37	.428	14.145	1.52	.547	1.86	.540
Marsh & McLennan	5.044	.56	.329	.56	.249	8.064	.48	.169	.64	.198
Martin Marietta	10.294	1.33	.448	1.60	.482	6.887	.79	.621	.87	.494
Mary Kay Cosmetics	12.586	1.06	.189	1.01	.129	—	—	—	—	—
Maryland Cup	9.202	.82	.211	.80	.151	11.594	1.30	.594	1.32	.406
Maryland National	6.936	.94	.487	.96	.379	13.499	1.40	.508	1.78	.547
Masco Corp.	8.715	1.27	.568	1.40	.515	12.534	1.28	.497	1.86	.687
Massey-Ferguson Ltd.	12.268	.92	.149	.79	.083	9.738	.74	.277	.85	.238
MassMutual M&R Inv.	5.843	.66	.342	.73	.312	11.776	1.09	.409	1.06	.253
Matsushita Elec. ADR	9.248	.59	.110	.66	.102	8.325	.29	.056	.36	.060
Mattel, Inc.	15.436	2.02	.456	2.36	.468	25.645	1.98	.282	1.78	.150
May Dept. Stores	7.216	.91	.424	1.00	.382	10.234	.93	.395	1.15	.397
Maytag Co.	5.718	.67	.367	.80	.395	7.715	.84	.559	.93	.454
MCA Inc.	7.734	.66	.196	.78	.205	11.250	.91	.310	1.04	.265
McCormick & Co.	9.676	.32	.029	.32	.021	—	—	—	—	—
McDermott Inc.	10.606	1.10	.286	1.51	.405	11.357	.55	.109	.97	.230
McDonald's Corp.	6.547	.65	.261	.67	.210	13.376	1.45	.554	2.08	.758
McDonnell Douglas	11.749	1.02	.202	1.17	.200	10.565	.82	.283	.96	.259
McGraw-Edison	9.063	1.03	.348	1.13	.312	9.619	.97	.485	1.07	.391
McGraw-Hill	8.414	.99	.367	1.12	.357	11.418	1.14	.474	1.21	.351
MCI Communications	14.438	1.46	.288	1.60	.258	—	—	—	—	—
McIntyre Mines	15.130	1.72	.344	1.98	.344	10.809	.85	.290	.97	.251
McNeil Corp.	7.412	.82	.324	.83	.248	7.163	.85	.660	.88	.468
Mead Corp.	8.920	1.21	.491	1.42	.504	9.270	.93	.472	.98	.349
Measurex Corp.	10.756	1.28	.377	1.27	.279	—	—	—	—	—
Media General	6.889	1.03	.592	1.11	.521	—	—	—	—	—
Medtronic, Inc.	10.495	1.19	.341	1.36	.334	13.923	1.20	.268	1.52	.309
MEI Corp.	8.072	.87	.307	.91	.254	12.651	.98	.284	.89	.156
Mellon National	6.698	.78	.362	.90	.361	7.871	.82	.516	1.06	.566
Melville Corp.	6.917	.76	.320	.78	.252	13.499	1.39	.504	1.40	.338
Mercantile Stores	5.385	.53	.255	.61	.253	10.576	.77	.249	.89	.223

| | January 1978–December 1982 | | | | | January 1973–December 1977 | | | | | Incomplete Data Series | |
| | Log (%) | VLIC | | NYSE | | Log (%) | VLIC | | NYSE | | Number | |
Stock	Std. Dev.	Est. Beta	R^2	Est. Beta	R^2	Std. Dev.	Est. Beta	R^2	Est. Beta	R^2	of Obs.	Period
Mercantile Texas	7.873	.97	.430	.97	.317	—	—	—	—	—	54	1978–82
Merck & Co.	6.119	.69	.340	.73	.282	8.205	.52	.191	.95	.424		
Meredith Corp.	8.028	1.08	.487	1.21	.452	10.165	1.11	.564	1.11	.372		
Merrill Lynch	11.084	1.78	.685	2.07	.696	13.499	1.44	.537	1.63	.455		
Mesabi Trust Ctfs.	5.901	.68	.357	.67	.259	8.983	.55	.175	.53	.111		
Mesa Petroleum	13.450	1.07	.168	1.37	.209	12.717	.86	.215	1.24	.296		
Metromedia Inc.	8.591	1.11	.449	1.17	.371	13.321	1.36	.497	1.51	.404		
Michigan Energy & Res.	6.369	.32	.067	.32	.050	7.904	.76	.436	.77	.294		
Michigan National	8.230	.54	.122	.46	.065	—	—	—	—	—	57	1978–82
Michigan Sugar	12.722	1.32	.289	1.46	.263	15.841	.87	.144	1.20	.180		
Mid-Continent Tel.	5.299	.50	.234	.48	.166	5.736	.30	.129	.33	.103		
Middle South Util.	5.386	.33	.100	.32	.094	7.965	.65	.313	.86	.361		
Midland-Ross	9.384	1.22	.450	1.31	.392	9.537	.92	.440	.87	.259		
Miller (Herman)	10.505	1.49	.539	1.60	.461	—	—	—	—	—		
Miller-Wohl	9.214	1.06	.350	1.07	.272	—	—	—	—	—		
Millipore Corp.	11.149	1.30	.360	1.50	.360	—	—	—	—	—		
Milton Bradley	12.333	1.63	.468	1.83	.440	16.160	1.73	.542	1.75	.367		
Milton Roy	8.748	.66	.154	.54	.077	—	—	—	—	—		
Minnesota Min./Mfg.	6.290	.76	.392	.99	.496	7.875	.71	.382	1.10	.606		
Minnesota Pwr. & Lt.	4.724	.35	.143	.39	.134	4.427	.46	.505	.50	.404		
Mirro Corp.	9.074	.70	.166	.60	.091	—	—	—	—	—	61	1978–82
Mission Ins. Group	9.329	1.11	.376	1.24	.351	14.292	1.34	.416	1.64	.413		
Missouri Pacific	8.381	1.10	.460	1.46	.604	8.257	.80	.450	.97	.429		
Missouri Public Sv.	5.320	.30	.087	.30	.064	7.135	.69	.441	.72	.322		
Mitchell Energy/Dev.	13.696	1.51	.324	1.91	.387	—	—	—	—	—		
MITE Corp.	8.572	.55	.110	.52	.073	—	—	—	—	—		
Mobil Corp.	7.841	.40	.068	.63	.130	7.184	.65	.392	.89	.478		
Mobile Home Indus.	16.835	1.66	.260	1.62	.185	20.336	1.77	.358	1.78	.239		
Mohasco Corp.	8.931	.94	.296	.90	.205	11.461	1.11	.442	1.15	.317		
Mohawk Data Sciences	14.155	1.92	.491	1.95	.378	19.666	2.05	.517	1.99	.321		

Mohawk Rubber	11.148	.99	.209	.96	.147	8.889	.86	.447	.80	.254	57	1978–82
Molson Cos. A	5.856	.46	.177	.56	.192	–	–	–	–	–		
Monarch Capital	10.036	.97	.249	1.05	.217	7.354	.58	.299	.53	.160		
Monarch Mach. Tool	11.303	1.46	.445	1.65	.428	12.477	1.07	.345	1.03	.214		
Monogram Indus.	10.410	1.20	.353	1.19	.263	14.096	1.52	.552	1.53	.370		
Monsanto Co.	7.011	.85	.395	.95	.367	8.572	.89	.508	1.15	.566		
Montana-Dakota Util.	5.920	.61	.286	.84	.400	6.106	.54	.370	.66	.366		
Montana Power	6.195	.63	.276	.73	.281	5.270	.40	.269	.53	.312		
Montgomery St. Inc. Sec.	4.484	.34	.154	.36	.132	–	–	–	–	–		
MONY Mtg. Inv.	6.085	.76	.421	.91	.447	10.457	.95	.391	.96	.263		
Moog, Inc. A	13.406	1.44	.311	1.52	.272	–	–	–	–	–		
Moore Corp. Ltd.	5.828	.64	.320	.67	.263	7.200	.57	.300	.91	.495	50	1978–82
Moore McCormack Res.	9.788	1.24	.425	1.33	.368	13.773	1.32	.432	1.58	.413		
Moran Energy	17.401	1.96	.359	2.59	.502	–	–	–	–	–	47	1978–82
Morgan (J.P.)	5.918	.52	.206	.58	.192	8.330	.79	.429	1.11	.556		
Morrison Inc.	9.577	1.15	.383	1.16	.292	–	–	–	–	–		
Morrison-Knudsen	10.781	1.42	.463	1.57	.425	11.721	1.14	.448	1.36	.422		
Morse Shoe	11.027	1.20	.316	1.35	.298	15.012	1.40	.412	1.50	.313		
Motorola Inc.	7.909	1.01	.438	1.12	.402	10.338	1.04	.482	1.32	.509		
Mountain Fuel Supply	7.343	.70	.245	.96	.339	11.779	.77	.200	1.00	.225		
Munford, Inc.	11.627	.73	.104	.70	.072	10.458	1.07	.495	1.15	.380		
Munsingwear Inc.	6.383	.22	.033	.30	.044	7.628	.72	.419	.79	.336		
Murphy (G.C.)	7.919	.71	.214	.76	.185	7.018	.68	.439	.65	.270		
Murphy Oil	12.033	1.21	.268	1.74	.418	11.268	1.04	.404	1.24	.381		
Murray Ohio Mfg.	8.212	.83	.270	.70	.146	10.218	.76	.265	.79	.188		
Mutual of Omaha	4.735	.38	.168	.41	.149	4.310	.36	.324	.37	.223		
Myers (L.E.) Gr.	13.420	1.37	.276	1.31	.190	14.015	1.15	.317	1.01	.162		
Nabisco Brands	5.499	.56	.278	.62	.257	8.019	.75	.414	.86	.360		
Nalco Chemical	6.611	.74	.337	.78	.278	11.617	1.22	.523	1.65	.631		
Narco Scientific	15.197	1.53	.269	1.60	.221	14.599	1.68	.628	1.70	.424		
Nashua Corp.	11.389	1.37	.387	1.39	.299	13.004	1.02	.289	1.12	.230		
Nat'l Can	9.103	1.13	.414	1.24	.372	9.649	.99	.502	1.11	.411		
Nat'l City Corp.	6.212	.72	.355	.80	.329	–	–	–	–	–		
Nat'l Data	11.713	1.39	.398	1.46	.352	–	–	–	–	–		
Nat'l Distill. & Chem.	6.205	.85	.504	.97	.487	7.210	.75	.511	.69	.333	47	1978–82
Nat'l Fuel Gas	5.591	.42	.151	.43	.118	5.946	.56	.414	.56	.281	49	1973–77

| | January 1978–December 1982 | | | | | January 1973–December 1977 | | | | | Incomplete Data Series | |
| | Log (%) | VLIC | | NYSE | | Log (%) | VLIC | | NYSE | | Number | |
Stock	Std. Dev.	Est. Beta	R²	Est. Beta	R²	Std. Dev.	Est. Beta	R²	Est. Beta	R²	of Obs.	Period
Nat'l. Gypsum	8.755	1.12	.439	1.28	.425	9.730	1.04	.539	1.00	.329		
Nat'l. Homes	13.007	1.45	.332	1.47	.256	18.696	1.92	.499	1.81	.295		
Nat'l. Medical Care	11.023	1.33	.385	1.44	.341	17.086	1.73	.479	1.92	.454	50	1973–77
Nat'l. Medical Enter.	12.142	1.70	.523	1.79	.436	10.521	1.14	.503	1.12	.381	44	1973–77
Nat'l. Mine Service	10.257	1.14	.328	1.11	.235	13.584	1.02	.205	1.12	.177	41	1973–77
Nat'l. Patent Dev.	14.355	1.73	.386	1.96	.372	—	—	—	—	—		
Nat'l. Presto Indus.	8.810	.78	.206	.80	.165	8.650	.61	.232	.65	.178		
Nat'l. Semiconductor	12.550	1.36	.312	1.50	.284	18.601	1.70	.396	1.94	.342		
Nat'l. Service Indus.	6.006	.82	.495	.95	.500	9.445	1.03	.559	1.03	.370		
National-Standard	7.919	.91	.355	.84	.225	11.778	1.23	.513	1.11	.280		
Nat'l. Steel	6.979	.87	.416	.96	.380	6.004	.52	.349	.55	.259		
Nat'l. Util. & Indus.	7.847	.51	.113	.53	.092	8.722	.52	.169	.52	.112		
Natomas Co.	10.837	1.31	.390	1.79	.547	13.937	.52	.067	.77	.096		
NBD Bancorp.	6.040	.75	.415	.83	.374	5.705	.67	.650	.77	.569		
NCH Corp.	9.050	1.07	.375	1.08	.284	11.911	.99	.327	1.39	.428		
NCNB Corp.	8.508	1.01	.376	1.03	.295	13.033	1.34	.499	1.82	.608		
NCR Corp.	9.450	1.24	.461	1.37	.423	11.671	1.21	.511	1.46	.487		
Nevada Power	5.638	.41	.139	.45	.128	7.777	.75	.438	.84	.362		
New England Elec. Sys.	5.942	.47	.167	.51	.145	7.804	.75	.438	.80	.330		
Newhall Land/Farming	10.183	1.05	.283	1.04	.209	11.504	.93	.306	.92	.199		
Newmont Mining	11.831	1.51	.436	1.76	.443	8.419	.74	.369	.93	.382		
Newpark Resources	14.169	1.62	.348	1.95	.377	—	—	—	—	—		
New Process	11.585	1.14	.260	1.18	.207	13.805	1.22	.370	1.16	.248	51	1973–77
New York State E & G	4.731	.29	.099	.30	.080	6.378	.68	.541	.75	.433		
New York Times	7.633	.95	.412	1.04	.368	10.056	.98	.446	.97	.294		
Niagara Mohawk Pwr.	5.159	.27	.075	.26	.050	7.098	.69	.444	.71	.312		
Niagara Share	6.888	.88	.435	1.03	.450	5.948	.51	.343	.65	.371		
NICOR Inc.	5.783	.66	.352	.88	.465	5.450	.58	.534	.67	.467		
Nielsen (A.C.) A	8.217	1.01	.406	1.06	.335	11.976	1.13	.420	1.36	.460	50	1973–77
NL Indus.	10.304	1.25	.394	1.71	.548	8.493	.90	.535	.92	.365		

Noranda Mines	9.409	.94	.267	1.01	.230	8.424	.71	.337	.92	.373	
Norcen Energy Res.	8.746	.72	.182	.72	.137	8.712	.71	.317	.73	.221	
Nordstrom, Inc.	9.618	.98	.277	.98	.207	—	—	—	—	—	
Norfolk Southern	8.148	1.03	.430	1.22	.451	5.664	.40	.241	.58	.333	
Norlin Corp.	9.531	.62	.113	.52	.059	8.684	.89	.497	.85	.301	
North American Coal	11.451	1.07	.234	1.10	.186	13.544	.88	.200	1.24	.264	
North Amer. Philips	7.756	1.08	.514	1.17	.452	10.015	1.14	.615	1.22	.466	
Northeast Utilities	5.591	.37	.117	.43	.116	7.993	.77	.435	.89	.387	
Northern Indus. Pub. Ser.	5.715	.35	.100	.35	.073	7.096	.59	.323	.71	.312	
Northern States Pwr.	5.511	.39	.133	.42	.115	6.369	.60	.425	.80	.492	
Northern Telecom Ltd.	8.644	1.06	.401	1.08	.310	—	—	—	—	—	
Northern Trust	6.136	.75	.400	.82	.357	6.946	.64	.360	.76	.401	44 1973–77
Northgate Exploration	13.700	1.29	.238	1.50	.239	15.556	1.08	.227	1.09	.155	
Northrop Corp.	11.292	1.38	.397	1.57	.388	9.873	.47	.106	.57	.103	
Northwest Airlines	10.402	1.20	.354	1.20	.264	12.756	1.43	.594	1.76	.594	
Northwest Bancorp.	7.158	.78	.315	.93	.339	9.626	.99	.496	1.35	.613	
Northwest Energy	10.276	1.10	.308	1.38	.359	8.429	.82	.409	.64	.190	44 1973–77
Northwest Industries	9.174	.81	.210	.91	.195	9.238	1.09	.663	1.12	.463	
Northwest Natural Gas	6.100	.69	.339	.84	.375	6.861	.60	.378	.63	.279	60 1973–77
Northwestern Steel/Wire	7.161	.84	.369	.86	.288	8.973	.70	.292	.75	.217	
Norton Co.	7.409	.85	.355	.97	.341	7.964	.80	.481	.84	.350	
Norton Simon	7.507	.64	.193	.61	.132	11.625	1.22	.525	1.55	.555	
Nova, An Alberta Corp.	8.374	.93	.326	1.02	.296	—	—	—	—	—	
Noxell Corp.	8.539	.99	.360	.92	.232	15.868	1.46	.416	1.65	.406	47 1973–77
Nucor Corp.	10.845	1.56	.549	1.70	.494	12.904	1.45	.600	1.49	.417	
Oak Indus.	12.668	1.17	.229	.94	.111	13.006	1.31	.481	1.30	.311	
Oakite Products	6.393	.61	.240	.64	.198	9.241	.94	.495	1.13	.472	
Occidental Petroleum	8.283	.93	.340	1.21	.429	10.714	.95	.372	1.08	.316	
Ocean Drill & Expl.	11.780	1.23	.289	1.62	.379	—	—	—	—	—	
Offshore Logistics	11.418	1.26	.323	1.57	.376	—	—	—	—	—	
Ogden Corp.	8.646	1.26	.563	1.47	.580	10.288	1.13	.569	1.24	.453	
Ogilvy & Mather Int'l	6.947	.87	.423	.89	.331	—	—	—	—	—	
Ohio Casualty	7.585	.90	.379	.96	.320	10.336	.60	.159	.97	.277	
Ohio Edison	5.547	.41	.149	.45	.133	7.687	.64	.333	.61	.195	
Oklahoma Gas & Elec.	5.324	.33	.101	.37	.097	7.167	.51	.239	.67	.276	
Olin Corp.	10.555	.93	.209	1.02	.187	12.812	1.00	.287	.97	.181	

	January 1978–December 1982					January 1973–December 1977					Incomplete Data Series	
	Log (%)	VLIC		NYSE		Log (%)	VLIC		NYSE			
Stock	Std. Dev.	Est. Beta	R^2	Est. Beta	R^2	Std. Dev.	Est. Beta	R^2	Est. Beta	R^2	Number of Obs.	Period
Olympia Brewing	7.645	.38	.067	.41	.058	10.051	1.02	.490	.91	.258		
Omark Indus.	8.911	1.20	.486	1.45	.528	9.665	1.05	.558	1.09	.400		
Oneida Ltd.	12.863	1.59	.406	1.65	.327	6.950	.60	.350	.68	.303		
ONEOK Inc.	8.967	1.07	.379	1.31	.424	6.451	.56	.363	.65	.317		
Opelika Mfg.	7.578	.46	.099	.37	.047	7.451	.75	.479	.72	.295		
Orange/Rockland Util.	5.212	.20	.041	.17	.021	15.347	1.18	.279	.92	.126		
Orange-co Inc.	10.999	1.10	.265	1.12	.208	—	—	—	—	—	51	1973–77
Orion Capital	9.977	1.14	.348	1.19	.283	15.818	1.27	.306	1.14	.162		
Orion Pictures	17.276	1.65	.242	1.74	.203	4.955	.45	.384	.60	.454		
Otter Tail Power	5.207	.45	.195	.47	.163	13.910	1.42	.496	1.47	.352		
Outboard Marine	11.417	1.21	.299	1.06	.173	9.655	1.00	.506	.94	.297		
Outlet Co.	11.302	1.61	.539	1.83	.522	—	—	—	—	—		
Overhead Door	8.431	1.05	.415	1.20	.406	12.166	1.25	.501	1.41	.421		
Overnite Transp.	9.249	1.21	.459	1.29	.386	10.866	.81	.262	.87	.203		
Overseas Shipholding	10.645	1.45	.496	1.75	.541	9.925	1.04	.520	1.30	.537		
Owens-Corning Fiber	9.563	1.14	.382	1.26	.348	7.723	.80	.505	1.00	.530		
Owens-Illinois	6.825	.80	.369	.91	.358	—	—	—	—	—		
Oxford Indus.	9.809	.95	.250	1.04	.225	—	—	—	—	—		
Ozark Air Lines	13.289	1.55	.378	1.65	.318	11.512	.86	.263	1.11	.288		
Pabst Brewing	10.589	.90	.194	1.05	.196	—	—	—	—	—	61	1978–82
PACCAR Inc.	7.555	1.01	.473	.97	.331	—	—	—	—	—		
Pacific Gas & Elec.	4.716	.22	.058	.23	.046	5.724	.43	.271	.61	.354		
Pacific Lighting	5.553	.32	.090	.41	.111	5.257	.48	.388	.41	.193		
Pacific Lumber	8.564	1.09	.429	1.25	.423	7.024	.54	.287	.59	.264	47	1973–77
Pacific Pwr & Lt.	4.684	.41	.203	.47	.202	5.847	.60	.499	.65	.390		
Pacific Tin Consol.	11.055	.86	.162	.88	.126	9.934	.64	.194	.64	.129		
Paine Webber	15.953	2.43	.621	2.91	.664	15.464	1.79	.636	1.86	.453		
Pall Corp.	7.954	1.01	.432	1.18	.440	—	—	—	—	—		
Palm Beach	11.073	.85	.155	.73	.086	12.960	1.33	.502	1.22	.278		
Pan Am World Airway	10.836	1.12	.285	1.01	.173	17.534	1.81	.506	2.15	.471		

Company										
							1973–77		1973–77 1978–82 1973–77	1978–82
							41		62 48 50	62
Panhandle Eastern	8.496	.89	.290	1.23	.416	8.395	.81	.444	.98	.429
Pantry Pride	19.320	1.23	.108	1.19	.076	9.601	1.00	.517	.91	.283
Papercraft Corp.	8.403	1.03	.404	1.15	.377	14.103	1.53	.554	1.53	.367
Pargas, Inc.	9.607	.97	.271	1.01	.220	8.599	.82	.434	.82	.286
Parker Drilling	12.031	1.43	.378	1.79	.444	–	–	–	–	–
Parker-Hannifin	8.628	1.02	.375	1.21	.395	10.749	1.04	.446	1.04	.291
Parker Pen	9.747	1.06	.318	1.23	.320	11.208	1.12	.476	1.27	.402
Parsons Corp.	12.005	1.49	.411	1.80	.449	–	–	–	–	–
Patrick Petroleum	12.751	1.21	.239	1.34	.269	14.793	.90	.134	.97	.111
Payless Cashways	9.558	1.28	.479	1.48	.395	–	–	–	–	–
Pay Less Drug St. NW	9.134	1.20	.461	1.32	.415	11.397	1.20	.522	1.33	.425
Pay'n Save	8.782	1.16	.464	1.25	.402	10.045	1.05	.521	1.10	.383
Penn Central	12.491	1.25	.280	1.60	.364	–	.75	–	–	–
PennCorp Financial	12.141	1.13	.229	1.03	.144	17.631	.75	.086	.79	.072
Penney (J.C.)	7.318	.63	.199	.62	.142	9.350	.88	.422	1.12	.449
Penna Power & Light	4.575	.35	.134	.39	.125	5.419	.58	.549	.59	.372
Pennwalt Corp.	6.060	.82	.493	.98	.522	9.329	.93	.474	1.01	.370
Pennzoil Co.	9.834	1.01	.282	1.33	.367	10.758	1.06	.460	1.27	.434
Pentair Inc.	9.282	1.01	.316	.91	.192	–	–	–	–	–
Peoples Drug Stores	9.096	1.01	.331	1.11	.300	14.035	1.53	.561	1.76	.494
PepsiCo Inc.	6.623	.76	.347	.77	.272	9.135	.86	.418	1.32	.654
Perkin-Elmer	10.127	1.25	.409	1.48	.424	10.654	1.07	.478	1.43	.564
Petrie Stores	8.650	1.02	.369	1.06	.301	10.593	.85	.303	1.09	.332
Petrolane Inc.	8.326	1.02	.399	1.29	.480	12.407	1.20	.441	1.14	.263
Petroleum & Resources	8.017	.88	.321	1.22	.464	7.642	.59	.279	.84	.378
Petrolite Corp.	8.606	.59	.127	.56	.085	–	–	–	–	–
Pfizer, Inc.	6.455	.64	.259	.80	.303	9.109	.67	.253	1.14	.487
Phelps Dodge	11.199	1.50	.480	1.71	.468	7.336	.51	.233	.67	.265
PHH Group	8.264	.94	.343	1.09	.351	–	–	–	–	–
Philadelphia Elec.	5.116	.44	.201	.49	.186	7.577	.73	.443	.81	.359
Philadelphia Nat'l	6.344	.77	.398	.95	.449	7.897	.85	.554	.93	.432
Philip Morris	7.009	.82	.363	.94	.357	8.139	.44	.136	.92	.398
Philips Indus.	13.054	1.73	.470	1.70	.337	16.790	1.88	.591	1.84	.375
Philips NV	6.007	.58	.258	.60	.206	–	–	–	–	–
Phillips Petroleum	9.776	.97	.263	1.37	.390	9.144	.61	.214	1.10	.454
Phillips-Van Heusen	10.206	1.18	.357	1.10	.232	13.687	1.49	.558	1.61	.434

Stock	January 1978–December 1982					January 1973–December 1977					Incomplete Data Series	
	VLIC			NYSE		VLIC			NYSE		Number of Obs.	Period
	Log (%) Std. Dev.	Est. Beta	R²	Est. Beta	R²	Log (%) Std. Dev.	Est. Beta	R²	Est. Beta	R²		
Phoenix Steel	14.745	1.50	.274	1.44	.189	14.530	1.01	.228	.96	.136		
Piedmont Aviation	13.853	1.62	.364	1.53	.244	—	—	—	—	—		
Piedmont Nat. Gas	6.054	.54	.215	.56	.172	5.854	.52	.379	.52	.243		
Pier 1 Imports	14.776	1.52	.281	1.51	.208	28.760	1.97	.221	1.78	.119		
Pillsbury Co.	6.887	.67	.253	.72	.219	8.330	.81	.450	.94	.399		
Pinkertons B	7.347	.88	.384	.89	.296	13.421	1.05	.292	1.18	.244		
Pioneer Corp.	10.354	.96	.227	1.32	.325	7.496	.60	.306	.73	.294		
Pioneer Electron ADR	10.719	.77	.136	.70	.085	—	—	—	—	—		
Pioneer Hi-Bred Int'l	7.926	.68	.198	.81	.207	10.066	.78	.282	.71	.171	52	1973–77
Pitney Bowes	8.731	1.09	.419	1.23	.398	11.952	1.19	.470	1.23	.334		
Pittsburgh National	6.404	.77	.413	.79	.343	—	—	—	—	—	47	1978–82
Pittston Co.	8.953	1.13	.426	1.25	.387	11.101	.85	.275	1.02	.267		
Pittway Corp.	6.578	.72	.324	.77	.272	9.961	1.00	.498	1.09	.391	60	1973–77
Planning Research	14.632	1.85	.426	1.99	.371	16.585	1.66	.472	1.64	.306		
Plantronics Inc.	10.506	1.31	.414	1.46	.383	—	—	—	—	—		
Playboy Enterprises	17.957	1.29	.139	1.36	.114	15.849	1.64	.506	1.66	.342		
Plessey Co. plc ADR	8.471	.55	.114	.62	.109	12.797	1.12	.363	1.24	.296		
PNB Mortgage	9.214	1.16	.422	1.28	.385	—	—	—	—	—		
Pneumo Corp.	12.475	1.64	.462	1.81	.423	9.422	.75	.230	.51	.076	41	1973–77
Pogo Producing	11.181	1.12	.268	1.42	.320	9.603	.31	.038	.67	.128	41	1973–77
Polaroid Corp.	10.732	1.21	.339	1.29	.290	15.102	1.41	.412	1.96	.527		
Ponderosa Inc.	13.657	1.61	.371	1.64	.289	20.284	2.12	.534	2.51	.501	60	1973–77
Pope & Talbot	10.605	1.39	.457	1.54	.424	—	—	—	—	—		
Portec, Inc.	8.146	1.04	.434	1.08	.352	10.861	1.04	.437	1.26	.421		
Portland General Elec.	5.161	.40	.157	.46	.161	5.754	.61	.533	.60	.341		
Potlatch Corp.	9.221	1.16	.425	1.31	.403	9.541	.87	.392	1.05	.376		
Potomac Elec. Power	5.165	.29	.087	.32	.077	6.201	.58	.418	.59	.280		
PPG Indus.	8.231	1.20	.571	1.32	.513	8.705	.88	.485	.92	.348		
Precious Metals Hldg.	12.695	1.15	.219	1.29	.206	—	—	—	—	—		
Premier Industrial	6.708	.63	.239	.66	.192	11.901	1.00	.337	.92	.188		

Company											
Prentice-Hall	7.273	.91	.417	1.00	.382	9.276	.81	.363	.92	.305	
Presley Cos.	15.481	1.82	.368	1.85	.287	—	—	—	—	—	
Prime Computer	15.373	1.98	.440	2.28	.441	—	—	—	—	—	
Procter & Gamble	4.990	.50	.269	.59	.276	7.094	.51	.242	.87	.472	
Prod. Research & Chem.	10.780	.91	.190	.99	.168	12.342	1.00	.311	.95	.186	
Proler Int'l.	9.763	1.12	.354	1.14	.272	10.639	.87	.327	1.09	.346	60 1973–77
PSA, Inc.	11.212	.74	.117	.88	.122	14.904	1.59	.542	1.68	.398	
Public Sv. (Colorado)	5.289	.36	.121	.40	.115	6.194	.56	.391	.71	.408	
Public Sv. (Indiana)	5.825	.29	.068	.28	.045	6.719	.57	.343	.84	.485	
Public Sv. (New Hampshire)	5.605	.34	.099	.37	.089	8.098	.77	.424	.86	.351	
Public Sv. (New Mexico)	5.346	.24	.054	.23	.036	6.384	.67	.516	.74	.426	
Public Sv. Elec. & Gas	5.323	.29	.082	.29	.057	7.012	.60	.349	.62	.248	
Pueblo Int'l	10.618	1.23	.356	1.22	.262	12.648	1.05	.326	.78	.118	
Puget Sound Pwr. & Lt.	5.369	.35	.112	.32	.071	5.070	.49	.447	.51	.314	
Pulte Home	14.332	1.92	.522	1.98	.443	—	—	—	—	—	45 1978–82
Puritan-Bennett	10.635	1.31	.407	1.35	.323	—	—	—	—	—	
Purolator, Inc.	10.201	1.10	.308	.99	.187	12.290	1.21	.462	1.46	.441	
Putnam Duofund Cap.	8.176	1.27	.645	1.47	.645	11.537	1.25	.555	1.42	.476	
Pyro Energy	15.789	1.51	.245	1.67	.224	15.983	.32	.018	.58	.046	
Quaker Oats	6.729	.76	.342	.91	.369	10.749	.74	.227	.82	.183	50 1973–77
Quaker State Oil Ref.	10.114	1.35	.476	1.67	.544	11.420	1.28	.596	1.51	.549	
Quanex Corp.	13.278	1.25	.237	1.54	.270	8.648	.56	.200	.62	.162	
Rainier Bancorp.	6.899	.76	.321	.76	.245	—	—	—	—	—	
Ralston Purina	7.305	.82	.339	.90	.303	6.660	.52	.290	.75	.397	
Ramada Inns	13.892	1.39	.267	1.42	.210	15.682	1.71	.564	1.79	.407	
RAMPAC	7.997	.99	.417	1.10	.438	—	—	—	—	—	40 1978–82
Ranco, Inc.	9.215	1.07	.361	1.20	.340	12.035	1.04	.352	.92	.184	
Ranger Oil Ltd.	15.041	1.42	.254	1.91	.369	—	—	—	—	—	46 1978–82
Rank Organ. plc ADR	10.145	.55	.078	.79	.121	15.699	1.31	.335	1.72	.384	62 1973–77
Raychem Corp.	8.799	1.13	.458	1.17	.367	—	—	—	—	—	61 1978–82
Raymark Corp.	12.787	.85	.117	.77	.073	9.414	1.02	.559	1.13	.450	
Raymond Int'l.	11.435	1.51	.467	1.61	.395	13.844	1.32	.430	1.33	.288	
Raytheon Co.	8.695	1.10	.429	1.28	.432	8.888	.85	.428	1.10	.476	
RCA Corp.	7.570	.89	.368	1.05	.382	9.614	1.18	.709	1.30	.572	
Reading & Bates	12.921	1.61	.417	2.12	.541	14.156	1.18	.327	1.76	.483	
Recognition Equip.	17.442	2.08	.379	2.18	.311	—	—	—	—	—	

Stock	January 1978–December 1982					January 1973–December 1977					Incomplete Data Series	
	Log (%) Std. Dev.	VLIC Est. Beta	VLIC R²	NYSE Est. Beta	NYSE R²	Log (%) Std. Dev.	VLIC Est. Beta	VLIC R²	NYSE Est. Beta	NYSE R²	Number of Obs.	Period
Redken Labs.	13.157	1.51	.353	1.52	.266	—	—	—	—	—		
Redman Indus.	13.007	1.76	.486	1.91	.430	22.969	2.26	.459	2.17	.280		
Reece Corp.	9.507	.88	.231	.92	.188	10.855	.98	.401	.82	.189	60	1973–77
Regency Electronics	14.691	1.70	.348	1.80	.301	16.320	1.63	.430	1.77	.392	44	1973–77
Reichhold Chemicals	8.015	.93	.357	.96	.289	9.651	.83	.353	.77	.201		
Republic Airlines	13.995	1.26	.218	1.09	.121	10.717	.99	.419	.86	.213	60	1973–77
RepublicBank Corp.	8.274	.83	.267	.83	.203	10.376	1.11	.542	1.42	.589		
Republic Corp.	11.579	1.58	.500	1.62	.391	14.565	1.43	.459	1.36	.274		
Republic Fin'l. Serv.	9.920	.76	.156	.86	.151	9.028	.94	.533	.99	.393	60	1973–77
Republic N.Y.	11.637	1.54	.535	1.60	.456	—	—	—	—	—	43	1978–82
Republic Steel	7.033	.83	.369	.86	.297	8.219	.78	.424	.86	.341		
Research-Cottrell	9.929	1.25	.420	1.31	.347	18.464	1.39	.278	1.61	.251	60	1973–77
Resorts Int'l. A	17.663	1.44	.177	1.43	.130	—	—	—	—	—		
Revco Drug Stores	7.177	.91	.425	.96	.360	14.753	.84	.153	1.13	.185		
Revlon, Inc.	8.812	.87	.260	1.06	.290	7.004	.67	.430	.89	.508		
Rexham Corp.	9.652	1.30	.487	1.31	.369	12.500	1.15	.398	1.22	.297		
Rexnord, Inc.	7.702	.85	.321	.94	.301	9.547	.91	.430	1.01	.350		
Reynolds & Reynolds	8.652	.75	.200	.87	.217	—	—	—	—	—	50	1978–82
Reynolds (R.J.) Indus.	6.304	.67	.303	.88	.393	5.696	.52	.394	.66	.424		
Reynolds Metals	7.921	.98	.404	.99	.315	11.027	1.11	.483	1.27	.417		
Richmond Tank Car	15.941	1.25	.194	1.31	.170	—	—	—	—	—	41	1978–82
Riegel Textile	7.347	.96	.452	.98	.356	8.902	.77	.353	.76	.230		
Rio Grande Indus.	11.438	1.37	.381	1.66	.421	11.501	1.06	.406	1.22	.354		
Rite Aid	8.417	1.19	.529	1.25	.443	17.007	1.52	.380	1.69	.309		
Rival Mfg.	7.824	.88	.337	1.02	.341	13.241	1.62	.543	1.84	.503		
Roadway Services	7.870	.91	.359	.91	.268	9.107	.62	.221	.90	.307		
Robertshaw Controls	10.147	1.14	.338	1.07	.221	10.954	1.10	.481	1.16	.351	41	1973–77
Robertson (H.H.)	9.420	.80	.192	.77	.135	8.210	.83	.482	.92	.391		
Robins (A.H.)	7.595	.83	.319	.85	.253	11.889	1.04	.365	1.41	.441		
Rochester Gas & Elec.	5.251	.35	.122	.37	.098	6.050	.61	.476	.67	.380		

Rochester Telephone	6.007	.51	.190	.55	.166	7.328	.54	.257	.43	.106		
Rockcor Inc.	13.043	1.53	.369	1.65	.318	—	—	—	—	—		
Rockwell Int'l.	8.108	.92	.346	1.08	.356	7.412	.56	.274	.62	.220		
Rohm & Haas	8.111	1.14	.528	1.13	.386	10.132	.95	.421	1.24	.472		
Rohr Indus.	14.340	1.70	.377	1.81	.320	13.708	.99	.249	1.00	.167		
Rollins Inc.	9.048	1.15	.428	1.43	.496	14.285	1.51	.530	1.75	.469		
ROLM Corp.	14.012	1.48	.297	1.61	.263	—	—	—	—	—		
Ronson Corp.	15.094	1.42	.236	1.38	.167	12.823	1.00	.290	.79	.119		
Roper Corp.	8.341	1.15	.511	1.21	.424	10.350	.97	.416	1.05	.324		
Rorer Corp.	8.339	.72	.200	.76	.166	—	—	—	—	—		
Rouse Co.	11.646	1.21	.306	1.18	.215	—	—	—	—	—	58	1978–82
Rowan Cos.	11.462	1.17	.278	1.57	.376	12.623	.73	.163	.96	.191	60	1973–77
Royal Crown Cos.	8.245	.60	.141	.51	.078	12.325	1.33	.553	1.50	.462		
Royal Dutch Petrol.	6.389	.57	.209	.83	.336	5.992	.55	.407	.74	.479		
RTE Corp.	9.496	1.20	.423	1.16	.298	14.957	1.35	.387	1.33	.247		
Rubbermaid, Inc.	7.319	.79	.310	.73	.199	11.541	.78	.215	1.05	.261		
Russ Togs	6.656	.87	.458	.94	.399	10.033	.89	.374	.84	.221		
Ryan Homes	11.434	1.47	.438	1.58	.383	16.560	1.65	.486	1.94	.451	60	1973–77
Ryder System	9.914	1.42	.551	1.56	.493	17.278	1.79	.511	2.23	.523		
Sabine Corp.	10.428	1.09	.294	1.41	.367	—	—	—	—	—		
SAFECO Corp.	6.930	.94	.486	.98	.400	9.775	.40	.062	.82	.186	41	1973–77
Safeway Stores	7.198	.69	.247	.67	.172	6.692	.54	.307	.56	.220		
Saga Corp.	10.066	1.03	.278	.96	.181	15.795	1.65	.527	1.87	.448	62	1973–77
St. Joseph Lt. & Pwr.	5.010	.27	.079	.34	.092	6.820	.59	.358	.67	.303		
St. Paul Cos.	7.064	.67	.241	.73	.212	12.320	.81	.207	1.18	.290		
St. Regis Paper	6.501	.94	.554	1.06	.528	9.657	.96	.471	1.23	.510		
Salant Corp.	10.207	1.01	.259	1.09	.230	14.234	1.45	.492	1.50	.346		
Sanders Associates	11.001	1.33	.393	1.45	.347	16.804	1.98	.658	2.04	.460		
San Diego Gas & Elec.	5.615	.32	.088	.36	.080	6.386	.63	.460	.66	.337		
Santa Fe Indus.	9.305	1.00	.307	1.43	.470	7.985	.60	.272	.85	.354		
Sargent-Welch Scient.	7.785	.83	.300	.88	.258	13.088	1.34	.498	1.32	.318		
Savannah Elec. & Pwr.	5.236	.30	.087	.28	.059	7.434	.70	.417	.83	.391		
Savin Corp.	13.120	1.32	.270	1.17	.160	22.494	2.23	.467	2.15	.285		
SCA Services, Inc.	14.829	1.79	.391	1.98	.357	17.580	1.80	.514	1.81	.347	60	1973–77
Scherer (R.P.)	11.271	1.26	.335	1.25	.245	—	—	—	—	—		
Schering-Plough	6.554	.73	.335	.75	.265	9.368	.69	.255	1.08	.413		

Stock	January 1978–December 1982					January 1973–December 1977					Incomplete Data Series	
	Log (%) Std. Dev.	VLIC Est. Beta	VLIC R^2	NYSE Est. Beta	NYSE R^2	Log (%) Std. Dev.	VLIC Est. Beta	VLIC R^2	NYSE Est. Beta	NYSE R^2	Number of Obs.	Period
Schlumberger, Ltd.	7.634	.90	.369	1.24	.531	7.742	.32	.079	.73	.275		
Scientific-Atlanta	11.008	1.11	.273	1.24	.255	—	—	—	—	—		
SCM Corp.	8.890	1.02	.352	1.00	.255	10.998	1.31	.668	1.35	.469		
SCOA Indus.	9.491	1.07	.337	1.14	.286	10.945	.99	.390	.90	.211		
Scot Lad Foods	10.221	.90	.205	.74	.104	12.777	1.35	.532	1.59	.482		
Scott & Fetzer	7.804	1.11	.535	1.17	.447	11.858	1.34	.607	1.58	.558		
Scott Paper	8.599	.99	.354	1.18	.375	9.934	.98	.458	1.19	.452		
Scotty's Inc.	9.563	1.38	.554	1.49	.487	15.152	1.42	.430	1.67	.454	47	1973–77
Scovill Inc.	6.384	.70	.320	.66	.217	11.580	1.19	.497	1.18	.324		
SeaCo Inc.	12.862	1.51	.367	1.57	.297	13.244	1.36	.385	1.32	.258		
Seafirst Corp.	8.414	.88	.291	.97	.265	9.502	.98	.505	1.14	.451	41	1973–77
Seagram Co. Ltd.	7.922	.76	.247	.99	.311	7.379	.52	.237	.64	.233		
Sealed Air	12.983	1.22	.249	1.09	.159	—	—	—	—	—	47	1978–82
Sealed Power	9.576	.92	.249	.93	.188	11.510	1.05	.391	1.01	.243		
Searle (G.D.)	8.039	.83	.285	.87	.235	11.001	1.09	.463	1.36	.476		
Sears, Roebuck	6.720	.72	.305	.76	.259	7.428	.72	.441	.98	.545		
Security Pacific	8.656	1.08	.417	1.19	.380	7.219	.77	.539	.82	.405		
SEDCO, Inc.	12.099	1.23	.278	1.65	.369	12.696	.82	.198	1.28	.318		
Service Corp. Int'l.	11.648	1.35	.421	1.38	.351	—	—	—	—	—	41	1978–82
ServiceMaster Indus.	6.828	.65	.263	.66	.215	—	—	—	—	—	45	1978–82
Service Merchandise	11.895	1.42	.379	1.37	.267	—	—	—	—	—		
SFN Cos.	9.368	1.15	.401	1.34	.408	9.719	.73	.269	.82	.221		
Shaklee Corp.	14.138	1.79	.427	1.98	.394	—	—	—	—	—		
Shapell Indus.	10.082	1.43	.538	1.55	.472	16.854	1.89	.597	1.95	.420		
Shared Medical Sys.	8.903	1.19	.473	1.29	.421	—	—	—	—	—		
Shell Canada A	9.261	.32	.032	.37	.035	—	—	—	—	—	49	1978–82
Sheller-Globe	9.273	1.05	.344	.94	.207	13.000	1.40	.550	1.39	.358		
Shell Oil	10.321	.84	.175	1.33	.330	9.274	.64	.226	1.08	.427		
Shell Transport	7.148	.50	.132	.75	.222	9.218	.82	.379	1.01	.375		
Sherwin Williams	8.627	1.08	.420	1.21	.392	8.832	.77	.365	.88	.312		

Shoney's Inc.	8.989	1.09	.389	1.12	.312	—	.60	.523	.63	.377
Showboat, Inc.	11.625	1.07	.226	1.23	.224	5.773	.93	.451	1.09	.409
Sierra Pacific Pwr.	4.714	.28	.097	.31	.085	9.525	1.30	.536	1.35	.382
Signal Cos.	9.785	1.38	.527	1.56	.507	12.232	1.21	.224	1.72	.296
Simmonds Precision	14.487	1.73	.382	1.88	.337	17.678	1.25	.418	1.32	.312
Simplicity Pattern	8.883	.93	.290	.85	.184	13.261	1.21	.357	1.32	.280
Singer Co.	12.699	1.40	.323	1.45	.260	13.948	1.08	.576	1.06	.365
Skyline Corp.	10.608	1.48	.516	1.61	.462	9.803	.95	.248	1.53	.427
Smith (A.O.)	7.812	1.05	.481	1.12	.413	13.136	.58	.249	.93	.422
Smith Int'l.	10.190	.94	.225	1.26	.304	8.059	.59	.207	.71	.196
SmithKline Beckman	7.238	.73	.274	.90	.306	8.915	.63	.268	.72	.270
Smucker (J.M.)	8.617	.73	.194	.94	.236	8.327	.88	.420	.91	.298
Snap-On Tools	9.025	1.15	.436	1.17	.334	9.315	.67	.154	.83	.153
Sonat, Inc.	8.663	.88	.276	1.18	.370	11.805	.31	.097	.38	.098
Sony Corp. ADR	9.239	.70	.153	.79	.146	6.818	1.83	.459	1.66	.249
Soo Line Railroad	7.616	.55	.137	.76	.197	18.633	.79	.528	.89	.445
South Atlantic Fin'l.	17.986	1.15	.108	1.05	.069	7.455	1.21	.457	1.56	.498
South Carolina Elec. & Gas	5.311	.39	.142	.41	.120	12.359	1.09	.500	1.15	.372
Southdown, Inc.	11.347	1.19	.294	1.37	.291	10.597	.78	.293	.61	.121
Southeast Banking	7.207	.98	.491	1.02	.403	9.897	.44	.300	.58	.347
Southeastern Pub. Ser.	6.997	.37	.074	.31	.039	5.523	.61	.346	.69	.288
Southern Cal. Edison	4.493	.22	.062	.29	.081	7.145	.56	.493	.56	.318
Southern Co.	5.007	.23	.055	.26	.052	5.523	.43	.431	.47	.339
Southern Indiana Gas & Elec.	5.390	.44	.180	.48	.160	4.533	.61	.433	.68	.357
Southern New Eng. Tel.	4.511	.42	.235	.46	.205	6.374	.87	.502	.98	.421
Southern Pacific	8.445	1.11	.461	1.34	.501	8.424	.57	.442	.54	.265
Southern Union	8.901	.91	.276	1.19	.358	5.851	.96	.394	1.14	.365
South Jersey Indus.	6.047	.65	.312	.68	.254	10.519	1.74	.174	1.51	.086
Southland Corp.	7.990	.85	.303	.93	.273	28.804	—	—	—	—
Southmark Corp.	17.441	1.54	.209	1.67	.183	—	—	—	—	—
Southwest Airlines	12.231	1.40	.350	1.32	.233	—	.44	.329	.55	.347
Southwest Bancshares	6.952	.79	.344	.89	.330	5.224	1.55	.630	1.44	.357
Southwestern Pub. Ser.	4.620	.17	.037	.14	.019	13.469	.84	.303	.82	.194
Southwest Forest Indus.	12.083	1.74	.552	1.86	.476	10.469	—	—	—	—
Sparton Corp.	11.232	1.24	.323	1.31	.273	—	—	—	—	—
Spectra-Physics	10.162	1.05	.288	1.21	.285	—	—	—	—	—

| | January 1978–December 1982 | | | | | January 1973–December 1977 | | | | | Incomplete Data Series | |
| | Log (%) | VLIC | | NYSE | | Log (%) | VLIC | | NYSE | | Number | |
Stock	Std. Dev.	Est. Beta	R²	Est. Beta	R²	Std. Dev.	Est. Beta	R²	Est. Beta	R²	of Obs.	Period
Sperry Corp.	8.284	1.23	.590	1.38	.558	8.693	.92	.528	1.29	.686		
Springs Indus.	8.925	1.22	.495	1.31	.430	7.772	.67	.350	.75	.289		
SPS Technologies	13.535	1.64	.393	1.76	.336	11.433	.84	.256	.84	.171		
Square D	7.132	.93	.457	1.12	.495	9.227	.83	.385	.89	.290		
Squibb Corp.	8.142	.81	.263	.84	.215	10.533	.57	.139	.94	.249		
Staley (A.E.) Mfg.	10.807	1.10	.278	1.42	.345	11.942	1.02	.348	1.16	.295		
Stanadyne, Inc.	9.225	1.01	.319	1.01	.237	—	—	—	—	—		
Standard Brands Paint	8.568	1.00	.363	1.09	.323	10.214	.89	.363	1.27	.482		
Standard Motor Prod.	11.148	1.44	.445	1.53	.376	—	—	—	—	—		
Standard Oil of Cal.	8.694	.52	.096	.90	.214	7.160	.56	.292	.85	.437		
Standard Oil of Indiana	9.391	.63	.121	1.11	.278	6.103	.37	.179	.61	.308		
Standard Oil of Ohio	10.921	.89	.178	1.43	.343	7.231	.16	.023	.38	.089		
Standard-Pacific	15.010	1.55	.286	1.85	.303	—	—	—	—	—		
Standard Register	6.206	.71	.352	.80	.328	7.528	.80	.537	.82	.384	62	1973–77
Standex Int'l.	8.161	.86	.299	1.05	.333	9.406	.74	.292	.65	.148		
Stanley Works	8.497	1.09	.440	1.25	.434	10.315	1.03	.471	.99	.289		
Stanwood Corp.	11.256	.74	.116	.90	.127	28.399	1.74	.177	1.33	.069		
Starrett (L.S.)	7.963	.83	.288	.99	.309	8.088	.58	.247	.63	.189		
Stauffer Chemical	9.313	1.16	.413	1.25	.357	9.295	.86	.404	1.05	.398		
Stelco Inc. A	6.484	.55	.191	.62	.184	6.597	.52	.296	.65	.303		
Sterchi Bros. Stores	6.271	.77	.403	.68	.237	7.243	.63	.360	.62	.227		
Sterling Bancorp.	8.372	.93	.333	1.03	.302	4.956	.20	.074	.11	.016		
Sterling Drug	8.693	.78	.216	.97	.250	9.327	.35	.068	.75	.205		
Stevens (J.P.)	7.526	1.06	.528	1.11	.438	8.377	.76	.390	.90	.364		
Stewart-Warner	7.366	1.00	.493	1.07	.418	6.774	.75	.578	.82	.459		
Stokely-Van Camp	9.909	.82	.185	.81	.134	8.118	.80	.463	.79	.298		
Stone Container	13.614	1.46	.305	1.51	.246	10.772	1.03	.432	1.16	.364		
Stone & Webster	8.781	.88	.270	1.04	.280	12.140	.95	.290	1.22	.314		
Stop & Shop Cos.	8.543	.75	.208	.73	.144	8.673	.91	.522	1.03	.439		
Storage Technology	13.168	1.39	.297	1.41	.229	13.268	1.26	.326	1.56	.361	41	1973–77

Company											Rank	Period
Storer Broadcasting	9.048	1.08	.377	1.21	.359	13.378	1.31	.455	1.52	.405		
Stride Rite	9.424	.71	.152	.68	.103	9.063	.68	.265	.63	.151		
Suave Shoe	11.673	1.44	.403	1.47	.316	19.955	1.81	.391	1.74	.237		
Suburban Propane Gas	9.059	.85	.233	1.03	.259	10.594	1.07	.485	1.10	.339		
Sullair Corp.	18.897	1.49	.195	1.62	.185	—	—	—	—	—	41	1978–82
Sun Banks of Fla.	8.820	1.09	.409	1.13	.327	11.676	1.26	.550	1.27	.370		
Sun Chemical	9.636	1.18	.403	1.23	.328	6.878	.43	.184	.57	.212		
Sun Co.	10.320	.99	.244	1.38	.355	14.289	1.46	.492	1.64	.412		
Sundstrand Corp.	9.235	1.19	.442	1.44	.485	—	—	—	—	—		
Sun Electric	12.155	1.52	.419	1.53	.317	13.579	.74	.142	.94	.151		
Sunshine Mining	15.613	1.46	.234	1.88	.290	—	—	—	—	—		
Super Food Services	7.964	.65	.192	.70	.180	9.804	.62	.189	.69	.176	45	1978–82
Superior Electric	10.127	.84	.184	.94	.172	9.716	.54	.147	.73	.176	50	1973–77
Superior Oil	9.727	.98	.269	1.30	.356	13.242	1.09	.319	.97	.167		
Supermarkets Gen'l.	8.500	.97	.347	1.08	.324	17.888	1.79	.467	1.98	.419		
Superscope, Inc.	14.296	1.66	.360	1.67	.273	10.377	1.20	.638	1.37	.547	52	1973–77
Super Valu Stores	7.423	1.02	.503	1.16	.485	10.204	.77	.269	.86	.220		
Swank Inc.	7.994	.86	.306	.92	.266	10.884	1.22	.594	1.43	.542		
Sybron Corp.	7.815	.94	.382	1.05	.362	11.248	.65	.157	1.05	.272		
Syntex Corp.	7.631	1.01	.468	1.13	.439	—	—	—	—	—		
Sysco Corp.	8.227	1.09	.494	1.23	.469	13.089	1.53	.644	1.60	.466	57	1978–82
Taft Broadcasting	7.901	1.09	.511	1.14	.417	10.249	1.02	.469	.90	.242		
Talley Indus.	9.115	.82	.217	.71	.122	11.301	.80	.237	1.21	.357		
Tampax Inc.	6.551	.54	.183	.59	.161	16.976	1.79	.525	2.00	.434		
Tandy Corp.	11.429	1.45	.431	1.59	.388	—	—	—	—	—		
Tandycrafts, Inc.	11.520	1.06	.240	1.15	.226	12.554	1.28	.491	1.24	.307	47	1978–82
TDK Electronics	8.599	.79	.235	.75	.171	9.292	.90	.442	.99	.357	48	1978–82
Technicolor, Inc.	13.677	1.36	.264	1.38	.204	10.941	.88	.309	1.15	.349		
TECO Energy	5.456	.35	.111	.35	.081	15.090	1.17	.285	1.43	.281		
Tektronix, Inc.	7.985	.95	.375	1.04	.339	20.820	1.00	.110	.27	.005		
Teledyne Inc.	9.796	1.35	.508	1.50	.470	6.720	.58	.347	.75	.388		
Telex Corp.	15.936	2.19	.503	2.22	.388	16.075	1.56	.460	1.80	.409		
Tenneco, Inc.	6.566	.84	.433	1.10	.564	10.007	.76	.272	.98	.301		
Teradyne Inc.	12.050	1.52	.424	1.55	.332	—	—	—	—	—	60	1973–77
Tesoro Petroleum	13.482	1.33	.258	1.48	.241	—	—	—	—	—		
Texaco Canada	12.838	.85	.119	1.00	.133	—	—	—	—	—	49	1978–82

| | January 1978–December 1982 | | | | | January 1973–December 1977 | | | | | Incomplete Data Series | |
| | Log (%) | VLIC | | NYSE | | Log (%) | VLIC | | NYSE | | Number | |
Stock	Std. Dev.	Est. Beta	R²	Est. Beta	R²	Std. Dev.	Est. Beta	R²	Est. Beta	R²	of Obs.	Period
Texaco Inc.	6.072	.35	.089	.64	.219	6.949	.72	.505	.91	.532		
Texas Air	14.314	1.83	.456	1.80	.328	—	—	—	—	—	61	1978–82
Texas Commerce Bkshr.	5.982	.74	.404	.76	.323	7.466	.66	.367	.82	.418	51	1973–77
Texas Eastern Corp.	8.394	.95	.343	1.26	.452	9.500	.87	.394	1.02	.359		
Texas Gas Trans.	8.426	1.13	.481	1.48	.616	7.188	.69	.441	.66	.265		
Texas Indus.	10.938	1.37	.416	1.48	.368	9.595	.91	.429	.89	.268		
Texas Instruments	7.775	1.03	.470	1.16	.444	8.854	.74	.328	1.03	.426		
Texas Int'l.	18.582	1.62	.202	1.91	.210	—	—	—	—	—		
Texas-New Mexico Pwr.	6.436	.33	.079	.25	.037	—	—	—	—	—	42	1978–82
Texas Oil & Gas	10.660	1.09	.278	1.59	.444	13.693	1.24	.391	1.53	.389		
Texas Pac Land Tr. Sub.	10.992	.99	.218	1.38	.313	6.965	.43	.180	.51	.171		
Texas Utilities	5.344	.26	.062	.31	.066	8.545	.67	.293	.86	.318		
Texfi Indus.	19.152	1.37	.137	1.29	.090	17.343	1.14	.204	.77	.061		
Textron, Inc.	7.872	1.25	.667	1.38	.614	10.343	1.10	.538	1.18	.406		
Thackeray Corp.	13.781	1.36	.258	1.25	.165	24.878	2.17	.359	2.16	.237		
Thermo Electron	10.100	1.28	.445	1.37	.378	—	—	—	—	—	61	1978–82
Thomas & Betts	7.156	.92	.442	1.02	.407	8.630	.93	.554	1.16	.564		
Thomas Indus.	10.319	1.28	.408	1.41	.373	13.169	1.32	.478	1.32	.317		
Thrifty Corp.	10.207	1.21	.376	1.14	.249	8.948	.95	.538	.99	.384		
Tidewater Inc.	11.387	1.29	.342	1.74	.467	10.527	.66	.188	1.01	.286		
Tiger Int'l	11.830	1.35	.348	1.33	.251	14.467	1.48	.497	1.45	.315		
Time Inc.	8.101	1.13	.523	1.24	.468	9.778	.96	.454	1.08	.385		
Times Mirror	7.813	1.21	.638	1.26	.516	10.315	1.06	.500	1.34	.525		
Timken Co.	6.026	.70	.356	.75	.307	7.398	.80	.561	.80	.367		
Todd Shipyards	12.681	1.44	.346	1.60	.319	14.462	.86	.169	.69	.072		
Tokheim Corp.	10.629	1.35	.432	1.57	.434	—	—	—	—	—		
Toledo Edison	5.252	.32	.097	.30	.065	5.610	.58	.506	.74	.546		
Tonka Corp.	13.858	1.67	.387	1.93	.387	12.701	1.26	.468	1.34	.351		
Tootsie Roll Indus.	8.469	.71	.187	.66	.121	10.663	1.06	.471	1.16	.373		
Torchmark Corp.	6.625	.57	.198	.59	.161	—	—	—	—	—		

Toro Co.	12.281	1.23	.268	1.22	.196	13.548	1.34	.462	1.61	.443		
Tosco Corp.	16.926	1.58	.232	1.92	.256	—	—	—	—	—	57	1978–82
Total Petroleum N.A.	12.888	1.12	.201	1.29	.201	14.174	1.19	.333	1.20	.226	41	1973–77
Toys R Us	9.498	1.09	.371	1.14	.300	—	—	—	—	—		
Tracor Inc.	11.407	1.62	.536	1.76	.477	14.177	1.43	.372	1.28	.212		
Trane Co.	9.462	1.05	.326	1.07	.256	12.851	1.29	.474	1.29	.316		
Transamerica Corp.	7.797	1.12	.546	1.24	.505	9.070	.96	.534	.90	.311		
Transam. Realty Inv.	10.410	1.41	.493	1.44	.382	17.462	1.65	.421	1.68	.291		
Transco Energy	9.969	1.03	.287	1.48	.441	11.216	1.16	.509	1.09	.298		
TRANSOHIO Fin'l.	11.574	1.34	.359	1.46	.318	13.040	1.30	.473	1.29	.343	51	1973–77
Transway Int'l.	6.412	.81	.423	.88	.376	9.662	1.13	.650	1.09	.398		
Trans World	14.660	1.83	.417	1.74	.282	16.973	1.92	.606	2.49	.674		
Travelers Corp.	7.153	.83	.361	.88	.299	9.873	.85	.353	1.05	.356		
TRE Corp.	12.369	1.71	.508	1.83	.437	17.046	1.85	.561	1.92	.399		
Triangle Indus.	8.975	1.19	.471	1.29	.411	9.387	.91	.450	.96	.331		
Triangle Pacific	11.667	1.71	.576	1.81	.482	12.970	1.21	.410	1.08	.218		
Tri-Continental	5.393	.82	.622	.95	.626	6.611	.71	.540	.86	.525		
Trinity Indus.	12.004	1.47	.397	1.75	.426	13.640	1.26	.405	1.40	.328		
Tri-South Inv.	12.659	1.54	.394	1.62	.328	31.404	2.14	.221	2.19	.152		
TRW Inc.	6.513	.81	.413	.90	.382	8.824	.92	.517	1.11	.572	49	1973–77
Tubos De Acero ADR	16.580	1.50	.219	1.67	.203	—	—	—	—	—		
Tucson Elec. Power	5.611	.24	.050	.34	.074	6.745	.61	.391	.68	.315		
Tyco Laboratories	11.357	1.55	.494	1.77	.487	13.080	1.15	.362	1.35	.371	51	1973–77
Tyler Corp.	10.981	1.06	.250	1.18	.229	10.948	1.18	.547	1.36	.484		
Tymshare, Inc.	12.573	1.62	.443	1.77	.394	15.777	1.94	.549	2.52	.663	41	1973–77
Tyson Foods	11.591	1.07	.227	1.10	.181	—	—	—	—	—		
UAL Inc.	11.746	1.49	.427	1.42	.291	12.535	1.21	.442	1.54	.472		
UGI Corp.	7.658	.91	.378	1.11	.421	7.081	.73	.497	.75	.355		
UMC Indus.	8.114	.89	.319	.96	.281	8.740	.97	.583	.88	.319		
UNC Resources	13.416	1.25	.232	1.30	.188	15.186	1.15	.272	1.28	.224	61	1973–77
Unilever N.V.	4.759	.45	.238	.51	.229	7.323	.56	.285	.71	.301	61	1973–77
Unilever plc	7.630	.43	.085	.47	.077	10.598	.65	.182	.78	.175		
Union Camp	6.307	.74	.370	.88	.393	9.259	.77	.331	1.01	.372		
Union Carbide	6.227	.93	.601	1.08	.598	8.483	.77	.395	1.05	.480		
Union Corp.	12.884	1.55	.385	1.44	.251	16.377	1.64	.473	1.61	.302		
Union Electric	5.031	.46	.227	.51	.209	6.011	.60	.468	.69	.416		

| | January 1978–December 1982 | | | | | January 1973–December 1977 | | | | | Incomplete Data Series | |
| | Log (%) | VLIC | | NYSE | | Log (%) | VLIC | | NYSE | | Number | |
Stock	Std. Dev.	Est. Beta	R²	Est. Beta	R²	Std. Dev.	Est. Beta	R²	Est. Beta	R²	of Obs.	Period
Union Oil of Cal.	10.564	.88	.184	1.38	.342	7.514	.57	.270	.83	.384		
Union Pacific	10.487	1.11	.299	1.64	.488	7.519	.47	.184	.80	.351		
Uniroyal Inc.	11.298	1.39	.403	1.32	.271	8.595	.96	.586	1.06	.480		
United Asbestos	18.942	.94	.065	.89	.044	21.176	.58	.035	.53	.022	51	1973–77
United Brands	12.407	1.46	.371	1.42	.263	15.436	1.31	.341	1.30	.223		
United Energy Res.	9.394	.92	.257	1.25	.355	10.529	1.06	.436	1.24	.463	44	1973–77
United Illuminating	6.035	.40	.118	.44	.108	6.858	.71	.512	.79	.414		
United Industrial	10.438	1.20	.354	1.36	.337	12.451	.95	.276	.87	.154		
United Inns	10.464	1.50	.546	1.63	.482	17.040	1.72	.483	1.77	.336		
United Jersey Banks	6.134	.64	.290	.60	.191	6.567	.54	.318	.45	.149		
United Merchants/Mfr.	13.299	.89	.118	.80	.072	—	—	—	—	—		
U.S. Bancorp.	6.699	.65	.248	.71	.227	8.517	.80	.421	1.12	.543		
USF&G Corp.	6.855	.76	.324	.88	.327	7.170	.83	.634	.95	.555		
U.S. & Foreign Secur.	5.782	.89	.628	.99	.590	8.965	.93	.513	.90	.314		
U.S. Gypsum	7.677	1.09	.536	1.11	.418	17.170	1.85	.548	1.82	.353		
U.S. Home	13.393	1.72	.440	1.90	.401	12.932	1.19	.398	1.10	.225		
U.S. Indus.	9.057	.87	.245	.91	.204	17.164	1.75	.492	2.07	.453		
U.S. Leasing Int'l.	8.670	1.18	.497	1.21	.388	11.087	.97	.362	1.00	.254		
U.S. Shoe	9.759	1.09	.335	1.18	.291	7.915	.62	.294	.82	.336		
U.S. Steel	8.395	.95	.339	1.01	.288	—	—	—	—	—		
U.S. Surgical	11.841	1.17	.259	1.18	.199	7.428	.71	.428	.82	.385		
U.S. Tobacco	6.113	.65	.301	.78	.322	7.827	.64	.321	.68	.238		
United Technologies	8.131	1.09	.484	1.24	.462	5.977	.53	.374	.67	.395		
United Telecom. (Kan.)	6.814	.65	.239	.70	.208	—	—	—	—	—		
United Va. Bankshs.	5.762	.65	.349	.65	.261	11.308	.78	.223	.78	.148	61	1978–82
Unitrode Corp.	10.536	1.35	.438	1.50	.406	—	—	—	—	—		
Univar Corp.	11.119	1.16	.289	1.30	.274	—	—	—	—	—		
Universal Foods	7.478	.30	.044	.23	.020	—	—	—	—	—		
Universal Leaf Tobacco	7.653	.66	.197	.85	.249	7.083	.57	.312	.71	.311		
Upjohn Co.	8.079	.88	.318	1.02	.320	10.807	.40	.066	.74	.146		

Company												
USAir Inc.	14.026	1.40	.265	1.48	.224	13.538	1.51	.612	1.68	.502	60	1973–77
USLIFE Corp.	9.086	1.25	.507	1.36	.446	12.993	1.32	.486	1.53	.437		
Utah Power & Light	4.765	.35	.144	.43	.159	5.011	.41	.323	.52	.340	41	1973–77
Valley Indus.	13.269	1.57	.374	1.89	.404	13.717	1.00	.195	1.44	.286		
Valley Nat'l. Corp.	8.075	.95	.372	.95	.278	10.865	.98	.387	1.25	.412		
Varian Associates	9.315	1.11	.378	1.10	.281	13.928	1.63	.650	1.79	.516		
Varo Inc.	12.165	1.68	.510	1.72	.401	—	—	—	—	—		
Vendo Co.	15.219	1.43	.235	1.21	.126	13.071	1.45	.583	1.41	.362		
Vermont American	9.164	1.08	.372	1.14	.311	—	—	—	—	—		
Vernitron Corp.	12.171	1.71	.532	1.86	.498	—	—	—	—	—	50	1978–82
VF Corp.	7.613	.76	.269	.89	.271	12.197	1.23	.479	1.58	.525		
Viacom Int'l.	8.492	.99	.360	1.06	.313	16.918	1.49	.369	1.37	.207		
Victoria Station	13.252	1.08	.176	.83	.078	—	—	—	—	—		
Virginia Elec. & Pwr.	5.346	.37	.126	.39	.105	7.827	.67	.347	.71	.260		
Virginia Nat'l Banksh.	7.383	.98	.467	1.06	.412	—	—	—	—	—		
Vornado Inc.	13.615	1.56	.350	1.48	.236	15.098	1.37	.391	1.24	.212		
Vulcan Materials	7.188	.68	.241	.68	.177	7.723	.75	.446	.91	.434		
Wachovia Corp.	6.588	.71	.312	.73	.244	10.901	1.15	.527	1.32	.460		
Wackenhut Corp.	12.203	1.41	.356	1.29	.223	12.262	1.20	.456	1.31	.356		
Wainoco Oil	16.280	.94	.093	1.25	.134	—	—	—	—	—	47	1978–82
Walgreen Co.	8.455	1.21	.546	1.22	.417	7.186	.75	.513	.81	.397		
Wallace Computer Svc.	7.822	.97	.411	1.00	.325	9.206	.50	.142	.47	.083		
Wal-Mart Stores	9.013	1.24	.502	1.36	.456	13.903	1.08	.284	1.19	.230		
Walter (Jim) Corp.	8.872	1.05	.376	1.14	.329	10.671	1.03	.442	1.22	.410		
Wang Labs B	12.497	1.67	.477	2.04	.534	—	—	—	—	—		
Warnaco Inc.	10.549	1.21	.354	1.33	.320	9.718	.77	.300	.73	.175		
Warner Communic.	9.845	1.13	.353	1.22	.305	12.575	1.30	.508	1.35	.360		
Warner-Lambert	7.225	.88	.392	.92	.323	8.972	.81	.383	1.18	.542		
Washington Gas Lt.	8.580	.48	.083	.49	.066	8.272	.64	.281	.57	.151		
Washington Nat'l	10.931	1.20	.321	1.32	.292	8.137	.61	.274	.66	.213	62	1973–77
Washington Post B	7.102	.85	.385	.90	.323	9.771	.99	.501	1.08	.403	60	1973–77
Washington Water Pwr.	4.912	.37	.152	.43	.150	3.584	.32	.382	.34	.284		
Waste Management	8.729	1.32	.611	1.45	.549	14.176	1.17	.326	1.41	.312	63	1973–77
Watkins-Johnson	10.467	1.24	.373	1.36	.339	14.935	1.09	.251	1.02	.125		
Wayne-Gossard	10.345	1.02	.257	1.21	.275	11.085	1.20	.556	1.21	.375		
Wean United	9.529	1.14	.382	1.19	.310	13.702	1.23	.381	1.00	.166		

| | January 1978–December 1982 | | | | | January 1973–December 1977 | | | | | Incomplete Data Series | |
| | Log (%) | VLIC | | NYSE | | Log (%) | VLIC | | NYSE | | Number | |
Stock	Std. Dev.	Est. Beta	R²	Est. Beta	R²	Std. Dev.	Est. Beta	R²	Est. Beta	R²	of Obs.	Period
Webb (Del E.) Corp.	18.395	1.79	.252	1.88	.209	14.205	1.32	.411	1.25	.247		
Weis Markets	4.982	.41	.179	.47	.175	7.272	.68	.415	.90	.476		
Wells Fargo	7.468	.86	.352	.92	.306	11.196	1.29	.626	1.55	.601		
Wells Fargo Mtg.	8.420	.83	.257	.97	.266	17.885	1.82	.490	1.72	.291		
Wendy's Int'l.	11.987	1.35	.339	1.30	.234	—	—	—	—	—		
Westburne Int'l. Indus.	12.850	1.41	.354	1.55	.339	—	—	—	—	—	45	1978–82
Westcoast Transmis.	6.498	.61	.234	.65	.197	6.907	.46	.212	.66	.283		
Western Air Lines	13.964	1.44	.282	1.43	.209	11.921	1.28	.549	1.55	.529		
Western Co. No. Amer.	13.400	1.47	.319	1.83	.371	13.967	.63	.097	.99	.176	51	1973–77
Western Deep Levels ADR	14.267	1.37	.247	1.74	.296	—	—	—	—	—		
Western Holdings ADR	15.305	.92	.096	1.12	.106	—	—	—	—	—		
Western Pacific Indus.	11.018	.76	.127	.83	.115	13.177	1.39	.531	1.33	.318		
Western Union	10.017	1.11	.325	1.41	.395	11.310	1.10	.450	1.17	.338		
Westinghouse Elec.	7.599	1.04	.500	1.17	.471	11.026	1.05	.430	1.13	.328		
Westmoreland Coal	10.318	.90	.204	1.05	.208	13.325	.77	.162	1.05	.203	60	1973–77
West Pt.-Pepperell	7.012	.87	.407	.94	.363	8.054	.68	.342	.86	.355		
Westvaco Corp.	7.182	1.07	.597	1.16	.522	8.443	.80	.429	.92	.369		
Wetterau Inc.	9.466	.87	.225	.97	.210	8.597	.82	.456	.87	.338	60	1973–77
Weyerhaeuser	7.778	1.13	.566	1.23	.497	8.392	.74	.371	1.10	.533		
Wheelabrator-Frye	9.536	1.35	.532	1.47	.475	11.272	1.24	.575	1.43	.505		
Wheeling Pitts. Steel	12.781	1.40	.321	1.31	.208	11.599	1.07	.403	1.23	.353		
Whirlpool Corp.	7.535	.87	.352	.91	.291	11.748	1.21	.503	1.61	.586		
White Consol. Indus.	7.396	.95	.438	.92	.309	10.823	1.19	.575	1.22	.397		
Whittaker Corp.	13.374	1.91	.546	2.15	.515	15.429	1.58	.496	1.48	.289		
WICOR, Inc.	5.309	.45	.191	.44	.138	—	—	—	—	—		
Wieboldt Stores	11.767	.72	.099	.67	.064	9.059	.81	.380	.75	.213		
Willamette Indus.	9.672	1.20	.413	1.24	.330	15.708	.61	.065	.58	.045	44	1973–77
Williamhouse-Regency	10.409	.88	.225	.78	.139	—	—	—	—	—	41	1978–82
Williams Cos.	10.683	1.26	.368	1.51	.397	9.476	.57	.173	.83	.240		
Wilshire Oil Texas	10.693	1.36	.432	1.47	.378	9.449	.96	.490	1.03	.431	49	1973–77

Winn-Dixie Stores	5.316	.34	.107	.33	.076	7.903	.65	.324	.76	.290	
Winnebago Indus.	18.227	1.96	.309	2.31	.320	19.693	1.90	.442	1.85	.276	
Winter (Jack)	7.648	.74	.249	.65	.144	11.628	1.00	.270	1.03	.205	41 1973–77
Wisconsin Elec. Pwr.	5.696	.20	.034	.25	.040	6.554	.41	.187	.65	.311	
Wisconsin Pwr & Lt.	6.311	.16	.017	.24	.028	6.288	.62	.456	.70	.391	
Wisconsin Pub. Ser.	5.929	.41	.129	.49	.138	4.994	.46	.407	.49	.304	
Witco Chemical	7.106	1.03	.556	1.03	.418	9.872	.86	.360	.94	.285	
Wolverine World Wide	11.228	1.29	.352	1.43	.322	14.927	1.44	.444	1.25	.219	
Wometco Enter.	10.591	1.14	.308	1.19	.253	11.396	1.26	.580	1.45	.507	
Woods Petroleum	10.790	1.12	.287	1.51	.391	—	—	—	—	—	60 1973–77
Woodward & Lothrop	6.633	.42	.108	.36	.058	10.178	.79	.293	.79	.200	
Woolworth (F.W.)	7.940	.83	.295	.86	.236	10.113	1.08	.543	1.20	.444	
Worthington Indus.	10.489	.99	.250	1.02	.212	—	—	—	—	—	47 1978–82
Wrigley (Wm.) Jr.	6.067	.55	.223	.57	.174	6.042	.27	.092	.40	.139	
Wurlitzer Co.	15.467	1.28	.182	1.25	.130	11.314	.87	.278	.87	.185	
Wyle Laboratories	12.348	1.75	.534	1.96	.501	—	—	—	—	—	
Wyly Corp.	16.121	1.61	.267	1.60	.198	22.385	1.90	.342	1.63	.166	
Wyman-Gordon	10.606	1.41	.499	1.44	.383	—	—	—	—	—	57 1978–82
Wynn's Int'l.	13.784	1.11	.190	.92	.104	—	—	—	—	—	45 1978–82
Xerox Corp.	7.113	1.00	.527	1.17	.540	10.006	.93	.411	1.32	.547	
XTRA Corp.	12.135	1.85	.619	1.91	.495	14.681	1.51	.498	1.52	.334	
Yellow Freight Sys.	9.889	.75	.152	.64	.085	10.934	.85	.289	1.06	.292	
Zale Corp.	8.536	.95	.334	1.11	.339	11.027	1.21	.569	1.35	.473	
Zapata Corp.	11.950	1.47	.403	1.75	.427	11.003	.86	.287	.91	.214	
Zayre Corp.	10.328	1.34	.450	1.32	.328	17.057	1.68	.458	1.52	.248	
Zenith Radio	10.811	1.45	.483	1.49	.378	—	—	—	—	—	
Zimmer Corp.	13.371	1.66	.413	1.73	.335	19.932	1.56	.292	1.31	.136	
Zions Utah Bancorp.	8.028	.77	.244	.90	.252	13.038	1.35	.503	1.45	.440	50 1973–77
Zurn Indus.	9.568	1.19	.410	1.25	.343	11.973	1.44	.682	1.38	.415	

References

Aber, John W., *Beta Coefficients and Models of Security Return* (Lexington Books, Lexington, Massachusetts, 1973).

Ansbacher, Max G., *The New Options Market* (Walker & Co., New York, 1979).

Arditti, Fred D., and Haim, Levy, "Portfolio Efficiency Analysis in Three Moments: The Multiperiod Case," *Journal of Finance,* June 1975, pp. 797–810.

Arnold Bernhard & Co, Inc., "The Value Line Stock Market Averages, 1961–1981," 711 Third Avenue, New York, New York 10017, 1982.

Arnott, Robert D., "Modeling Portfolios with Options: Risks and Returns," *Journal of Portfolio Management,* Fall 1980, pp. 66–73.

Arrow, Kenneth J., *Essays in the Theory of Risk-Bearing* (Markham, Chicago, 1971).

Arrow, Kenneth J., "Limited Knowledge and Economic Analysis," *American Economic Review,* March 1974, pp. 1–10.

Asay, Michael R., "Implied Margin Requirements on Options and Stocks," *Journal of Portfolio Management,* Spring 1981, pp. 55–59.

Balch, William F., "Market Guides, Indexes of Stock Prices Lately Have Multiplied," *Barron's,* September 22, 1966.

Baron, Martin, "Investing Too Dull? Risk Takers Find Hot Item in Stock-Index Futures," *Los Angeles Times,* May 2, 1982, p. 3.

Bear, Robert M., "Margin Levels and the Behavior of Futures Prices," *Journal of Financial and Quantitative Analysis,* September 1972, pp. 1907–1930.

Bearman, Arlene Erlich, and Betsy Epstein Kuhn, "A Test of Efficiency: Cash Versus Futures Markets," *Journal of Portfolio Management,* Fall 1981, pp. 44–47.

Bernstein, Peter L., "Dead—Or Alive and Well?," *Journal of Portfolio Management,* Winter 1981, p. 4.

Bierman, Harold, Jr., "How Much Diversification is Desirable?" *Journal of Portfolio Management,* Fall 1980, pp. 42–44.

Black, Fischer, "Equilibrium in the Creation of Investment Goods Under Uncertainty," in *Studies in the Theory of Capital Markets,* M. Jensen, Ed. (Praeger, New York, 1972), pp. 249–265. (a)

Black, Fischer, "Capital Market Equilibrium with Restricted Borrowing," *Journal of Business,* July 1972, pp. 444–455. (b)

Black, Fischer, "Fact and Fantasy in the Use of Options," *Financial Analysts Journal,* July–August 1975, pp. 36–41, 61ff.

Black, Fischer, "The Pricing of Commodity Contracts," *Journal of Financial Economics,* III, 1976, pp. 167–179.

Black, Fischer, and Myron Scholes, "The Pricing of Options and Corporate Liabilities," *Journal of Political Economy,* May 1973, pp. 637–654.

Blume, Marshall E., "On the Assessment of Risk," *Journal of Finance,* March 1971, pp. 1–10.

Blume, Marshall E., "Betas and Their Regression Tendencies," *Journal of Finance,* June 1975, pp. 785–795.

Blume, Marshall E., "Inflation, the Pricing of Capital Assets, and Real Balance Effects," in *Inflation and Capital Markets,* M. Sarnat, Ed. (Ballinger, Cambridge, Massachusetts, 1978), Chapter 7, pp. 101–112.

Blume, Marshall E., and Irwin Friend, "A New Look at the Capital Asset Pricing Model," *Journal of Finance,* March 1973, pp. 19–33.

Blume, Marshall E., and Irwin Friend, "Risk, Investment Strategy and the Long-Run Rates of Return," *Review of Economics and Statistics,* August 1974, pp. 259–269.

Blume, Marshall E., and Irwin Friend, "The Asset Structure of Individual Portfolios and Some Implications for Utility Functions," *Journal of Finance,* May 1975, pp. 585–603.

Blume, Marshall E., Jean Crockett, and Irwin Friend, "Stock Ownership in the United States: Characteristics and Trends," *Survey of Current Business,* November 1974, pp. 16–40.

Bogle, John C., and Jan M. Twardowski, "Institutional Investment Performance Compared: Banks, Investment Counselors, Insurance Companies, and Mutual Funds," *Financial Analysts Journal,* January–February 1980, pp. 33–40.

Bogue, Marcus C., III, "The Estimation and Behavior of Systematic Risk," unpublished Ph.D. dissertation, Stanford University, 1973 (University Microfilms, Ann Arbor, Michigan).

Bowman, Robert G., "The Theoretical Relationship Between Systematic Risk and Financial (Accounting) Variables," *Journal of Finance,* June 1979, pp. 617–630.

Brainard, William C., and James Tobin, "Pitfalls in Financial Model Building," *American Economic Review,* May 1968, pp. 99–154.

Bryant, Edward C., *Statistical Analysis* (McGraw-Hill, New York, 1960).

Burns, Joseph M., *A Treatise on Markets: Spot, Futures, and Options* (American Enterprise Institute for Public Research, Washington, D.C., 1979).

Butler, H. L. and J. D. Allen, "Dow Jones Industrial Average Re-Reexamined," *Financial Analysts Journal,* November–December 1979, pp. 23–30. (Note: Title is kooky, but correct!)

Cagan, Phillip, "Financial Futures Markets: Is More Regulation Needed?," *Journal of Futures Markets,* Summer 1981, pp. 169–189.

Calderwood, Stanford, "The Truth About Index Funds," *Financial Analysts Journal,* July–August 1977, pp. 36–47.

Camp, Robert C. and Arthur A. Eubank, Jr., "The Beta Quotient: A New Measure of Portfolio Risk," *Journal of Portfolio Management,* Summer 1981, pp. 53–58.

Capozza, Dennis R., and Bradford Cornell, "Treasury Bill Pricing in the Spot and Futures Markets," *Review of Economics and Statistics,* November 1979, pp. 513–520.

Carpenter, Michael D., and Davis E. Upton, "Trading Volume and Beta Stability," *Journal of Portfolio Management,* Winter 1981, pp. 60–64.

Castanias, Richard P., II, "Macroinformation and the Variability of Stock Market Prices," *Journal of Finance,* May 1979, pp. 439–450.

Caves, Richard E., "Organization, Scale, and Performance of Grain Trade," *Food Research Institute Studies,* XVI, 3 1977–1978, pp. 107–123.

Cesta, John R., "Financial Futures and the Social Benefit Hypothesis," paper presented at the 1980 Midwest Finance Association, March 28, 1980.

Chen, Son-Nan, "Beta Nonstationarity, Portfolio Residual Risk and Diversification," *Journal of Financial and Quantitative Analysis,* March 1981, pp. 95–111.

Chen, Son-Nan, "An Examination of Risk-Return Relationship in Bull and Bear Markets Using Time-Varying Betas," *Journal of Financial and Quantitative Analysis,* June 1982, pp. 265–281.

Chicago Board of Trade, "Financial Instruments Markets: Cash-Futures Relationships," Chicago, 1980.

Chicago Board of Trade, "U.S. Treasury Bond Futures," Chicago, undated (1980 or 1981).

Chicago Mercantile Exchange, "Before You Speculate," International Money Market, Chicago, April 1977.

Chicago Mercantile Exchange, "Trading in Tomorrows," International Monetary Market, Chicago, April 1978.

Chicago Mercantile Exchange, "Inside S&P 500 Stock Index Futures," Index and Option Market, Chicago, 1982. (a)

Chicago Mercantile Exchange, "Opportunities in Stock Futures," Index and Option Market, Chicago, 1982. (b)

Cohen, J., and E. Zinbarg, *Investment Analysis and Portfolio Management* (Irwin, Homewood, Illinois, 1967).

Cohen, Kalman J., and Bruce P. Fitch, "The Average Investment Performance Index," *Management Science,* February 1966, pp. B195–215.

Cohn, Richard A., Wilbur G. Lewellen, Ronald C. Lease, and Gary G. Schlarbaum, "Individual Investor Risk Aversion and Investment Portfolio Composition," *Journal of Finance,* May 1975, pp. 605–620.

Commodity Futures Trading Commission, "Futures Trading in Financial Instruments," Division of Economics and Education, by Ronald B. Hobson, Washington, D.C., October 1978. (a)

Commodity Futures Trading Commission, Hearings in the Matter of: "Application of the Kansas City Board of Trade for Designation as a Contract Market in Transactions for Future Delivery Based Upon 30 Industrial Stocks Average Index," Hoover Reporting Co., Inc., Washington, D.C., October 25–26, 1978, pp. 1–426. (b)

Commodity Futures Trading Commission, "Survey of Interest-Rate Futures Markets," Division of Economics and Education, by Naomi L. Jaffe and Ronald B. Hobson, Washington, D.C., December 1979.

Cooley, Philip L., Rodney L. Roenfeldt, and Naval K. Modani, "Interdependence of Market Risk Measures," *Journal of Business,* July 1977, pp. 356–363.

Cootner, Paul H., "Returns to Speculators: Telser Versus Keynes," *Journal of Political Economy,* April 1960, pp. 396–404.

Cootner, Paul H., Ed., *The Random Character of Stock Market Prices,* revised edition (M.I.T. Press, Cambridge, 1964).

Cootner, Paul H., "Stock Market Indexes—Fallacies and Illusions," *The Commercial and Financial Chronicle,* September 29, 1966, pp. 18–19.

Cootner, Paul H., "Speculation and Hedging," Proceedings of a Symposium on Price Effects of Speculation in Organized Commodity Markets, *Food Research Institute Studies,* Supplement to Vol. VII, 1967, pp. 65–104.

Cornell, Bradford, and Kenneth R. French, "Taxes and the Pricing of Stock Index Futures," UCLA Graduate School of Management Paper 5-82, Los Angeles, California 90024, October 1982.

Cornell, Bradford, and Kenneth R. French, "The Pricing of Stock Index Futures," *Journal of Futures Markets,* Spring 1983, pp. 1–14.

Cox, Charles C., "Futures Trading and Market Information," *Journal of Political Economy,* Vol. 84, No. 6, 1976, pp. 1215–1237.

Cox, John C., and Stephen A. Ross, "The Valuation of Options for Alternative Stochastic Processes," *Journal of Financial Economics,* III, 1976, pp. 145–166.

Dusak, Katherine, "Futures Trading and Investor Returns: An Investigation of Commodity Market Risk Premiums," *Journal of Political Economy,* December 1973, pp. 1387–1406.

Ederington, Louis H., "The Hedging Performance of the New Futures Markets," *Journal of Finance,* March 1979, pp. 157–170.

Eitemen, W., C. Dice, and D. Eitemen, *The Stock Market* (McGraw Hill, New York, 1966).

Elgers, Pieter, Joanne Hill, and Thomas Schneeweis, "Research Design for Systematic Risk Prediction," *Journal of Portfolio Management*, Spring 1982, pp. 43–52.

Elia, Charles J., "Swinging Stocks: Market's Volatility Has Grown in Decade," *Wall Street Journal*, March 30, 1979, p. 1 ff.

Elton, Edwin J., Martin J. Gruber, and Thomas J. Urich, "Are Beta's Best?," *Journal of Finance*, December 1978, pp. 1375–1384.

Fama, Eugene F., "Efficient Capital Markets: A Review of Theory and Empirical Work," *Journal of Finance*, May 1970, pp. 383–417.

Fama, Eugene F., "Risk, Return, and Equilibrium," *Journal of Political Economy*, January–February 1971, pp. 30–54.

Fama, Eugene F and Richard Roll, "Some Properties of Symmetric Stable Distributions," *Journal of the American Statistical Association*, September 1968, pp. 817–836.

Farrell, James L., Jr., "Analyzing Covariation of Returns to Determine Homogeneous Stock Groupings," *Journal of Business*, April 1974, pp. 186–207.

Figlewski, Stephen, and Stanley J. Kon, "Portfolio Management with Stock Index Futures," *Financial Analysts Journal*, January–February 1982, pp. 3–11.

Fisher, Lawrence, "Some New Stock-Market Indexes," *Journal of Business*, January 1966, pp. 191–218.

Fisher, Lawrence, and James H. Lorie, "Some Studies of Variability of Returns on Investments in Common Stocks," *Journal of Business*, April 1970, pp. 99–134.

Fogler, H. Russell, "Common Sense on CAPM, APT, and Correlated Residuals," *Journal of Portfolio Management*, Summer 1982.

Fosback, Norman G., *Stock Market Logic* (Institute for Econometric Research: Fort Lauderdale, Florida, 1976).

Fox, Edward A., "Comparing Performance of Equity Pension Trusts," *Financial Analysts Journal*, September–October 1968, pp. 121–129.

Frankfurter, George M., "The Effect of 'Market Indexes' on the Ex-Post Performance of the Sharpe Portfolio Selection Model," *Journal of Finance*, June 1976, pp. 949–955.

Frankfurter, George M., and Thomas J. Frecka, "Efficient Portfolios and Superfluous Diversification," *Journal of Financial and Quantitative Analysis*, December 1979, pp. 925–938.

Frankfurter, George M., and Herbert E. Phillips, "MPT Plus Security Analysis for Better Performance," *Journal of Portfolio Management*, Summer 1982, pp. 29–36.

Frankfurter, George M., Herbert E. Phillips, and John P. Seagle, "Bias in Estimating Portfolio Alpha and Beta Scores," *Review of Economics and Statistics*, August 1974, pp. 412–414.

Friend, Irwin, "The Demand for Risky Assets: Some Extensions," in *Financial Decision Making Under Uncertainty*, H. Levy and M. Sarnat, Eds., (Academic Press, New York, 1977).

Friend, Irwin, and Marshall Blume, "Measurement of Portfolio Performance Under Uncertainty," *American Economic Review*, September 1970, pp. 561–575.

Friend, Irwin, and M. E. Blume, "The Demand for Risky Assets," *American Economic Review*, December 1975, pp. 900–932.

Friend, Irwin, Yoram Landskroner, and Etienne Losq, "The Demand for Risky Assets Under Uncertain Inflation," *Journal of Finance*, December 1976, pp. 1287–1297.

Gerschenkron, Alexander, "Soviet Heavy Industry: A Dollar Index of Output, 1927–1937," *Economic Backwardness In Historical Perspective: A Book of Essays* (The Belknap Press of Harvard University Press, Cambridge, Massachusetts, 1962).

Goldberger, Arthur S., *Econometric Theory* (John Wiley & Sons, New York, 1964).

Goldman, M. Barry, Howard B. Sosin, and Lawrence A. Shepp, "On Contingent Claims That Insure Ex-Post Optimal Stock Market Timing," *Journal of Finance*, May 1979, pp. 401–413.

Gonedes, Nicholas J., "A Note on Accounting-Based and Market-Based Estimates of Systematic Risk," *Journal of Financial and Quantitative Analysis*, June 1975.

Grant, Dwight, "How to Optimize with Stock Index Futures," *The Journal of Portfolio Management*, Spring 1982, pp. 32–36. (a)

Grant, Dwight, "Market Index Futures Contracts: Some Thoughts on Delivery Dates," *Financial Analysts Journal*, May–June 1982, pp. 60–63. (b)

Gray, Roger W., "Price Effects of a Lack of Speculation," Proceedings of a Symposium on Price Effects of Speculation in Organized Commodity Markets, *Food Research Institute Studies*, Supplement to Vol. VIII, 1967, pp. 177–194.

Grossman, Sanford J., "The Existence of Futures Markets, Noisy Rational Expectations and Informational Externalities," *Review of Economic Studies*, October 1977, pp. 431–449.

Grube, R. Corwin, O. Maurice Joy, and Don B. Panton, "Market Responses to Federal Reserve Changes in the Initial Margin Requirement," *Journal of Finance*, June 1979, pp. 659–674.

Hadar, Josef, and William R. Russell, "Rules for Ordering Uncertain Prospects," *American Economic Review*, March 1969, pp. 25–34.

Hamada, Robert S., "The Effect of the Firm's Capital Structure on the Systematic Risk of Common Stocks," *Journal of Finance*, May 1972, pp. 435–452.

Hanoch, G., and H. Levy, "The Efficiency Analysis of Choices Involving Risk," *Review of Economic Studies*, July 1969, pp. 335–347.

Hanoch, G., and H. Levy, "Efficient Portfolio Selection with Quadratic and Cubic Utility," *Journal of Business,* April 1970, pp. 181–189.

Hieronymus, Thomas A., *Economics of Futures Trading* (Commodity Research Bureau, New York, 1971).

Horn, F. F., *Trading in Commodity Futures* (New York Institute of Finance, New York, 1969).

Houthakker, Hendrik S., "Can Speculators Forecast Prices?," *Review of Economic and Statistics,* May 1957, pp. 143–151.

Houthakker, Hendrik S., "The Scope and Limits of Futures Trading," in Abramovitz and Others, *The Allocation of Economic Resources,* Essays in Honor of Bernard Francis Haley (Stanford University Press, Stanford, California, 1959).

Houthakker, Hendrik S., "Systematic and Random Elements in Short Term Price Movements," Frontiers in Uncertainty Theory, *American Economic Review,* **51,** 1961, pp. 164–172.

Hudson, Richard L., "Taking a Chance on Stock-Index Futures," *Wall Street Journal,* January 26, 1982.

Hurtado-Sanchez, Luis, "Short Interest: Its Influence as a Stabilizer of Stock Returns," *Journal of Financial and Quantitative Analysis,* December 1978, pp. 965–985.

Jean, William H., "The Extension of Portfolio Analysis to Three or More Parameters," *Journal of Financial and Quantitative Analysis,* June 1971, pp. 505–514.

Jean, William H., "More on Multidimensional Portfolio Analysis," *Journal of Financial and Quantitative Analysis,* June 1973.

Jean, William H., "The Geometric Mean and Stochastic Dominance," *Journal of Finance,* March 1980, pp. 151–158.

Jensen, Michael C., "Random Walks: Reality or Myth—Comment," *Financial Analysts Journal,* November—December 1967, pp. 77–85.

Jensen, Michael C., "Risk, the Pricing of Capital Assets, and the Evaluation of Investment Portfolios," *Journal of Business,* April 1969, pp. 167–247.

Joehnk, Michael D., and William J. Petty, II, "The Interest Sensitivity of Common Stock Prices," *Journal of Portfolio Management,* Winter 1980, pp. 19–25.

Johnston, J., *Econometric Methods* (McGraw-Hill, New York, 1963).

Jones, Frank J., "The Economics of Futures and Options Contracts Based on Cash Settlement," *Journal of Futures Markets,* Spring 1982, pp. 63–82.

Kansas City Board of Trade, "The Future Is Here," in four booklets, (1) "Futures Trading & The Value Line Stock Index"; (2) "Hedging and Speculating in Value Line Futures"; (3) "Value Line Composite Average: The Index Behind the Futures"; (4) "Option Strategies and Stock Index Futures," KCBT, 4800 Main Street, Suite 274, Kansas City, Missouri 64112, 1982.

Kaufman, P. J., *Commodity Trading Systems and Methods* (Ronald Press, John Wiley & Sons, New York, 1978).

Kaufman, P. J., Ed., *Technical Analysis in Commodities* (Ronald Press, John Wiley & Sons, New York, 1980).

Kim, Moon K., and J. Kenton Zumwalt, "An Analysis of Risk in Bull and Bear Markets," *Journal of Financial and Quantitative Analysis,* December 1979.

King, Benjamin F., "Market and Industry Factors in Stock Price Behavior," *Journal of Business,* January 1966, pp. 139–190.

Klemkosky, Robert C., and Terry S. Maness, "The Impact of Options on the Underlying Securities," *Journal of Portfolio Management,* Winter 1980, pp. 12–18.

Klemkosky, Robert C., and John D. Martin, "The Effect of Market Risk on Portfolio Diversification," *Journal of Finance,* March 1975, pp. 147–154.

Kon, Stanley J., and Frank C. Jen, "The Investment Performance of Mutual Funds: An Empirical Investigation of Timing, Selectivity and Market Efficiency," *Journal of Business,* April 1979, pp. 263–289.

Latane, Henry A., and Donald L. Tuttle, "Criteria For Portfolio Building," *Journal of Finance,* September 1967, pp. 359–373.

Latane, Henry A., and Donald L. Tuttle, *Security Analysis and Portfolio Management* (Ronald Press, New York, 1970).

Latane, Henry A., and William E. Young, "Test of Portfolio Building Rules," *Journal of Finance,* September 1969, pp. 595–612.

Latane, Henry A., Donald L. Tuttle, and William E. Young, "Market Indexes and Their Implications for Portfolio Management," *Financial Analysts Journal,* September–October 1971, pp. 75–85.

Lavely, Joe, Gordon Wakefield, and Bob Barrett, "Toward Enhancing Beta Estimates," *Journal of Portfolio Management,* Summer 1980, pp. 43–46.

Lee, Cheng F., "On the Relationship Between the Systematic Risk and the Investment Horizon," *Journal of Financial and Quantitative Analysis,* December 1976, pp. 803–814.

Levhari, David, and Haim Levy, "The Capital Asset Pricing Model and the Investment Horizon," *Review of Economics and Statistics,* January 1977, pp. 92–104.

Levy, Haim, "Portfolio Performance and the Investment Horizon," *Management Science,* August 1972, pp. B-645–653.

Levy, Haim, "Equilibrium in an Imperfect Market: A Constraint on the Number of Securities in the Portfolio," *American Economic Review,* September 1978, pp. 643–658.

Levy, Haim, "The CAPM and Beta in an Imperfect Market," *Journal of Portfolio Management,* Winter 1980, pp. 5–11.

Levy, Haim, "The CAPM and the Investment Horizon," *Journal of Portfolio Management,* Winter 1981, pp. 32–40.

Levy, Robert A., "Random Walks: Reality or Myth," *Financial Analysts Journal,* November–December 1967, pp. 69–76.

Levy, Robert A., "On The Short-Term Stationarity of Beta Coefficients," *Financial Analysts Journal*, November–December 1971, pp. 55–62.

Lilliefors, Hubert W., "On the Kolmogorov-Smirnov Test for Normality with Mean and Variance Unknown," *Journal of the American Statistical Association*, June 1967, pp. 399–402.

Lintner, John, "The Valuation of Risk Assets and the Selection of Risky Investments in Stock Portfolios and Capital Budgets," *Review of Economic and Statistics*, February 1965, pp. 13–37.

Lintner, John, "Inflation and Security Returns," *Journal of Finance*, May 1975, pp. 259–280.

Lorie, James H., "The Second Great Crash," *Wall Street Journal*, June 2, 1980, p. 24.

Lorie, James H., and Mary T. Hamilton, *The Stock Market: Theories and Evidence* (Richard D. Irwin, Homewood, Illinois, 1973).

Mains, Norman E., "Risk, the Pricing of Capital Assets, and the Evaluation of Investment Portfolios: Comment," *Journal of Business*, July 1977, pp. 371–384.

Malkiel, Burton G., "The Capital Formation Problem in the United States," *Journal of Finance*, May 1979, pp. 291–306.

Malkiel, Burton G., George M. von Furstenberg, and Harry S. Watson, "Expectations, Tobin's *q*, and Industry Investment," *Journal of Finance*, May 1979, pp. 549–564.

Markowitz, H., "Portfolio Selection," *Journal of Finance*, March 1952, pp. 77–91.

Martell, Terrence F., and Jerrold E. Salzman, "Cash Settlement for Futures Contracts Based on Common Stock Indices: An Economic and Legal Perspective," *Journal of Futures Markets*, Fall 1981, pp. 291–301.

Melamed, Leo, "The Futures Market: Liquidity and the Technique of Spreading," *Journal of Futures Markets*, Fall 1981, pp. 405–411.

Merton, Robert C., Myron S. Scholes, and Mathew L. Gladstein, "The Returns and Risk of Alternative Call Option Portfolio Investment Strategies," *Journal of Business*, Vol. 51, No. 2, 1978, pp. 183–242.

Modest, David M., and Mahadevan Sundaresan, "The Relationship Between Spot and Futures Prices in Stock Index Futures Markets: Some Preliminary Evidence," *Journal of Futures Markets*, Vol. 3, No. 1, Spring 1983, pp. 15–41.

Moore, Thomas Gale, "Stock Market Margin Requirements," *Journal of Political Economy*, April 1966, pp. 158–167.

Moriarty, Eugene J., Susan M. Phillips, and Paula A. Tosini, "A Comparison of Options and Futures in the Management of Portfolio Risk," *Financial Analysts Journal*, January–February 1981.

Murray, Roger F., "A New Role For Options," *Journal of Financial and Quantitative Analysis*, November 1979, pp. 895–899.

New York Futures Exchange, "Introducing New York Stock Exchange Index Futures," in various booklets and pamphlets: "The Market Will Fluctuate

. . ."; "Notebook"; and other accompanying pamphlets, NYFE, 20 Broad Street, New York, New York 10005, 1982. (a)

New York Futures Exchange, "New York Stock Exchange Financial Index Futures Contract," NYFE, 20 Broad Street, New York, New York 10005, 1982. (b)

New York Stock Exchange, "Fact Book: 1981," New York, June 1981.

Niederhoffer, Victor, and M. F. M. Osborne, "Market Making and Reversal on the Stock Exchange," *Journal of The American Statistical Association,* December 1966, pp. 897–916.

Niederhoffer, Victor, and Richard Zeckhauser, "Market Index Futures Contracts," *Financial Analysts Journal,* January–February 1980, pp. 49–55.

Officer, R. R., "The Distribution of Stock Returns," *Journal of the American Statistical Association,* December 1972, pp. 807–812.

Officer, R. R., "The Variability of the Market Factor of the New York Stock Exchange," *Journal of Business,* No. 46, 1973, pp. 434–453.

Options Clearing Corporation et al., "Understanding the Risks and Uses of Listed Options," 200 South Wacker Drive, 27th Floor, Chicago, Illinois 60606, October 1982.

Pettit, R. Richardson, and Randolph Westerfield, "A Model of Capital Asset Risk," *Journal of Financial and Quantitative Analysis,* March 1972.

Pettit, R. Richardson, and Randolph Westerfield, "Using the Capital Asset Pricing Model and the Market Model to Predict Security Returns," *Journal of Financial and Quantitative Analysis,* September 1974, pp. 579–607.

Petzinger, Thomas, Jr., "Speculators in Financial Futures Embrace Intermarket Spreads to Reduce Their Risk," *Wall Street Journal,* August 17, 1982, p. 36.

Phillips, Susan M, and Paula A. Tosini, "A Comparison of Margin Requirements for Options and Futures," *Financial Analysts Journal,* November–December 1982, pp. 54–58.

Powers, Mark J., "Hedging an Underwriting," *Commodities,* April 1980, pp. 54–59.

Powers, Mark J., and David J. Vogel, *Inside the Financial Futures Markets* (John Wiley & Sons, New York, 1981).

Putka, Gary, "Arbitragers Devise New Strategies Combining Trading of Shares Against Stock-Index Futures," *Wall Street Journal,* August 23, 1982, p. 33.

Reddig, William M., "How to Bet on a Stock Index: The Latest Wrinkle on the Old Commodity Contract is Scheduled to Appear in February. Beware the Odds," Investing, *New York Times,* December 20, 1981.

Reinganum, Marc R., "A New Empirical Perspective on the CAPM," *Journal of Financial and Quantitative Analysis,* November 1981, pp. 439–462.

Reinganum, Marc R., "A Direct Test of Roll's Conjecture on the Firm Size Effect," *Journal of Finance,* March 1982, pp. 27–35.

Rendleman, Richard J., and Christopher E. Carabini, "The Efficiency of the

Treasury Bill Futures Market," *Journal of Finance*, September 1979, pp. 895–914.

Renshaw, Edward F., "Portfolio Balance Models in Perspective: Some Generalizations That Can Be Derived from the Two-Asset Case," *Journal of Financial and Quantitative Analysis*, June 1967, pp. 123–149.

Rolfo, Jacques, "Optimal Hedging Under Price and Quantity Uncertainty: The Case of a Cocoa Producer," *Journal of Political Economy*, February 1980, pp. 100–116.

Roll, Richard, "A Critique of the Asset Pricing Theory's Tests," *Journal of Financial Economics*, 1977, pp. 129–176.

Roll, Richard, "Performance Evaluation and Benchmark Errors," *Journal of Portfolio Management*, Summer 1980, pp. 5–19. (a)

Roll, Richard, "A Possible Explanation of the Small Firm Effect," UCLA Graduate School of Management Working Paper, October 1980. (b)

Roll, Richard, "Performance Evaluation and Benchmark Errors (II)," *Journal of Portfolio Management*, Winter 1981, pp. 17–22.

Rosenberg, Barr, "The Capital Asset Pricing Model and the Market Model," *Journal of Portfolio Management*, Winter 1981, pp. 5–16.

Rothstein, Marvin, "On Geometric and Arithmetic Portfolio Performance Indexes," *Journal of Financial and Quantitative Analysis*, September 1972, pp. 1983–1992.

Rubinstein, Mark, "The Strong Case for the Generalized Logarithmic Utility Model as the Premier Model of Financial Markets," in *Financial Decision Making Under Uncertainty*, H. Levy and M. Sarnat, Eds., (Academic Press, New York, 1977).

Rutz, Roger D., "The Economics of Performance Margins in Futures Markets," Chicago Board of Trade Research Study, 1982.

Ryan, James C., and Mack Kritzman, "Catch 500: The Irony in Indexing," *The Journal of Portfolio Management*, Winter 1980, pp. 30–32.

Sarnat, Marshall, "Capital Market Imperfections and the Composition of Optimal Portfolios," *Journal of Finance*, September 1974, pp. 1241–1253.

Schlarbaum, Gary G., Wilbur G. Lewellen, and Ronald C. Lease, "Realized Returns on Common Stock Investments: The Experience of Individual Investors," *Journal of Business*, April 1978, pp. 299–325.

Scholes, Myron S., "The Economics of Hedging and Spreading in Futures Markets," *Journal of Futures Markets*, Summer 1981, pp. 265–286.

Schrock, Nicholas W., "The Theory of Asset Choice: Simultaneous Holding of Short and Long Positions in the Futures Markets," *Journal of Political Economy*, March–April 1971, pp. 270–293.

Schulz, John W., "Pale Blue Chips," *Barron's*, February 11, 1980, pp. 11 ff.

Scott, Elton, and Stewart Brown, "Biased Estimators and Unstable Betas," *Journal of Finance*, March 1980, pp. 49–55.

Sharpe, William F., *Portfolio Theory and Capital Markets* (McGraw-Hill, New York, 1970).

Sharpe, William F., "The Capital Asset Pricing Model: A 'Multi Beta' Interpretation," in *Financial Decision Making Under Uncertainty,* H. Levy and M. Sarnat, Eds. (Academic Press, New York, 1979), pp. 127–135.

Sharpe, William F., "Factors in New York Stock Exchange Returns, 1931–1979," *Journal of Portfolio Management,* Summer 1982, pp. 5–19.

Sharpe, William F., and Guy M. Cooper, "Risk-Return Classes of New York Stock Exchange Common Stocks, 1931–1967," *Financial Analysts Journal,* March–April 1972, pp. 46 ff.

Simkowitz, Michael A., and William L. Beedles, "Diversification in a Three-Moment World," *Journal of Financial and Quantitative Analysis,* December 1978, pp. 927–941.

Simonson, Donald G., "The Speculative Behavior of Mutual Funds," *Journal of Finance,* May 1972, pp. 381–391.

Smith, Keith V., "Stock Price and Economic Indexes For Generating Efficient Portfolios," *Journal of Business,* April 1964, pp. 326–336.

Standard & Poor's Corporation, "Stocks in the Standard & Poor's 500," 345 Hudson Street, New York, New York 10014, September 29, 1978.

Statman, Meir, "Betas Compared: Merrill Lynch vs. Value Line," *Journal of Portfolio Management,* Winter 1981, pp. 41–44.

Stevens, Guy V. G., "On the Impact of Uncertainty on the Value and Investment of the Neoclassical Firm," *American Economic Review,* June 1974, pp. 319–336.

Stoll, Hans R., "Commodity Futures and Spot Price Determination and Hedging in Capital Market Equilibrium," *Journal of Financial and Quantitative Analysis,* November 1979, pp. 873–894.

Stone, Bernell K., *Risk, Return and Equilibrium* (The MIT Press, Cambridge, 1970).

Stone, James M., *One Way for Wall Street* (Little, Brown, Boston, 1975).

Telser, Lester G., "Margins and Futures Contracts," *Journal of Futures Markets,* Summer 1981, pp. 225–253.

Telser, Lester G., and Harlow N. Higinbotham, "Organized Futures Markets: Costs and Benefits," *Journal of Political Economy,* October 1977, pp. 969–1000.

Theobald, Michael, "Beta Stationarity and Estimation Period: Some Analytical Results," *Journal of Financial and Quantitative Analysis,* December 1981, pp. 747–757.

Tole, Thomas M., "How to Maximize the Stationarity of Beta," *Journal of Portfolio Management,* Winter 1981, pp. 46–49.

Tosini, Paula A. and Eugene J. Moriarty, "Potential Hedging Use of a Futures Contract Based on a Composite Stock Index," *Journal of Futures Markets,* Spring 1982, pp. 83–103.

Tsiang, S. C., "The Rationale of the Mean-Standard Deviation Analysis, Skewness Preference, and the Demand for Money," *American Economic Review,* June 1972, pp. 354–371.

Vandell, Robert F., "Is Beta a Useful Measure of Security Risk?," *Journal of Portfolio Management,* Winter 1981, pp. 23–31.

Vasicek, Oldrich A., "A Note on Using Cross-Sectional Information in Bayesian Estimation of Security Betas," *Journal of Finance,* December 1973, pp. 1233–1239.

Veit, E. Theodore, and John M. Cheney, "Are Mutual Funds Market Timers?," *Journal of Portfolio Management,* Winter 1982, pp. 35–42.

Von Furstenberg, George M., and Burton G. Malkiel, "The Government and Capital Formation: A Survey of Recent Issues," *Journal of Economic Literature,* September 1977, pp. 835–878.

Wallace, Anise, "Is Beta Dead?," *Institutional Investor,* July 1980.

Weiner, Neil S., "The Hedging Rationale for a Stock Index Futures Contract," *Journal of Futures Markets,* Vol. 1, No. 1, Spring 1981, pp. 59–76.

Yates, James W., Jr., and Robert W. Kopprasch, Jr., "Writing Covered Call Options: Profits and Risks," *Journal of Portfolio Management,* Fall 1980, pp. 74–79.

Yeaney, Woodrow Wilson, Jr., "Investment Characteristics of Commodity Futures Contracts," unpublished Ph.D. thesis, Pennsylvania State University, 1978.

Young, William E., and Robert H. Trent, "Geometric Mean Approximations of Individual Security and Portfolio Performance," *Journal of Financial and Quantitative Analysis,* June 1969, pp. 179–199.

Yule, G. Udny, and M. C. Kendall, *An Introduction to the Theory of Statistics* (Charles Griffin, London, 1965).

Zweig, Martin E., "Perfect Hedge," *Barrons,* February 22, 1982.

Index